WITHDRAWN

Date Due			
Feb 5 '4			
May 6 '54			

REBEL AT LARGE

REBEL AT LARGE

Recollections
of Fifty Crowded Years

BY

GEORGE CREEL

G. P. PUTNAM'S SONS • NEW YORK

Copyright, 1947, by George Creel

MANUFACTURED IN THE UNITED STATES OF AMERICA
VAN REES PRESS • NEW YORK

TO ALICE

ACKNOWLEDGMENTS

I should like to express my deep appreciation to the editors of *Collier's* for their gracious permission to use the material quoted from that publication.

I should also like to thank the following publishers for kindly allowing me to quote from their books here mentioned: *The Making of a State* (published in the United States under the title *Memories and Observations*), by Dr. Tomáš Garrigue Masaryk, G. Allen & Unwin, Ltd., and Frederick L. Stokes Company; *Memoirs,* by Robert Lansing, and *My Memoirs,* by Mrs. Woodrow Wilson, Bobbs-Merrill Company; the *Autobiography* of William Allen White, The Macmillan Company; and *Intimate Papers of Colonel House,* edited by Charles Seymour, Houghton Mifflin Company.

CONTENTS

REBEL AT LARGE

CHAPTER 1

A Bit of Background

*H*igh in the list of my distastes are those diapers-to-dotage autobiographies, biographies, and reminiscences that begin at birth, prattle along through infancy and adolescence, and reach the middle of the book before coming to the years that have meaning and any approach to general interest. However, when one sets himself up to deal authoritatively with public figures, policies, and events, laying down flat statements and passing judgments, a certain amount of background is demanded by common honesty.

By way of a frank start, it must be admitted that the open mind was no part of my inheritance. I took in prejudices with mother's milk, and was weaned on partisanship. Born and bred in western Missouri, I had reached my tenth year before I knew any adult males except "Southern colonels" and realized the existence of a peculiar political sect that called themselves Republicans. All through my early schooling I had to learn two separate and distinct versions of the War between the States, for when I came home, Mother would ask me about the day's history lesson, and then indignantly instruct me in the true gospel.

"The battle of Antietam, indeed! Why, honey, it was the battle of Sharpsburg, and we *whipped* them."

Strangely enough, Missouri was not regarded as part of the solid South, yet no state below the Mason and Dixon line ever gave more devoted allegiance to the Confederate cause. Daniel Boone, probably the first white man to explore the wilderness beyond St. Louis, lacked the youth for new ventures, but his glowing reports of rolling prairies and great forests of hickory, walnut, persimmons, and papaws excited the restless in Virginia, Kentucky, and Tennessee. A small trickle of immigration became a flood as the Southerners wagoned in, the Cavalier strain filing on the savannas and rich bottom lands, and lean mountaineers from the Appalachians picking homes in the Ozarks.

All of my forebears were Virginians. The McClenahans, Austins, Morrises, and Facklers—my mother's people—crossed the Atlantic in 1735 and took up acreage in Augusta County. Alexander McClenahan, a great-great-grandfather, came from Ireland, and the record shows him to have been quite a fighting man. He commanded a company in the famous battle at Point Pleasant in 1774, when Virginia volunteers defeated the Shawnees, Mingoes, and Delawares, compelling Chief Cornstalk to sue for peace. Among the first to enlist after the shot at Concord, he served as colonel of the Seventh Virginia Continental regiment, and letters prove that he enjoyed the confidence of General Washington.

My mother's grandfather left Virginia for Missouri in 1842, together with nine of his ten children, and settled in Saline County. There, like all of the Southerners who had preceded him, he built a white-pillared home and slave quarters, plowing the virgin soil, planting orchards, and collecting the usual pack of foxhounds. He was a man of considerable enterprise nevertheless, for he brought the first threshing machine into the state, and waged victorious battle against the white farm hands who tried to smash it. A third son, my grandfather, after completing his medical studies in St. Louis, went back to Staunton to marry Amanda Parkes Austin, a childhood sweetheart, and returned to hang out his shingle. Left a widower, he handed a small boy and two little girls over to the care of his sisters and quit his profession for land speculation.

Judging from accounts, that early Missouri life must have had much the same charm and graciousness that marked the Virginia plantations. The fertile soil yielded rich harvests, and with slave labor necessitating no more than supervision on the part of the masters, there was the ample leisure that permits culture. Every home had its library, and New York newspapers and even London and Edinburgh quarterlies were exchanged and discussed.

My mother, her sister, various cousins, and the daughters of neighbors went to school at the home of a relative, where they were given the usual Southern education with its emphasis on Greek, Latin, and the classics. "Auntie" Hill, the teacher, was still alive in my ninth year, but it was long afterward before I

4

learned that she was not a real aunt, but only a maiden lady who had found loving shelter with Cousin Selina Creel, a school friend. The thoroughness of her instruction may be measured by the fact that my mother at eighty and after years of toil still had her languages, and knew ancient and modern history better than I did.

The War between the States brought an instant and violent end to Arcadian simplicity. All of the young men, my uncle Wylie among them, dashed off to fight for the Confederacy, and the women and elders, left behind, soon knew all the horrors of border warfare. Lane and Jennison, with their Jay-hawkers and Redlegs, raided across the line to ravage Missouri communities, and Quantrell and his guerrillas raided back, killing and burning in Kansas with equal ferocity. As a youngster I saw any number of "Jennison's Tombstones," as they called the lone stone chimneys left standing after the houses had crumbled into ashes.

My mother, then in her early teens, lived through days that were never without terror and danger. Looting stripped the homes of Southern sympathizers, and Kansas bands destroyed what they could not take away, even turning on the taps of sorghum barrels. As border ruffianism increased, men were shot down in their doorways or else hung to a tree in the yard while the families looked on.

The story with which she thrilled us most, however, had to do with the time when her brother rode up from Arkansas with General Jo Shelby, that dashing, golden-bearded cavalry leader who was the Jeb Stuart of the West. As most of his command were from Lafayette and Saline Counties, he gave them leave for a night, and all scattered to their homes. Unfortunately, a Union detachment cut Uncle Wylie off from rejoining Shelby, and after turning his horse out into the wood pasture he hid in a hemp shock with his saddle and rifle. The Yankees hung around for three whole days, and each evening Mother walked out into the field as dusk fell, dropping the food and water bottle that she carried under her skirt.

By the time it was safe to leave, Shelby and his riders were far to the south, so Uncle Wylie disguised himself as a harvest hand and wormed a slow, cautious way to Virginia. There he fought under Jeb Stuart and saw his beloved commander fall at Yellow Tavern. After Appomattox, he and several other

5

young Missourians took a contract to supply beef cattle to Fort Laramie in Wyoming, and he was never heard from again. The Cheyennes were on the warpath at the time, and there is little doubt that he met his end at their hands.

After initial Southern successes the tide of battle turned, and the Union forces won full control of western Missouri. Bitter proof of it came in August, 1863, when General Thomas Ewing issued his infamous Order Number 11. Under its cruel terms all of the Southerners in three populous counties were driven from their homes and permitted to take away only what they could carry in their hands. Hundreds of families were herded into the highways by bayonets as the torch set fire to houses and barns, and not until the war's end were they allowed to return to their ravaged homesteads.

It was such brutal inhumanities, and not the conflict itself, that left scars on my mother's heart and soul, preventing "reconstruction." In later years Woodrow Wilson was another who drove home the intensity of resentment engendered by savageries that went beyond the necessities of war. I knew that he was born in Virginia, of course, but as I had never thought of him as a Southerner, the realization came as a surprise. One day during the war, while discussing the work of the Committee on Public Information, I told him of my decision not to play up German atrocities, believing it a criminal blunder to base our propaganda on hate. The President approved, but added grimly that there was still another reason. "The Germans," he said, "might remind us of Sherman's march through Georgia."

Saline County did not come under Order Number 11, but continuing outrages and drastic laws made life intolerable for Southerners. In May, 1864, as a consequence, my grandfather joined with some twenty others, and the group set forth for California with their women and children. The majority traveled in covered wagons, but Mother liked to stress that she and her sister and several aunts rode royally in a specially constructed spring wagon with a canvas top, drawn by four fine mules.

The start was made from St. Joseph, and the way led through the northeast corner of Kansas, bordered the Kickapoo reservation, and then shot straight for the sod houses of Fort Kearney, a distance of 267 miles. From this point the Overland Trail, fairly well beaten by years of travel, followed the Platte to its

6

junction, forded the South Platte at Julesburg, meandered on to Fort Laramie, and then climbed higher and higher until it wound through the tortuous defiles of South Pass to Fort Bridger and Salt Lake. Beyond the Mormon capital stretched miles of desert and the steep ascent of the Sierras.

I still have Mother's diary, full of rhapsodies over the beauties of nature and brimming with classical allusions and excerpts from the poets. For example:

The desert, contrary to expectations, is a gorgeous flower bed. I wish I could press some, but that seems an impossibility. I cannot think there is anyone wholly impervious to the subtle, spiritualizing influence of flowers. As an eloquent writer has said, "they are evangels of purity and faith, if we but unlock our hearts to their ministry, and they weave rosy links of imagination more binding than steel, and sometimes of incalculable value." Another has styled them "chalices of divine workmanship."

And again:

This morning dawned clear and beautiful. The mountains, except for the snowy crests of Fremont's and Pike's Peak, were wrapped in the early shadows. Amy [her sister] and I did a large washing. I brightened my tins and made a huge cherry dumpling for dinner. After everything was in order again, I made myself tidy, and spent the remainder of the day with Mrs. Jones, sewing while she read "Locksley Hall" aloud. I do not know when I have enjoyed anything so thoroughly, and forgot all bodily fatigue in delight with the poem. Mrs. J. reads beautifully; her voice is clear, gentle, and sweet, a most excellent thing in woman.

In Salt Lake, where the party stopped for several weeks to rest the mules, Mother was much impressed by the courage and industry of the Mormons, but formed a poor opinion of Brigham Young. "A huge man with disgusting habits," she recorded, "for even in the pulpit he hawked and expectorated." At Dayton, Nevada, then the most prosperous town in the new state, owing to its smelter, my grandfather was induced to stay over through the winter, as an epidemic made his professional services a desperate need. The bonanza kings, drunk with their nuggets, were "rough, common swaggerers" in Mother's eyes. Not only did she feel that they did not "know how to make wise use of their wealth," but feared that they might well turn out to be "bad examples for the rising generation." San Francisco, however, stirred her to enthusiasm, for she opined that "the majestic beauty of the hills and the bay" was bound to "exert an ennobling influence on the people." In fact, she went so far as to hazard the belief that Pacific coast culture might someday match that of Missouri.

My grandfather and his daughters went home from California by way of New York, taking a steamer to Panama, crossing the Isthmus by train, and boarding another ship at Aspinwall. After a week in New York, where Mother waxed ecstatic over concerts and art galleries, they rode in day coaches to St. Louis. As the Mississippi had not yet been bridged, the party sleighed across over the ice and journeyed to Saline in spring wagons. Even with peace restored, conditions were unhappy, for carpetbaggers were running the state with a high hand. Not until 1875, when Southerners regained the right to vote, was there an end to brutal intolerance.

So much for my mother's people. On my father's side, the Creels were of Scotch-Irish stock and came to Virginia in 1690. First settling near Richmond, the family removed to what is now Prince William County in 1724, taking up land around Manassas. There they lived until 1797, when my great-grandfather, George Creel, bought 1,400 acres on the Little Kanawha, seven miles from Parkersburg.

An older son went ahead to clear, build, and plant, and the rest of the clan followed in detachments. The removal must have been something like the flight of a Tartar tribe, for there were six sons, four daughters, forty slaves, and the household goods accumulated over the span of a century. The main body boarded flatboats at Wheeling, floating down the Ohio to Parkersburg, but Alexander Herbert Creel, then a boy of thirteen, drove the horses overland, a toilsome journey of one hundred miles through the wilderness.

This grandfather of mine seems to have been quite a handy man with the pen, for his journals give spirited accounts of pioneer life, and also deal in detail with the politics and political figures of the time. He tells with gusto of his part in the capture of Blennerhasset Island, headquarters of Aaron Burr and his conspirators, and proudly relates the spirited behavior of a cousin, Colonel Anthony Buckner, when called as a juror to try Burr for treason.

8

"Did you not say repeatedly," asked counsel for defense, "that you would give five pounds for Aaron Burr's head?"

"Yes," shouted Colonel Buckner, "I did, and by God, the offer still stands." Naturally, he was challenged for bias.

Alexander Herbert grew up to be something of a marvel in those leisurely days, for he was at once a lawyer, a surveyor, a farmer, and a businessman. He dammed the Little Kanawha, putting up flour mills; formed Pleasants County in 1847; and two years later laid out the town of St. Marys, where there is now a monument to his memory. For a while it looked as if the little community would become a city, but the Baltimore and Ohio decided to run through Parkersburg, and St. Marys lost its chance to grow.

My grandmother was a Neale, descended from the Daniel Neale who settled in Virginia prior to 1640, and I was never allowed to forget that she was the first cousin of General Thomas J. Jackson's mother. The great Stonewall himself spent a summer at the Creel plantation, and my father had many stories to tell of his austerity. More Puritan than Cavalier, he believed implicitly in a personal God, and retained that faith throughout years of blood and battle. Curiously enough, General Jeb Stuart and Chinese Gordon, two other soldiers, held to the same conviction.

Although a slaveholder, Grandpa Creel could not have had much sympathy with the institution of slavery, for he named my father after Henry Clay, the ardent champion of emancipation. My mother's people were also opposed to slavery, convinced that it was even more of a curse to the white man than the black, but when war came they upheld the South's right to secede.

The son of a Catholic, my father naturally received his education at St. Xavier's in Cincinnati, one of the best schools in the West at the time. Soon after his graduation he was elected to the Virginia House of Delegates, but any hope of a political career soon petered out, for he fell in with Richmond's wild set, and roistering left little time for lawmaking. Doubtless as a measure of reformation, my grandfather packed him off to Missouri in 1860 along with two body servants, buying a large tract of land in the wilds of Osage County.

The stay, however, was short, for when Virginia left the Union, Father hurried home and enlisted. His first service was

9

with a brother-in-law, General William Jackson, but after getting a captain's commission he changed to General Jubal Early's command and fought through to Appomattox. Left at a loose end, and doubtless believing that Virginia would have a hard time recovering from the devastation of war, he decided on a return to Missouri.

His father scraped together $10,000, figured as a son's share of the estate, and with this capital the former captain bought a farm in Lafayette County, and one that was close to my mother's home. She was slim and lovely and he was romantically handsome, and in 1868 the two were married. And there on the farm three sons were born to them—Wylie, George, and Richard Henry, never called anything but Hal.

CHAPTER 2

Harry Truman's Town

*M*y father, in his new role as a tiller of the soil, was a flop from the first. Reared as a "gentleman," with all of its antebellum implications, he knew agriculture only from the back of a horse, and had neither training nor industry. Without slaves and an overseer to do the work, the farm proved a losing venture, and he went back to diligent drinking as an escape from his failure.

Finally selling out at a loss, he decided to try cattle raising in southeastern Missouri, somebody having told him there was money in it. I have only the dimmest memory of Hickory County, but when I traveled through years later there were no railroads, the houses still had earth floors, and people borrowed a shovel of hot coals from a neighbor when the fire went out. A primitive region, and yet from it came Sally Rand, the fan dancer, and Zoë Akins, that very sophisticated playwright.

The cattle-raising experiment lost what was left of the family fortune, and our next move was to Independence, where my poor mother began the dreary business of taking in "paying guests." This packed the little cottage to bursting, and by way of adding to congestion, every now and then we would have a long visit from some old "mammy" formerly owned by my grandfather or some great-uncle. Born snobs, these turbaned crones would sit around with their corncob pipes and bemoan the low estate to which "Miss Virgie" had fallen.

Where Father got the money I never learned, but by some hook or crook he managed to go on regular sprees. I can remember being awakened by the noise when saloon friends brought him home late at night, and having Mother hurry me back to bed with the whisper that Papa was "sick." But how could he be sick, I wondered, when he was yelling and laughing?

Missouri may have been Southern, but Independence was super-Southern. Most of the men had worn Confederate gray, and memories of Order Number 11 still festered. As an illustration, when Frank J. James surrendered after Jesse's assassination and was brought to Independence for trial, community leaders engaged the leading lawyers of the section to defend him on the ground that the James boys had been driven into a life of crime by "Yankee persecution."

Colonel Elijah Magoffin, my cousin by marriage, was one of the group, and he took me to the jail to meet the "poor victim of Northern hate." I was scared out of my shoes, but the outlaw patted me on the head, and I rushed home as fast as legs could carry me, bearing the news that his hands were *soft*. Even my mother's Southern blood could not swallow the visit, and Cousin Lije was laid out for taking a child to see a "murderous bandit." Anyway, Frank was duly tried and just as duly acquitted, a verdict that took some of the sting out of Appomattox.

Independence is now famous as President Truman's home town, but it had a high place in American history before that distinction. The site was laid out as early as 1826, and along with the erection of a log courthouse costing $150, Samuel Weston started a blacksmith shop and wagon factory. Then came the "mountain men," and soon the bustling hamlet was the last outfitting point before jumping off into the West. Kit Carson and Jim Bridger were familiar figures, and when Father De Smet, the great Jesuit missionary and pathfinder, first set forth into the wild Oregon country, it was Weston who advised and aided.

Years later I did the story of Father De Smet, and in the

11

course of research discovered that he was undoubtedly the first white man to find gold in the wild reaches of the West. Crossing the Bitterroot Range, he stopped to drink at a mountain stream and looked down through the clear water to see a golden glitter among the pebbles. For a moment he knew a singing of the heart, for his knowledge of mineralogy told him that here was wealth more than ample for all of his missionary labors among the Kootenays, the Chaudières, the Coeur d'Alênes, the Flatheads, and the Blackfeet.

Then, as though a shadow blotted the sun, he remembered his days among the Osages, the Potawatomi, and other Missouri River tribes and saw again the drunkenness and degradation worked by the greeds of white men. One word of his discovery, and he knew that the mountains would fill with adventurers drawn from every quarter of the globe, debauching the Indians and ending forever his dream of conversion. Dropping the nuggets back into the stream, the Black Robe wiped his hands as though they had been soiled, and ran as from an imminent peril.

Mormons followed the mountain men, Joseph Smith claiming to have had a vision that revealed Independence as the new Zion. With 1,500 of his followers the Prophet arrived in 1832, and after laying the cornerstone of the temple, established a weekly paper and launched a vigorous campaign of evangelization. The Missourians stood it for a while, but when the meaning of polygamy finally stood clear, they "riz up." Mormon homes were burned, the newspaper plant was thoroughly wrecked, and after tarring and feathering the leaders they drove the rest across the Mississippi into Illinois, where Smith founded Beautiful Nauvoo.

The old temple was one of our playgrounds, and as none of us youngsters had more than a vague idea as to who or what the Mormons really were, there was always the delicious fear that something might rush out and get us. Another favorite spot was the "Vaile place," a mile or so north of Independence. This huge, imposing pile of brick had been built by one of the men who swindled the government out of millions in connection with overland postal services, aided by senators and high federal officials. Not only were the cedar trees in the yard pruned into fantastic shapes, but there were rumors that the ceiling in every room was covered by paintings of half-dressed women.

The Mexican War gave Independence quite a setback, for some nine hundred men left the farms of Jackson and Clay Counties when Colonel Alexander Doniphan shouted his call in 1846. Organized as the First Regiment of Mounted Missouri Volunteers, the little company rode away to the Rio Grande, crossing the dreaded *Jornado del Muerte,* and after conquering five Mexican states, galloped home again. A Homeric march of five thousand miles within the year! At the battle of the Sacramento one man in seven was assigned to hold the horses, but when bugles sounded the charge, not a Missourian stayed at his post.

"Darn your ornery hides," roared Doniphan, "go on and do what I told you."

"Like hell!" came the indignant answer. "We can hold horses back home."

Soon after the war's end, the first mail coach line started from Independence to Santa Fe, and in 1849 the town had a fresh burst of prosperity as gold hunters streamed through on their way to California. Westport Landing, however—ten miles away and on the riverbank—got the cream of the trade, and began the phenomenal growth that was to make Kansas City the real gateway to the West. By the middle fifties Independence had accepted its fate, settling down as a quiet country seat and the prosperous center of a rich farming region.

Not until the War between the States was there a return to excitement, for the transplanted sons of Virginia, Kentucky, and Tennessee enlisted at the first call. From Fort Sumter to Appomattox, Missouri was a major battleground, some six hundred important engagements being fought, but as all of the correspondents were with the armies on the Potomac, few of the battles made front pages.

There may have been some grown men in Independence who had not worn the gray, and some may have been privates, but if so I can't recall them. Colonels rocked on every front porch, held forth in the courthouse yard on summer afternoons, delivered all of the Fourth of July orations, and gave the town its thrills and laughter. Fat colonels, lean colonels, blustery colonels, quiet colonels with faces like nicked sword blades,

13

and swashbuckling colonels eager for a quarrel—all living in a past that they refused to put behind them.

The one I remember best was Colonel John, a mountain of a man who dealt only in superlatives. Gargantuan in his appetites, he loved to boast that he could eat more and drink more than any other living man. Waiters were always instructed to bring him the *whole* ham, and to serve his lettuce in a tub. And when he was speaking at a Democratic rally, what a bellow went up when his cry for water brought nothing larger than a pitcher! "Take it away! If I put it to my mouth I'd inhale it. Fetch me the *rivah!*" Woe indeed to the presumptuous varlet who dared to grow familiar. "Off with your hand, suh! I killed a dog this morning for putting a paw on me." Once I went with a friend to ask if we could go swimming in the small pond on his place, and I can still see his purpled face.

"My *what?*" he roared.

"Why, Colonel, your pond," I quavered.

"My ocean, you young whelp. My *ocean!*"

The Colonel had two sons about my own age, and mischievous to a point where they often came under the stern eye of the town marshal. When he received word that one of them was in trouble, it was Colonel John's invariable habit to leap forth, let out a shout that could be heard for miles, and invite the citizenry to "follow the Roman father."

In the course of an hour's oration, usually delivered from the end gate of a wagon, he would start off with his courtship, dwelling fondly on the ecstasies of young love; tell of his joy in expectant fatherhood, describe in detail the books on Napoleon, Washington, and Jefferson that he read to his wife while the little life was forming, and so on up to the moment when they came to him and cried, "Lo, a man-child has been conceived." And then the peroration, heartbreaking in its anguish, as he pointed to the calaboose where the man-child cowered for the high crime of stealing a chicken.

Where the Colonel really shone, however, was when he fought the war all over again, ignoring every fact that took away from drama. Of a summer evening it was his habit to enthrone himself on a chair in front of the drugstore or hotel, armed with a palm-leaf fan, and tell of heroic encounters in a cause that though lost was still cherished in every true heart.

14

His favorite, as my father used to tell it, had to do with a battle fought at some creek.

"There we were," rumbled the Colonel, "a young band of Southrons hastily gathered from home and field to beat back the iron heel of the invadah, armed only with squirrel guns, hoe handles, pitchforks, and other rude agricultural implements hastily fashioned into weapons of defense. As we sat in the cold gray light of early dawn, munching the parched corn that had been our sole subsistence for days, over the hill poured the Yankee hosts, outnumbering us by twenty to one, and equipped with every device known to military science.

"But did fear clutch at our vitals? Was there the quiver of a lip or the lowering of a crest? As well ask if there was a poltroon at Thermopylae or impugn the valor of the immortal Six Hundred. With the indomitable courage that has ever marked the Southron, we fell upon the blue-bellied hordes and beat them into dastardly flight."

"Why, John," piped up an old Confederate whose long beard did away with the need of collar and tie, "I was in that fight, and the Yankees whipped hell out of us."

"Oh, Lord!" groaned Colonel John. "Another great story ruined by a goddam eyewitness."

As a rule, most of the veterans of the Lost Cause settled down peacefully enough, even though less than industriously, but there were those who proved less adaptable. The most notorious of the lot was Jim Crow Chiles, one of Harry Truman's uncles, having married a sister of the President's mother. After Appomattox, Chiles had followed General Jo Shelby across the Rio Grande, and the wild, freebooting life of the Missourians in Mexico did nothing to counteract the turbulence of his war years.

Returning to Independence, he became the town's "bad man," terrorizing the entire community by his violent temper and ready revolver. Not the least of his many lawlessnesses was a threat to "kill any nigger that gets to windward of me," and several poor wretches were careless enough to forget the warning. One particularly cold-blooded murder, that of a colored boy, was witnessed by two men from a second-floor window, whereupon Jim Crow went up to their offices and gave them twenty-four hours to leave town. Parker, a dentist, had the courage to refuse, but the other, St. John by name, skedaddled for Kansas, where he rose to be governor.

Finally fed up with Jim Crow and his rampages, the people put in Jim Peacock, also a veteran, as an assistant to the town marshal. Chiles took it as a personal affront, and when the new peace officer announced that there was going to be no more "pistol totin' and killin'," he let it be known that he would take advantage of the very first opportunity to slap Mr. Peacock's ears loose from his head.

The chance came on a quiet Sunday morning when most of the townspeople were in church. Accompanied by his young son, Lije, Jim Crow marched into a drugstore on the public square where Peacock made his unofficial headquarters, and swaggered out again when told that the marshal was sunning himself across the way. Charlie Peacock, Jim's son, happened to be in the store at the time, and followed close after borrowing a revolver.

Curiously enough, no gun was drawn as the two duelists came together. Arms at his sides, Jim Crow walked forward as if to engage in talk, but on getting close he whaled away and gave the slap he had promised. Peacock, a powerful man, grappled at once and threw Chiles to the ground, but on the instant Lije Chiles pumped a bullet into his back. Before he could shoot again, Charlie Peacock let loose a volley, sending Lije to the ground with mortal wounds. Rushing to his father's aid, however, Charlie managed to snag the revolver in his pants, and a shot in the leg put him out of the fight along with Lije.

Jim Peacock, although spouting blood from the hole in his back, nevertheless struggled desperately to make his man a prisoner, but when Jim Crow reached for his gun, he pulled his own. A bullet, right through the head from ear to ear, ended the bloody struggle, and nothing remained to be done except cart away the bodies.

Quite a commotion, but highly satisfactory as to outcome. Jim Peacock recovered after long weeks in the hospital, and took up where he had left off. With both Jim Crow Chiles and young Lije out of the picture, the rest of the gun-toters decided to call it a day, and either watched their steps or else left town. And a grateful people kept iron-bodied Mr. Peacock in office until he died of old age.

A vanished breed, these "colonels" that I saw and of whom

I heard. Perhaps it is just as well, but their passing took a lot of color out of life. Years later I sat by the bed of Colonel John Calhoun Moore, the last of the lot. Then in his nineties, but with ice-blue eyes undimmed by age, he still wore the long black coat, the billowy shirt front, and the flowing tie that were the badge of his tribe. Loving the gaunt old man, I was murmuring some words of false cheer when he cut me short with an impatient wave of his hand.

"Don't bother, son," he said. "I'll be glad to go, for life hasn't been worth living in this country since they abolished dueling. When blackguards had to answer for it with their lives, they kept a decent tongue in their cheeks."

CHAPTER 3

Three Boys and a Mother

*I*f I came to voting age with a passionate belief in equal suffrage, it was because I *knew* my mother had more character, brains, and competence than any man that ever lived. It was not only that she brought up three sons by her toil and sacrifice, imbuing them with something of her own indomitability and pride, but my father was ever a burden on her aching back. I remember nothing of the farm and very little of Hickory County, but during the years that came under my seeing eye he never lifted a useful hand.

We were poor in Independence, but there was no feeling of poverty, for the town was more like a family than a community. Moving away from all that neighborly kindness must have been a wrench for Mother, but Kansas City offered larger opportunity for a boardinghouse. There was also the prospect of wage earning for Wylie, while I could sell papers after school hours. Things worked out according to plan. The barn of a house filled with "paying guests," Wylie carried a paper route both morning and evening, I picked up quite a few pennies, and during the summer vacations Hal joined us at berrypicking.

17

It was in Kansas City that full realization of our circumstances came to me. There were cooks and maids in the families of my playmates, and I could see their mothers on the front porch with books or fancy work, or dressed up to go out. Mine was always in the kitchen, harassed, worn, and flushed with heat from the big coal range. Thank God, the boardinghouse proved a failure, despite her drudgery, and in my twelfth year we moved to Odessa, a little town forty miles to the east, where her father owned a piece of property.

Looking back, I am reluctantly forced to the conclusion that this grandfather of mine, while about the meanest man that ever lived, was rather remarkable in many ways. As early as 1850 he realized the importance of teeth to health, and supplemented his medical education with a course in dentistry. He never came to see us without giving long talks on the "liquification of food," watching every mouth to see that nothing slipped down without adequate chewing. He was also a pioneer in calisthenics, and I still remember my mortification at the laughter of neighbors when the Doctor went out on the front porch of a morning and "aerated" his blood by exercise and deep breathing.

Quitting practice shortly after the war, he made a fortune in land speculation, riding various booms in Missouri, Kansas, Florida, and Texas, but neither in Independence nor Kansas City did a dollar ever come to us. From the first he had hated my father as a dissipated incompetent, and when Mother refused to consent to a separation, the cruel, intolerant old man left us to our poverty. All through the boardinghouse years, when drudgery wasted Mother to a wisp, he did not offer a helping hand, and it was not until Odessa that there came the grudging grant of a monthly pittance. A gambler, for all of his morning and evening prayers, he was caught overextended in a panic and died penniless.

Things went much better for us in Odessa. Wylie, staying in Kansas City, sent home half of his small earnings, Mother took in sewing, and the back yard was large enough for a truck garden. Hal and I peddled the milk from Bess, our little Alderney cow, and went into the fields during summer vacations. At twelve I shocked wheat side by side with grown men, and Hal, although his bare legs were hardly long enough, rode lead horse to the binder.

Odessa, like Independence, was 100 per cent Southern, and

with the same neighborhood spirit. If we came upon bad times, the long-bearded grocer gave us credit and so did the butcher. Mrs. McLaughlin and Mrs. Williams, the two community leaders, took Mother to their hearts at first sight, and as a member of the Modern Priscillas she again enjoyed the companionship of cultivated people.

It was not only that Mother had the gift of making tasks and hardships seem a game, but she colored our lives with her own eager interest in everything. Night after night, when she must have been ready to drop, she told us stories that made dead heroes live again, and actually had us believing that it was a privilege to learn the poems of Scott and Longfellow. When I reached the "dime novel" stage, she did not forbid them, but simply crowded them out by giving me Dickens' *Child's History of England* and juvenile versions of the *Iliad*. To this day Hengist, Horsa, Achilles, and Ulysses are real to me.

Her rare understanding of childhood's intensities was another of Mother's gifts, and only God and His angels will ever know the sacrifices she made to give her boys the little pleasures that saved heartache. No matter how empty the family purse, she always managed to find a dime when a troupe came to the hall over the grocery store that went under the name of Opera House.

There was the time in Kansas City when a contemptible hound waited until school was out and distributed dodgers advertising a show at which "valuable presents" would be handed out to every boy and girl buying a ticket. The list was long and impressive, and I was among the first purchasers, happening to have fifteen cents I had earned that morning by sweeping snow off a neighbor's sidewalk. Poor Mother tried to tell me that such costly articles could not possibly be given away for so small a price, but she could not shake my faith in the printed word. Giving up at last, she gently refused my offer to pick a rocking chair for her, thus letting me decide on a pair of roller skates for myself.

For a full week I swept the boardwalk regularly, so that I could start skating without a second's wait, and even practiced fancy glides on the way to school. At last the Big Afternoon came, but when I marched up to get my prize, all the wretched creature gave me was a tin badge something like a tobacco tag. I burst into tears and made quite a scene, but when I reached home, still sobbing, there was Mother with the roller skates she had pinched herself to buy.

It was an understanding that reached deep into the hearts of her children, helping us to get over hurts that might have left a scar. In Odessa I passed a note during school hours to a current fancy, assuring her that she was still my girl even if I had walked home with Dora the day before. The teacher intercepted the note and sent it up to the principal, who came down to our room with a wolfish leer I still remember. First he read it aloud, not once but twice, rolling his eyes and mincing his tone, and then gave me a brutal switching that raised welts. I told Mother all about it that night, and early the next morning she took me with her to the principal's home.

"Georgie deserved punishment for breaking a rule," she said, "but discipline does not involve humiliation. If you knew anything about children, you would know that what you did to him was cruel and unforgivable."

Realizing what it would mean to me to go back to face the laughter and jeers of my mates, Mother took me out of the public school and put me in another that called itself a "college." The tuition fee, although small, added another burden, but never once did she refer to it.

Then there was the tragic afternoon at the home of Roe McLaughlin, my favorite companion. His mother and Mrs. Williams were chatting on the front porch while we played at the side of the house, and I heard Mrs. McLaughlin say that it was such a pity that Georgie was "so homely."

"Yes," Mrs. Williams agreed, "but he's quite attractive."

I had only a vague idea as to the meaning of "attractive," but I knew what "homely" meant, and after a few painful minutes, raced for home as fast as my legs could carry me. "Mamma! Mamma!" I cried, throwing myself in her arms. "Am I *ugly?*" Between sobs I managed to give an account of what had happened.

"Why, darling," she said, holding me close, "it isn't the face that matters. Mouth, lips, and nose have nothing to do with looks. If you are handsome *inside,* it will shine through your eyes and make you handsome *outside.*" There was much more to it than just that, and while I didn't quite grasp it all, I did get a soothing conviction that in the course of years, if things went well, I could make myself into something rather spectacular.

More than anything else, as I look back, there was the tender care with which she guarded my father's bruised pride and battered self-esteem. She always addressed him as "Mr. Creel," deferring to him as though he were really head of the house, and while her skilled fingers made our clothes out of castoff garments, his suits were bought brand-new. The only sternness I can remember was when one of us would show curiosity as to why Papa did not go to an office or store in the morning like other men.

Strangely enough, considering her sound sense in everything else, she held unchangeably to the false standards of a dead era. Once at school in Kansas City the teacher asked each pupil to tell what his father did. All I could remember was that he had made me a sled, so I answered that he was a carpenter. When I told that to Mother she went to school with me the very next morning and told the teacher that Papa was *not* a carpenter, but a gentleman farmer temporarily retired on account of ill health.

Poor, unhappy man! During my teens when he was hurt by some word or look he would threaten to go to work as a day laborer, or even as a street sweeper. It always impressed me as a sound idea, but when I applauded he would fly into a rage and order me out of the house. Invariably on my return at night I would find a note from Mother tucked under the door, the envelope inscribed "Read, ponder, and digest," and inside this appeal: "Darling, apologize to your father in the morning. Someday you will understand." Not until I was fully grown, however, did understanding come to me. As he was without a trade or profession, and physically deteriorated by years of hard drinking, there was no work that he *could* do, and Mother knew it.

My bitterness against him hurt her at the time, and there was also another thing that gave her pain. A devout Episcopalian, believing implicitly in the apostolic succession, she found her religion a strength and a comfort, and my stubborn refusal to receive confirmation wounded her deeply. It was the cruelty, even savagery, of the Old Testament tales heard in Sunday school that first turned me against so-called Christian teaching. Particularly that choice bedtime story about how Elisha called

21

two she-bears down from the mountain and had them eat up forty-two little children who had done no more than laugh at his bald head.

I liked the poetry of the Psalms, but thought King David a lecherous, treacherous old man. To this day I can remember the horror I felt at hearing how he lay with Bathsheba, and got her with child, and then sent the husband off to war with secret instructions to have him killed. If that was Christianity, I wanted no part of it.

Later on I came to believe in God the Creator, and bowed before Christ as a great teacher, but I could not swallow denominationalism, or get over my distaste for those who made their own particular brand of devotion to the Galilean an excuse for hateful intolerances. Nowhere in the New Testament could I find that He who delivered the Sermon on the Mount ever made mention of Catholics, Episcopalians, Methodists, Baptists, Presbyterians, etc., etc.

Even so, I did not know what to call myself until I wrote a book on Thomas Paine in 1932, eager to do something toward restoring the author of the *Crisis* and *Common Sense* to his proper place in American history. As a deist, Paine rejected the idea of God as a mean, narrow sectarian, but believed in Him as a Supreme Being whose tenderness embraced *all* humanity. Moreover, no less than George Washington, Thomas Jefferson, and Benjamin Franklin were also deists, standing fast against attacks.

"Deism, *that* is atheism," sneered an eminent divine of the time.

"Chalk, that is charcoal," amiably jeered Franklin.

Knowing Mother's hurt, and eager to soothe it by some assurance that at least I was not an atheist, I found the chance in 1907. The *Rubáiyát* was then at the height of its popularity with sentimental women and self-indulgent men, and I decided to write a "Christian answer." Working on streetcars, and often late at night, I threw together some 120 quatrains that attested a religious faith, although steering clear of sectarianism.

Paul Elder, the San Francisco publisher, brought out the little book with a preface by Julian Hawthorne, and to my amazement and relief, the reviewers did not chide me for impudence or deride me for daring to enter the lists against Fitzgerald. Better than everything else, however, was Mother's joy in the verses, and pride in the dedication where I paid tribute to her "inspiring companionship."

By no means was this just a phrase. Even as she gave joy and color to my boyhood, so was Mother the help and strength of my early manhood. In Kansas City she made a home just for Father and me, for Wylie was traveling out of St. Louis, and Hal, having worked his way through a medical school, had entered the Public Health Service. First in San Francisco, then in New Orleans, and after that in the Philippines, he was one of those who fought and whipped the plague.

It was not only that Mother, with her amazing memory, supplied dates and quotations, but her high standards kept me from many a cheapness and compromise. More often than not, my intense partisanship led to confusions, but she could always be counted on to point out the dividing line between the true and the false.

I was making money enough to rent a nice place and hire a cook, and how she blossomed! Instead of complaining when I flooded the house with politicians, poetesses, "nuts," actresses, prize fighters, musicians, and touring celebrities, she loved it. And every one of the strangely assorted company that I gathered loved her. Her one little demur was that oftentimes I did not know the last names of my guests.

Father died in 1907, and in our conversations just before his death he paid a debt long overdue. Since he had been born and bred a Catholic, I asked him if he wanted me to call in a priest. "No," he said. "Your mother has been the most wonderful wife that ever blessed a man, and it will please her to have the last rites administered by her rector. God knows it is little enough for me to do for her after all she has done for me."

On reading over this chapter, I have the feeling that the stress on our struggle may give the impression of an unhappy childhood. Far from it. If I could go back and live those earlier years again, I would make no change except in the matter of greater ease and comfort for my mother. Our poverty brought us close, for love was all we had to give one another, and the determination to justify her sacrifices and hopes developed ambitions and energies. Certainly this was true in my case, for I was born with a streak of vagabondage. In the schoolroom I was always thinking of the sun and open fields outside, and to this day I cannot see a train or plane without aching to be on board.

As for Independence and Odessa, those two blessed small towns, they helped to drive home the essential meaning of Americanism. There, throughout my formative years, I saw democracy in action—not just a word but something you could *feel*. No dividing line between the rich and poor, and no class distinctions to breed mean envies. The wealthiest merchant stood behind his counter, and the banker walked home of an evening with the round steak for supper tucked under his arm.

The march of industrialism had not yet transferred skill from the worker to the machine, and each town had its cobbler, tailor, saddler, etc., making products complete in themselves and in which they took pride. Self-sustaining and self-respecting, for the automobile had not yet come with its plague of hot-dog stands, filling stations, "tourists' homes," and the obliteration of boundaries.

The aged lived in the homes of married sons or daughters, where they were loved and honored, and illness was the common concern. When Mother came down with a fever, the neighbors flooded in with broths and extra sheets and blankets, and in turn I ran my legs off carrying little delicacies to sick friends. "Miz' Jones, here's something Mamma thought you might relish."

Character was the bed rock on which the community rested. When people married they stayed married, not leaping to another bed at the first irritation or disagreement, for the home was the keystone in the social arch. Children were a sacred charge, entailing high obligations, and if youngsters went beyond the usual run of mischief, the blame was placed on the parents.

Judgments were tolerant except with respect to shiftlessness and dishonesty. Work was the common lot, and a man's word took the place of written contracts. Pride went bone-deep, people asking nothing and wanting nothing that they had not earned. If anybody had ever said charity to my mother, she would have put her gentleness aside and reached for a broom. All in all, a kindly, gracious existence. Life presented no soul-tearing problems necessitating a call for psychiatrists, for there were things that decent people did and things they did *not* do. And all knew what they were.

24

CHAPTER 4

Last of the Cavaliers

*I*t was in 1896—my twentieth year—that I quit odd jobs, put by indecisions as to a career, and became a reporter on the Kansas City *World* at the princely salary of $4 a week. Not an easy choice by any means, for while the itch to write had been with me from boyhood, I also fancied myself as a third baseman, pulling off brilliant plays and poling out home runs for some major-league teams while thousands shouted my name.

From the first, however, I looked on my employment merely as a springboard to "literature," and planned the earliest possible departure for foreign lands. Where else but in Europe did life hold anything worth writing about? Kings and queens, titled beauties, silks, satins, and swords, and the intrigue of courts!

What an unutterable jackass! At my hand, had I the eyes to see, were ready-made dramas that flamed with high adventure. Not a one of my Independence colonels but had a story, and where any more thrilling epic than General Jo Shelby's reckless dash across the Rio Grande after Appomattox? Six hundred Missourians braving the dangers of war-torn Mexico rather than live under Yankee rule! Nor am I able to offer the excuse of ignorance, for many of the principals were still alive, and it was from their mouths that I had the full account dinned into me without the skip of a detail.

I was particularly well instructed by General Shelby himself, then United States marshal for the district of western Missouri. President Cleveland's appointment of such a famous "rebel" caused quite a stir in the eastern press, and there was even more of a flutter when the General named a Negro as one of his deputies. At last, they cheered, the "man and brother" had been given recognition, and by a former slaveholder and great Confederate leader. It was a good thing that New England editors never visited the General's office, for while Ol' Bob did have the title of United States deputy marshal, his real job was to wait on Mars' Jo, and see to it that the mint juleps were properly frosted.

Still "unreconstructed," General Shelby didn't like my employment, and made no bones about saying so. "Every one of your menfolks served under the Stars and Bars," it was his habit to rumble, "and the women of your family never failed in courage and sacrifice. Why, your own uncle fought side by side with me. Yet here you are working on a Yankee paper and not ashamed of it."

The federal building was on my beat, and when I dropped in to see the General, it was usually an hour before I could get away. As a rule, members of his old command sat with him, and when dispute occurred as to a date or incident, they turned to their bible, Major John N. Edwards' chronicle of the expedition. I had it all, with nothing to do but set down their words, but I held unshakably to my conviction that Europe was the only source of material for a *real* author. I write it now, fifty years later, not only because the story deserves to be told, but as a warning to young authors who scorn their environment.

On the news of Lee's surrender, Confederate commanders west of the Mississippi gathered to confer about the future. There was much talk of continuing the war, but Shelby drove against this farrago with the cold steel of facts. The South was *whipped,* and it was stupid to evade the bitter truth. The choice was between surrender and flight. Nor need the flight be aimless. Across the Rio Grande lay Mexico, where Maximilian of Austria, put upon a tinsel throne by Napoleon III, was fighting for life and empire against the republican army of Benito Juárez.

What better opportunity ever offered to men of spirit and courage? Full fifty thousand men could be gathered from the scattering forces of "Pop" Price and Kirby Smith, and once on the ground, they could decide whether to take service with Maximilian or with Juárez. Or in the event that they chose to elect neither cause, they could fight both, seize the country, and establish a Confederate States of America of their own.

A great cheer rang out as Shelby finished speaking, and with waving swords the conference fixed the date and place for a rendezvous at San Antonio. The whole of our history might

26

have been changed had the Southerners marched as they planned, for fifty thousand was indeed a number that could have worked its will in Mexico. Price's command disintegrated, however, Kirby Smith gave an order to concentrate at Shreveport for surrender, and in the end only Shelby and six hundred of his cavalrymen crossed the border.

Equipment was not lacking, for Texas was an arsenal, and the Missourians outfitted themselves with artillery, rifles, revolvers, munitions, and wagon trains. At Piedras Negras, on the Mexican side of the Rio Grande, the Juaristas were assembled in force, and Governor Biesca came out for parley. At first he demanded surrender, but when this was refused contemptuously, Biesca offered Shelby the military control of Coahuila, Tamaulipas, and Nuevo León if he would espouse the cause of Juárez. Calling a council, the General told of the offer and urged its acceptance. As a matter of fact, there seemed to be no choice. Biesca's forces outnumbered the Southerners five to one, and the Juaristas held the country for miles around. The nearest royalist force was at Monterrey, and there were deserts to cross and mountains to climb.

Not only this, but the end of the empire was plain to be seen. England and Spain had already composed their differences with Mexico, and the French people were demanding the abandonment of a disastrous adventure. Even if Napoleon III did not heed the anger of his own people, the United States would soon take steps to make him, for with the Civil War ended, nothing was more certain than that Lincoln would enforce the Monroe Doctrine.

The men listened quietly, and when General Shelby had finished Colonel Ben Elliott rose as their spokesman. He agreed that the doom of the Austrian appeared to be sealed and victory for Juárez a certainty. General Shelby was still their leader, and if his honor had been pledged to Biesca in any degree, he might depend upon them to see that his word was not forsworn. But a human equation was involved that he felt sure the General had overlooked. According to report, the Empress Carlota, Maximilian's wife, was one of the fairest and noblest of her sex. "A woman twice crowned, once by God with beauty and character, and again with the golden diadem of temporal power." If ever a lady stood in need of supporting swords, it was Carlota. Were they to fail her? Was it to be left for history to write down that Southrons had remained deaf to the call of chivalry?

Bowing low, General Shelby rendered his apologies for a forgetfulness that had brought him so close to shame. The next morning, as nonchalantly as though he were refusing a dinner invitation, he informed Governor Biesca that his men had decided to fight for Maximilian and against Juárez. However, as the way to Monterrey was rough, he might be inclined to sell his artillery and wagon trains. The dazed Biesca accepted and the deal was closed for $60,000—$20,000 in cash and the rest in Juárez scrip.

"But, General," I exclaimed when this was told me, "the Juaristas outnumbered you five to one, according to your own admission. And you had just told them you were going to join the enemy. When they got your artillery, what was to prevent them from taking back the money and annihilating you?"

"You seem to forget, sir," was his icy reply, "that we still had our side arms."

Nevertheless, the departure from Piedras Negras was not entirely peaceful, for as the Southerners saddled, some Mexicans went up to Ike Barry and insolently claimed the horse that he rode. "You don't say so!" laughed the Missourian. "Well, you'll have a hell of a time ridin' him." With that he swung his heavy sword and severed the Mexican's right arm at the shoulder. In the fight that followed, many were killed, and the Southerners recaptured the artillery they had sold that morning.

"We wanted to sleep," Major Edwards explained, "and for fear of Vesuvius we took the crater to bed with us."

Order restored and the artillery given back, Shelby and his men set forth on the long journey across mountain and desert. Throughout the march, as Major Edwards told it, no man was ever killed that the wail of a woman did not float out upon the still air—"such a wail as may have been heard in David's household when back from the tangled brushwood they brought the beautiful Absalom." It was also invariably the case that the "white moon looked down in compassion from a benignant sky." Stilted, to be sure, and laughable now in these days when we spend only the copper in our purse of language, but in those times a gentleman was known by his culture as well as by his courage.

Burning by day and freezing by night, regularly attacked

28

from ambush, and compelled to give bloody battle at every ford, the Missourians struggled on, coming finally to Monterrey in late July, 1865. General Jeanningros, who held the city for Maximilian with five thousand soldiers, ruled with a hand of iron, and the dead wall against which he shot his prisoners was never free from blood. On receiving word that Shelby had sold his artillery and munitions to the hated Juaristas, Jeanningros swore mightily and made public vow that he would hang the Southerners as common guerrillas. No sooner had Shelby made camp before the walls than he threw out his guards and dispatched the following note:

General:

I have the honor to report that I am within one mile of your fortifications with my command. Preferring exile to surrender, I have left my own country to seek service in that held by His Imperial Majesty, the Emperor Maximilian. Shall it be peace or war between us? If the former, and with your permission, I shall enter your lines at once, claiming at your hands that courtesy due one soldier to another. If the latter, I propose to attack you immediately.

Very respectfully yours,
Jo. O. SHELBY

Disarmed by the frank courage of the note, the Frenchman received the adventurers kindly, and in the soft air of the hill city the exhausted Southerners healed their wounds and recovered strength and spirits. Jeanningros, while eager to accept Shelby's aid, could not do so except with the consent of Marshal Bazaine, head of the French forces and Louis Napoleon's check on Maximilian. Since no other course was left them, Shelby and his men marched away to Parras, where free passage into Sonora was requested of Colonel Depreuil. In furious, insulting fashion, the Frenchman told Shelby he had received orders from Marshal Bazaine to bar their way and send them on to the City of Mexico. Far gone in liquor, he cursed the Americans for murderers and robbers, and expressed the opinion that all should go forward in irons.

Shelby, returning his hat to his head, said: "I imagined that when an American soldier called upon a French soldier, he was visiting a gentleman. I am mistaken, it seems. At least I can keep my hands clean, and I wash them of you because you are a slanderer and a coward."

"Off with your hat!" Depreuil shouted, insane with anger.

"Only to beauty and to God," was the stern reply. "To a coward, never!"

The duel was quickly arranged. Shelby, wounded in his right arm, was unable to handle a sword, and Depreuil agreed to pistols. At the very moment when the men were about to take their places, Jeanningros arrived in Parras, heard the story, and forced Depreuil to apologize. Sadly enough, however, he was compelled to admit that Bazaine's order was a fact.

Turned back from Sonora, therefore, the Southerners now commenced the dreary march to the city by way of San Luis Potosí and Querétaro. A thousand adventures marked the march. From general to private, every man in the company was a throwback to Cavalier ancestors, living and thinking in terms of medieval chivalry. Adventure of any kind was a delight, but it became ecstasy when touched with romance or concerned with damsels in distress.

Five days out from Parras, James Wood and Yandell Blackwell heard that a beautiful young American girl was being held as a slave in the harem of a Spanish *hacendado*. Daughter of a Californian gold hunter and an Indian, the fair Inez was possessed of beauty that was matched only by her virtue. Carefully concealing their intentions from Shelby, Wood and Blackwell gathered twenty men and led an attack upon the hacienda at night, taking advantage of a heavy storm. The stables were carried, and then a log, used as a battering ram, broke down the great door leading into the main hall.

One by one, the hacendado, Rodríguez, and his retainers were killed in hand-to-hand fighting, and when Shelby arrived the place was a shambles. Figuring it as a base adventure in pillage, the General swore that every man concerned in the outrage should face a firing squad. When Wood had explained, however, Shelby sent for the beautiful captive and heard her story. Her wishes were accepted as commands, and the next morning, with her women about her, the fair Inez went forward with the expedition.

Every mile of the way was a battle, with only now and then a friendly city in which rest and entertainment might be found. As the days went by, heavy with dangers and fatigues, hot tempers took on a bitter edge, and not even the iron hand of the General was able to prevent bloody encounters among the men.

At last the mountain heights were won, and the Missourians looked down on "fair Tenochtitlan," even as Cortez and the conquistadors had stared three hundred years before. In the city Shelby found two old comrades in high place. Commodore Matthew Fontaine Maury, the famous hydrographer, was now Imperial Commissioner of Immigration, and General John B. Magruder, beau sabreur of the Confederacy, lorded it as Surveyor General of the Empire. The one had captivated Maximilian by his scientific attainments, and the other by his dash and charm.

The two arranged at once for Shelby to meet with the Emperor and Marshal Achille François Bazaine. In 1870 the Marshal was to be blamed for having lost the war with Germany and sent to prison as a traitor, but at the time his star rode high. The real master of Mexico, with Maximilian a puppet, he ruled royally with the fortune brought him by a Mexican wife.

The Emperor, at first glance, was an impressive figure with his billowy golden whiskers and majestic air, but a closer look revealed the weakness of the chin, and there was irresolution in the large blue eyes. He had not wanted the Mexican throne, preferring his mimic court at Trieste, where he ameliorated the cares of state by gardening and the perpetration of bad poetry, but Carlota wanted to wear a crown.

Speaking directly to the Emperor, Shelby laid down a plan to recruit forty thousand Americans against the time when the French soldiers would be withdrawn. Maximilian asked at once why he thought the French troops would be sent home, and received this crisp answer: "Because the Civil War is over and the United States is now in a position to enforce the Monroe Doctrine. France will have to get out of Mexico or fight."

Bazaine listened and said nothing. As for Maximilian, the prospect of French withdrawal was a joy to him, for his proud spirit deeply resented the overlordship of Bazaine. And yet if he accepted Shelby's offer, permitting the mobilization of forty thousand Confederates, might it not be that he would merely exchange one master for another? Above all, the brother of Franz Josef, Emperor of Austria and King of Hungary, felt a high Hapsburg confidence in his destiny, and believed that

31

it was only a question of time until the Mexicans would acknowledge his divine right to reign.

At every point Maximilian thought of the country in terms of Italy. He had ruled successfully in Lombardy and Venezia, and saw no reason why the same results could not be achieved in Mexico. What he did not remember was that an Austrian army had gone into Italy before him, and that the brutal campaigns of Radetzky had left the Italians without spirit or resources. Moved by these joint considerations, he refused the aid that Shelby offered, courteously enough but still definitely. Friendless and penniless exiles in a strange land, the Southerners were indeed in a desperate plight.

"There is but one thing to do," Shelby laughed. "Learn enough Spanish to get a Mexican wife with an acre of breadfruit, twenty-five tobacco plants, and a handful of corn."

Marshal Bazaine, appreciating their straits, generously dipped into his military chest and gave each man fifty dollars. At one last rally vows were exchanged, and then General Shelby dissolved the company. Some of the Missourians marched to the Pacific and took ship for California or Japan or the Sandwich Islands. Others went off treasure hunting, inflamed by tales of streams that ran gold and of rocks studded with precious stones, and by legends of tombs where the bones of Aztec emperors were so covered with jewels that they lighted the catacombs like stars in a moonless sky.

A party under the leadership of General Sterling Price settled near Córdoba, where the Emperor had set apart a tract of land for American immigrants. General Slaughter established a large sawmill at Orizaba. General Bee engaged extensively in the raising of cotton. General Hindman, having mastered Spanish in the short space of three months, commenced the practice of law in Córdoba. General Stevens, the chief engineer of General Lee's staff, was given a similar post with the Mexican Imperial Railway. Former Governor Reynolds of Missouri was appointed superintendent of two short-line railroads running out from Mexico City. General Shelby and Major McMurtry became large freight contractors, with headquarters at Córdoba. Former Governor Allen of Louisiana, assisted by the Emperor, founded the *Mexican Times,* a paper printed in English and devoted to the interests of colonization. General Lyon of Kentucky and General McCausland of Virginia were appointed government surveyors. General Watkins was taken into the diplomatic service and sent to Washington on a special mission. Everywhere Americans were honored and promoted, but only in civil life. The army, where they could have been of real service, was closed to them.

Among the French, Austrians, Germans, and Belgians that crowded the city, the Missourians soon stood out as the most reckless and the most deadly. Duelists all, they had a code of conduct, especially with respect to women, that brought them into almost daily conflict with the Europeans. One day the Princess Salm-Salm walked into the dining room of the Hotel Iturbide, where many of the Foreign Legion sat over their cognac. The princess was an American, and the rumor was that she had been a circus rider before her marriage to the Austrian. As she entered, a huge Belgian, far gone in drink, uttered a derisive "Hoop-la!" Before the words were well out of his mouth, Hazel, a young Missourian, was at his side. Seconded by Jim Wood of Sedalia, he met his adversary the next morning at dawn, and his shot was so close to the heart that the Belgian balanced on the grave's edge for months.

So the days went by, full of fighting and adventure for the Southerners, and heavy with doom for Maximilian. In December, 1865, Secretary Seward had notified Napoleon III that friendly relations would be endangered unless France should leave the Mexican people to the "free enjoyment of the republican government they have established for themselves, and of their adhesions to which they have given what seems to the United States to be decisive and conclusive as well as touching proofs." Not only this, but the menace of Prussia made it imperative for Louis Napoleon to concentrate every ounce of strength in France. As a consequence, the order for withdrawal was sent to Bazaine early in 1866.

Gone now were Maximilian's dreams of peaceful rule, and when Bazaine told him of his instructions, the mercurial Hapsburg planned to renounce the crown. Carlota, hoping with all her proud heart to avert the humiliation, begged delay while she went to Paris in an attempt to persuade Louis Napoleon to keep his promises. The Empress sailed from Vera Cruz on July 13, 1866, never to return, for in Paris her poor, disordered mind gave way.

Maximilian, first inclined to flee, finally resolved to remain at his post until the end. The privileged classes promised men and money, and Miramón, Mejía, and Marquez, his three generals, vowed to build the throne on granite. The pledges were as empty as the boast. Upon withdrawal of the French army, it was as if a dike had burst, for the advance of Juárez was a flood that carried everything before it. With reverse following reverse, Maximilian sent for General Shelby and asked him if it was still possible to rally his countrymen. "Too late" was the answer given him.

"It is no longer a throne to be saved," said the Missourian, "but your life. Quit listening to false reports and empty promises, and face the fact of defeat. The one hope is to fight a way to Vera Cruz and board the Austrian warship of your royal brother."

Thanking him for his candor, the Emperor took off the gold cross of the Order of Guadelupe that he wore and pinned it on Shelby's breast. The two then embraced and parted, never to meet again. Indecision lost Maximilian his chance for flight, and the tragedy rushed swiftly to its tragic conclusion. Marching to the relief of Querétaro, the Emperor and his army were surrounded by the Juaristas, and after weeks of siege, a traitor opened the gates at night.

During Maximilian's imprisonment while awaiting trial the Princess Salm-Salm planned his escape, but the attempt came to nothing, and on the morning of June 19, 1867, the Hapsburg and his two generals—Miramón and Mejía—were placed against a stone wall on the Hill of the Bells. A harsh command, and a volley from the rifles of a firing squad ended forever Europe's dream of an American empire.

Juárez, like Maximilian, saw the danger of letting war-trained Americans get a foothold in Mexico, and soon made it clear that they were unwelcome guests. Under this pressure, General Shelby and a majority of his men drifted back to Missouri, many of them as casually as though they had only stepped next door. One bearded colonel, walking into his home after an absence of four years, merely threw down his hat and complained, "Good Lord, Sally. Dinner not ready yet?"

This was the story I did not have the sense to write.

CHAPTER 5

Up from Journalism

I still wonder why the city editor of the *World* ever hired me, for my qualifications would not have gained admission to the kindergarten class in a modern school of journalism. Loathing mathematics, resenting routine, and liking only what interested, I had successfully fought off every effort to provide me with a well-rounded education. Thanks to my mother, I had a fair knowledge of history and the classics, and knew by heart the poems of Scott, Longfellow, and Tennyson, as well as those of Father Ryan and Henry Timrod, two bards of the Confederacy. Aside from that, there was only a brief postgraduate course in "literature" that I had given myself.

A couple of years before, beating back to Missouri from Texas, I happened to pass a secondhand bookstore on the way to the station and saw a set of Ouida, forgotten now, but then at the height of her popularity as a romanticist. Ten volumes, and so badly battered that they were tied together with a rope, but *only two dollars.* I leaped at the bargain, and after buying an excursion ticket, invested the rest of my capital in apples, bananas, and gingersnaps. For three days and two nights I wriggled around on the hard cane seat of an ancient smoking car and gulped down *Moths, Chandos,* and *Under Two Flags.* The end of the journey found me pretty gaunt and sore in every bone, but happy in the conviction that I had acquired a *style.*

The *World* was a Scripps paper, among the first in a chain that now stretches from coast to coast, and back of it was the hope of edging into the rich territory long held in fee simple by William R. Nelson and his *Star.* The venture folded up after several brave years, for the *Star* came close to being Holy Writ in Kansas and western Missouri, but the failure was not inglorious. Since then various publishers have tried

35

to invade the Kansas City field with even less success, all dropping tens of thousands where prudent E. W. Scripps lost only hundreds.

What got me my job, in all probability, was the paper's lack of money with which to hire more than three trained men. As a cub, I covered the federal building, undertakers, and the railroad offices, and served as "leg man" for the star reporters. My ambition, however, was backed up by demoniac energy, not to mention the conceit of ignorance, and inside of a few months I was turning out feature articles suggested by Mrs. Whitney and Miss Bishop, two fine women who ran the public library. Stuff so old that it was new, such as the travels of Sir John Mandeville, Richard Burton's journey to Mecca, George Washington's early affairs with Alequippa, the Half Queen, and the voyages of Marco Polo.

More than that, I started a book-review column and passed pontifical judgments on William Dean Howells, Mrs. Humphrey Ward, Hall Caine, and other great authors of the period. I shudder to think how bad the stuff must have been, for it followed Ouida faithfully, but the editors were glad to have space filled at no added cost.

In time, however, the *World* decided to cover social happenings, something that had not been done before, and being the least important member of a small staff, I drew the assignment. Going to balls and banquets after a long, hard day might have seemed a chore to some, but I loved it, particularly as it never occurred to me that I was not an honored guest as much as any other. Had I not always been invited to everything in Independence and Odessa, the towns where I grew up? As a result, I hoofed it with the best at every dance, and sat down at tables with never a thought that I might be unwelcome. What ended this happy unconsciousness was the city editor's casual remark that he wished he had my "cast-iron nerve."

"What do you mean?" I demanded, reddening at once.

"Your gall," he repeated, grinning nastily. "Butting in on parties as though you were a regular guest and not just a reporter."

To this day I can recall my agony of shame, and there were weeks when I could not go on the streets without thinking that fingers of scorn were being pointed at me. From that

36

moment I hated the job of which I had been so proud, but it required another incident to give me the courage for a break.

The daughter of a local magnate ran away with the coachman—chauffeurs had not yet come into the social picture—and I was rushed up to the home for full details. I rang the bell, and the father himself came to the door. He was a small, chunky man with pepper-and-salt whiskers, and eyes red from crying.

"I'm sorry, son," he said, his voice breaking, "but I don't want to talk about it."

"I know just how you feel, sir," I assured him, my own throat choking up. "It's *terrible*. What on earth got into Miss Nannie?"

With that we went into the parlor, sat down, and had a long talk, going over the sad affair from start to finish. Returning to the office, I carefully explained that Mr. So-and-So and his wife were deeply distressed, and would appreciate it if nothing was said in the paper about the elopement.

"To hell with him," rasped the city editor, a hard-boiled importation from the East. "Hustle around to the back door and get the story from the cook." Reared in the best Southern tradition, I coldly informed him that I was not in the habit of going to back doors, a dignified rejoinder that earned me the boot.

Now came the great decision to proceed to New York and take up where Edgar Allan Poe had left off. Mother argued cautiously that it might be well for me to try for a job on some other paper, building up a larger stock of experience, but nothing could stop me. The kindly city passenger agent of the Wabash provided a pass to Chicago, and there I made arrangements with the Erie Railroad for the rest of the trip, agreeing to ride herd on a car of cattle in return for free transportation.

What a nightmare! I took off nothing but my hat for five horrible nights, and as a capsheaf to wretchedness, nearly perished from actual starvation. I had figured on buying food at the various stations, and learned too late that freight trains stopped only in the yards, often miles away from a store of any kind. The trainmen, however, were a decent lot and tossed me scraps from their own meals, so I managed to keep body and soul in some sort of contact.

I landed in the wilds of Jersey City around four o'clock on a bitter cold February morning, and took the Cortlandt Street ferry over to New York. Walking with difficulty, for I was still twisted out of shape by the cattle car, I wandered up to City Hall Park and crouched miserably on a bench until daylight. A copy of the *Tribune* furnished the address of a boarding-house on the lower East Side, and by eight o'clock I had bargained for a room and meals at $3 a week. A dingy hole, reeking with queer smells, but after the freight train it had the look of a palace.

Having been taught to believe in the early-bird theory, right after breakfast I fared forth with my bundle of manuscripts, fruit of Kansas City nights. The telephone book gave me a list of magazines, and deeming it best to start humbly, I steered clear of *Harper's* and the *Century* and picked the smaller ones. Before the week was out I doubted the existence of editors, for all I ever saw were office boys. There was no such uncertainty about my rejections, for they were swift and explicit. I burned the entire collection not long afterward, and, thank Heaven, cannot remember much about them.

The double weight of homesickness and failure was rapidly getting me down when I met a savior in the saloon where I was sipping a glass of beer and making heavy inroads on the free lunch. Our talk developed that he was a joke writer, and on hearing my sad story he told me of a regular gold mine that had just been opened up. Hearst and Pulitzer were getting out comic supplements, entering the field in competition with *Puck* and *Judge,* paying a dollar for squibs and twenty-five cents a line for verse.

"There's nothing to it," he declared. "After you get on to the trick, they just roll out."

Hustling up to the public library, I sweated over every output of humor I could find, gaining confidence as little of the stuff gave me so much as a titter. Finally believing that I had the hang of it, I invented a couple by the name of Dasherly and Flasherly, and began turning out what I hoped were brilliant bits of wit and repartee. The business of marketing was quite simple, for at both the *World* and the *American* there was a "joke editor" who pawed through your offerings at top speed.

With what sick expectancy I watched them read my squibs

and jingles, and how my heart sank as they shook their heads! This went on day after day, and by the end of the month my small savings had dwindled to a point where there were not enough nickels to make a noise in my pocket. But lo, even as I faced the prospect of park benches, there came a manifestation of the divine providence that even watches the sparrow's fall. Overnight a heavy snowfall blanketed New York, and the morning found me on hand to get a shovel.

The harvest fields of Missouri, thank heaven, had given me strong arms, and I earned $6, enough to pay my board bill for another two weeks. Unhappily, the editors continued to regard my jokes with what was close to loathing, and the weatherman reported no more snow in sight. Broke again, I went to my landlady, a buxom widow in her forties, and mumbled that I would have to get out unless she felt like trusting me.

"Of course!" she exclaimed, clucking sympathetically. "Why, Mr. Creel, a man of your ability is bound to succeed. Stay right here until things get better. And I'll move you down from that little old room at the top of the house to the back parlor. Right next to me."

From there she went on to murmur something about being a lonely woman, for as I could see for myself, the other boarders were not her type. Also something to the effect that companionship was a vital human need. Even with my utter lack of sophistication I got the basic idea, and while I heard myself saying, "Yes'm," I thought only of flight, never having read Benjamin Franklin's advice to his nephew.

Back upstairs in my cubbyhole I went to work with the concentration bred by panic, grinding out jokes and verse in a steady stream. All day long I kept at it, and in the late afternoon, when I knew that preparations for dinner were under way, I packed my few poor belongings and slipped out of the front door with all the stealth of an Iroquois. I spent the night on a bench in Madison Square, getting a loathing for that sylvan spot that has endured to this day. The next morning, after spending my last dime on coffee and doughnuts, I trudged down to Park Row with my fresh output. Once again a higher power intervened in my behalf, for the man at the *Evening Journal* took *four,* and arranged for immediate payment.

From that time on I hit the jackpot regularly, and soon sold to *Puck, Judge, Truth,* and *Life,* as well as the comic supplements and back pages of the *Evening World* and *Evening Journal.* Selling to any of the weeklies was proof that a joke writer had arrived, for aside from paying $2 per squib, they were regarded as the top level in humor. I also had the good luck to team up with four or five artists, furnishing the ideas for their drawings. Before long I was not only able to send regular remittances to my mother, but could even chide her for earlier doubts. Going over papers after her death, I found all of my letters, tied up with ribbons, and in one of them was this juvenile boast:

So you see, Mamma, darling, that I was right about coming to New York. It isn't just the money, although $25 a week, and sometimes more, is a lot better than the beggarly $4 paid me by the *World.* I am now meeting some of the very finest figures in art and literature, and can actually feel myself *grow* by contact with these towering personalities. Next Friday, for example, I am invited to the home of Ella Wheeler Wilcox, the great poetess. She has a salon, like the famous authoresses of the Old World, and just to be seen at one of her soirees is a *distinction.*

Early in 1898 the *American* made me an offer to go on the staff of the comic supplement, and with the right to sell independently to the back page of the *Evening Journal.* Lumped together, it looked like a weekly wage of $40, and since it was surer than free-lancing, I accepted. Although our product— *The Katzenjammer Kids, Foxy Grandpa,* and *Buster Brown*— may not have been any challenge to Mark Twain, at least they had the merit of trying to be funny, and I'll back them against the incredible strips that pass for comics today.

My new job gave me a first sight of William R. Hearst, very Western in his black, broad-brimmed Stetson, and dashing here and there in pursuit of the political career that was to elude him. It also brought me into association with Morrill Goddard, head of the whole Sunday supplement and the real father of yellow journalism. A gaunt, nerve-racked man with a pair of mad eyes, he frankly confessed that his idea of a good paper was to have the reader reel back after one look at the first page, screaming, "My God! Oh, my God!" Mr. Goddard liked some of the verse and captions that I did, and suggested that I quit jokes for page thrillers, but after seeing what it had done to him, I respectfully declined.

Arthur Brisbane, then zooming the circulation of the *Evening Journal* up to dizzy heights, also made me an offer, but a day in his office ended that. At one and the same time he dictated to his secretary, hammered away on a typewriter, and talked into a recording machine. The city room, catching the fever, had all the quiet of Bedlam. Nevertheless, he remained the object of my passionate envy, for no writing man was ever more richly dowered. He was the son of a father who belonged to the Brook Farm community, and all that was fine and brilliant in American life passed through his home; in Paris he knew and learned from Fourier and Saint-Simon; while still a young man he represented Charles Dana's New York *Sun* in London, enjoying the friendship of England's greatest; and before coming to Hearst, he had sat at the right hand of Joseph Pulitzer.

In late April the Spanish-American War broke out, and Park Row, rather than Cuba, was the battleground. Hearst and Pulitzer each claimed the conflict as his own personal property, and rivalry reached the stage of utter madness. Both reared tier after tier of scaffolding before their buildings, and singers, speakers, artists, and musicians, perched on these platforms, created pandemonium from morning until night. If the *World* hired four bands, the *American* employed eight, and if the *American* had five artists painting battle scenes, the *World* engaged ten. One editor went raving crazy, and why the rest escaped is one of life's mysteries.

There was a chap in our crowd who had the most amazing facility for turning out doggerel, and one morning he came into our favorite saloon with the news that he had just been told to write a war poem that would be spread over the entire front page of the *Evening World*. It sounded incredible, of course, but John showed the order, and hurried off to turn out the epic by morning. And he did! Unfortunately, on reaching the office with his masterpiece he found that the editor had just been carted off to the asylum. Poor John! For weeks he insisted that the man was completely sane, and hinted darkly at a Spanish plot.

Catching the war fever in its most aggravated form, I enlisted in a regiment being organized by William Astor Chanler, but

41

after two months of drilling, the Republican governor refused to accept the services of a Democratic colonel. Hearing that John Jacob Astor was getting together a mountain battery for the Philippines, I begged a letter of introduction from Arthur Brisbane, but here again my patriotism was thrown back for a loss. The last man of the hundred was chosen five minutes before my arrival.

What with one thing and another, I came to hate what I was doing and the life I was leading. I saw myself clearly as the cheapest sort of hack, and no longer fooled myself that the tosspots I drank with in Park Row saloons were the "finest figures in art and literature." Twenty-two years old, and nothing more than a penny-a-liner! Life half gone and a failure!

About this time I began to see a good deal of Arthur Grissom, a young poet who contributed verse and vignettes to the magazines. He had married the daughter of Kansas City's richest banker, by a whirlwind courtship snatching her right out of the arms of the businessman to whom she was engaged. After considerable outcry, the outraged parents accepted the situation, and around Christmas the Grissoms agreed to make Kansas City their home.

Arthur and I corresponded regularly, and in the course of time he broached the idea of a weekly paper. Not the usual boiler-plate affair, but a high-class "journal of opinion." William Marion Reedy's *Mirror* was a brilliant success in St. Louis, and it was a certainty that we could do equally well in Kansas City. The scenario sounded good, and there was also his explicit statement that his wife's father, the millionaire banker, had agreed to come across with the necessary capital. Homesick, and even sicker of Park Row saloons and comic supplements, I finally wrote him my agreement to go in on the venture as associate editor.

CHAPTER 6

In Search of a Faith

*W*hen Arthur Grissom assured me that his rich father-in-law would put up the money for our weekly paper, I have no doubt that he wrote in good faith. On reaching Kansas City, however, he met me with the gloomy news that the miserly old man had reneged, refusing to risk a cent of his fortune on two writers without any business training. My face fell with a thud that startled the station porters, but Arthur argued persuasively that it was only a temporary setback. A personal canvass for subscriptions would give us cash enough for preliminary expenses, and leading merchants had promised support.

There was nothing for me to do but agree. Having left New York with a blare of trumpets, I could hardly sneak back again. Mrs. Grissom was off somewhere with her parents, and since the venture called for constant association, I went to live with Arthur in the handsome home that the banker had been good enough to provide. Deciding to call our venture *The Independent,* we laid out a sixteen-page dummy and began the round of office buildings and stores.

The response from subscribers and advertisers was generous beyond expectations, and on March 11, 1899, we made our bow. All of the dailies commented favorably on the first number, and the people seemed to like it. Starting off with a vigorous editorial page, we covered the theaters, books, sports, and social news, and plunged headfirst into local and national politics. Arthur and I wrote all of it with the exception of contributions from New York friends who came to our aid. Not a bad lot, either, for among the artists who helped us were Jimmy Swinnerton, C. T. Anderson, Tom Allen, and Billy Marriner, and such writers as Edwin Markham, Julian Hawthorne, Ada Patterson, and Winifred Black.

Every prospect pleased. Mother was overjoyed to have me back, and even Father showed a mild pleasure. Unhappily, a large bluebottle fly soon began to buzz around in our ointment. Mrs. Grissom continued to stay away, claiming ill health, and as the days went by, our home became the scene of mysterious disappearances. First a picture would be missing, and then silver, rugs, and pieces of furniture. For a while Arthur insisted that it was all part of spring cleaning, but when we reached the house one evening to find that our beds had been carted off, the conclusion forced itself that dear old Papa-in-law wanted us out.

I went home, convinced that the skids were being readied for poor Arthur, but he clung pathetically to the hope that his little lovebird would return to the nest. In December, however, the banker quit stalling and let him have it right between the eyes. The marriage, he said, had always been hateful to him, for a scribbler was not his idea of a son-in-law, and at last he had succeeded in winning the wife's consent to a divorce. Arthur sued the old man for breaking up his marriage, and on getting $40,000 out of a compromise settlement, hopped off for New York, where he started the *Smart Set*. And there was I, left holding the bag.

Mother was delighted, of course, having resented the fact that I was under Arthur, but sole ownership brought me up with a jerk. Out of a naïve respect for the printed word, I believed that every editor, even the humblest, had it in his power to be a Molder of Public Opinion, a Light for the Feet of the People. Sophomoric, to be sure, but I was only twenty-three. Like every youth with any generosity of spirit, I knew that I wanted to fight for the underdogs of life, but had no very clear idea how to go about it.

What was the right gospel for me to preach in order to be a True Guide? Should I keep on with my inherited devotion to the Democratic party, or was there some other faith that held greater promise? Bowed under the weight of my responsibility, and with a flash of sound judgment that still amazes, I sat down to do the thinking that might help me decide on a course.

In New York I had come into fairly close relations with a wild-eyed, shockheaded writer who called himself a Communist, and quoted incessantly from men named Marx and Engels. One of his lines, about how workers had nothing to lose but their chains, made a great impression. Remembering him, I searched around until I found a copy of *Das Kapital,* and pored over those dreary, turgid volumes until every nerve ached in protest.

The theory of "surplus value" made a certain appeal, but everything else revolted me. Hate oozed from every line—hate of the competitive struggle, hate of achievement, hate of demonstrated superiorities—with only wholesale bloodletting as the satisfaction of that hate. At every point the Marxian class war had its base in monstrous envies. Arbitrarily and without distinction, owners were all exploiters, and nonowners the helpless, unhappy victims of their greeds. Instead of regarding ownership as the reward of initiative and industry, Marx and Engels set it down as the result of evil, conspiratorial practices; instead of urging honest effort as the open road to ownership, they preached the gospel of revolution, confiscation, and liquidation.

Denying that the state had any natural and legal functions, Marx and his followers attacked government as another cunning, sinister device to protect private ownership and continue the slavery of the exploited. In the same breath they sneered at religion as "the opiate of the people," spat at the idea of God, and rejected Christ's teaching even while bawling about the brotherhood of man.

Aside from the gross materialism of the Marxian program, the thing that most repelled was the derision of "bourgeois morality." Honor and honesty were repudiated as rules of life in dealing with the capitalistic class, and every infamy was justified if used for the advancement of communism. Not only lying, hypocrisy, and treachery, but even theft and assassination. Nothing was ever more shameless than the open advocacy of falsehood and bad faith as a fixed policy.

Then, too, there was the confident prediction of what would happen when the violences of revolution had liquidated the owning class, done away with private property, and lifted the proletariat into power. The state would disappear, leaving every man and woman a free agent in a free society. On the instant, and even while their hands dripped blood, the victors would be cleansed of every evil passion and live side by side in love and fraternity. Production, by some miracle, would take care

45

of itself, each producing "according to his abilities," and each using "according to his needs."

The whole Communist gospel filled me with loathing, and every passing year has added to it. In nothing that Lenin ever wrote was there a single dissent from the commandments of Marx, and even while Stalin joins in the discussion of plans for a new and democratic world order, the party is told that 100-per-cent Marxism—the overthrow of capitalist states—remains the goal of communism.

After communism I explored socialism, and sweated over heavy doctrinal expositions until I had the luck to run across the clearer, simpler literature of the Fabians as put forth by H. G. Wells, Shaw, and the Webbs. For a time I was almost persuaded, being particularly impressed by their emphasis on democratic processes rather than the hates and violences of Marx and Engels.

What appealed particularly was the public ownership of natural resources and such utilities as were natural monopolies. Why should a man claim title to oil and coal deposits by the mere fact of discovery? Or a wandering prospector be permitted to own rich mining properties because his mule chanced to paw up a nugget while hitched to a piñon? Even the Roman Empire had the sense to rule that the owners of land had only surface rights.

What repelled was the dogmatism and an unwillingness to appreciate the value of intelligent opportunism. Such leaders as I talked with reminded me of nothing so much as hens sitting on porcelain eggs. It was their angry insistence that the program must be taken as a whole or not at all. Worst of all was their demand for the surrender of the individual will. The party was to do the thinking for its members, and any dissent carried all the horrid implications of heresy.

Time, of course, has worked changes in my early faiths. Today I reject socialism as an economic philosophy in irreconcilable opposition to the American system and every other form of free society. As proved by Russia, Italy, and Germany, where socialism paved the way for communism, fascism, and nazism, the program leads inevitably to totalitarianism. There is no "middle way" between collectivism and democratic processes, for one or the other must go down in the struggle. But at twenty-three, brimming over with the optimism of youth, I

46

thought that socialization could be taken in small doses, failing to see that it was habit-forming.

Next in order came *Progress and Poverty,* and after the hate and muddle of *Das Kapital* and the doctrinaire gospel of the Socialists, the clarity and force of Henry George was heaven. My conversion was complete, and an object lesson provided by Joseph Fels helped mightily. As I remember it, he bought a large tract of land near Philadelphia and left for England after giving instructions to resist every improvement.

"Make the land a public dump," he told his agent. "Do everything possible to make it unsightly. Fight the extension of car lines and water mains. Bring suits to keep out telephones and electricity. Be the worst sort of citizen."

The agent did just that, but when Mr. Fels returned some years later, the city had spread out to take in his lots, and he sold them for ten times the original purchase price. "Certainly it was not I who created the increased value," crowed Mr. Fels. "People were taxed for the homes they built, and taxed for every improvement, but I, who did nothing to promote the growth of the community, now reap a huge profit by reason of that growth. I feel like a thief, but as long as Philadelphia is stupid enough to let me get away with it, what can I do?"

If anybody at that time had told me that the day would come when the single-tax movement could be housed in a telephone booth, I would have hooted.

Out of my thinking and research, jumbled though all of it may have been, came a number of definite decisions. First of all, I came to the belief—and it is a belief that has never changed— that the American form of government is the best system ever devised by man. If evils persist, it is either the negligence or the indifference of the citizen, for the ballot is at hand as a method of correction.

While rejecting socialism, I made up my mind to stand for the highest degree of socialization short of a deadening level that did away with the incentive motive and denied proper rewards for initiative, industry, and ability. In addition, I would fight for the single tax, and end the monstrous injustice of having individuals appropriate the wealth created by the community.

As I viewed it, both socialization and single tax called for the use of existing political parties rather than the laborious

47

organization of new ones. This compelled a choice between the Republicans and the Democrats, and that was not difficult. A Democrat by inheritance, I was also wholeheartedly convinced that the Democratic party was closer to the people and more likely to stand for human rights rather than property rights. William J. Bryan was no Jefferson, but by every progressive standard he was infinitely better than McKinley, owned by Mark Hanna and his plunderbund.

What faced me, however, was not a choice between the two parties, but a choice between factions. From the Civil War right on down, Missouri had gone Democratic with pious regularity, and Jackson County had helped to swell majorities. Lacking Republicans to fight, Democrats battled each other, and elections were contested with a vigor that stopped short only at mayhem. In Kansas City, dominating the county by its larger vote, Joe Shannon, a handsome, black-muzzled Irishman, led the Rabbits against the Goats of Jim Pendergast, a rotund saloonkeeper who controlled the river wards.

From the first *The Independent* favored the Rabbits, and on coming to sole control, I dumped all of my eggs in the Shannon basket. The fact that Pendergast and his Goats were controlled by the brewers and the public-service corporations was not the only consideration that moved me. At Joe Shannon's right hand, and the brains of the faction, stood Frank P. Walsh, a man who had won my love and admiration at our initial meeting.

A great lawyer, a persuasive speaker, and the most authentic liberal I have ever known, Frank could have aspired to any office, but he waved political preferment away out of his conviction that "an agitator outside" was far more valuable than a plodding administrator inside. Only Woodrow Wilson ever won him over to officeholding, and then because the jobs were anything but routine. In 1913 the President made him head of the Commission on Industrial Relations, and his searching inquiries into the reasons for unrest opened the way for the splendid labor laws that followed.

In 1918 Frank was again called to the colors, President Wilson appointing him and former President Taft as the co-chairmen of a National War Labor Board that was, in effect, a supreme court for industry as a whole. The Taft-Walsh board, ruling on disputes between workers and management, handed down decisions so eminently just that only twice were they

48

defied. No two men were ever more unlike than Taft the conservative and Walsh the radical, yet at the end of their association the former president publicly praised Frank as the "finest type of American."

Billy Lyons was another of my inseparables, and the three of us were faithful observers of the Eleventh Commandment, "Thou shalt not take thyself too seriously." Among many joyous memories, there was the time when the intelligentsia of Kansas City decided to organize a University Club. The promoter came to Frank, Billy, and me, and while not one of us had gone beyond the eighth grade, we approved the idea with enthusiasm. Yes, indeed! What the town needed was a place where men with academic backgrounds could forgather for mutual stimulation. Eventually questionnaires came, asking us to name our college, and we answered that our alma mater was the International School of Correspondence at Scranton.

Back from the secretary, of course, came a letter stating that Scranton was not recognized and that our applications could not be considered. Frank, Billy, and I got together at once and addressed an indignant reply, using the letterhead of Frank's law firm. What we demanded was a bill of particulars. Why was Scranton denied equal rank with Harvard, Yale, and Princeton? We too had our traditions, and while collective action was not possible, each student was under strict instructions to haze himself at the opening of a term.

The young secretary, a newcomer, replied apologetically that he had nothing to do with the rules, and we branded the letter as "evasive." Out of love for our alma mater, we must insist on a categorical explanation. If not, there were laws in the land that applied to slander and calumny. Unfortunately, just as we were beginning to enjoy the correspondence the president of the club called us up.

"Quit deviling that poor sap of a secretary," he ordered. "And if you want the truth, I don't think any one of you three bums ever took a course from Scranton." And he was right!

I have never quite made up my mind as to whether I missed or benefited by my lack of a formal education, for I have known both regret and thanksgiving. On the whole, a bit more of the latter, for as Woodrow Wilson complained, most of the colleges and universities fail to relate their courses to life. The ideal arrangement, as I have come to see it, is this: after high school a year or so of work so as to give some idea of what is *wanted* out of further schooling. That is what I had in mind for myself, but somehow I could never find either the time or the money.

The turn of the century was an ideal time for my advent as a "reformer." Theodore Roosevelt was beginning to lift the voice of insurgency; Lincoln Steffens and Ray Stannard Baker were racing from city to city with their muckrakes, exposing corruption, and dynamic progressives were springing up at key points: Tom Johnson, Newton Baker, and Fred Howe in Cleveland; Golden Rule Jones and Brand Whitlock in Toledo; Ben Lindsey in Denver; Frank Heney on the Pacific Coast; and in Oregon W. S. U'Ren was preaching the initiative and referendum as a means of insuring responsible as well as responsive government.

Brashly enough, I wrote them all, and all were generous enough to answer. As a result we started a chain of letters something on the order of Jefferson's Committee on Correspondence, permitting an exchange of views and experiences. Nowhere was there any doubt as to the means of salvation. "Kick the rascals out"; municipal ownership; laws for the protection of labor; and the return of power to the people through the initiative, the referendum, the recall, and the direct primary.

Since the Goats were our rascals in Kansas City, furnishing the votes for monopolists and franchise grabbers, I ranged myself at the side of Walsh and Shannon, and addressed myself briskly to the task of kicking them out.

CHAPTER 7

The Rabbits and the Goats

*I*f anybody had come to me in those early days and prophesied that Tom Pendergast was destined to be a national figure, a member of the Democratic high command, and a welcome White House visitor, I would have laughed in his face. We looked on cunning, resourceful Jim as smartest of the smart, and dismissed Tom, his younger brother, as a thick-skulled, heavy-jowled oaf.

I would have had an equally hearty laugh if it had been predicted that James A. Reed, then the mouthpiece for the Goats, would go to the United States Senate and play no small part in helping the Republicans to defeat the League of Nations. Outside of a Byronic ensemble and an amazing gift for vitriolic oratory, he was without ability. As some wit said of him at the time, "Open Reed's front door and you're in his back yard."

Therefore, when *The Independent* stood forth as the organ of the Rabbits in 1900, the one target for attack was Jim Pendergast. From his saloon near the water front he controlled the three river wards, and his "vote mills" furnished the majorities that elected councilmen who did the bidding of the brewers and the corporations. Our course, quite obviously, was to elect a mayor who would clean house, and when Pendergast named Reed as his candidate, the Rabbits offered an elderly merchant of considerable standing.

And what a licking we got! Reed's gab made our man seem tongue-tied, but the real cause of defeat was the vote of the river wards, where the Goats stuffed ballot boxes until they had to be tied with ropes. Our screams rang to high heaven, but the noise we made was our sole satisfaction. Beaten in the city, we now turned to the fight for sheriff, judges, assessor, and other county offices.

According to custom, the convention was held in Independence, the old county seat, the embattled factions gathering in a circus tent. The vote of the districts outside Kansas City, chiefly rural, gave the Rabbits control, but Pendergast refused to abide by the result and put forward a man named Williams as his choice for permanent chairman. Yelling, hitting, and kicking, the Goats came down the aisle in flying wedge formation.

I was on the platform and rose with other Rabbits to defend our position, but I can't say my heart was in it. Leading the charge were Billy Burgoyne and Jack Pryor, two Goats with a bad reputation for gunplay, and behind them were Pendergast's "muscle boys." With a heave-ho they lifted up their chairman, but just as his face rose above the level of the platform a bony fist shot out and landed squarely on Williams' nose, squashing it all over his face.

"That does it," I groaned to myself, burying my head deeper in the planks of the platform, but instead of the expected rush, a sudden silence fell. Getting the courage to look up, I saw that the blow had been struck by the one man in the tent who could get away with it. The fist was that of Jim Pryor, Jack's father, and a faithful Rabbit despite his son's high standing among the Goats.

"Lay off," rumbled Jack, catching hold of Burgoyne's arm and waving back the muscle boys, who were about to charge. "He's an old man and has damned few amusements."

Our chairman, crawling out from under the table, took possession of the ice-water pitcher and called for the next order of business. Deciding against further battle, Pendergast led his Goats to the back of the tent, where they held a rump convention and named an opposition ticket. The courts gave our nominees the nod, but Pendergast bolted when the election came around, putting Republicans in the county offices for the first time in forty years.

As the dismal returns rolled in on election night, a few of us adjourned to a near-by grogshop owned by a devoted Rabbit and sat late drowning our sorrow. As a result, the next morning found me anything but chirpy, and a sympathetic bartender advised an absinthe frappé. Just as I was lifting it to my mouth, however, I found myself holding nothing but the stem of the glass, while a shrill voice shattered my eardrums with the cry of "Hell's broth!"

Looking around, I saw a little gray-haired old lady, bonnet tied under her chin, who announced herself as Mrs. Carry Nation. Having neatly sliced away my drink with her hatchet, she sank her weapon in the mahogany bar and then threw it through the mirror at the back. The Kansas lady's reign of terror lasted for a week, and then she journeyed east, leaving wreckage and innumerable cases of nervous prostration behind her.

Two losing campaigns, bitterly fought, were not so good for *The Independent*. Circulation went up but advertising went down, for under pressure from the city hall, many merchants withdrew their patronage. Instead of enlarging my staff, as I had hoped, I was forced to make reductions. I kept Colonel

John Calhoun Moore to help out with editorials, and also, a couple of canvassers, but the advertising manager and assistant editor had to be released.

Not only did I hustle ads, racing from store to store, but wrote almost everything in the paper. Girl friends contributed gossip for a Lucy Grey page, and Mother aided in a fashion page that I did under the name of Maid Marion, but all the rest was up to me. Sports, theaters, local stuff, politics, comic verse, burlesque, and even fiction and a six-installment serial. Strange as it may seem, I found time to take up baseball again, playing third base for the Kansas City Athletic Club, and I boxed regularly with Tommy Ryan, then the great middle-weight champion.

Restored to solvency in some degree, I turned again to politics as a major activity and sat down with Frank Walsh to discuss tactics and strategy. With his usual clarity, he pointed out the mistake that all of us had been making. Viewed properly, Pendergast and Reed were pawns in the game, for behind them, and responsible for their power, stood a state machine. This ring, for there was no one boss, ruled Missouri as viceroys for the corporations, issuing them licenses to plunder and controlling local machines by the denial of home rule. For example, the police commissioners and election commissioners in both Kanas City and St. Louis were appointed by the governor, thus letting city bosses get away with murder at every election.

Frank's analysis seemed to make sense, so off we started on a campaign to clean up the state. Luck was with us, for former Governor William J. Stone chose that moment to quarrel with Colonel William H. Phelps, lobbyist for the Missouri Pacific Railroad and a higher-up in the ring. Angered out of his usual silence by the attack, the Colonel spilled the beans with his bitter comment that "we both suck eggs, but Stone hides the shells."

Following up this lead, we interviewed members of the Legislature and finally struck pay dirt in the person of a simple soul named Cardwell. What he told of his experiences in Jefferson City was hair-raising, and we lost no time in putting it all into a speech for public delivery. In precise detail, Cardwell related how state officials had ordered him and other legislators to kill bills disliked by the corporations, explaining that their campaign contributions "entitled them to immunity from un-friendly legislation."

The scandal rocked Missouri, and before it could die down the Secretary of State foolishly burst out with a letter in which he called Cardwell an "infamous and absolute liar." We made the young legislator sue, of course. Frank Walsh was his counsel, and high officials were dragged to the witness stand and forced to make damaging admissions. Former Governor Stone himself, thereafter known as Gumshoe Bill, was exposed as the paid lobbyist for the schoolbook trust, the baking-powder trust, and various other privileged interests.

Unhappily, Cardwell suddenly accepted a compromise settlement of $7,500, and the case came to an abrupt stop. Public indignation soon died down, and in the spring of 1902 Jim Reed was re-elected mayor. The Shannon forces won out in the fall, the entire county ticket winning by a large majority, but it was poor consolation for the loss of the city.

Worse was still to come, for the Legislature now proceeded to name Stone to the seat in the United States Senate left vacant by the retirement of Senator George Vest. And there he stayed, coming to evil prominence in March, 1917, when he and ten other "willful men," as President Wilson stigmatized them, successfully filibustered against the bill to arm our merchant ships.

What made the action of the Legislature more shocking was that it put the admitted lobbyist in the chair long held by a great statesman. Senator Vest threw back to Benton, Webster, and Calhoun, and for thirty years or more had been an honor to both his state and the nation. A thousand and one stories were told about him, for few figures were more picturesque, but the one I liked best had to do with a speech during the Cleveland campaign.

The Republicans made much of the charge that the Democratic candidate had had an affair with his housekeeper, and even broadcast this bit of doggerel: "Maw, Maw, where's Paw? He's in the White House, haw-haw-haw." Party chieftains, scared to death, backed away from any answer, but not Senator Vest. At a great mass meeting in Missouri he met the charge head on.

"What of it?" he thundered. "What of it? We did not enter

our man in this race as a gelding." And Cleveland carried the state.

Once again, however, as in the case of Cardwell, we had a lucky break. The street railroads in St. Louis were asking new franchises, and with their usual simple directness they bribed the local boss and bought the votes of council members, laying cash on the barrelhead. All was going well until one high-powered financier made the mistake of double-crossing a dumb German. After giving this councilman $5,000 for his vote, he borrowed it back "just for a few hours." Then, when the poor fool asked for it, the millionaire briber shook his head and said, "I don't know what you are talking about."

The Dutchman, of course, yelled his head off, and his squawks came to the ears of Joseph W. Folk, the young and vigorous circuit attorney, and soon whole batches of indictments were being returned. Newspapers and orators bemoaned the disgrace of it all, but for me the light of the trials was this priceless bit from the lips of Butler, the convicted boss.

"If I had to do it over again," he said, "you'd never find me taking bribes. I'd be a lawyer and call 'em fees."

The bribery cases, brilliantly and successfully prosecuted, brought Folk into the limelight, and our crowd was quick to see him as a gubernatorial possibility. Frank Walsh and I made repeated trips to St. Louis, and every talk strengthened our belief in the honesty, courage, and very real ability of the man. Like us, he was enthusiastic over the initiative, referendum, recall, short ballot, direct primary, and commission government, and in every way looked like the answer to prayer.

The announcement of Folk's candidacy brought screams from the state and city machines, and Jim Reed was chosen by them to save Missouri from "demagogues" and "foul birds." The election was in the bag from the first, for the rural sections were aroused at last, and with all pressure removed we took time out for a little good clean fun. As a senator, Reed became noted for his vituperative tongue, but in those days he was flowery to the point of absurdity.

Knowing his humorlessness, I printed speeches that he was supposed to have delivered, and while all stirred him to protest, one in particular brought furious denials. In it I charged him with having said that "when God poured out the milk, the cream ran over and made Missouri." Day after day he begged audiences to believe that no such words had ever passed his lips, and always I came back with a wealth of supporting affidavits.

Folk was swept into office by a landslide, Reed carrying only one county, but disaster befell the rest of the ticket, for Missourians turned away from sacred traditions and put Republicans in state, county, and city offices. The Cardwell revelations had something to do with the result, but the main reason was the colorful personality of Theodore Roosevelt as contrasted to the stodginess of Alton B. Parker. Where Bryan had carried the state by a handsome majority in 1900, Parker lost it by 50,000.

The outcome held no element of surprise. I attended the Democratic national convention in St. Louis, and the gathering had about as much excitement and enthusiasm as an undertaking parlor. Disheartened and disorganized by Bryan's two defeats, the progressives lacked the spirit to resist Wall Street domination; and as if Parker's nomination was not strain enough on Democratic gullets, the convention gave him a doddering millionaire reactionary for running mate. On the way home, Frank Walsh summed up the situation in this crisp sentence: "What chance have we got to lick the Republicans when we're playing their game?"

Aside from disgust, my one positive emotion was pity for Mr. Bryan, pushed aside and even avoided, where only four years before he had been the party's idol. I followed him around Missouri during the 1900 campaign, and at the first note of his organ voice audiences reared back and bayed like coon dogs. I can still recall both my admiration and my envy as I listened to his speeches and saw his shirt and coat wet with sweat. I was just beginning to make platform appearances at the time, and aside from difficulty in getting my upper lip loose from my teeth, I suffered from a sense of extreme cold.

By sheer force of will, I became a fluent speaker in time, but never a good one. Always more interested in what I was saying than in the way I said it, I took no pains to study delivery, and contracted several unfortunate mannerisms that were never lost. Not the least of these was the habit of speaking through my clenched teeth, and while aware of it, I made no effort at correction until 1935. In that year H. G. Wells came over from England to do some articles for *Collier's,* and spent two weeks with me in Washington. After several days of cordial companionship, I felt that I knew him well enough to talk frankly, and pointed out that while his voice was inaudible enough, he made it worse by keeping a hand over his mouth.

"Perfectly true, my dear fellow," he said. "Perfectly true. Many times, while on the platform, I have found myself speaking through my mustache to my tie. But since you have brought the matter up, may I say that your own speech gives an effect of mastication, thereby entailing inevitable parentheses."

"All right," I laughed. "Let's make a bargain. I'll quit eating my words if you'll stop inhaling yours."

The election result desolated my mother, but I myself was tickled pink. With Roosevelt in the White House, there was bound to be a shaking of dry bones, not only in Washington but throughout the nation. Moreover, Herbert Hadley had been elected Missouri's attorney general, and by reason of our close friendship, I knew that a militant progressivism underlaid his Republicanism.

Poor Herbert! Elevated to the governorship in 1908, beating Folk by a narrow margin, he came close to the Republican presidential nomination in 1912, for the Taft delegates offered to accept him as a compromise candidate. Stricken with tuberculosis, he was compelled to quit public life, and died in Colorado soon after. Had Herbert Hadley kept his health, I still believe that he would have been the Republican nominee in 1920.

CHAPTER 8

Federal Judges and Crooked Cops

*T*here is an unhappy wretch in Greek mythology, Sisyphus by name, whose doom it was to roll a stone up a hill, only to have it roll down again whenever he reached the top. If I thought of him at all, it was vaguely, but our experiences in Jefferson City gave me a warm fellow feeling for the poor creature.

No sooner had the legislature convened than our group descended on the capital, fairly sway-backed under the weight of progressive measures and full of confidence that Governor Folk's election meant their passage. Alas for high hopes! Pendergast's boys, together with the St. Louis gang and a bunch of rural legislators bought by railroad passes, formed a bloc strong enough to throw us back for a loss. All of our major proposals were defeated, and it was only by a fluke that we pushed through a maximum-freight-rate bill and a two-cent-fare law.

A gain, to be sure, but even while we rejoiced over our success in bringing the railroads under some measure of control, their lawyers marched into the federal court. A few brief arguments, not nearly so long or convincing as the selling talk of a Fuller brush man, and injunctions were granted against the operation of both laws. There was nothing that we could do about it, for in those days a federal judge ranked only a little lower than Moses.

Even as we licked our wounds in the silence bred by awe, however, Providence intervened. A few nights after the issuance of the injunctions, the state game warden happened to be at the Union Station and saw a Pullman porter hurrying by with a load of snipe, prairie chickens, and geese. On investigation, it developed that the porter was taking the out-of-season game to a private car that contained this distinguished company: Judge John F. Phillips, presiding over the Western District of Missouri; Judge Smith McPherson of the Southern District of Iowa; Judge John C. Pollock of Kansas; Gardiner Lathrop, general solicitor for the Santa Fe; O. M. Spencer, general attorney for the Burlington; and Samuel Moore, general solicitor for the Kansas City Southern. These men—the lawyers who had asked the injunctions and the judges who had granted them—were headed for a week of tarpon fishing off Tampico as the guests of Mr. Lathrop.

It was as though the heavens had opened, letting us hear the song of the seraphim. With Frank Walsh's help I went over Missouri records for the last twenty-five years and discovered that 244 cases against the railroads had been taken away from the state into the federal courts. Of this number, 14 were decided in favor of the railroads, 21 remanded, and 209 summarily dismissed.

Going on from there, I proved that the so-called "temporary injunction" usually lasted from two to five years, and sometimes gained permanency by old age. After that I figured the saving to the people if the maximum-freight-rate bill and the two-cent-fare law had been permitted to operate, and laboriously worked out the cost of each tarpon that might be caught by the judges and the general solicitors. It ran up into the millions.

In order to bolster my attack, I ran from one leader of the bar to another, begging an expression of opinion, but if there is any greater coward than a doctor, it is a lawyer. Only at the last did I have the luck to find a man of courage, and he turned loose with this blast:

"I do not hesitate to say that I believe that those general solicitors would not have invited the men they did had not those men been judges. No doubt the invitation was fairly and innocently worded. But men of the caliber of the three judges ought and must have known that there was dope in the middle of the sugar-coated bait held out to them. Such an affair as the Tampico pleasure jaunt begets in the people a disregard for judges and a consequent disregard for law."

The grave and reverend seigneurs ignored my attacks for a while, but finally Judge Phillips issued a public statement deploring the "spirit of intense demagoguery" that seemed to be abroad, and offering this explanation: "It is true that we rode in a special car, just as I would have gone fishing in the private wagon of a friend, standing my proportion of the grub and bait."

I accepted the explanation without argument, but as a concession to the "spirit of intense demagoguery," begged the Judge to tell the exact amount paid by him and the other two judges as their share of the "grub and bait." Not a guess, but the *exact* amount. When he preserved a dignified silence, I pressed the question again and again. It was my hope, of course, to be sent to jail for contempt, but the judges were too shrewd for that, and the whole thing soon died out.

What it did do, however, was breed certain convictions that afterward found expression in my advocacy of the recall of judges and also of decisions that set aside laws as unconstitutional. A desperate remedy, perhaps, but not more desperate than the evil of an uncontrolled and autocratic judiciary translating social and economic prejudices into law and pushing the Congress to one side as though it were not a co-ordinate branch of government.

Nor is it that judges are in agreement as to what is or is not constitutional. A district judge is overruled by circuit judges, and these in turn are overruled by the Supreme Court, usually by a split decision, the dissenting justices disputing everything said by the majority. Even then the decision is not irrevocable, for nothing is more common than for the august tribunal to reverse itself.

One member, Justice Robert Jackson, is actually on record with the bitter gibe that the acrobatics of the Supreme Court have made the law of the land like a railroad ticket—"good for this day only."

Impeachment is a farce. The Constitution, of course, states explicitly that all judges, "both of the Supreme and inferior courts, shall hold their offices during good behavior." Unhappily, what constitutes good behavior is still one of the great mysteries of American life. Never at any time has it been given any exact definition, for the Senate, which sits as a high court of impeachment, is anything but a judicial body. It makes its own rules, heeds no precedents, and each of the ninety-six senators votes his purely personal opinion.

Since the adoption of the Constitution, only ten federal judges have been impeached, and of the number, just half were found guilty and stripped of their robes. All of the cases were marked by bewildering differences of opinion as to what did or did not soil the judicial ermine, for while some senators were harsh in their judgments, others gave evidence of believing that nothing was misbehavior short of mayhem, arson, and mass murder.

In the course of forty years, some of my views have suffered radical alteration. For example, after watching the operation of the direct primary, particularly with reference to United States senators, I am beginning to doubt its infallibility. The old system, at least, saved us from hillbilly singers. In no degree, however, have I changed with respect to the wisdom of the recall for officials, including judges. Today, as a matter of truth, it is even more necessary, for during the last decade every appointment to the federal bench has been purely political, not stopping at ambulance chasers or the mouthpieces of city gangs. To pick one illustration out of many, President Roosevelt draped the judicial ermine about a notorious hench-man of Frank Hague, despite a roar of protest from every county in New Jersey. Governor Charles Edison, the worthy son of a great father, not only denounced the appointment as a disgrace but went to the White House with a personal appeal.

The defeat of our measures by an opposition bloc in the legislature had its value, for it taught us a lesson. What stood plain was that mere enthusiasm had no chance against organi-zation, so we decided to build a people's machine that would function just as effectively as that of the gangs. A lobby in the public interest! Under the leadership of Frank Walsh and Phil R. Toll, a brilliant young businessman, a score of citizens agreed to go to Jefferson City when the legislature convened and *stay on guard* until the end.

What's more, it *worked,* for out of the session came these laws: the direct primary, the initiative, and the referendum; a child-labor law; a law prohibiting railroads from removing cases to the federal courts; factory inspection; registration of lobbyists; and a law compelling all railroads doing business in the state to incorporate in Missouri. All may seem rather ordi-nary today, but at the time they were spectacular achievements, putting Missouri in the van of progressivism.

Our one failure was the defeat of the act under which every city, town, and village would be given the right to regulate the charges of public-utility corporations. No Missouri muni-cipality possessed the power, and rates were what the companies chose to fix. Governor Folk, therefore, called a special session of the legislature, and after a hard fight the people's lobby won again. By way of good measure, we also got the recall, although judges were carefully excluded.

Unhappily, no such successes attended our local battles. Jim Pendergast's vote mills in the river wards kept us from getting control of the council. A new city charter was beaten, and our campaign for a three-cent carfare went down to defeat before the solid opposition of the "business element." We had asked Tom Johnson to come to Kansas City for a mass meeting, but when the bankers and merchants denounced him as a "dan-gerous demagogue" we told him to stay away. Even my pet proposal, the use of the public schools as social centers, was rejected as "newfangled nonsense."

That was, and still is, one of my most ardent enthusiasms. Just as the political parties had their permanent organizations and all-year-round headquarters, so was it imperative that the citizenship set up similar machinery. And what more obvious than the use of the public schools for such purpose? Even as each school is the center of a neighborhood, with attendance taking no account of politics, race, or creed, so would the gathering of adults in the buildings at night be a nonpartisan, nonexclusive meeting of the citizens of the neighborhood.

An end to the wretched system of discussing public business only in the heat of a campaign, and then taking information from excited partisans orating in a hall hired by party funds. In the community center there would be continuous discussion of public business by the people themselves, with Democrats, Republicans, Socialists, independent voters, poor men, rich men, employers, workers, etc., etc., all touching elbows and subjecting their opinions to the test of debate.

The Board of Education—as is the case in many cities today—was entirely willing to have the schools used as recreation centers, or for lectures on noncontroversial subjects, but the members stood immovably against the organization of *community centers*. Lacking the money to hire halls, we could not reach the people as a whole, and after the excitement of the election died down, our Kansas City movement lost impetus.

True, Governor Folk appointed new police commissioners, but one of them was the "loyal citizen" type who insisted that a thorough house cleaning might give the town a bad name. As a result, he teamed up with the Republican mayor and prevented any reorganization of the department. All of my howls went unheeded until there came another of those lucky breaks that had favored me in the past.

A famous pickpocket, Dawson by name, was caught while ripping through a train with his mob, and suffered a fractured ankle when he jumped through the car window. Slipping into Kansas City, Dawson was given tenderest care by the police surgeon, and detectives took him daily gifts of fruit and flowers. A hospital nurse tipped me off, and I broke the story with a bang.

Investigation proved that the town had become a rendezvous

for criminals; that pictures of notorious thieves had been taken out of the rogues' gallery; that policemen sheltered bank robbers; that plain-clothes men helped to market loot, taking diamond rings and watches as their pay. At that, there was nothing yellow about the rascals, for even in the face of daily exposures they fought back. Witnesses were beaten with black-jacks, one man was shot, and others received death threats. Right in the middle of the trials the chief of police sent word that he had "something on me" and would turn it loose if I didn't "lay off."

"Has he?" Both Frank Walsh and Joe Shannon came to me with the question.

"Well," I answered, "I don't think so."

"Then go on down and call his bluff." The two of them, sitting there comfortably, had no doubt as to my course and would not listen to any excuse. So off I went, but at a snail's pace, and doing my best to think of some good sudden ailment.

To get to the chief's office I had to pass through a large room where the detectives loafed when off duty, and out of the corner of my eye I saw many I had been accusing. All of them started up at sight of me, and it took every ounce of will power not to break into a mad gallop. At every step I could feel a club coming down on my head or a slug burying itself in my back. Maybe there are men who do not know the meaning of fear, but I am not one of them. When I finally reached the side passage, after what seemed years, my shirt was wringing wet.

Recovering somewhat, I entered the chief's office with a fairly bold face and demanded to know what it was that he had on me. The Big Fellow, as they called him, blustered and threatened for a while, but at the last he began to whine and wanted to know why we "couldn't be friends." After thunder-ing my defiance, I walked out of the station with the knee action of a drum major. By way of ending the story, the "loyal citizen" commissioner was dismissed, the chief kicked out, and the department completely reorganized.

CHAPTER 9

Incursions and Excursions

Politics and political reforms, while a major activity, did not take up all of my time by any means. Between campaigns, and with an omniscience that pains me to remember, I took a whack at everything from Marriage and the Home to Manners, Morals, and the Duties of Parenthood. Others might entertain doubts as to their infallibility, but I had the solution for all social problems, and not even Lord Macaulay was ever more pontifical or sure of himself.

Now and then, however, I planted my feet on fairly firm ground, and also managed to keep a sense of humor. Particularly in battles against the excessive puritanism of the period. The younger generation, with navels bared to the sun, will find it hard to believe, but in those days the female body was assumed to stop abruptly at the chin, only taking up again at the instep. Virtue and chastity were measured in bolts of cloth, and women swathed themselves so thickly that they had to begin undressing for bed at four o'clock in the afternoon. In many cases such quantities of material were used that the poor creatures had to be marked with crosses showing where the body could be found.

Kansas City, although well on its way to metropolitanism, still held to the village note where legs were concerned. For example, the pulpits of the town broke out in a fever of indignation over the *Black Crook,* a highly decorous spectacle except that the chorus girls wore tights. Not the diaphanous things of today, mind you, but a kind of thick woolen union suit that buried the flesh beyond the sight of anything but X rays. And when the first alfresco performance of *As You Like It* was given at Fairmount Park, public discussion raged as to the exact amount of thigh that Rosalind could show, and the poor actress

64

finally compromised on a robe that had all the protective value of a tent.

Week in and week out I rang the changes on these incredible pruderies. Why should a woman lose her reputation for no greater crime than the exposure of an ankle? Where was there justice in committing a girl to a religious institution because her dress came open in the back? By elaborate measurements I proved that it took the wool of eighteen sheep to make a female bathing suit, compelling women to enter the water early in the morning if they wanted to get wet the same day. And how I went to town in talking about the riding habit of a lady! It had to be so modest that it hid not only her legs but also the horse's.

How far away it seems from the present day, when a woman has to be vaccinated on the tonsils if she doesn't want the scar to show! I do not flatter myself that my articles in *The Independent* brought about the change, but I am proud to have had a part in it.

My favorite crusade, however, was against the moldy tradition that woman's one and only proper place was the *home*. A hermetically sealed home at that, through which no wind of change was ever allowed to blow. Out of love and admiration for my mother, I resented it, and with Chivalry vs. Justice as a battle cry, I clamored that women had just as much right as men to be regarded as *people*.

Here again changes have been so fundamental as to make the past unbelievable, and yet right up to a date well after the turn of the century, marriage was the one trade or profession open to women. Their sole employment was to make some good man happy by a lifetime of incessant, unselfish service, and in the discharge of that pious mission they found the justification for their existence.

Now and then, when thought of Mother intruded, I boiled over, but for the most part I kept to satire and plain "josh." As I loved to point out, even the right to stay young was exclusively a prerogative of the male. Any girl that reached the ripe old age of twenty-five without bagging a husband, or making some sort of kill, had her hunting license taken away, and automatically became an Old Maid. Queer little shawl-bearing animals, herbivorous by habit and uttering a frightened cry at the sight of a man.

65

As all of the trades and professions were closed to women, the Old Maid usually went to live with some relatives, where they called her "Auntie" to distinguish her from the help that got regular wages and Thursdays off. At thirty she was generally regarded as an aged crone, and at fifty there were violent arguments whether the head of the family ought to chloroform her himself or send for the vet.

Married women, as a matter of truth, were not much better off than the Old Maids when it came to retaining good looks. A certain interest in personal appearance was tolerated during the honeymoon, but after that anything more than mere cleanliness was viewed with dark suspicion by both the husband and the community. Any woman caught with a rouge pot or lipstick would have been prayed for in open church, and as for powdering, the Bible was assumed to read, "Let your nose so shine that men may see your good works."

Nobody, I argued, ever dreamed of considering a married man merely as a Husband and a Father, but the minute a woman left the altar she ceased to be *people,* and took her place in the formless and faceless army of Wives and Mothers. A few rebellious struggles, and public opinion forced her into heavy underwear and shoes that fitted. In a little while she slicked her hair back, let the waistline go, and found her pleasure in afternoon teas, church socials, and trading recipes and dress patterns. For the most part, however, sick headaches kept them busy, and burning brown paper soaked in vinegar was often their one emotional expression.

All of this, I conceded, was fine for the lord and master. The Wife and Mother was a trifle hard on the eyes, to be sure, but he contrived not to see much of her, and while he himself wandered far and free, he had the comfort of knowing that she was safely parked in the home, with no larger or more attractive manifestation of life than a slow, rhythmic movement of the gills.

All in all I had a grand time. Curiously enough, however, my mother, primarily responsible for the crusade, never liked it. To the day of her death she frowned on equal suffrage and could not abide my insistence that divorce was the one remedy when a marriage shattered on the rocks.

My main tilt, however, and one of which I am still proud, was against quacks and quackery. Kansas City at the time was the country's most favored stamping ground for magnetic healers, cancer ghouls, lost-manhood harpies, and scores of like charlatans who preyed on credulity and despair, promising quick and permanent cure of everything from dandruff to leprosy. All of the dailies, even Colonel Nelson's papers, carried their advertisements, and the staid *Journal* even ran them as straight reading matter.

Various pathetic cases called the creatures to my attention, and after deciding on attack I picked on a Dr. Carson as the target for my opening guns. A huge, pompous ass, he featured sideburns that had the spread of lace curtains, for those were the days when the common man still retained an almost religious faith in the virtue of whiskers. From behind this facial jungle the Good Old Doctor shouted pledges to cure "all diseases" by the simple laying on of hands. Here, for example, is the way he applauded himself for his success with appendicitis:

Patients are brought to him from every part of the country suffering from this dread disease, most of them having been given up by the attending physicians, although some had held out to them the vague hope that, under certain conditions, a surgical operation might perhaps save life. Patients have been carried into his office helpless, laid out on a stretcher, suffering the most excruciating agonies of the dread disease, and been raised up as if by magic after a few treatments at his hands, and without the use of drugs or the even more deadly knife.

Gallstones, Bright's disease, typhoid, and even tuberculosis and cancer were also made the subjects of Carson's extravagant claims; but cripples were his speciality. The so-called Temple of Health, occupying a prominent corner, had the yard piled high with crutches supposedly discarded by persons that Carson's healing hands had cured.

Investigation disclosed that the wretched victims did not come merely from Missouri and Kansas, but traveled in from almost every state in the Union, pouring a golden stream into Carson's pockets. Another of my discoveries was that the flood of patients had compelled a change in treatment. Finding himself unable to lay hands on all of the thousands, the cunning old fraud changed over to the "vitalization of tissue." Slips the size of cigarette papers were alleged to receive the "magnetic and electrical power" that flowed from his hands, and all that the sufferer had to do was to pin one between his shoulder blades at night. By this means Carson could minister to scores in a day, shoveling out the tissue in lieu of massage.

I learned about this from a youngster brought into my office by his father. The boy was then being treated by competent physicians for a diseased hip joint, and this was the story he told: "Dr. Carson gave me these," holding out a bunch of tissue slips, "and said that all I had to do was to pin one on my shirt whenever I hurt, and think for an hour of my papa and mamma who loved me."

On digging into Carson's past, I found that his only diploma came from the American College of Health in Cincinnati. Ohio officials informed me that this had been a notorious quackery mill operated years before by a John Bunyan Campbell. According to their report, Campbell divided all human ailments into red diseases and blue diseases. Patients, therefore, were placed under either a blue window or a red window, and by a system of stroking with his hands, Campbell "got the pizen out of the system by drawin' it down" into the copper plates on which the sufferers stood.

On the face of things, Carson looked like a push-over, but my confidence soon got a jolt. His bankers, his printers, his attorneys, all hastened to give the old fraud certificates of character, and the daily papers printed them in their advertising columns. It was only after a year of constant attack that I managed to have a warrant issued for his arrest on the ground that he was practicing medicine without a license. Colonel Nelson's *Star* and *Times* printed the bare fact, but the *World* and *Journal* carried long statements by Carson and his attorneys attempting to prove that it was not a criminal prosecution, but a "mere technicality."

Where the Good Old Doctor overplayed his hand, however, was in accusing me of trying to blackmail him and getting my printer to refuse further publication of *The Independent*. Managing to switch shops almost overnight, I leaped at the chance to bring Carson into court and sued him for libel. When the taking of depositions began, the Doctor was flanked by five leaders of the Kansas City bar, with Jim Reed in the role of hatchet man. In my corner, serving without pay, Frank Walsh stood alone.

68

Reed's humorlessness played right into our hands, and from the first Frank treated the whole business with contemptuous mockery. Under merciless questioning and over screamed objections, Carson was forced to admit that he claimed to cure heart disease, cancer, and curvature of the spine by the laying on of hands; also that the "magnetic power" that flowed from his hands was helped out by vaseline mixed with red pepper.

Where Frank really went to town was in the matter of the tissue slips. How did the Doctor know how, if, and when the "magnetic and electric power" passed out of his mitts into the papers? Was there some sort of spigot attachment, and could he turn it off and on? If not, wasn't it possible that the "healing energy" gushed out into the newspapers as he read them? Or even into the tissues that he used when Nature called? These were typical questions and answers:

A. If you will tell me what the fox leaves on the ground so that a dog may follow the trail twenty-four hours later, I will tell you what I impart to the slips.

Q. Oh, so it's a sort of smell?

A. No, sir. It isn't. I pass my hands over and across that piece of paper and then enfold it in an envelope. It leaves a certain something that we call magnetism or power.

Q. Did you not give specific guarantee that your method could cure St. Vitus' dance, spinal disease, tuberculosis, cancer, nervous prostration, insomnia, paralysis, cholera infantum, stomach trouble, and rheumatism?

A. I did treat all those diseases. I have been treating those diseases for a long time, for years.

So it went on for several weeks; but after dragging every possible admission from Carson, I dropped the libel suit and turned attention to the criminal proceeding. Eventually the judge found the creature guilty of a misdemeanor, and imposed the ridiculous fine of $500. The *Journal of the American Medical Association* supported my crusade vigorously, but with the usual cowardice of the learned professions, not a doctor would come forward as a witness.

Next on the order of business came the ghouls who claimed to cure cancer with "balmy oils." All were venerable and heavily bearded in their advertisements, but when we brought them out into the open, the majority proved to be clean-shaven, brassy young charlatans who had never studied medicine even for a day. "Good Old Dr. Johnson," for example, a man in his early thirties, admitted that he diagnosed not only cancer, but also the type, entirely by aid of his "educated eye." Under examination he showed utter ignorance of anatomy, for he could not even describe the location of the glands, and finally confessed that his "treatment" consisted of iodine of potassium and digitalis "for the kidneys."

The lost-manhood swindlers were also put on the grill. Their trick was to get hold of poor youngsters who had reached the stage of emissions, and scare them to death by painting horrible pictures of impotency and idiocy. To arrest this "physical and mental decay," the "doctors" simply applied an electric buzzer to the small of each back at $5 a throw.

Not Carson nor any of the others ever went to prison, but an aroused public sentiment did bring about a certain measure of reform. The bankers, merchants, and lawyers withdrew the testimonials they had been signing, and Colonel Nelson quietly issued an order barring all quack advertisements from the columns of the *Star* and the *Times*.

Another crusade had less to show for it. That had to do with the social evil, or as a lighthearted friend of mine referred to it, the "sociable evil." I thought that the whole problem of prostitution should be made the subject of study and that the statistics of venereal disease ought to be brought out into the open. According to the physicians with whom I talked, our red-light district, although carefully tucked away in the slum section, was pouring out a steady stream of poison.

The trouble with the crusade was that I myself had no very clear idea as to the remedy, nor did I get any help from city officials and the ministers that I consulted. The police commissioners were of the opinion that keeping the girls within a restricted area was about the best way to handle it; and the ministers, while condemning prostitution, felt that it would shock the sensibilities of their congregations to have the problem dealt with from pulpits.

I reproached them for their stand, but when it came to writing the articles, I found myself absolutely unable to put such words as gonorrhea and syphilis into cold print. As a consequence, I skated all around the subject, getting more and more vague and involved, and accomplishing nothing except to have a number of subscribers rebuke me for my "preoccupation with prurience."

As a last resort, I wrote to Brand Whitlock, then mayor of Toledo, and he sent back a long, long letter that traced prostitution back to Greece and Rome, telling how both Solon and Augustus failed, and how the Puritans of New England found that the flogging, branding, and even burning of bawds did not result in abatement. Dismissing punitive laws and the police as a cure, he went on to talk about a "single standard of morals," and the value of some sort of competent and judicious sex education, although he did not know who would impart it, since no one knew much about it. His letter, addling me still more, ended the crusade.

CHAPTER 10

The University Militant

Gautier, in his preface to *One of Cleopatra's Nights*, laments the "dullness of modern uniformity," with its loss of individual color and the dreary sameness of the human pattern. True enough in the main, but the Frenchman might have written less morosely had he visited western Missouri during the days of my youth. Then it was possible to scare four or five "characters" out of every brush pile, and not the phonies of today, but wildly radical departures from type. Of all the ones I knew or met, I think that Charles Ferguson was the prize specimen, not even excepting General Shelby or Colonel John.

The pastor of a small suburban church in Kansas City's outskirts, he came into our group in 1906, and by way of introduction made casual mention that he had also been a lawyer and a journalist. "As you will see," he added, "I have triangulated my problem by submission to the contrasting disciplines of the three sociological professions—the Law, the Church, and the News." Although he did not say so, it was plain that he felt competent to diagnose the ills of the world as a result of the triangulation.

Charles spoke little of the past, seeming to have dismissed it, and only bit by bit were we able to trace his life story. There was no question but that he had studied at universities in this country and Europe—Oxford and Heidelberg, among others— and that he had learned law under James Coolidge Carter, the great constitutional authority. Why and when he switched from the bar to religion never received explanation, but for a while he was rector of the Church of the Carpenter in Boston, with Edward Everett Hale as his friend and sponsor.

Next came a move to Toledo—the reason for it was never made quite clear—where he worked intimately with Golden Rule Jones and Brand Whitlock, and also with Tom Johnson and Newton Baker of the Cleveland progressive group. Even more of a mystery was why he had changed over to journalism, but friends in San Francisco informed us that Charles had lived there, writing editorials for the Hearst chain and sitting close to the throne. What swung him back to religion and brought him to a humble Unitarian pulpit in Kansas City was something he never discussed, and to which we failed to find an answer.

A slender little man with china-blue eyes, dull yellow hair parted in the middle, and an ageless face, he wasn't much to look at, but when he opened his mouth the change was instant and electric. He seemed to grow to commanding proportions, and his rich, powerful voice had as many stops as a pipe organ. Joe Shannon, after the first meeting, shook his head and said, "I don't know what Ferguson's talking about, but hell, he makes better music than an Irish harper."

Charles had small use for our reform laws and legislative program, branding them as a false approach to democracy's problems. What he urged was a university militant, "a new intellectual and spiritual establishment strong enough to withstand both the seductions of the money power and the assaults of the mob." As he set it forth, the Old World had three great visions of universal order. First, the Roman Empire sought to put the will of all mankind in the service of pure intellect, but the effort failed, for Rome's legions broke and were shattered against the indomitable instincts of humanity. Next came the vision of Augustine and Ambrose, of Hildebrand and Innocent, who dreamed of a Holy Catholic Church that should arise more terrible and glorious than armies, to beat down that tyranny of intellect which had bruised and broken the hearts of men, and win the whole world to the sway of suffering but imperious love. The majestic fabric fell into ruins because emotion without intellect is as impracticable as intellect without feeling. Then out of the rubble arose the vision of a world-wide republic of the arts and sciences—the university.

Why had it failed? Charles supplied the answer without being asked. The universities of the Middle Ages were clogged with all the morbid traditions of the past. They made a tremendous effort to bring the scientific spirit into effectual correspondence with the humanistic spirit, to heal the immemorial breach between the intellect and the emotional forces of life, but the confused currents of the time were too strong for them. The most they could accomplish was to rough-sketch the design of a true civic order and leave it for the future to work out. That, he insisted, was *our* job.

How we were to do it was always skimmed over. When pressed for a blueprint, Charles would simply dismiss details as immaterial, and urge us to "see things in the large." About the nearest he ever came to a concrete plan was the suggestion that we ask the government to establish a university in the desert lands of the West, "free from the greeds of private initiative and the raids of the freebooting money-maker."

Had we forgotten that the famous cities of the antique world were for the most part founded upon the practice of irrigation and nursed in the desert? That the Old World was scientific enough to prefer its rainless lands—Egypt and Palestine, Asia Minor and Syria? What of the agricultural miracles worked by the Carthaginians and the Moors, the Incas and the Aztecs? In countries of abundant rainfall the soluble plant foods were mainly washed away and wasted, while in arid areas these elements accumulated in the soil, creating an inexhaustible bank account. So, he argued, a university city built in the great American desert would have "solid elemental underpinning."

Interrupting him when in full flight was almost an impossibility, but once I brought him down to earth with the following story: A Wyoming rancher invited some eastern friends to go with him on a camping trip, but on the morning of the start his cook quit him. Not to disappoint his guests, he decided to do the cooking himself, and when the chuck wagon stopped that night he got out with his coffeepot. As there was no firewood in sight, he began lighting the bunch grass that grew at irregular intervals, holding the pot first over one clump and then over another. The coffee finally boiled, but by that time he was fifteen miles from camp.

Just as Charles was contemptuous of our political approaches to social problems, so did he shake his head in sorrow over the "triviality" of *The Independent*. What he urged, constantly and persuasively, was a change to what he called *The Newsbook*, making it the mouthpiece of a "great national movement that would point the way to escape from the ruins of the old religious and political superstitions." Day in and day out, persistently and persuasively, he doped me with the organ music of his voice and dazzled me with word paintings that had the glow of a Titian. Did I not remember how Abelard, rejected in the musty schools of Paris and driven forth alone into the wilderness, built for himself that cabin of reeds and stubble to which the generous youth of Europe flocked that they might breathe his catholic and cosmopolitan air? And had not Lamennais, Lacordaire, and Montelembert, speaking through *L'Avenir*, worked wonders in healing the schism between rich and poor? What a privilege to follow in their steps, taking up the torch that had fallen from those mighty hands!

What people wanted was a higher standard of living and a public organ to articulate that demand. The necessaries of life to be cheaper and the graces more attainable. And what are they getting? From the monthly and weekly magazines nothing more than mental lunches and literary vaudeville, and from the press an infinite outpour of anodynes, a million inducements to spend their time and money, and to relax and scatter their wills.

The newspaper, as Charles explained it, swung between sensationalism and insipidity—a prodigy of moral and intellectual passivity, a sort of spineless cactus framed for the ruminants. The truth that people did get from the press was for the most part unavailable, because there was no known system of public assay whereby readers could pick out the truth from the mass of reports that were not true.

Did I not see that journalism—meaning the intellectual comprehension of passing events—was bound to be the dominant force in our national life, if not the sovereign power, when divorced from the profit motive? *The Newsbook,* owned and controlled by an association created in the spirit that exulted in artistic and scientific achievement, would blaze the way.

For a long while I beat him off; but at last, in the closing months of 1907, he wore me down, and over the protests of Frank Walsh I agreed to his proposition. Having gained my assent, Charles entered at once into impassioned correspondence with all the friends he had collected during his many moves, and by the New Year the National Fellowship of the University Militant had come into being. An imposing list, for among the members were Edwin Markham, Brand Whitlock, Elbert Hubbard, Ray Stannard Baker, Julian Hawthorne, Charles Zueblin, then professor of sociology in the University of Chicago, Ida Tarbell, Louis Sullivan, the famous Chicago architect, Margaret Deland, the novelist, Edward Everett Hale, Gerald Stanley Lee, and Henry M. Alden, editor of *Harper's Monthly.*

Ten of the number met in New York at the National Arts Club on January 11, and on motion of Dr. Ferguson I was given "the difficult task of leadership in the journalistic branch" of the undertaking. My *Newsbook* was to be "the first link in a projected chain of weekly newspapers localized in the chief cities of the country," and this Municipal University Press was named formally as "the principal agent and executor" of the National Fellowship's propaganda.

The aim of this propaganda, as phrased by Dr. Ferguson, was to

win and hold the balance of power in American communities, for an institution—the municipal university or university of the people —that shall subordinate all sects, parties, and special interests to the paramount interest of civilization, to wit, the raising of the general standard of living through the practical advancement of science and the humanities. We believe that such an institution is the predestined crown and complement of our national system of free schools.

In the midst of a situation that threatens the gravest social disappointments—through the separation of the intellectual and emotional forces of life, the deepening contradiction between the money power and the creative energy of the people—we undertake to raise in every city an ensign of conciliation and construction. We invite all sensible men and women to a social adventure that can certainly break the commercial deadlock into which we are sinking, and open up a new and interminable era of prosperity. *Our hope lies not in the fever of egotism or the frenzy of sacrifice, but in the response of a sane people to the summons of a more wholesome, expansive, and interesting life.*

The Newsbook made its bow on March 7, 1908, and died on June 27; and I make bold to doubt if in a field of comparable size there was ever such a monumental flop. Not only did we fail to make the diggers think and the thinkers dig, but we confused readers to a point where they canceled subscriptions in droves. As for advertisers, they wanted to know what in hell I thought I was doing, and turned away coldly from my explanations.

It was not that Charles and other members of the National Fellowship failed to make contributions. They poured them in, ransacking their files for essays that had never been able to get publication. As I couldn't understand half of it myself, the idea gradually dawned that maybe my fellow Kansas Cityans were having the same difficulty. Finances also had something to do with my decision to go back to *The Independent*, for debts were piling up and the bank was beginning to show a definite distaste for overdrafts.

Charles for once indulged in no long-winded dissertation when I broke the news to him. "George! Oh, George!" he intoned sadly but still musically. "What a mess you've made of it!" Soon afterward he shook the dust of Kansas City from his feet and established himself in New York as the center of an adoring group. His gift of captivation must have remained unimpaired, however, for Woodrow Wilson fell for his blank verse and sent him abroad to make certain economic studies. As far as I have been able to learn, that was his last conquest, for nothing more was ever heard of him.

Recapturing readers and advertisers was a grim business, but I invaded stores and office buildings with all the ferocity of a starved timber wolf and managed to regain some measure of solvency. The New Year, in fact, found me out of debt, and this happy condition, together with other considerations, brought on an aggravated attack of itchy feet. All of the laws for which we had fought were now on the statute books of the state, and the election of an antimachine mayor gave promise of an honest, progressive administration. The Goats seemed to be dehorned, and Jim Reed, my pet detestation, had accepted employment as trial lawyer for the streetcar monopoly and looked to be dead politically.

Where, then, was the point in staying put? *The Independent,* despite trials and tribulations, had a value, and several people came forward as purchasers; but when the deal hung fire, I broke out in one of my usual sweats. Calling in Clara Kellogg and Katherine Baxter, two fine women who ran a job-printing shop, I gave them the paper, lock, stock, and barrel.

CHAPTER 11

Mexico and the Mexicans

Giving away *The Independent* in a burst of impatience was headlong business, for in my eagerness to get foot-loose I had not even thought about where I would go or what I would do. Also a bad business, for while I balanced the possibilities of new fields, who should buttonhole me but Arthur Stillwell. Another "character"! My experience with Charles Ferguson should have given me sense enough to break away and run, but instead of that I found myself agreeing to go with him to Mexico.

I still marvel at the sheer incredibility of the man. In middle life, and after a succession of minor failures, he suddenly decided to become an empire builder and launched the project of a railroad from Kansas City to the Gulf of Mexico. The closest he had ever been to a railroad was a Pullman car, but boldly careering off to Holland, he raised the necessary capital, fascinating the Dutch with his golden whiskers, clear blue eyes, and persuasive speech.

Wall Street soon took the Kansas City Southern away from him by some chicane, and Stillwell's next venture was the Kansas City, Mexico, and Orient. According to his own account, the idea came to him in a dream, for as he slept a map of the United States and Mexico flamed before him. Then out of the darkness came a shining angel shape, and with fingers of fire traced a line from Kansas City to a Mexican port called Topolobampo.

"Build a railroad!" This was the order of the seraph, delivered in ringing tones, and on waking, Stillwell set about it. Another succession of journeys to Europe procured the money for the purchase of several small lines planned as links, and in the years that followed he brought over a steady stream of Dutch and English capitalists. All were carried luxuriously in private cars to the Mexico City, where President Porfirio Díaz not only wined and dined them, but also extolled Señor Stillwell as a man of vision and genius. Few of the foreigners ever got away without buying a bunch of bonds.

Not satisfied to rest content with his fame as an empire builder, Don Arturo panted for eminence in other fields. Particularly literature and music. An organist was already in his employ, hired to help him with a few oratorios, symphonies, and operas; and my job was to give the "finishing touches" to a novel that he had in mind. As it turned out, he had gone no further than deciding on Russia as the locale, leaving everything else up to me.

The trip started off pleasantly enough, but changed for the worse when we crossed the border. For long years Americans had been led to believe that Porfirio Díaz was a great and inspired ruler who had brought peace, justice, and prosperity to a distracted land. I myself had swallowed the fulsome speeches of Elihu Root and President Taft without any distension of the gullet. What opened my eyes was Chihuahua, where the Terrazas family owned a stretch of land twice the size of Massachusetts, a vast domain where unhappy peons lived in mud huts and slaved for an average wage of twelve cents a day. This condition, I discovered later, was fairly general.

The governor of Chihuahua, Enrique Clay Creel, was a cousin of mine, for his father was a Virginian who had fought under General Scott in 1847 and had stayed in Mexico after the war. The son, marrying a Terrazas, was not only one of the richest men in the country but one who stood closer to Díaz than all but a very few. He was an affable, courteous man, and our relations were most cordial until we fell into argument over Mexican conditions.

It was not only what I saw—the grinding poverty and the visible degradation of the people—but what I heard from intelligent Mexicans. After thirty years of Díaz rule, with a brimming treasury always at hand, 85 per cent of the population could neither read nor write, and peonage was an organized and accepted system. True, Don Porfirio gave peace; but it was the peace of the grave, for he crushed every voice of protest with ruthless ferocity.

Although Francisco Madero did not rise until 1910, revolution was in the air, and I annoyed Mr. Stillwell excessively by predicting it. As a result, the Great Novel ceased to be mentioned, and on the return trip I spent most of the time in the baggage car so that the ears of the capitalists would not be horrified by my dire prophecies. Needless to say, our parting was not marked by tears and fond embraces. I never saw Don Arturo again, but developments proved that the angel had made a mistake with respect to the feasibility of the Kansas City, Mexico, and Orient, for the line was never completed.

By reason of the visit, I continued to follow events in Mexico with fascinated interest, cheering when Madero overthrew Díaz and screaming editorially when he and his vice-president were assassinated by drunken Huerta. It was not until October, 1920, however, that I crossed the border again, sent by President Wilson to attempt a settlement of the bitter differences between Mexico and the United States. Although Carranza had succeeded Huerta by American aid, the suspicious old man hated the Colossus of the North and played Germany's game throughout the war.

Carranza's death and Álvaro Obregón's election to the presidency worked a change in the picture that gave President Wilson the hope of friendly relations, and I carried the terms on which the new administration would be recognized by the United States. They were generous, and after I had been a week with Obregón and his advisers, full agreement was reached. Unhappily, negotiations collapsed just as recognition was about to be extended, for American oil interests in Mexico started a vicious attack and the State Department suddenly claimed to have intercepted cables that proved Obregón's bad faith.

Out of the mess came an embarrassing experience that left my face red for weeks. At the height of the controversy over the cables I went to Washington for a conference with Bainbridge Colby, Secretary of State, and put up at his home for the night. The interview ended on a note of such complete disagreement that I would have liked to leave the house, but stayed on because of the lateness of the hour.

At the time I had a removable bridge in the back of my mouth, made to replace a lost molar, and on retiring I placed it carefully in the drawer of a bedside table. I forgot it, of course, when I hurried away the next morning. After parting with the Secretary in high dudgeon, I prayed for the earth to open and swallow me up when I had to go back and ask him to bring down my tooth.

Anyway, the second visit to Mexico gave me the idea of writing the country's history, and in 1924 I began a series of journeys that carried me into every state. My book *The People Next Door* may not have been the best ever written, but at least it told the truth about our war with Mexico. Instead of the United States inciting the Texas rebellion, and aiding it by men and arms, Sam Houston had only 783 men at the decisive battle of San Jacinto, and faced a Mexican army of 1,600. Instead of annexing Texas, as requested by the Texans, Congress voted a contemptuous rejection, and for nine years the Lone Star republic held its place as a sovereign power, with a president, a congress, an army, and a navy, and was recognized by the nations of the world.

Not until 1845 was Texas annexed, and it was then that *Mexico* declared war. President Polk, instead of accepting the challenge, went sick with dismay. Not only was the United States without an army, a navy, and money, but there was the fear that England and France, eager for a further foothold in the New World, would back Mexico in her war. As an escape from his plight, Polk hurried emissaries to Mexico with instructions to pay $5,000,000 for a "satisfactory Rio Grande boundary." Before Herrera, the Mexican president, could receive the proposal, he was overthrown by General Paredes, who rushed additional troops to the border, bombastically announcing that the "Mexican flag would soon be waving over the ancient palace of George Washington."

Now for the war itself: General Zachary Taylor, with only

80

2,400 men, whipped 4,000 Mexicans, first at Palo Alto and then at Resaca de la Palma; for Paredes' army budget of $21,000,000, twice that of the United States, had been stolen by the "generals," leaving soldiers without arms or ammunition. Again at Buena Vista, where Taylor faced 17,000 with a force of 5,000, the Mexicans were defeated by the incompetency and corruption of their officers. Even greater were the odds against General Winfield Scott. With an army of less than 10,000 effectives, he climbed from Vera Cruz to the City of Mexico, a steep ascent of 8,000 feet, and captured a country with a population of 7,000,000.

In the hour of complete victory, what were the terms imposed by the United States? The English had no other idea than that we would keep Chihuahua, Coahuila, and Tamaulipas, and France even assumed that President Polk would regard the whole of Mexico as proper spoils of war. Instead of that, the Treaty of Guadalupe turned back states and ports, and not only waived indemnity but gave Mexico $15,000,000 for her rehabilitation, besides assuming her obligations in the matter of long-standing claims. The total of $20,000,000 was $5,000,000 more than the price paid for the Louisiana Purchase.

On his recent visit to Mexico, President Truman earned cheers by placing a wreath on the graves of the six military cadets killed during Scott's assault on Chapultepec, Mexicans hailing it as repentance for a crime. As a matter of truth, they should have been ashamed to have the incident recalled. A mile away from Chapultepec was a city of 200,000, and directly at hand was an army of 20,000. How, then, was Scott to know that boys figured in the garrison that defended a key position?

It was not until 1934 that I visited Mexico again, going down for *Collier's* to report on just how "red" Lázaro Cárdenas really was. No one could have been more shocked at the suggestion of communism than the suave, smiling President, whose face plainly showed his Tarascan blood. True, he was a Socialist, but his brand of socialism did not run to confiscation. Of course, all public utilities should be owned by the people, and there must be full satisfaction of every peasant's need for land and water, but honest payment would be made for all expropriations. And what would be the nature of the payment? Well, that was something that remained to be determined.

And what about the Six Year Plan's insistence on "socialistic education" in the public schools? Why, nothing more than a combination of academic and vocational training. And how false to assume that his government aimed at atheism! The one purpose was to break the political power of the Church, and when that was accomplished, every citizen would be guaranteed the right to liberty of conscience and freedom of worship.

Mexican friends howled at my report of the talk. "Bosh!" they exclaimed. "Go call on Tomás Garrido Canabal, and then drop down for a look at things in Tabasco."

And who was this Tomás? Secretary of Agriculture at the moment, but for ten years the dictator of Tabasco, and still unquestioned ruler of the state. And what was his record as a dictator? Well, in the whole of Tabasco there was not a church, for he had razed every religious structure and either killed or deported every priest. His favorite outdoor sport, in fact, was the public burning of altars and images, or as he phrased it, *"la incineración de fetiches."* Marriage was recognized only as a social contract, all industry was socialized, and even prostitution rated as a legal business.

Interviewed in his office in the Department of Agriculture, the Scourge of Tabasco proved cordial and very, very frank. Was it indeed true that he had driven priests out of the state and torn down every church? "But yes, señor, and with reason." His shrug was eloquent with wonder at the question. How could any sane person read history without coming to the conclusion that religion had been humanity's great curse? And did he kill priests outright? "But no, señor. I am a sportsman. Always I gave each padre a start of one hundred yards. If he had led a godly, temperate life, he usually had the speed to beat me to the frontier. If, however, he had been gluttonous and a loose liver, I caught him easily. But why rest content with secondhand reports? Why not go to Tabasco and see things for yourself?"

A committee of notables met me at the airport in Villa Hermosa, eager to show me the accomplishments of Don Tomás in his crusades against religion and *los reaccionarios.* A tennis court was pointed out as the site of a church that had been demolished, and on another corner a swimming pool replaced the ancient cathedral. Truly, señor, they chatted happily, the "incineration of the fetishes" was a most inspiring

82

occasion. And was there no resistance? No cry of protest? No arm lifted to strike? "But no, señor. Such as were hopelessly *fanático*—too blind to see the light—either fled the state or took refuge in the mountains; that is, if they were lucky. As one can plainly see, this purged the population, leaving only the rational behind."

A rather potent incentive to "rationalism," I discovered later, were the *Jóvenes Revolucionarios*—revolutionary youths —who paraded the streets of towns and villages, hunting for *fanáticos* and even searching homes and digging up yards in search of *santitos*. Many old people still held to their superstitions, but thanks to the splendid educational system introduced by Don Tomás, the boys and girls were receiving "rational" instruction. Every school had its walls hung with obscene and antireligious paintings, and every program given in my honor contained songs or speeches attacking religion as "humanity's curse." Here was one triumphal chant sung on all occasions:

> The genuine Man of the Revolution,
> The Liberating Sun that has risen,
> For the good of Tabasco and all the nation
> Is the tremendous figure of Tomás Garrido.
> He defends the worker and puts down the bourgeoisie,
> Snatches from the clergy all their power,
> And stands potent and superbly unmoved
> Before a flood of cruel calumny.
> He closed the saloons and the centers of vice,
> Where the worker parted with his daily wages,
> He developed new guides for humanity
> By destroying the priests and the feudal lords.
> He solved the agrarian problems in the land,
> Giving to farmers the rights justly theirs.
> And for these things he merits the name Liberating Sun,
> Which will ring with pride through the twentieth
> century.

Before two years had passed, the true intent of Cárdenas stood clear. His expropriation of the property of seventeen foreign oil companies had a certain justification, for the owners were both stupid and arrogant, but there was no such excuse for the confiscation of more than 29,000,000 acres of land for distribution to individuals and communities. Nor was there anything picayunish or piecemeal about the seizures, for among them was the Laguna tract of 1,105,812 irrigated acres in Coahuila and Durango; broad stretches in the Yaquí, Mayo, and Mexicali valleys; the German-owned coffee plantations in Chiapas; and the rich henequen properties in Yucatán. Americans, British, and Spaniards were hardest hit, although many "antisocial" Mexicans suffered along with them.

Expropriating all private ownership in the National Railways of Mexico, Cárdenas handed them over to a worker administration. In addition, many strikes ended by the expropriation of factories on the bland theory that it was the only way to "restore tranquillity." And at the right hand of the President stood Vicente Lombardo Toledano, leader of the federated unions and a flaming disciple of Karl Marx, Lenin, and Stalin.

In 1938 *Collier's* sent me across the border to report on the Cárdenas program, and if I ever had any doubt as to the fallacy of communism, it would have been removed by the failure of Mexico's adventure in collectivization. The nationalized petroleum properties showed a deficit of $20,000,000 since expropriation; communal agriculture had dropped production below a subsistence level, forcing the importation of corn, wheat, and beans; the railroads were streaks of rust, and the once flourishing sugar industry was only a memory.

In the spring of 1941 I went again to Mexico for *Collier's*— this time to have a heart-to-heart talk with Manuel Ávila Camacho, Cárdenas' successor. Although he had been in office less than a year, vast changes had already taken place, with communism giving way to a sane progressivism. The National Railways were now operated by a strictly business management, and instead of the disastrous system of collectivized agriculture, each farmer had clear title to his allotment of land. Even more significantly, Mexico's communistic labor laws had been drastically revised and socialistic education thrown out of the schools. Holding that the separation of Church and State had been completed, the government again guaranteed freedom of conscience, and churches and cathedrals were open and crowded.

These were not the only radical departures from the red ideology of Lázaro Cárdenas. As I sat with President Camacho on the veranda of his small farmhouse near Cuernavaca, he professed a desire for close relations with the United States and backed it up by a pledge of alliance if war came to the Western Hemisphere. Over and over he stressed collective defense against communism, fascism, nazism, and all other kinds of totalitarianism.

CHAPTER 12

Tammen, Bonfils, and Bedlam

*B*ack in Kansas City after the Mexican jaunt with Stillwell, the idea of Europe again appealed; but when Mother argued against it, I decided to have a go at the magazines in New York. Right in the middle of packing and farewell parties, however, who should bob up with the offer of a job but Fred Bonfils and Harry Tammen. Two more characters! At the time these two owners of the Denver *Post* dominated the Rocky Mountain region, and the bankrupt paper, acquired in 1895 for $12,500, had come to be a $10,000,000 property.

Bonfils, of Corsican stock and with a West Point background, was darkly handsome and dynamic, but had the feral eye of a man-eating tiger. The start of his fortune, according to open accusations, came from shady deals in Oklahoma land and oil, but principally from the operation of the Little Louisiana lottery in Kansas City, Kansas. Tammen, in direct contrast with Bonfils, was blond, short, fat, and had the round pink face and the unwinking blue eyes of a kewpie. He had started life as a bartender, without other capital than a "Dutch haircut and white watch," and according to his own admission, acquired his first stake by knocking down on the boss.

"There were no cash registers in those days," he loved to boast, "and I tossed up the dollars as they rolled in. If they stuck to the ceiling, the house got 'em."

Bonfils had dignity and reticence, but Tammen went in for clowning and made his rascalities engaging by the frankess with which he confessed them. Many of the stories about black-mailing had their source in his cackled brags, for he liked to tell how he and Bon had made this or that department store come across, or forced a politician to "roll over and play dead."

Knowing the men and their paper, I turned the offer down; but Bonfils explained that a brand new policy was in the making. Henceforth the *Post* would be "dedicated to the public service without favor, fear, or faltering"; and as he talked, his face glowed with the zeal of Peter the Hermit. When he chose to turn it on, few men had more charm; and, as in the case of Ferguson and Stillwell, I found myself consenting. It may be an essential weakness, but I have never been able to resist characters. My eagerness to meet Ben Lindsey also had something to do with it, for the Little Judge's fight against the corrupt Colorado machine had made him one of my idols.

On landing in Denver, I found that the *Post* more than lived up to its reputation as the Coney Island of journalism. Bon and Tam also owned a circus, and there was always a doubt as to whether we worked on a paper or under the big top. Bands, Indians, baby llamas, bearded ladies, and pygmy elephants cluttered up the building; "human flies" crawled over the façade; and when the balcony was not occupied by singers, evangelists, or acrobats, Bonfils would rush out with a canvas bag and scatter pennies to the populace.

Prize exhibit of all was this red-lettered inscription spread across the whole front: "O Justice, when expelled from other habitations, make this thy home." Spencer, a clever artist on the *Republican,* came out one day with a cartoon showing Bon and Tam going through the window, carrying the glass with them, and closely pursued by the majestic figure of Justice. As they whirled in mid-air, this anguished question ballooned from Tammen's mouth: "Say, Bon, who in the hell *is* that dame?"

Aside from the bedlam, I had little cause for complaint. My signed articles were daily features, and in the Sunday edition I had a whole page to do with as I liked. Not only was Denver a delight with its mountain ranges and winy air, but Ben Lindsey and his group furnished stimulating companionship, and the *Post's* staff also furnished friends. Particularly Winifred Black, whom I had known in New York when she was Hearst's prize "sob sister"; and Lyulph Ogilvie, a gaunt, grizzled Scot.

Lyulph was only the younger son of a noble house who had run through his money, but Tammen insisted that he sign his stuff "Lord Ogilvie." Years later, at a luncheon in London given by H. G. Wells, I sat at the side of Mrs. Winston Churchill, and when we talked about Denver, the name of Ogilvie came up. Thank heaven, I spoke of him with affection, for she turned with a smile and said, "He is my uncle."

Pleasant enough, but I was not given the editorial control that had been promised, and Bon and Tam kept stalling with respect to crusades. After six months I was pretty well fed up, but, when I announced an intention to quit, Bonfils came forward with a great idea. This was in February, 1910, and Theodore Roosevelt was about ready to come out of Darkest Africa, where he had gone on a hunting trip after seeing Taft inaugurated as his successor. The two of us would meet him in Khartoum, bearing an invitation to visit Colorado on his return to the States. If T.R. accepted, the *Post* would launch him as the Republican candidate in 1912 and begin the fight for all of the reform measures with which his name had been associated. As editorial writer, signing everything, I would be allowed to go as far as I liked. What could be fairer?

An advance of $1,000 was made to me, but in the last-minute rush to the station I either dropped the wallet or had my pocket picked. From the first I had heard stories about Bon's penny pinching, but until then I had never seen evidence of it. When I told him of my loss he came close to bursting a blood vessel, and his moans kept up even when I pointed out that the $500 in traveler's checks could be recovered, and that I stood ready to pay back the rest out of salary. On the train, still pale and shaken, he called the Pullman conductor and started to make arrangements for just one lower berth.

"Not on your life!" I protested. "Take away the shoes and I'll sleep under it. But *not* in it!"

My howls finally got me an upper, but there remained the problem of pocket money, for he insisted that I could not be trusted with any more cash. Every meal witnessed a fight with the waiter over the tip. He refused to give the porter more than a quarter after three days of service, and in New York he stabled us in one small room, overruling my pathetic plea that no two people ever wanted the light turned out at the same time.

This kept up on the steamer and even in Europe, until I was fit to be tied. Gene Fowler, writing about Tammen and Bonfils

87

in 1933, devoted several chapters of *Timberline* to the African trip, but got the train and hotel incidents all mixed up. As he told it, I jumped out of my upper berth and landed on Bonfils as he slept comfortably in a lower. It wasn't that way at all, for where my revolt came was in a Paris hotel. Determined to get a room of my own, I waited until Bon's snoring reached crescendo and then shot high into the air, coming down on his stomach with a yell that rattled the windows.

"Nightmare!" I mumbled as he writhed in pain. "Thought I was over them, but I reckon they're coming back."

After that we had separate rooms, but the added expense deepened his insistence on economy. There were constant quarrels over tips, and in Naples it took the police to save us from being mobbed by angry porters. Up to that time I had never been able to understand miserliness, but Bonfils made me see avarice as a passion that gave more sheer pleasure than the love of women or the applause of men. Saving a nickel actually bathed him in happiness and content.

We reached Khartoum a full week before former President Roosevelt's arrival, and nothing would satisfy Bonfils but a trip up the White Nile in a chartered steamer. I didn't want to go, having met some nice people on the journey from Cairo, particularly an old Turk who traded in ivory and ostrich feathers. He wanted to take me out into the desert for bargaining with the sheiks; and as if this were not temptation enough, I had leased a racing camel and bought a complete Arab costume that I was dying to wear.

Bonfils, however, stressed his rights as an employer, so off we went on a wood-burning junk pile that stopped at every huddle of huts to buy fuel, goats, and guinea hens. Fortunately, the authorities let me carry a rifle, and between shots at the crocodiles that lined the banks I counted the hours until we reached the "jungle." By some curious mental twist, I kept thinking of it in terms of Kipling—dense forests, pythons, orchids, etc.—and fancied myself as a Mowgli.

And what finally broke on my sight? A grassy plain, covered with thorn trees; the air thick with Baltimore orioles and turtle doves; guinea hens cackling like mad, and a herd of deer in the distance that looked exactly like Jersey cattle. Jungle, my eye! It was a Missouri pasture. And just to give the picture a last touch of realism, a small antelope jumped up under my feet and bounded off with flirts of a snowy behind. A cottontail!

As anticipated, the trip turned out to be a nightmare. Egotistical and contentious, Bonfils disputed every statement, accepting no authority, and we were barely on speaking terms by the time of our return to Khartoum. Curious how irritation develops littleness in a man. At a wood station I picked up the back of a crocodile, freshly killed and dismembered by some native. I had no intention of keeping it, but when Bon yelled at me to throw the "dirty thing" away, I took it to my bosom. What's more, I toted the damned nuisance through Europe and clear back to Denver, reveling in his angry yawps.

T.R. reached Khartoum in due course, attended by a small army of correspondents, and was escorted to the Sirdar's palace with all the pomp of royalty. Several interesting days followed, for we were taken over the battlefield of Kereri near Omdurman, where Kitchener in 1898 defeated the Arab horde that had held the Sudan in subjection for sixteen years. The tour was conducted by Sir Rudolph Slatin, or Slatin Pasha, an Austrian in the Egyptian service, who had been held captive by the dervishes from 1883 to 1895. Unlike heroic Chinese Gordon, who died defending Khartoum, Slatin surrendered early and saved his life by turning Mohammedan.

I kept my camel right up at the front, and as T.R. listened to the gory details of the engagement, the approving click of his teeth was punctuated by cries of "Bully!" It seemed to me more like a butchery than a battle. Armed only with swords, spears, and inferior rifles, the Arabs charged with all the madness of fanatics, and British fire laid them down in windrows. At the end of the day the dervish casualty count was 11,000 dead, 16,000 wounded, and 4,000 prisoners. Against this the British loss was 25 killed and 106 wounded, plus 21 killed and 235 wounded in the Egyptian army.

All of the professional hunters who had been on safari with Roosevelt accompanied him into Khartoum. A lean, picturesque lot, carrying a strong suggestion of our own frontiersmen. One night I had the luck to dine with them, and at the stage of pleasant exhilaration ventured to ask about the Colonel's marksmanship. Blind in one eye, and myopic in the other, how *could* he hit anything? The answer was very simple. When he leveled his gun, three other guns also leveled at the same instant. As the leader of the safari explained, "Mr. Roosevelt had a fairly good idea of the general direction, but we couldn't take chances with the life of a former president." All agreed, however, as to his courage.

Some years later an Oklahoma character by the name of Buffalo Jones vowed that he would go to Africa with two cowboys and rope and ride everything that Roosevelt had shot. He did just that, bringing back motion pictures to prove it. I saw a private showing, and laughed myself sick. Lions, leopards, rhinoceroses, and other like animals are sprinters rather than long-distance runners, and Jones and his cowboys simply ran them ragged with their swift ponies and then swung two ropes on them. It was side-splitting to see the bewhiskered old boy drag the exhausted creatures into the shade and fan them a while with his hard-boiled hat before straddling their backs. So side-splitting, in fact, that somebody put up the money to have the films suppressed—probably the motion-picture industry, eager to protect the romance of big game hunting.

Colonel Roosevelt accepted our invitation and came out in August for Frontier Days in Cheyenne. Senator Borah, Gifford Pinchot, Medill McCormick, James Garfield, and other Roose-veltians also swarmed in, and I have always believed that it was at this meeting that the Colonel decided to push La Follette out of the way and make the race against President Taft himelf.

Whatever I may have done to Bonfils on the trip was repaid with interest when we sat down for a financial settlement. In addition to the $500 that I had lost, he added every penny spent for cigarettes, drinks, and entertainment, and then assessed me $100 as my share of the steamer for the White Nile trip. Having thus wound me around with a chain of debt, he welshed on an agreement to raise my salary. Each week saw a deduction in my pay check until the last dollar had been paid off, and yet two years later, when we were at each other's throats, he published a front-page attack plainly intimating that I had *stolen* the money. A lie and also unintelligent, for it gave me the chance to tell the whole story, and did I put in every humiliating detail!

The phony accounting was a bitter pill to swallow, but it

had a sugar coating. Bon and Tam lifted me to the high post of editorial writer and piously endorsed these campaigns: the initiative, referendum, and recall; the direct primary for senators; the commission form of government for cities; a railroad commission with teeth; legislative endorsement of the constitutional amendment permitting an income tax; the headless ballot, and municipal ownership of public utilities.

Quite a list of chores, but we set about the doing of them with vigor and dispatch. Bonds for the purchase of the water company carried handsomely, and Governor Shafroth was induced to call a special session for the enactment of our proposals. Unhappily, a federal judge held up the bond issue by the usual injunction, and eleven Democratic senators blocked action in the legislature. By a fluke, the initiative and referendum were submitted to the people and approved, but every other measure was hamstrung.

Day after day, searching my soul for new screams, I branded the eleven as traitors, pinned the Scarlet Letter on each breast, and carried their names on a Roll of Dishonor. In one editorial I even went so far as to shout that lynching would be a good thing. Finally, one of the eleven sued the *Post* for libel, asking $100,000 damages. Formerly a coal miner, and an honest man at heart, the poor fool had been seduced rather than bought. First elected to the exclusive Denver Club, he was then given a degree by Denver University, and as a last touch, the corporation press began to praise him as a "strong man, brave enough to withstand demagogic clamor."

Bonfils and Tammen, who had been out of town, were a worried pair on hearing of the suit, but took heart when I produced my evidence. The trial was a slaughter! Not only did we show that the senator had asked votes on the very platform he afterward repudiated, but proved that he borrowed money from corporation lawyers on unsecured notes and collected mileage while traveling on railroad passes. On taking the stand I was permitted to answer every question with a stump speech; and when attorneys for the plaintiff tried to interrupt, the judge warned them against "browbeating." Some of my violences still appall me. For example, my lawyer asked if it was not true that I used the word "rope" in a purely figurative sense. "No," I yelled at the top of my voice. "The *hemp!* The *hemp!*"

At the end of four days the jury returned a verdict in our favor, holding that the Senator deserved everything I had said about him. As we were leaving the courtroom I spoke to Tammen in warm appreciation of the judge, saying that I had never seen one fairer or more fearless. "Why not?" he barked. "Who in hell do you think put him on the bench?"

At the very outset of our crusade I urged the organization of a Citizens party that would make its own nominations for state and county offices when the fall election came round. Bonfils and Tammen endorsed the idea, and with the promise of *Post* support, hundreds of men and women enlisted under the new banner. Our particular concern was with the offices that controlled the election machinery, and three splendid men declared their candidacies.

With a full Citizens ticket finally decided upon, it was planned to print the full list of names on the Saturday before election. I urged an earlier date, but Bonfils and Tammen favored a last-minute bang. On Friday night, therefore, I sat down to write the editorial lead. I have the yellowed page before me now, and a quotation will show the intensity of our feeling in those days:

On Tuesday every man and woman will have opportunity to strike a blow for a free state, a free city. What soul with so little life and light to hold back? There is joy in this thing! And beauty! And inspiration! The ballot becomes a gleaming sword and the shabbiest jacket a gift of splendid armor. It is an adventure—this fight for equal justice—the Great Adventure which has ever enlisted all that was best and truest in the human heart. For the People! Say that word over. People! *People!* Why, it grows electric! It thrills! Not this banker, not that bricklayer, but all who toil in patience or impatience, courage or despair, sorrow or happiness, struggling that tomorrow may be made better than today.

I could hardly wait for Saturday's paper, but when I saw it the pit of my stomach fell out. All the Citizens ticket was there except our nominees for sheriff, county clerk, and coroner. In these key places had been inserted the names of three machine men, one notorious for his election frauds in the past. I raced at once for the Bucket of Blood, as Bon's office was called, but both he and Tam had disappeared. There was nothing to do but resign, and I did so in a public statement, backing

92

it up by public speeches. There was not time, however, to straighten out the confusion, and on election day the people voted the Citizens ticket as instructed, not catching the changes.

A thing that hurt, and also mystified, was the attitude of my fellow newspapermen. A few applauded but the majority condemned, and one woman wrote a letter in which she accused me of disloyalty and "shaming our noble profession." In my answer I asked if it was not conceivable that Bonfils and Tammen owed *me* loyalty? Or was loyalty always a one-way street for employers only? She never replied.

I could have had another newspaper job in Denver, but journalism was a bad taste in my mouth and once again I decided on a literary life in New York. En route I stopped off in Toledo for a bull session with Brand Whitlock, and in Cleveland to visit with Newton Baker, then making his successful campaign for mayor. Curiously enough, both men hated officeholding. Brand wanted nothing so much as to give all of his time to writing, and Newton yearned for the peace of a leisurely law practice that would give him time for philosophical research. When Woodrow Wilson took over the White House, however, one of his first acts was to send Brand as our ambassador to Belgium, and as storm clouds gathered he called Baker to his side as Secretary of War.

Poor Newton! At the end he was praised by General Pershing, General Dawes, and General Harbord as "the greatest Secretary of War in war that our country has yet produced," but throughout the conflict he was beaten on by a storm of ridicule and abuse. Washington correspondents, used to judging figures by weight, refused to believe that mind, courage, and character could possibly be housed in a five-foot frame, and when Newton foolishly confessed to a love of flowers, they nicknamed him Pansy. One night during the war, as we sat together in his office, he spoke of the handicap imposed by his small stature, and wryly remarked that someday he meant to write an essay on the "hypnotism of beef." Standing only five feet seven myself, I begged the privilege of collaboration.

CHAPTER 13

The Walls of Jericho

*T*he only thing predictable about Theodore Roosevelt was his unpredictability. His teeth-gnashing denunciations of "predatory wealth" and the corruptions of city gangs and state machines were almost entirely responsible for the reform wave that swept the country in the earlier years of the century. It was with his approval, if not actual blessing, that *McClure's*, *Everybody's*, the *Cosmopolitan*, and even the staid *Saturday Evening Post* devoted their pages to the exposure of evil conditions and gave a free hand to Lincoln Steffens, Ray Stannard Baker, David Graham Phillips, Charles Edward Russell, and Ida Tarbell. Both in Kansas City and Denver, I never had any other thought than that I was the humble sharer in a great national crusade led by T.R. himself.

Imagine, then, the shock when he changed attitude overnight, delivering a speech before the Gridiron Club in which he spoke of "yellow magazines" and compared their writers to the Man with the Muckrake in Bunyan's *Pilgrim's Progress*. Having coined "muckrakers" as an epithet, and highly delighted with it, he rang the changes on it in speech after speech, shaming those that he had once praised.

When I reached New York in the spring of 1911, the effects of his turnabout were plain to be seen. Editors had gone off the raw-meat diet, convinced that T.R.'s speech reflected a more conservative public opinion, and were looking about for a less controversial brand of articles. Only Hearst's *Cosmopolitan* still believed in the value and righteousness of exposing rotten conditions wherever rottenness could be found, and dear old Charles Edward Russell hounded the editors until they took me on.

One of my first assignments was Mississippi, where James K. Vardaman had just been elected to the Senate after a battle in which ugly charges had been made against big business. Another character! Not only did "Jeems K" wear his hair in a mane that fell below the shoulder blades, but as the champion of White supremacy he wore white linens and rode in a white cart drawn by snow-white oxen. The hillbillies adored him, and prominent in the crowd that worshiped at his feet was a jug-eared, bull-voiced young state senator by the name of Theodore Bilbo. Although I refused to accept Bilbo's assurance that Vardaman was a "demigod," I did swallow the story of "corporation skulduggery" without investigation, a credulity of which I came to be ashamed.

My parting with the senator-elect, owing to a bad *faux pas* on my part, was anything but cordial. On the last night of my stay he took me into the parlor, and after praising me as a man of wide experience and rare discernment, asked for suggestions as to his course on taking office. "As far as my poor abilities permit," he said, "I want to be of the greatest possible service to my country."

"Well, sir," I said, "do you want an honest answer?" On being assured that he did, I advised him to get a haircut. There was nothing smart-alecky in it, but real sincerity; for I knew how the newspapermen would seize on his Indian-medicine-man make-up, and that he would start off in the Senate with two strikes against him. Unfortunately, the Senator chose to regard it as a rudeness, if not an insult, and there was no delegation at the station to see me off.

A Cincinnati assignment brought me up against my first *real* boss, for George Cox made Jim Pendergast and the Denver gang look like baby-faced amateurs. Bankers, merchants, politicians, leaders of the bar, all crawled to pay court to the gross creature as he sprawled at his sloppy table in a local beer hall, weeping with delight when he gave them a smile and trembling with fear at his frown, à la Ben Bolt. Openly and arrogantly, he nominated and elected and levied tribute on every transaction, public and private.

Grown vain and garrulous, weaknesses that were to overthrow him eventually, Cox talked freely; and some of his rumbled comments were startling. For example, when I mentioned the great names in Ohio politics and referred to them as his lieutenants, he grunted contemptuously. "Lieutenants! That's a laugh. They're my *dogs*."

95

Evidently Cox repented his frankness after sobering up, for he demanded to see the finished article. I refused, of course; whereupon he told me that it didn't matter a goddam anyway, as the piece would not be printed. How he did it I never learned, but the article was suppressed. The blow drew blood, for in my description of Cox I had written that the saloon-keeper's only starting capital was "a gift of sullen silence that passed for force among the fluid souls of ruined men." I had worked over that sentence with all the patience of a lapidary, and when the editor informed me that the rhetorical jewel was doomed to blush unseen, I died the death.

Between assignments I lived in Greenwich Village, supposedly the habitat of the radical movement's intelligentsia. Maybe it was, but not to my simple Western way of thinking. One day Emma Goldman and her anarchism were all the rage, and the next day "Big Bill" Haywood held the center of his stage with his International Workers of the World, heaping scorn on achievement and glorifying the proletariat. The works of Freud and Jung had just been discovered, and at every so-called *salon* the talk was of psychoanalysis and sex. After Frank Walsh, Brand Whitlock, and Ben Lindsey, it was all pretty cheap and frowsy.

In September the *Cosmopolitan* sent me west on a story, and I stopped off in Denver to see old friends. While we were still embracing, former Senator Thomas M. Patterson sent for me and offered me the job of editorial writer for the *Rocky Mountain News,* Colorado's leading morning paper. As I had no wish for another Tammen-Bonfils experience, I suggested that we sit down and find out whether we saw eye to eye.

What I outlined was a finish fight against the corporations that had a strangle hold on Colorado and its cities. The tramway company, the water company, the telephone company, the coal companies, the smelters—all operating as a unit—controlled both parties and named both tickets in every election. The Supreme Court, members of the legislature, mayors, county officials, and councils were "hired hands," taking their orders from the Big Mitt. As a result, the public-utility companies grabbed franchises and charged exorbitant rates, while the industrial corporations were able to defeat all laws having to do with the protection of life, limb, and health and limiting the work day.

96

Senator Patterson was seventy years old at the time and had quite a reputation for thrift, yet when I had finished he beamed approvingly through his thick lenses and told me to "shoot the works." Not once in the months that followed did he ask me to pull a punch, even though boycotts often threatened his ruin.

Another source of strength, aside from Senator Patterson, was one of the most remarkable groups ever gathered together in any community. Heading it was Judge Lindsey, of course, and at his side stood Edward P. Costigan; William MacLeod Raine, the novelist; Randolph Walker, son of the John Brisben Walker whose *Cosmopolitan* pioneered in the field of the fifteen-cent magazines; and Josephine Roche, not long out of Vassar and a Lindsey coworker. Karl Bickel, then running a paper in Grand Junction, came to Denver for our meetings, as did Tom Tynan, the humane warden of the state penitentiary. A traveling salesman until his appointment, and without any training in penology, Tom had already inaugurated the "honor and trust" system that was to pave a way for the penal reforms of Thomas Mott Osborne and Warden Lawes. *All* of us young and strong in the faith, we marched forth to blow our rams' horns before the walls of the Big Mitt's Jericho.

Our first decision was to kick out Mayor Bob Speer, operator of the Denver machine that provided the Big Mitt with its majorities. As the best and quickest way of doing it, we agreed on a campaign for the commission form of government. Our plan did away with the mayoralty and reduced the number of elective officials from forty-nine to nine. This done, we began the circulation of petitions.

The *News*, of course, was the spearhead of the movement; and in addition to heated editorials, I filled the front page with attacks and appeals. The corporations, fighting back, ordered an advertising boycott, but while it made a sizable dent in revenues, Senator Patterson stayed put. The churches were also scared into opposition by rich parishioners, and only Father O'Ryan and Rabbi Kauvar, two dauntless souls, gave us pulpit support. Speer's board of education refused us the use of the schoolhouses, but we topped that hurdle by asking the people to open their homes, and neighborhood meetings proved most effective.

By early December we had thirty thousand signatures for the commission form as an amendment to the charter, and presented them to the city council. It was the plain duty of the body to call a special election; but, instead of that, Speer's gangsters threw our petition into the wastebasket. We shook Pike's Peak with our screams, of course, protesting against "brazen defiance, shameless venality, and depraved servility"; but what to do about it was a problem.

It was this trying time that Lincoln Steffens picked for a visit, stopping off on his way back from Los Angeles, where he had figured spectacularly in the trial of John and James McNamara, accused of dynamiting the *Times* building and killing twenty-one employees. The brothers were officials of the Structural Iron Workers, and General Harrison Gray Otis, owner of the *Times,* was organized labor's bitterest foe.

Shortly before, Lincoln had discovered Christ, and barged into Los Angeles with the golden rule as his cure for a hate-filled situation. Dismissing the crime as a "social manifestation" of a condition, he proposed that the prosecution be dropped, after which labor and management would sit down in the Christ spirit and uproot the causes of industrial war. I do not think there is any doubt that Lincoln secured the consent of powerful business groups to such a settlement and had much to do with getting the McNamaras to plead guilty.

Whether the judge and prosecutor welshed on the agreement, or whether they were not parties to it, is still a matter of debate. Anyway, Jim got a life sentence and John fifteen years, and a country-wide man hunt eventually sent two other dynamiters to the penitentiary. The pleas of guilty sent organized labor into a tail spin, for every union in the country had gone on record that the McNamaras were the innocent victims of an employer frame-up. As for the conference at which workers and management were to follow Christ's teachings, it was never held.

The failure of the experiment had no power to dampen Lincoln's faith in the golden rule, and at his first meeting with our group he urged us to drop our fight, throw affectionate arms about Mayor Speer and his gangsters, and join in a lion-and-lamb act. "There are no *bad* men," he smiled indulgently, "just victims of social maladjustments. The way to straighten them out is for everybody to stop calling names and get together." All of us held Lincoln in love and admiration, but

98

when we finally put him on the train for New York our sighs of relief had the roar of a cyclone.

In spite of many efforts, I have never been able to accept nonresistance as a workable rule of life. Not to fight evil is to encourage evil. Neither in the first World War nor in the second did I have any sympathy for "conscientious objectors," believing implicitly that their philosophy was an open invitation to aggression. All of the breed, of course, quote Christ at length; but not one seems to remember that he scourged the moneylenders from the temple, or recalls his rage against the "devourers of widows' houses."

Some of our group were impressed by the Steffens gospel and urged a try at Mayor Speer's conversion, but fortunately an antidote happened to be at hand. A month or so before, Dr. Sun Yat-sen had been in Denver, soliciting funds for his "revolution" from the small Chinese colony, and a few of us had had the privilege of meeting him and hearing the story of his struggle. During the conversation I asked him how it was that his people had put by the doctrine of nonresistance, taught by their philosophers for two thousand years. "Because," answered Sun Yat-sen, "they came to see the truth that evil had to be *fought*."

While we cursed the council and debated the next move, Mayor Speer himself made the decision as to our future course. For some time Denver's assessor, one Henry Arnold, had been the gang's number one headache. He had cut off $650,000 secretly added to the assessment of small property holders by his predecessor, and followed this up with substantial increases in the valuation of the tramway, water, and gas company properties. Now, on the heels of the council's action, Arnold announced that he would not obey the Mayor's order to add $400,000 to the city's tax bill, branding it as "plain graft." That night, without any warrant in law, Speer deposed Arnold and named a corporation tool as his successor. This man, accompanied by some twenty armed thugs, proceeded at once to the assessor's office, broke down the door with crowbars, and threw Arnold into the street.

Dimly remembering something in the Bill of Rights that applied, I hunted for a copy and found the exact wording: "That the people have the right peaceably to assemble for the common good, and to apply to those invested with the powers

99

of government for redress of grievances by petitions and remonstrances." Out at once, therefore, went this call:

When officials desert the law they have sworn to uphold, and lend themselves to anarchy, lawlessness and riot, it becomes the high duty of the people to take counsel for the preservation of the public peace and the maintenance of the good order that is essential to the safety of institutions. All law-abiding citizens are hereby urged to gather at the east front of the State House Sunday afternoon to consider the many outrages perpetrated by Robert W. Speer and his venal council, particularly the crowning villainy of the midnight raid of thugs upon the courthouse, and the ruffianly ejection of Assessor Henry Arnold from an office to which he was elected by the people. Let every honest man and woman come! Let the children too be brought, that their young minds may be stamped with detestation of lawlessness.

The corporation papers denounced the call as an appeal to mob violence, but despite a snowstorm, more than twenty-five thousand answered. For three hours the throng listened to speeches, and then, quietly and solemnly, endorsed a resolution that asked the Supreme Court to take original jurisdiction of a suit to restore Arnold to his office. The justices refused even to hear arguments on the petition, and when an honest district judge issued a writ of mandamus ordering the council to set a day for the special election, the court again intervened. Completely protected by these decisions, the gang gaily set about the business of re-electing Speer and his fellow rascals.

There was nothing for us to do but meet the challenge, and we determined to put a complete Citizens ticket in the field, making a fight for every office. In the matter of a mayoralty candidate we had no choice, for Arnold stood out as the man of the hour. He had never been identified with our movement, and there were disquieting rumors about his past, but after we had made him our Galahad, it would have been suicidal to back away. The rest of the ticket, however, was beyond all question; and with Ben Lindsey running again for juvenile judge, we had a vote-getter without parallel.

At the very outset of the campaign our doubts with respect to Arnold were revived, for Tammen and Bonfils, with a loud shout, put the *Post* behind his candidacy. On the heels of this calamity, the air filled with charges that our hero had been guilty of forgery, embezzlement, swindling, etc., before coming to Denver. We grilled him, of course, but he had a plausible explanation for every charge, and with a roar of protest against "polecat fighting," we swept forward. Nevertheless, it was deemed wise to have an ace in the hole, and at a great mass meeting every candidate was made to hold up his right hand and take solemn oath that if elected he would do everything in his power to bring about commission government at the earliest possible date.

The election was not merely a defeat for the Big Mitt, but a rout, the walls of Jericho tumbling down with a loud crash. Arnold went in by an overwhelming majority, and Ben Lindsey, as usual, led the ticket. Shrewd old Senator Patterson, however, was not dazzled by the victory, having seen too many millennial dawns fade away into twilights. "Arnold," he prophesied, "will not keep his pledge, nor will any of the others after they have had a taste of office. We've got to put one of our own people on guard, and the strategic place is police commissioner."

At a meeting of the group I was selected as the sacrificial goat, and notice to that effect was duly served on the new mayor. Arnold did not like it one little bit, squirming like a worm on the hook; but when Senator Patterson put on the heat, he gave in. Taking my place on the board along with a fire commissioner and excise commissioner, I lost no time in smashing the machine by summary discharges and transfers. Ballot-box stuffers, thugs, and criminals were among the lot I kicked out; yet from the uproar it might have been thought that all were Knights of the Grail.

The presidential campaign, unhappily, split our movement wide-open, half streaming off after Theodore Roosevelt and the other half being just as enthusiastic for the Democratic ticket. My own devotion to Woodrow Wilson dated back to Kansas City days when I heard him speak to high-school students on the meaning of democracy. This admiration grew as I read his books and watched him perform as governor of New Jersey. Senator Patterson, fortunately, shared my belief in Wilson as the nation's hope, and let me go the limit in editorials and front-page stuff.

Ben Lindsey, Ed Costigan, and Josephine Roche, however, gave themselves to T.R. with an ardor that bordered on fanaticism, and were foremost among the Bull Moosers who shed their blood at Armageddon. The Little Judge was dubbed the

101

Bull Mouse, and Josephine made headlines as leader of the Moosettes. Back in Colorado they put a Roosevelt ticket in the field, with Costigan as their gubernatorial candidate, but Wilson swept the state.

The November election also furnished a first and successful test of the initiative. The Mothers' Compensation Act, the headless ballot, and an eight-hour law for women in industry —all proposed by our Direct Legislation League—were carried by large majorities. Where we lost out was in the fight to gain approval for the recall of judicial decisions, and the defeat was mainly due to Theodore Roosevelt.

The measure did *not* refer to private litigation, but was concerned only with laws duly enacted by the Legislature. Under it the State Supreme Court alone would have the power to declare a law unconstitutional, and the people would have the right to override the decision by majority vote. In Colorado it had been the habit for inferior judges, even justices of the peace, to nullify statutes by a scratch of the pen, and the initiated bill was our answer to the unlawful practice.

Ben Lindsey, while visiting Oyster Bay in the summer, made the mistake of telling T.R. about the measure, and overnight the recall of decisions was adopted as a plank in the Bull Moose platform. When it was made a national issue and distorted by every possible misrepresentation, even the people of Colorado were deceived. I was for the bill at the time, and today, when every branch of the American judiciary has been dragged down to an all-time low, I am for it more strongly than ever.

CHAPTER 14

Creel Lochinvar Runs Amuck

I took office as commissioner without other purpose than to smash the police machine that protected the Big Mitt's vote mills, thus opening the way for honest elections. This proved a fairly simple chore, and as our campaign for commission government was not yet ready for launching, it looked like a good idea to clean up some of the mess that Speer had left behind. A system of traffic control met with general approval, and there was no great outcry when I proceeded against the crooked gambling games that operated in every block, but the storm broke as the result of an order that took clubs away from the policemen.

Nobody listened when I pointed out that London's "bobbies" did very well without clubs, and no attention was paid to the long list of stupid brutalities I cited in support of my position. Not one criminal had ever been beaten up, the victims being drunks, half-grown boys, and citizens who made the mistake of "talking back." The opposition press and the Chamber of Commerce waxed hysterical in prophesying a "reign of terror" that would put every officer's life in jeopardy, and only after several peaceful months did the clamor die down.

A second furor arose in connection with an I.W.W. invasion, led by Big Bill Haywood. These "wobblies," with their American version of Europe's communism, had been turning other cities into bedlams by street meetings that invited arrest. Jail was exactly what they wanted, for it gave them the opporunity to raise a cry against "America's Cossacks" and attack the whole democratic process.

Knowing this, and happening to believe in free speech, I gave the wobblies the right to talk their heads off; whereupon every civic body passed resolutions denouncing me as Haywood's secret partner in his conspiracy to overthrow American institutions. As I had expected, nobody listened to Big Bill's orators after the first day, and he actually came to see me, begging for a "crack-down." When I refused, the hulking agitator and his followers left town. Incidentally, Haywood skipped out for Russia after the Lenin-Trotsky coup in 1918 and died of homesickness for capitalistic America. Emma Goldman, the high priestess of anarchism, was another who found the Soviet Union somewhat short of being heaven on earth. Persecuted and then deported by the Bolsheviks, she spent the rest of her life begging readmission to the United States.

In attacking my "crackpot ideas," the *Post* and the *Times* dealt in outright abuse, and only the stodgy *Republican* had the wit to introduce a note of ridicule. Spencer's cartoons were brilliantly satirical, giving me a laugh even while getting under my skin. Some anonymous poet also had a keen thrust, and his "Lochinvar Creel" parodies did me more harm than all the bludgeoning, convincing a good many people that I meant well but lacked balance. These were the two stanzas that started the series:

> George Lochinvar Creel came out of the West
> His ideas were naked, his reforms undressed,
> And save his good nerve, he weapons had none,
> But he boomed into office like a 13 inch gun.
> So erratic in politics, abnormal by far,
> There ne'er was reformer like Creel Lochinvar.
>
> He stayed not for horse sense, and stopped not for reason,
> He flew into air at most any old season,
> But ere he'd alight after some of his fits,
> The commissioners would shrink and always yell "quits."
> A reformer in peace and the real thing in war,
> No one could rave on like Creel Lochinvar.

The real fight, however, began over commercialized vice. Under Speer the infamous "crib system" had been tolerated and even encouraged. This was an artificial street lined on both sides with cubicles in which half-naked women sat for sale beside a soiled bed and a dirty washbowl. When a customer mounted the short flight of steps, a corrugated shutter was pulled down. Every night the street was packed and jammed with milling crowds, men for the most part, but with a high percentage of veiled women, and even more distressingly, many teen-age boys and girls.

Judge Lindsey blamed the district for the increase in juvenile delinquency, and from the health authorities I learned that there was more than a score of cases of syphilis and gonorrhea in the public schools. In Kansas City, as editor of *The Independent,* I had interested myself in the problem of prostitution; but it was a half-baked approach, unsupported by any real study. Now, faced by the horror of Denver's crib system, I burned midnight oil over the works of Lecky, Havelock Ellis, and various other authorities. More than this, I wrote to the police authorities in other cities, asking what they were doing.

Almost at the very outset, however, the ministers of Denver swooped down on me with a demand for the instant abolition of the red-light district. With this I was in full agreement, but where we split was with respect to method. When they urged arrest and imprisonment, I answered that jails had proved their powerlessness to solve the problem. As for "running the harlots out," where was I to run them? To other cities? Well and good, but only if they could bring me letters from the mayors of Pueblo and Trinidad, stating a willingness to receive them.

Others than the ministers badgered me with suggestions and insistences. One group urged segregation, talking largely of the "physiological necessity of the male" as justification for the recognition of prostitution as a legitimate industry. Businessmen, slipping in slyly, urged "hush-hush" policy on the ground that the discussion was giving Denver a bad name. Doctors even advocated reglementation, the French system of medical inspection, pointing out that it had been adopted by many American cities, notably San Francisco.

Holding off the ministers, businessmen, and physicians with one hand and turning the pages of Lecky and Ellis with the other, I finally reached certain definite convictions and conclusions. First and foremost, I rejected *in toto* the theory of "necessary evil," and looked on segregation and medical inspection as both infamous and useless. Only a few months before, at a conference in Brussels, the champions of reglementation had been forced to confess that it had proved a "lamentable failure."

What I proposed, therefore, was this: to take over a 266-acre farm owned by the city and equip it with hospitals and dormitories where Denver's human wreckage could be collected, treated, and sorted. Here treatment would be provided not only for disease, but for the rehabilitation of the drug fiends and the drunkards; also opportunity for a winnowing process that would separate the habitual and the occasional, the hardened and the semidelinquent, handling all with regard for nothing but purely social considerations.

Until the farm could be got in readiness, palliative measures would have to be relied on, and I stated that these orders would be issued at once: the closing of fake restaurants, "massage parlors," and disorderly houses in the residential section; barring minors from the crib district, forbidding the sale of liquor, and the abolition of the telephone-call system.

Believing that commercialized amusement had a very definite connection with commercialized vice, I appointed Josephine

Roche as a special officer to ride herd on dance halls and skating rinks. The daughter of a wealthy Colorado mine owner, she went from Vassar to do settlement work in the slums of New York, and had shown capacity and rare understanding. In 1912 even equal suffrage was being fought as "unwomanly," and as she was the country's first "lady cop," the appointment came in for a lot of publicity, much of it unfavorable.

From the first, however, Josephine flashed those qualities that were to make her a national figure. When she made her rounds, wearing a large, impressive star, she didn't say, "Do so-and-so or I'll throw you in jail." Instead of that she talked heart to heart with every proprietor, showing him the evil effects on children and appealing to his own love of family. Whereas wholesale arrests would have aroused resentment and resistance, her approach made a friend and supporter of every dance-hall man and rink owner. Gangs were a menace at the time, but she won the confidence of young hoodlums, and soon the tough kids were forming a guard of honor for the "lady cop" on her nightly tours.

A fine group of ministers, priests, and rabbis endorsed my plan but a pharisaical majority kept up their caterwauling, abetted by the thieves we had kicked out of office. As a result of their activity, a "stooge" judge called a "stooge" grand jury, and in September, when we had been in power only three months, this combination indicted every city official for "permitting the red-light district to exist." Never very calm when under fire, I gave full rein to my anger and contempt in this public statement:

Who does not remember when this street was a riot of naked women, and when Denver conditions were only rivalled by the infamous cribs of Havana? Did any judge or grand jury take action during those years? No indeed! Not until now, when a new administration has waged war on white slavers, cadets and prostitution itself—along with the corporations that pillage the city—does the eminent purist come forward. . . . While every energy will be devoted to the eradication of prostitution, I will not hound the individual prostitute. Most of them are the helpless victims of economic and industrial injustices, and when I see the prostitutions of self-respect going on in Denver every day by men of standing, I grow to a certain respect for those who sell their souls openly.

Two elements combine to embarrass the Board and its policies.

One is the corporation forces that seek to discredit the Arnold administration by hues and cries, thus stopping the investigation of their stealings. The other is formed by alleged Christians whose one manifestation of Christian activity is the demand that these women be thrown into jail or else driven out of town. They make no suggestion other than arrests, and their study of the problem is confined to nightly prowlings in and about the district.

Does anyone find these men investigating wages, hours of work or housing conditions? *No!* But every night finds their quivering noses pushed into bawdy houses, their moist eyes bathing in seminudity. Possessed by an infamous curiosity, such investigators come to be as much habitues of the district as those who go there frankly for a purpose.

My idea of reform does not entail intimate and sole concern with the habits and amusements of the individual. Not only have I never enjoyed that conviction of moral perfection that enabled me to sit in judgment on my fellows, but I am also of the opinion that such "reform" is not calculated to bring the best results. Good does not come from *without* but from *within*. People are not bettered by statutory enactment and municipal ordinances, but grow in goodness through their response to the summons of a finer, more wholesome and expansive environment. Men change with conditions, and as long as conditions are unjust and degrading, the law commands uplift without avail.

It is such conditions that I have sought to change through the securement of economic, social, industrial and political reforms, sincerely believing that the surface evils of modern living would disappear when the causal evils were eliminated. I have no sympathy whatever with the reforms that seek to make people good by ordering them to "stop doing things."

I make bold to call myself a Christian, and in my administration of the police department I am attempting to give practical application to the teachings of the Nazarene. As I play my small part in the great movement that has the changing of evil conditions as its objective, I try also to repress and remedy the vice and crime that these conditions have caused. If this honest endeavor meets the approval and cooperation of the avowedly religious element, I shall be glad and proud. But if such approval is dependent on my turning the police force into beadles, and giving all effort to measures that have no other than a punitive purpose, I must forgo it.

• Nothing was ever done about the indictments, as they were intended only to furnish ammunition for the guns of the *Post*, the *Times*, and the *Republican*, and the uproar finally subsided into whines.

CHAPTER 15

Blowing Off the Lid

*A*ll through these excitements, Mayor Arnold's support left nothing to be desired as far as public statements were concerned. On one occasion he even went so far as to wish that Denver had "a thousand Creels." Nevertheless, certain undercover happenings stirred our suspicions. More and more he avoided our group, and rumors began to circulate about his increasing intimacy with Tammen and Bonfils. Slyly at first, but then boldly, the *Post* praised Arnold as an able administrator whose plans for a greater Denver were being blocked by a bunch of wild-eyed reformers, naming me as a "tramp anarchist." There was no open change on the mayor's part, however, until I came out with a demand for the fulfillment of our commission-government pledge. Then he sidled into my office with some mumble about it's being a mistake.

"I'm for it, of course," he explained, "but what's the rush? Let's get things straightened out first."

"Why, Henry," I exclaimed, "have you forgotten our solemn promise to hold a special election at the earliest possible moment? Hands lifted to heaven, reverent voices, tear-filled eyes, and all that?"

"Certainly not," he hastened to reply. "But all the same, George, so many elections are pretty hard on the people. Why not give them a breathing spell?"

"Be of good cheer," I answered soothingly. "If the people are sick of elections, they can show it by not signing our petitions."

Judge Lindsey and I opened offices, getting the rent from a faithful few, and devoted men and women again started off on the drudging job of getting signatures for a special election. All of the old enthusiasm revived, but as the campaign got under way the *Post* attacked and Arnold showed his hand. Without a word to me, he instructed the fire commissioner and the excise commissioner to return clubs to policemen, branding the order as a "criminal blunder," and stating that its continuance might well result in the "wholesale murder of officers."

The poor fool left himself wide open, for I had a record to pull on him. Prior to the order, twelve policemen had been killed, while in the ten months of the "clubless" period, just two assaults were reported. A plain-clothes man, butting in on an Irish dance, got a punch in the nose for his rowdyism. Miss Roche, who happened to be present, picked him up, dusted off his clothes, and took the bully home after telling the young puncher to appear before me the next morning.

The other case involved a policeman who pushed into a social gathering and acted rudely to an expectant mother. The husband struck him, whereupon the officer knocked him down and proceeded to beat his face into a pulp with his fists. Had he possessed a club, there is little doubt he would have killed the man.

I threw these two cases into Arnold's face and dared him to make an answer. He preserved a discreet silence, but two weeks later came back with another sneaky attack. During my absence from the city he issued an order permitting the sale of liquor in the red-light district. Again I blasted him and my fellow commissioners, and again there was sullen silence.

"What's the matter with the fellow?" Senator Patterson came down to the office that night to ask the question.

"A reversion to tripe," I told him. "Living at a high level involved too much moral and mental strain. Bonfils and Tammen are his kind, and he's quit us to go with them. The three mean to start a new gang of their own."

I was for an instant break, but the wise old senator insisted that Arnold be given a bit more rope. "Push the commission-government election," he advised, "and make him come out into the open." This we did, obtaining signatures to our petition until enough were secured to force the city council to order a special election for February 14.

This done, I turned again to the red-light district, determined on decisive action. For eight months the administration had blocked every move to acquire the city's 266-acre farm as a laboratory and hospital center, and the uselessness of further effort stood apparent. Moreover, the problem had worsened. On June 1 there were approximately 700 professional prostitutes plying their trade in Denver. On December 1, by reason of repressive measures, the number had dwindled to 250. As a result of the permission to resume liquor selling, given in my absence by McGrew and Blakely, my fellow commissioners, many girls had returned, and on January 1 probably 350 were doing business in the district.

Appalling statistics, furnished by the hospital authorities, free dispensaries, and the medical profession, proved the unwisdom of further delay. All were alarmed at the spread of venereal disease, reporting a steady increase, with more cases coming in from the high schools. After consultation with Judge Lindsey and every other official having to do with the public health, I decided to sequestrate all cases of disease as a first step toward the abolition of the district. Any other course, quite obviously, meant scattering the plague over city and state.

With hospitals already overburdened, the problem of space arose; but Mother St. George, head of the House of the Good Shepherd, came forward with an offer of her old quarters at a nominal rental. Arnold, however, found an excuse for refusing to pay the small amount, and blandly assured me that the farm would be ready for occupancy in ten days or two weeks. Knowing this to be a lie, Judge Lindsey, Miss Roche, and I took our appeal elsewhere. Generously and enthusiastically, the sheriff renovated and enlarged the women's quarters in the county hospital; the commissioner of supplies ordered bedding, shower baths, and other necessities; and the medical department of the state university agreed to make Wassermann and antigen tests at cost.

The procedure mapped out was this: Each night a certain number of prostitutes would be taken into custody and arraigned in court the next morning. The judge was to continue the cases for ten days, during which time the blood tests were to be made. Upon rearraignment, such as were diseased were to be committed to the county hospital. The arrests began on the night of January 9, and 129 prostitutes had been removed from the district by February 1.

Nothing was more necessary than to gain the co-operation of the sullen, resentful women by convincing them that it was not a mere "moral crusade," but a reclamatory movement largely in their own interest. As always when a real job had to be done, I called in Josephine Roche, and her sympathy and

110

understanding won the great majority to the hope of a new and better life, many coming in voluntarily.

Of the 144 women first taken into custody, 95 were hospitalized for treatment; and the *Post, Times,* and *Republican* deafened the heavens with their outcry against the "expense to taxpayers." By way of adding to hypocrisy, they also moaned over the "cruel conditions" due to the overcrowded hospital. For twelve years the poor creatures had lived in cribs and hovels, yet now there was indignant outcry because a few were made to sleep on cots or pallets.

Nothing was more vital than an immediate report in order to stem the clamor, but here I ran against Senator Patterson's deep-rooted prejudices. At the mention of syphilis and gonorrhea he hit the ceiling, and vowed that such words should never soil the pages of the *News.* To do him justice, he was not alone in this attitude, for at the time venereal disease was a taboo in every newspaper office. It was only after long pleading and argument that I won his consent, and then he salved his conscience by refusing to read a word of what I wrote.

At the outset I expressed my disgust at the talk of expense.

If smallpox should develop in the city [I asked], what would be thought of the official who refused to quarantine cases on the score of expense? One of the women now in the hospital has both syphilis and gonorrhea, and on the night preceding her arrest she met thirty men. This, to be sure, was an unusual record. With "parlor-house girls," the average is ten; while the crib girls, who do not have to sing and dance, have an average of twenty-five. Think, then, of the disease that flowed daily from the 95 women sent to the hospital! Compare the cost to the taxpayers with the ruined lives, the rotted manhood and the curse laid on unborn generations.

Then followed this record:

Arrests	129
Voluntary surrenders	15
Total cases	144
Released	47
Diseased	95
Further examination	2
Syphilis	36
Gonorrhea	40
Both	19

Only a few months before, Denver had gone into spasms over the discovery of a leper. I recalled this, and pointed out that every woman of the ninety-five held more menace to the community than any leper, and that while there was no known cure for leprosy, we were curing the diseased prostitutes, and also treating drug addicts successfully. Although Miss Roche had been able to make a study of only forty cases, even this small number disproved the theory of "innate depravity," for this was her ascertainment of causes:

Couldn't get work	2
Wages under $5 a week ...	7
Family in want	1
Exhausting work	7
Causes from marriage	5
Ruined at 14 or 15	6
Lured by district	7
"Didn't think"	5

The forty-seven women released after examination, I admitted frankly, presented a problem, as the sheriff refused to keep them in jail for reclamatory effort. From various sources, however, Miss Roche was able to collect a little money, and with it she accomplished these results: four were returned to their families out of town; three to families in town; eleven went to manual jobs or to friends; and the rest, while marked down as doubtful, insisted that they had no intention of going back to the old life. The clergy, as a whole, commended the report, and many public meetings proved that the people were back of me.

I thought then, and still think, that I was on the right track. What confirms it is the fact that the trail we blazed is now a beaten road. The story of the Denver experiment received nation-wide notice, and had a great deal to do with breaking down the taboo against public consideration of the social evil and venereal disease. The fight against segregation—the city's partnership with commercialized vice—took on new vigor and won victories from coast to coast.

Only poor Senator Patterson remained unchanged. For weeks he went around, shaking his head and dolefully wondering what the world was coming to. What a blessing that he died before the smart set, breaking loose from all restraints, made "homos" and Lesbians a favorite topic of conversation.

Any doubt as to Arnold's stand on commission government was soon removed. He himself kept a closed mouth, but his personal appointees came out against the proposal, and at his order the fire commissioner and the excise commissioner took entire charge of the police department, making me a minority of one. To stay in office meant fighting with tied hands, so at a conference it was decided that I should break with the mayor and bring his double cross out into the open.

The first of February was fixed on as the date for the explosion, and as the match to touch it off, I chose McGrew, the fire commissioner and Arnold's intimate. No sooner had the board met than I rose and proposed this resolution:

"Whereas, we are in receipt of numerous complaints with regard to uniformed man frequenting saloons,

"Be it resolved that any member of the fire and police departments, from the Chief down, be forbidden to drink at any public bar while in uniform, and

"Be it further resolved that as an example and encouragement, this board shall submit themselves to the same discipline."

McGrew instantly roared a protest against the last paragraph as insulting, and I answered that it was the point of the whole resolution. "You have rarely drawn a sober breath since you came on this board," I continued, throwing the amenities overboard. "There have been mornings when you have lurched in here with your eyes blackened as the result of low saloon rows, looking like any bum. You have turned the department's automobiles into midnight joy wagons, and the fire chief into an attendant during your circle of bars and disorderly resorts."

He started up with doubled fists but sat down quickly, contenting himself with some mumble about "considering the source." By way of concluding the performance, I called attention to a completely vicious attack in the *Republican,* attributed to McGrew, and asked who wrote it for him.

"Nobody wrote it for me," he blustered. "I gave out the interview, and stand by it. I . . ."

"Nonsense," I interrupted. "You can't pronounce half of the words in it. I defy anyone who has been present at these meetings to recall a single intelligent or even intelligible sentence you have ever uttered."

As I had expected, Mayor Arnold made an immediate request for our resignations, but while the fire commissioner obliged at once, I refused, demanding an open trial. As a result, the Mayor ordered my suspension and named February 15 as the date of the hearing. I had hoped for a favorable public reaction, but not in such volume. From every pulpit came denunciation of Arnold, and officials and private citizens filled the columns of the *News* with commendation of my policies.

What gave me the most pleasure, however, was the action of old friends when McGrew went to Kansas City for the avowed purpose of "getting something" on me. The *Star* guyed him unmercifully, printing a series of depositions that charged me with all sorts of crimes from stealing jam and watermelons to breach of promise during my school days.

More seriously, Colonel William R. Nelson, the great newspaper's great owner, wrote an editorial entitled "Creel's Useful Enemies" and declared that "in Kansas City Mr. Creel was doing the same sort of fighting against shams and frauds and crookedness that he is doing in Denver." Nor was that all. Under date of February 7 I received the following telegram, signed by judges, civic leaders, editors, and every city and county official:

Kansas City, Mo., February 7, 1913

A man named McGrew is in Kansas City for the avowed purpose of getting something on you. Newspaper reporters have endeavored to have him specify what he wishes, but he refuses to do so. If it is your integrity, there are thousands in Kansas City and Western Missouri who would be glad to tell of your struggles from boyhood until you removed to Denver. It is a story of a winning fight against overwhelming odds, with every obligation manfully and honestly discharged. If he means your public life, we have a story of your fight of a decade against corruption and dishonesty, almost entirely at your own expense, with the result that the cause of higher civic ideals and the principle of honesty in public life were advanced immeasurably.

If it is against your private life, the legion that know you intimately and love you for what you are, stand ready to attest your beautiful loyalty to your parents, family and every human being having any claim of blood or friendship, the openness and cleanly character of

your intimate life, and your honorable conduct with your fellow
human beings.

I prized the tribute then, I prize it now, and I will prize it
to the day of my death. While the tears were still in my eyes,
dear old Senator Patterson entered the lists in my behalf.
Coming down to the office at night, he told me that he would
attend to the cartoon, and smilingly shut his door in my face.
Not until the next morning did I find out what he was doing.
There on the front page was a picture of me, incredibly noble
and unafraid, standing with folded arms while the *Post, Times,*
and *Republican* plotted my ruin in the background. A streamer
—"I Stand on My Record"—ballooned out of my mouth,
and a five-column box blared this endorsement of me and my
policies:

Past differences forgotten, W. G. Evans, owner of the Times,
F. G. Bonfils and H. H. Tammen, owners of the Post, and Crawford
Hill, owner of the Republican, are now fast friends and sworn allies.
The basis of this strange unity is a rancorous hatred of George
Creel, and a desperate determination to encompass his ruin. Bonfils
and Tammen have boldly announced their intention to run Mr.
Creel out of town, and Hill and Evans, through their agents, are
aiding and abetting them.

Every day sees the Post, the Times and the Republican filled with
the most shocking falsehoods against Mr. Creel, and every species of
vituperation and calumny calculated to wound, poison and vilify.
Why is there such concentration of malignity against this one man?
Why are these men, so recently locked in blackguardly combat, now
united in this campaign of slander and abuse? The people, undoubtedly, have already answered that question to their own satisfaction. If the attacks do not cease, these men will make George
Creel a giant in strength in this community if he is not that right
now.

The trial was duly held, and Senator Patterson insisted on
acting as my counsel. In his letter of suspension Arnold had
filed five counts—four dealing with attacks on my policies as
"disruptive and demoralizing," and the fifth concerned with
the "creation of dissension" by my "offensive charges" against
a fellow board member. What I wanted, of course, was to consider the first four counts in detail, but the city attorney moved
my discharge on the fifth count, ignoring the others.

For a full forty minutes Senator Patterson argued against the stand as unjust and arbitrary, insisting on my right to call witnesses and present testimony. His eloquence, backed by sound law, brought out the sweat on me, stirring the fear that Arnold might weaken, but while showing signs of unhappiness, he brazened it out. Dismissing the Senator's contentions, he ruled that the fifth count constituted sufficient cause for discharge, and that the other four need not be considered.

Not only was the special election just one week away, but the administration now came out into the open against the charter amendment, and the *Post, Times,* and *Republican* went the limit in abuse and falsehood. Senator Patterson, however, turned the *News* over to us, and the plain people opened their homes for our meetings and contributed their dimes to our pitiful campaign fund. The result was even more than any of us dared to hope, for commission government was carried by a vote of three to one.

Ten days after the election, Arnold came out with a vice policy of his own. An order by the Fire and Police Board closed the red-light district, and the inmates were given twenty-four hours to evacuate. When asked by a delegation what was to become of them, Arnold answered that he didn't know. Denver soon found out, for the women simply moved into side-street hotels and rooming houses, soliciting in broad day as well as at night. Not stopping with this blunder, the mayor then proceeded to discharge Josephine Roche.

With May 20 set as the date for the election of commissioners, Arnold announced his candidacy for the finance post, while others of his gang filed for the eight remaining commissionerships. In speeches and statements I analyzed the man and his career, ending up with this judgment: "There is not room for anger in the recital. It is too huge a tragedy. By the height and splendor of his opportunity, the depths and degradation of his failure may be measured. Some may ascribe it to venality and corruption. It is more true and more charitable to put him down as a fool with a homesickness for mud."

Again the election returns exceeded our fondest hopes. Neither Arnold nor any of his crew carried a single precinct, and the commissioners placed in office were all men of our choosing. Never was there plainer proof that the people, put

116

in possession of the facts, can be depended upon to vote intelligently.

What to do now was the big problem. In November of the year before I had married Blanche Bates, and she had given up her brilliant stage career to share my fortunes in Denver. Senator Patterson urged me to stay with the *News*, painting rosy pictures of a great political future, but they held no appeal, for I had returned to my old belief that a writer with convictions was far more valuable outside office than in. Even had this not been the case, there was my domestic situation.

I was almost penniless as a result of the various campaigns, and the prospect of improvement in my financial position was not bright, for newspaper salaries in Denver were not marked by prodigality on the part of publishers. Looking ahead, I could not see how $60 a week would be enough to support a household, and there was a deep prejudice against being supported by my wife.

The compelling consideration, however, was her unhappiness. Social ostracism was a favorite weapon of the Big Mitt, and along with Ben Lindsey and others of our group, I was barred from clubs and homes and treated as a pariah. This did not bother me, for there was the excitement of the battle, but to be regarded as an outcast was a new and miserable experience for my bride. Even worse than ostracism, however, was the ugliness of the Denver fight—the lies, the vileness of attacks, the hates, the obscenity of anonymous letters—and while she made no complaint, her distastes and actual misery were plain to be seen. It was because of this, more than anything else, that I decided to quit Colorado and try my fortunes once again in New York.

It was from the Atlantic seaboard, therefore, that I watched the rush of events in Denver after my exit. In October Senator Patterson, old and tired, sold the *News* to John C. Shaffer of Chicago, who then bought the *Republican* and killed it, thus leaving the *News* in sole possession of the morning field. When he placed some highly competent men in charge, particularly William L. Chenery as editorial writer, the people not only believed that Patterson policies were to be continued, but that the *Post*'s hold on the city would be broken.

Shaffer, unfortunately, proved to have small stomach for the knockdowns and drag-outs demanded by the Denver situation.

117

Bonfils and Tammen, old hands at infighting, first slugged him slap-happy and then bluffed him out of his breeches. For a while the *News* continued to make the fight against the Big Mitt, flat on its back as a result of the Citizens movement, but soon there were ominous signs of change. It was not until the strike of miners in the coal fields, however, that "Honest John" came out into the open. Over the protests of Bill Chenery, who resigned as a result, he championed the cause of the operators, and in twenty-four hours the circulation of the *News* was cut in half.

In 1926, whipped to a frazzle and sick of losses, Shaffer sold out to the Scripps-Howard chain, and Roy Howard, dynamic, aggressive, and highly articulate, burst upon the Denver scene. His opening gun, fired before a meeting of the Chamber of Commerce, had all the blare of Joshua's trumpet.

"We are coming to Denver with neither a tin cup nor a lead pipe," challenged Mr. Howard. "We will live with and in this community, and not on or off it. We are nobody's big brother, wayward sister, or poor relation. We come here simply as news merchants. We will run no lottery."

Bonfils and Tammen picked up the gage, and what followed was the newspaper battle of the century. Both papers doubled their size, careless of cost, and plunged into a circulation contest based on premiums rather than principles. Beauty contests, parades, prizes, and similar extravagances succeeded one another in frenzied succession, and at last came the famous "gasoline war." The *Post* first offered to give away two gallons of gasoline with every want ad, and when the *News* offered four gallons, the *Post* leaped to five. Both papers had to set up desks in the street, and clerks, sweating the clock around, were fed as they worked.

After two years of warfare, costing each paper approximately three millions, the exhausted battlers called a truce and agreed on peace terms. Bonfils and Tammen suspended the *Morning Post* and Howard junked the *Evening News,* and the treaty also contained provisions against the future offer of prizes and premiums.

So ended the Battle of the Century, and so ended Denver's revolt against corporation and gang rule. Under cover of the uproar, the Big Mitt overthrew the commission form of government, elected an amiable nonentity as mayor, and took up

118

where it had left off. With Ben Lindsey left to stand guard almost alone, and lacking newspaper support, the wolf pack bit and clawed until he was dragged down.

CHAPTER 16

Peace Hath Its Victories, but—

*F*ifteen years ago, or maybe it is safer to say twenty, Ben Lindsey enjoyed world-wide fame. European governments sent delegations to Denver for the study of his methods, and the Japanese took photographs of the furniture so that his courtroom might be reproduced in Tokyo. Parliamentary bodies praised him as one of the great benefactors of humanity. Today it is doubtful if the rising generation knows anything about his work or can even recall his name.

There is no greater paradox than that here in the United States, dedicated to freedom, the literature of democracy has no standing in our schools. The battlefields of war are dealt with in detail, and lengthy chapters perpetuate the memories of victorious generals, but those who fought the battles of peace, waging ceaseless struggle for the social justice without which free institutions may not endure, go unmentioned.

All of the "reformers" of that earlier day—Folk of Missouri, Tom Johnson and Brand Whitlock of Ohio, Francis Heney of California, La Follette of Wisconsin—were made to run a gantlet of abuse and defamation, but not one was ever called upon to undergo greater persecution than Ben Lindsey. As if grinding poverty were not enough—he lived in a half basement that a small salary might be poured back into his work— enemies pursued him until the end with tireless malignity.

Not even Francis of Assisi was more pure of life, and yet they accused him of vilest immoralities, bribing prostitutes to sign affidavits accusing him of the lowest form of vice; when his mother was operated on for cataract, they spread the report that her bandaged eyes came from the beatings Ben had inflicted in a fit of drunken rage; social ostracism was employed to break him; assassins threatened him; both political parties rejected him, and when he was elected as an independent, corrupt judges forced him to run again.

In the first years Denver had only admiration for the poor boy who had risen to be a county judge, studying law while he worked as a janitor. His initial reforms also had a large measure of popular appeal, for they did not affect the power of political machines or touch the great corporations that were the real masters of the state.

The arrest of a small urchin for stealing lumps of coal from the railroad tracks was the start of it all. Instead of passing sentence, as urged by the district attorney, Ben balked at sight of the shivering child and postponed the trial until he could do a bit of investigating. Down in the city jail he found mere children in filthy, verminous cells, locked up with adult criminals and subjected to the most degrading personal indignities. On visiting the industrial school at Golden he saw armed guards, boys shackled with ball and chain, and cruel floggings the usual punishment for infraction of rules.

The treatment of children as criminals coming under the criminal law shocked Ben by its barbarity, and he began poring over the statute books in search of a remedy. At last, in an obscure section relating to the disciplining of school children, he discovered something that might apply, and evolved the theory that juvenile offenders could be treated as wards of the state and corrected by the state as *parens patriae*. That was the beginning of the famous juvenile court of Denver, an idea that swept from state to state and eventually went around the world.

Public opinion applauded when Ben cleaned up the jails, ended the horrors of the industrial school, established a detention home, and clamored for playgrounds and public baths. Unfortunately for him, the Little Judge did not stop there. The lad that stole the coal was the son of a widow who had not received a penny in damages when her husband died of lead poisoning in a smelter. The mother of four youngsters, brought into his court and branded as "unfit" to keep her children, worked for twelve hours a day in a steam laundry.

Why, he began to ask himself, did the widow receive no compensation from the smelter? Why was it that the mother of four drudged twelve hours a day? Was it true, as he began to hear, that the corporations ran Denver for their profit, that there had not been an honest election in years, and that many officials were on the Big Mitt's pay rolls?

Those were the questions that made Ben Lindsey turn away from palliatives and begin the fight for fundamental reforms. It was not only that he campaigned against the machines and the corruptionists, but there was his incessant demand for laws that would take the loaded dice away from big business and put protective measures on the statute books that would lift some of the cruelties and injustices out of life. That was when the best people denounced him as a liar, a madman, and a degenerate. Only the plain people stayed with him, but their votes kept him in office year after year.

Ben's crowning offense, however, was committed in 1906 when the Denver Gas and Electric Company applied for a long-term franchise. Under the charter, the question could be voted on only by taxpaying electors, and even before election day rumors of gross frauds began to be circulated. It was freely charged that thousands of tax receipts were being issued for small amounts so as to qualify an army of dependable voters.

When the gas franchise carried by only five hundred votes, an investigation of the "ten-cent" receipts was demanded, and after many delays the case came before Judge Lindsey. As subpoenas went out, a general exodus started, high officials fleeing as well as vast numbers of clerks and minor employees who had been compelled to commit perjury to hold their jobs. Henry L. Doherty, president of the company, happened to be among those who did not get out of town, but when brought into court, he crossed his arms and arrogantly refused to testify.

Judge Lindsey straightway imposed a jail sentence until he did answer, and Mr. Doherty, to his rage and surprise, found himself in a cell. But not for long. The utterly lawless action of a notorious judge set him free, and he fled across the state line. With the franchise in his pocket, the financier went on to form the huge Cities Service Company and rise to heights of philanthropy as the first chairman of President Roosevelt's Birthday Balls.

Some months later, Mr. Doherty's right-hand man either lost his memorandum book or had it stolen from him. Pages from it, reproduced in Senator Patterson's paper, showed that he had paid $67,690 to candidates and leaders of both parties. For example, $4,500 to the mayor; $4,490 to the state oil inspector; $400 to a judge; $1,600 to the president of the Board of Supervisors; $550 to preachers, etc., etc. There was laughter in it as well as shock, for each page was headed by a nice bit from the Bible, such as "Suffer little children" and "Blessed are the meek."

Never was corruption more thoroughly exposed, but for his part in it Ben Lindsey was damned as never before. Out with a foul bird who shamed his town! To make himself still more odious to the best people, the Little Judge denounced the Legislature for daring to send Simon Guggenheim to the Senate and fought the re-election of the bribe-taking mayor.

This was the situation when I entered Denver, and it was my privilege to ease his lot materially. First in the *Post,* and later in the *Rocky Mountain News,* I gave him newspaper support against his enemies, championing the measures for which he had been fighting and supporting new ones such as mothers' pensions and the eight-hour day for women in industry. With my departure in 1913, however, along with Senator Patterson's sale of the *News* and the *Post's* permanent switch from tolerance to bitter enmity, Ben was left naked to attack.

Up to 1924 he held his own fairly well, but in that year the Ku Klux Klan swept the state, starting fires of bigotry in every town and village. Ben, with his usual courage, was one of the few officials to fight the hooded fanatics, speaking day and night at the risk of his life. He won in the election, but a narrow margin of three hundred votes furnished grounds for a contest. On the Supreme Court sat one Greely Whitford, a man he had denounced for years, and in January, 1927, this fellow and a majority of his associates handed down a decision that kicked Ben out of office. As if that were not enough, the justices ruled that he must pay back all of the salary he had received since January, 1925. The type of man who took over the juvenile court may be judged from the fact that he turned out to be a thief, committing suicide rather than face charges.

Even this did not satisfy the hate of his enemies. The Bar Association, picking up an old charge that had been thoroughly aired and disproved, filed a petition with the Supreme Court for Ben's disbarment, and once again he was face to face with

Whitford and his wolf pack. Coldly, brutally, he was denied a hearing before an impartial referee, with right to testify and summon other witnesses, and in December, 1929, the court ordered his disbarment.

Poor Ben! Butting stone walls had become so much a habit of life that he now picked another to run his battered head against. His book on "companionate marriage," as he called it, was seized on by his enemies as a chance to destroy him once and for all, and their propaganda branded it as an attempt to "legalize free love." Publicity-loving preachers took up the cry, and the press added to misunderstanding and prejudice by constant allusion to the idea as "pal marriage" and "week-end marriage."

All of which was miles away from the truth. Ben's program simply proposed to stabilize and to direct certain of the customs, privileges, and practices of modern marriage that were already in widespread use, but that had no legal status or guidance. The first plank was birth control; the second, divorce by mutual consent for persons without dependent children, but only after the failure of a court of domestic relations to reconcile the couple; the third was for the state to undertake the education of youth and married people in the laws of sex and life, the better to equip them for the serious duties of wedlock and parenthood. Marriage, he insisted, was an art that should be taught in the schools.

The furor was at its height in December, 1930, when Ben came to New York to address the Churchmen's Association, made up of Episcopal clergymen. Bishop Manning, however, that direct spiritual heir to the bigotry of Cotton Mather, ordered the association to cancel the meeting, and when the membership refused, announced that he would deliver a "chastisement sermon" on the following Sunday. I happened to be in New York at the time, and when Ben told me that he meant to go to the Cathedral of St. John the Divine to hear what Manning had to say, I begged him on bended knees to stay away.

"Let him spew his poison," I urged. "The more the better. Then you can hold a press conference Monday morning, and your answer will make every front page."

He agreed, but with Sunday came a change of heart. Nevertheless, as he told me afterward, he took a seat in the cathedral with firm determination not to open his mouth. "But, George, when the Bishop thundered that companionate marriage was a 'foul and wicked thing, a filthy propaganda for lewdness, promiscuity, adultered and unrestrained sexual gratification,' I could not contain myself." The scene that followed was without parallel.

"Bishop Manning," Ben shouted, getting to his feet in spite of hands that tried to pull him down, "you have falsely represented me. If this is not a house of justice it is not a house of God. I ask for five minutes to answer your unfair attack."

On the instant, the congregation of three thousand burst into an uproar. Dignified gentlemen hit him with their fists, elderly ladies beat him with umbrellas, and the Lord only knows what would have happened to him but for the intervention of the police. Hurried off to a near-by precinct station, Ben was released on his own recognizance, and the next morning I went with him to court. The judge dismissed the complaint, ruling that the charge of disorderly conduct was not properly drawn, but the case filled the newspapers for days and the howls of the wolf pack beat down my voice of defense.

Ben and his devoted wife stayed in Denver for a while, making a vain fight for reinstatement, but at last his friends prevailed on him to quit Colorado for California. Once again there was a bitter fight when he asked the right to practice in his new home, for all of his enemies rushed westward with their lies and calumnies. William G. McAdoo argued his case, and having come to be a resident of San Francisco, I was able to get the full story into the Scripps-Howard newspapers.

Ben Lindsey, I explained at length, could not be judged fairly without consideration of his whole life, for the disbarment was but the last blow in a campaign of hate covering three decades. Unanimously and sincerely, the Board of Governors held Ben guiltless of misconduct and gave him the right to practice. At the last, thank God, he knew some measure of happiness, for the Californians elected him to the bench and gave him love and faith.

There is still another tribute to be paid—another monument to be raised. Like Ben Lindsey, Ed Costigan could have had wealth and position by simple acceptance of things as they were, but instead of that he gave his life to just causes. In 1914 the governorship was his for the taking, but he lost it deliberately by his defense of the striking coal miners. In 1916, when almost every other Bull Mooser crept back into the Republican tent, he turned away from the conservatism of Hughes and campaigned for Woodrow Wilson.

Appointed a member of the Tariff Commission, he carried on into the administrations of Harding and Coolidge, finally resigning in 1926 with a burst of indignation that shook the country. Here is the closing paragraph of his letter of resignation:

I fully realize that the manipulation of the Tariff Commission is but a part of the total picture of present-day Washington. In an era which history may yet summarize as the age of Daugherty, Fall and Sinclair—in which another governmental body, the Federal Trade Commission, is widely looked upon as the legitimate prey of those who deal in the unfair practices which that Commission was created to destroy—in which even the National Senate is not immune against the trespass and dictates of powerful lobbies—the fate and fortunes of the Tariff Commission may be thought unimportant. Yet no part of the public edifice can be undermined without danger to the whole structure. Public service still demands public fidelity. And the ancient right of remonstrance remains. An official witness of law violations, I have successively appealed to the President and to Congress. One further dissent is in order. I am therefore returning my commission to the Government.

Returning to Denver, Ed engaged in the practice of his profession, but in 1930 the people of Colorado sent him to the Senate by an overwhelming majority, and this against the open opposition of the Republicans and the secret knifing of the Democratic organization. There, long before the yeasty emotionalisms of the New Deal, he advocated the great reforms that gave the Roosevelt administrations their sole distinction. He was the first to fight for a soil conservation law and reciprocal trade agreements; as early as 1931 he launched the drive for a WPA and a PWA, a wage and hour act and a social-security act. Stressing the importance of bringing holding companies under stricter control, he was the first to declare the need of a securities and exchange commission, and his was the first voice to demand a tax on undistributed profits.

Breaking under the terrific strain, Ed collapsed in 1935, and from his sickbed watched the tragedy of opportunism that subordinated fundamental reforms to political victories. To give the dying man the comforting assurance that what he said and did was not "writ on water," Josephine Roche brought out a book containing his major speeches, and I had the high honor of writing the foreword. This was the closing sentence: "All of us are firm in the belief that this volume, though it has its source in personal love, is indeed a contribution to the gospel of democracy, and proof irrefutable that there is a place in American public life for ideals and idealists."

CHAPTER 17

The Colorado Coal Strike

*T*hroughout my entire Denver stay, conditions in the coal fields were not the least of the many things that raised the blood pressure of our group. After an uprising in 1904, savagely suppressed by state troops, the operators replaced American, Scotch, Cornish, and Welsh miners by workers brought in from the Balkans, Italy, Finland, Mexico, Poland, and even Japan. These herded thousands, speaking twenty-six different languages and ignorant of the country's laws, were denied every right and soon reduced to a state of actual peonage.

Our Denver cleanup had no effect on the situation, for the coal properties were located in distant and thinly settled counties where the companies were able to control the courts and officials. At every election a bunch of us would journey to Huerfano County and try to compel an honest election, but it was never more than a gesture. During the day we were not allowed to go behind the barbed wire that guarded the voting booths, and at night we were held at a safe distance while the sheriff and his deputies counted the ballots.

In September, 1913, however, the strikebreakers of 1904 staged a walkout of their own, driven into revolt by an accumulation of wrongs. Ancient history now, to be sure, but to my mind a detailed story of the strike has high educational value. Just as it marked the abandonment of feudalism by

126

industry and gave a tremendous impetus to unionism, so did it set the labor movement in an ugly pattern that does much to explain the distrusts and resentments that mark industrial relations today.

Not more than a fourth of the twelve thousand strikers were members of the United Mine Workers at the time, but the union assumed entire responsibility for the care of all, housing some twenty-one thousand men, women, and children in tent colonies on the mountainsides when they were driven from their company-owned homes. By the employment of professional strikebreakers and border "bad men" and the purchase of rifles and machine guns, the allied operators organized a private army, and to their aid soon came the militia, called out by a servile governor. Military courts superseded civil authority, the writ of habeas corpus was suspended, and hundreds of miners were imprisoned without warrant and held without trial.

The reign of terror culminated on April 20, 1914, in what came to be known as the "Ludlow massacre." At a given signal, troops and mine guards opened fire on a tent colony and kept it up until dark. The strikers fought back from arroyos, while the women and children sought the refuge of safety pits dug under the tents—a ghastly blunder, as it turned out, for machine guns ignited the flimsy shelters. The flaming canvas then dropped down on the pits, scorching scores and burning two mothers and eleven children to a crisp.

Nor was that all. That night Louis Tikas and James Fyler, two strike leaders, were captured and brought before one Linderfelt, a bravo imported from Mexico as a mine guard and later inducted into the militia as a lieutenant. Both Tikas and Fyler were unarmed, and subsequent testimony proved that they had done their best to stop the fighting, but this did not save them. In a burst of rage Linderfelt broke his rifle over Tikas's head, and as he fell four bullets pierced his body. Fyler met the same fate, and others done to death were Bartoloti, Rubino, Costa, and Snyder, a mere boy. All that night and well into the next afternoon Tikas and Fyler were left lying in their blood as a warning.

I was in New York at the time, but on receipt of telegrams from strike leaders who remembered my efforts in their behalf, I entrained for Denver at once. With the state and even the

127

nation ablaze with indignation, what to do seemed quite obvious, and I urged a mass meeting on the statehouse lawn, such as had been so effective in the days when we used to "assemble to consult for the common good." I returned to my best Colorado style in writing the call, piling adjective on adjective and commanding the attendance of "all those to whom patriotism means more than profits, and in whom humanity still burns," so that they might "breathe their passion into the dead body of murdered justice."

More than ten thousand people answered the appeal in spite of a driving rainstorm, and although scores of policemen were ordered on duty, not even an angry argument disturbed the peace of the mass meeting. All of the speakers were miners except myself, but according to press report, I outdid them in violence of attack. What a wonderful thing to be young and free from the cautions and restraints of age! I can still feel Senator Charlie Thomas tugging at my legs and hear him pleading, "George! George! For God's sake, tone it down!"

John D. Rockefeller, Jr., controlling power in Colorado Fuel and Iron, was my main target, but I did not neglect the governor and lieutenant governor, branding them as "traitors to the people and accessories to the murder of babes," and shouting for a special session of the legislature to "impeach them as false to their oaths and to their God."

There were, however, some constructive suggestions mixed in with my excoriations; for example, the instant seizure of the coal mines by the state, pending an agreement between operators and strikers, and that this agreement be followed by steps to cancel the leases on 13,000 acres of school land for which the companies paid only a beggarly rental. Also that plans be laid for the early development of 473,000 acres of coal land owned by the state.

William L. Chenery, at a later date the brilliant editor of *Collier's,* and my dear friend, was then in charge of the *Rocky Mountain News,* and he ran the story of the mass meeting in full. Poor Bill! The Rockefeller company sued at once, asking damages in the sum of $600,000, and specifically branding my speech as "false, malicious, defamatory, and libelous." Parenthetically, the case was never brought to trial, but it did scare the owner of the *News* right out of his pants.

Public indignation, however, had small weight against the

128

control of elected officials by the companies and their fixed determination to crush the strike by force. Strike sympathizers were shot down in their homes, and on April 29, while the mass meeting still echoed, the militia and mine guards set out from Walsenberg to clear a hill of strikers. The bloody "battle of the Hogback" took place, and as a result President Wilson sent in federal troops, and some degree of order was restored.

Barred from further open violence, the companies now turned to the courts, and hand-picked grand juries indicted scores for entering into a conspiracy to commit murder. When an honest judge ruled that the juries were packed by a grossly prejudiced sheriff, the attorney general of the state stepped forth and filed informations to take the place of indictments.

Not until the late months of 1914, when the Commission on Industrial Relations began to hold hearings, were the miners given opportunity to tell their story. This body, created by Congress at the suggestion of President Wilson, was under direction to search out the causes of industrial war and to inquire into the general conditions of labor in the principal industries. Frank P. Walsh, my comrade in Kansas City days, was the chairman, and when he asked me to serve as a consultant, my first drive was to have an investigation of the Colorado coal strike. A hearing was held in New York in December, and John D. Rockefeller, Jr., was among those called to the witness stand.

In spite of my bitterness, I could not help feeling sorry for the man as he sweated under Frank's merciless questioning. In the same breath that Mr. Rockefeller confessed to having given huge sums for sanitation and health measures in China, and equally large amounts to provide a refuge for migratory birds in Louisiana, he was compelled to admit that not in ten years had he set foot on the Colorado properties where thousands toiled underground to make him the money for his philanthropies in other areas. He was unable even to name the counties in which they were located, to tell how many miners were employed, what rental the company charged for houses, or the length of the working day.

He did not know that his superintendents deported every worker suspected of "agitation"; that the prices in the company stores were twice as high as in outside stores; that the company built saloons, charging a 50-per-cent rental; that for years the men had been paid in scrip; that there was a "black list," and that no damage suit had been filed against his company for years because of company control of county officials and courts. A long list of settlements, read to him by the chairman, showed that the amounts paid to widows of men killed in the mines ran as low as $200. Chairman Walsh then inquired into Mr. Rockefeller's views on unionism, and these were some of the questions and answers:

Q. Can you conceive of effective protest against abuses in a large industry where it is without organization on the part of the employees?

A. My lack of practical experience makes it impossible for me to reply. . . . I think the prosperity of this country is being best conserved by large combinations in industries.

Q. Would or would not national organizations of employees be necessary from both a logical and practical standpoint?

A. There again you are getting into a technical question that I am sorry I have not the information with which to answer.

Q. Should not the representatives of such organizations of employees be permitted to exercise their functions without interference or restriction so long as they are lawful means?

A. I am not able to deal with the question.

Throughout his testimony, Mr. Rockefeller insisted that he, in common with other capitalists, interested himself only in the financial affairs of his corporation, leaving labor policies to administrative officers on the ground. The impression he sought to give was that the conduct of the strike was entirely in the hands of Mr. Welborn, president of Colorado Fuel and Iron, and that his own position was distant and detached. Against this, a letter from Mr. Welborn to Mr. Rockefeller was introduced in evidence. Written under date of July 27, 1914, three months after Ludlow, it contained this paragraph: "The knowledge that we have your support and confidence makes everything else easy."

This same Mr. Welborn, at a previous hearing, was asked if he did not think that society had an interest in the mining of coal. To this he made reply: "I am very sure it is my business." In an effort to get an equally frank statement from Mr. Rockefeller, Mr. Walsh put this question: "If abuses appear inevitable wherever unrestricted power develops, how can the worker be protected if the proposition is laid down, and strictly adhered to, that the owner of the industry cannot be interfered with?"

"I do not feel myself competent to deal adequately with that question," Mr. Rockefeller answered.

Unlike most of the federal commissions that come and go, probe and report, the Walsh group produced one immediate effect. Even prior to the hearings, the Rockefeller Foundation set aside $1,000,000 for an investigation of its own into the causes of industrial unrest, and employed W. L. Mackenzie King, the eminent Canadian, as director.

Meanwhile the allied operators in Colorado drove harder and harder to crush the strike. One of the means was the secret employment of Ivy Lee, publicity man for the Rockefellers, who proceeded at once to flood both the state and the nation with copies of a pamphlet called *Facts*. The falsehoods it contained were so easy of disproof that the campaign proved a boomerang, even the *Survey*, a publication far from unfriendly, exposing the lies in merciless detail.

Thrown back for a loss in the publicity sector, the operators turned to the courts. In the battle of the Hogback a Major Lester was killed, and the state entered a conspiracy charge against every striker alleged to have been on the ground. Even in prejudiced courts, however, a number of acquittals were returned, so in February, 1915, the legislature created a special judicial district and the governor appointed a coal-company attorney to be the judge. It was before this man that John Lawson, high official of the United Mine Workers, went on trial for the "murder" of one John Nimmo, a mine guard.

It was not charged that Lawson had done the killing or even been near the battlefield. The information simply declared that Nimmo had been shot by *some member* of the United Mine Workers, and that Lawson, as an officer of the organization, was responsible. The panel was not drawn from the jury box, as prescribed by law, but hand-picked by the sheriff, and it was from a list of eighty-three coal-company partisans that twelve men were chosen. Working with the precision of a machine, the jury returned a verdict of guilty, and the coal-company judge imposed a sentence of life imprisonment.

Even Rockefeller partisans were shocked by the lawlessness of the proceeding, and an outburst of public indignation eventually forced the State Supreme Court into action. A stern order prohibited the judge from presiding at any further trials, branding him as grossly biased, and a writ of supersedeas brought John Lawson out of his cell to plead anew. The utter baselessness of the murder charge stood so plain that the Attorney General himself made the motion for acquittal.

By some slip-up, one of the Lester cases was transferred to another county to be tried by another judge, and brilliant, devoted Edward P. Costigan stood forth as chief counsel for the defense. A host of coal-company attorneys opposed him, but at the end of eight bitter weeks the jury acquitted the four defendants, a verdict that resulted in the dismissal of all untried cases. Moreover, in due time Mr. Rockefeller proclaimed the "Mackenzie King plan" that provided correction for many of the evils that had driven twelve thousand miners into revolt. Not the least of the reforms was an agreement to submit all disputes to arbitration, along with a measurable approach to collective bargaining. Had these concessions been made in the beginning, there would have been no strike.

The thing that came clearest out of it all was the *high cost of hate*. Colorado's loss was heavy, on account of the employment of the militia and the disruption of industry, and there is no estimation of the monetary damages suffered by the companies. As for the United Mine Workers, the bills paid for relief, defense attorneys, and court costs ran up to $6,000,000, bringing the union close to bankruptcy.

CHAPTER 18

Long before Hollywood

*S*ome months ago I dropped into the Fairmont for luncheon and found the hotel fairly crawling with cameramen, actors, directors, and bug-eyed motion-picture fans. Inquiry developed that Orson Welles had come to San Francisco to shoot some scenes for *The Lady from Shanghai,* and that the comparatively small company with him was costing $22,000 a day.

Some time later the Chinese cook brought me the news that a lot of people were making "plenty big hell" on top of Russian Hill, just above our home. I climbed the steps to see what it was all about, and found Humphrey Bogart on location. A friendly dramatic critic, detached from the onlookers, explained that a San Quentin picture was in process of being filmed—the story of an escape and "full of the hard-boiled stuff that Bogy loves."

I mentioned the daily cost of Orson Welles's company, and he laughed at it as "chicken feed." Bogart's expenses ran twice as much, and with that he cited huge expenditures that brought a sense of dizziness. Hundreds of thousands for a run-of-the-mill picture, and millions for a supercolossal! "Why, just the reshooting of two scenes in an Ingrid Bergman film set Enterprise Pix back another one hundred G's." From that he went on to tell how one director spent $200,000 "on a scene that didn't come off. Nothing important, only a one-minute touch that might have added color."

As I turned away from the army of actors, directors, technicians, and authors, all stewing along without regard for time or cost, my mind shot back to a Denver day in 1910, during my *Post* travail, when a stranger walked into my office and introduced himself as G. M. Anderson, a partner in the Essanay Film Corporation. "Better known as Broncho Billy," he added significantly, bending forward to note the effect. I learned later that he was a star, every bit as much of a popular idol as W. S. Hart came to be, but at the time the name meant nothing to me. Nor did motion pictures, for that matter. I knew that small theaters were springing up all over town, but I had never been in one and thought that the whole business was still in the nickelodeon stage.

When I confessed ignorance, Anderson took time out for enlightenment. "The Essanay," he explained, "is one of the seven companies that practically control the industry in the United States. Believe it or not, our studio in Chicago occupies a *whole floor*. That's where we make plays that call for interiors, keeping actors on the pay roll all year round. At big salaries, too—the average is fifteen dollars a day.

"During the summer we make outdoor pictures in and around Chicago, but when fall comes, I take a photographer, a property man, and two or three principals, and follow the sun. Other people are picked up from local stock companies. Colorado's a great place for scenery and clear light, but some companies are trying to build up a motion-picture center out at a whistle stop in California called Hollywood. Anyway, I'm here in the Rockies now, shooting a bunch of Westerns, and we're running short of scenarios. What about writing some for us?"

My interest still failed to catch fire, but when Anderson went on to mention that he would be willing to pay $25 apiece for as many as I could turn out, my ears flapped forward. Campaign funds were a daily problem in the various fights we waged regularly, for all of the moneyed people were against us, and not even the sacrifices of our low-income group met expenses.

Anderson's offer came like a fall of manna, and my blood pressure went up as I did some swift mental arithmetic. A scenario a day for ten days would mean $250—untold riches— and what if it all went on for twenty days? Nevertheless, common honesty forced me to admit that I had never written a scenario, and had no idea how to go about it.

"There's nothing to it," shrugged Anderson. "We're making a picture tomorrow up at Mount Morrison. Come along and you'll see how it's done."

On board an early-morning train I was introduced to the company. Aside from the photographer and the property man, the Chicago group included Smith, a character actor, and O'Brien, a tall, handsome fellow who handled the heavy roles. The only local addition was the leading lady, a slender, very pretty girl borrowed for the day from a stock company. Not a very imposing cast, but the property man informed me that he pitched in when occasion required.

The more I looked at Broncho Billy, the less he appealed to me as the hero type. On the short side, bunchy rather than lithe, he had a twisted nose that added nothing to beauty. O'Brien, however, assured me that Anderson was a knockout, killing 'em dead in every picture, and already had a following bigger than any actor on the legitimate stage.

"Bigger than Edwin Booth?" I asked in a burst of whimsy.

"Booth?" O'Brien shook his head. "Funny, but I don't place him."

On pulling into Mount Morrison, we were met by a dozen or so cowpunchers, all saddled up and leading a bunch of extra bronchos. The real article, too, for all came from near-by ranches, and I recognized several as having roped and ridden at Cheyenne. Trooping up to the town's one hotel, the property man opened his trunks and handed out *chaparajos*, bandannas, boots, sombreros, and spurs. Soon dressed, the troupe clattered downstairs and climbed on the waiting mounts.

Our way led along brawling Bear Creek, and after a ride of two miles we came to a small ranch house tucked away in a grove of cottonwoods. Russell, the property man, had bargained with the owner some days before, paying $25 for the rent of the home and yard for the day. In addition, he was to have the use of a bunch of cattle pasturing farther back in the hills.

Broncho Billy, after approving the location, drew some crumpled sheets of note paper from his pocket and perched on the porch steps for a reading of the scenario. The rest of us sprawled on the grass. *The Heart of a Cowboy* was the title of the opus, and as he droned along, stopping now and then to make a point, I lost all doubt as to my ability to write for the silver screen. The plot was so simple as to be childish, and the action had about as much originality as a game of tag. That night Broncho Billy gave me the script as a souvenir, and when Welles and Bogart recalled my own motion-picture experience, I rummaged through an old file and had the luck to find it. Here are the twenty scenes:

1. Girl comes out of house, carrying some Kodak pictures of herself. Cowboy rides up, sees snapshots, and asks for one. She finally consents, writing "To Steve" on it. He tries to hold her hand, but she snatches it away.

2. As Steve goes out gate he meets his partner coming in, and they shake hands. Partner also named Steve, but he is as bad as the other is good.

3. Girl comes out and gives cry of joy as she sees Bad Steve. Throws herself into his arms. Playfully demands pencil, and gives him picture with "To my sweetheart" written on it.

4. Bad Steve in front of his dugout, looking at picture. Honest Steve rides up and wants to know what his partner is doing with picture. Shows his own to prove the girl is his sweetheart. Bad Steve points to what is written on his picture. Honest Steve can't believe it, and the two go to girl's house.

5. Call girl out. She puts her arms around Bad Steve's neck,

but holds out hand of friendship to Honest Steve. He shows heartbreak for a minute, but gives them his blessing.

6. Mexican rides up to Bad Steve's dugout and tells him of a chance to steal some cattle. After some talk the two go away together.

7. Bad Steve and Mexican cut bunch of cattle out of herd and drive them away. Steve drops his picture.

8. Bad Steve sends Mexican off to sell stolen cattle and goes to girl's house.

9. Rancher discovers his loss and sends the word to all of his neighbors. Also finds picture.

10. Ride of the vigilantes.

11. Vigilantes reach girl's house and find her sitting on step with Bad Steve. Leader of vigilantes accuses him of stealing cattle, and when he denies it, pulls picture on him. The girl jumps up, and as she protects Bad Steve, Honest Steve slips to partner's side. Takes picture out of his hat and forces it into partner's hand. Bad Steve shows it as proof of his innocence, and Honest Steve takes guilt on himself. Vigilantes throw rope around his neck and lead him away. Girl in arms of Bad Steve.

12. Bad Steve rides up to house and tells girl they must leave at once. As she hurries to pack her things, Mexican arrives and starts to divide money. Bad Steve stops him with a curse and takes him around to side of house.

13. Girl comes out, and hearing voices, stands still to listen. Gets enough of talk to arouse her suspicions, and creeps closer.

14. As Bad Steve and Mexican quarrel over division of money, girl confronts them. Mexican draws knife to stab her, but girl jerks gun out of Bad Steve's holster and covers them both. Makes them hand over money and write confession, and then orders them to ride double and get out of country.

15. Girl saddles up and gallops off to save Honest Steve from lynching.

16. Girl riding at top speed.

17. Shot of vigilantes in cottonwood grove, fixing rope to tall tree.

18. As they are about to hang their prisoner, girl dashes up and hands over money and confession.

19. Girl gives Honest Steve another picture with "To my future husband" written on it.

20. Girl and Steve embracing and vigilantes cheering.

Having finished the reading of the scenario, Anderson announced that the forenoon would be devoted to ranch-house scenes, regardless of sequence, and the afternoon to the rest. The cameraman unlimbered his apparatus, and things were about to start when O'Brien, the handsome heavy, made plaintive murmur that he didn't feel so good.

"Stomach upset, I reckon," he gulped, and then made a hasty dash for the back yard.

"A hell of a note!" For a second Broncho Billy was visibly upset, but suddenly his face cleared and he turned to me with an ingratiating leer. "How about helping us out, Mr. Creel?"

"Good Lord!" I gasped. "You must be crazy. The nearest I ever came to acting was when I suped for Richard Mansfield in *Richard the Third*. Even then I kept tripping over my spear."

"All you've got to do is to follow directions," he insisted. "And you can ride."

I tried to tell him that I held the record at Frontier Days in Cheyenne for staying on a bucker the shortest time of any living man, but he cut me off, and the others begged me to remember that my refusal meant the loss of a day. Giving in at last, I took over a pair of chaps, a sombrero, and a bandanna and braced myself for action. By way of a sketchy rehearsal, each scene was gone over once without the camera, Anderson calling directions and the property man laying down stones and twigs to mark each actor's exact position.

"Can we talk?" I asked.

"All you want," grunted Robbins, the photographer. "Only no cussing. People can read your lips."

By high noon all ten ranch-house scenes had been shot, and smoothly enough except for a few mishaps. My love scenes with the girl were a bit too strenuous, and in my quarrel with the Mexican over the money I bloodied his nose and almost choked him to death. The damned camera, whirring away, had me keyed to top pitch, and I couldn't even hear Broncho Billy bawling at me to loosen up.

Where the real trouble came was when the girl broke in on my quarrel with the Mexican and made us climb the same pony for our retreat from crime. Poor Smith didn't know one end of a horse from the other, and the broncho had never been taught to carry double. I stayed on by pulling leather, but Smith went off three times, without finding a soft spot to land. What finally saved the scene was not any horsemanship of mine, but the poor little cow pony's eventual exhaustion. The leading lady also had her bad moments, for even short skirts irritated her mount profoundly, compelling a switch to a bronc without sex prejudice.

A bite of luncheon, spread out on the grass, and then we rode up into the hills to spoil the afternoon nap of the Herefords. A look at the cattle, and then we inspected Bad Steve's "home," a dugout that showed every sign of having been abandoned by Kit Carson or some other hardy pioneer. Aside from rotted steps, a sag in the roof, and fallen timbers, a further peep showed about three feet of stagnant water.

"Not for me," I protested. "I'd have to have rubber boots, a boat, and some antirattlesnake serum."

"You don't have to go all the way down," Russell argued. "Just crouch down on the top steps out of sight and bob up when you're called."

Going back to the Herefords, Robbins set up his camera and then bent bushes and laid stones to show the exact area in which the steers had to be stolen. The Mexican and I grasped the idea at once, but it soon developed that the cattle were completely in the dark as to space limitations. The crazy creatures bolted all over the pasture, and by the time we got a dozen bunched, stolen, and duly photographed, Smith and I were good and sorry that we had ever taken up a life of crime.

This chore chored, the local cowpunchers took over as the vigilantes, gathering in the pasture at the call of the angry owner. With just the one camera, and only Robbins' legs for transportation, there were no long rides over hill and dale. First the vigilantes raced up and down within a narrow range, and then there was a short move to another field, where the girl dashed back and forth until Robbins had footage enough to show her furious gallop for the rescue of Honest Steve.

The last shot was taken just as twilight began to fall, and it was a weary lot that rode back to Mount Morrison, hoarse from yelling and bone tired from long contact with Texas saddles. When I muttered something about a Sunday page that had to be written that night, the leading lady let out a derisive hoot.

"What about me! I go on at eight o'clock, and for three hours

138

suffer perils and persecutions at the hands of a blackhearted villain who is more beast than human. The way I feel now, I think I'll let him kill me in the first act."

Rolling back to Denver on the train, I ventured a timid request to Anderson for comment on my performance. While good enough to say that I hadn't done so badly, he made it quite clear that the only thing that counted in the picture was his own role. "They come to see Broncho Billy," he said, not immodestly, but simply stating a fact. That little matter disposed of, we discussed the workings of the film industry.

The Heart of a Cowboy, he explained, would be sent back to the head office in Chicago, where it would be leased to "renters," and these, in turn, would lease it to theaters at so much a day. All leases ran for six months only, as that was about the life of a picture. Then the film was returned to Chicago and melted up for the silver. Not an inconsiderable item, Anderson beamed, netting as much as $2,000 a year. Yessir!

Warming up, Broncho Billy went on to paint a great future for the motion-picture industry. "Two years ago," he boasted, "a fifty-foot film was considered big. Now five hundred feet is the minimum, and one thousand feet is coming to be average. There are now more than twelve thousand movie houses in the United States, and it won't be long before you'll see one in every town. Present admission prices range around a dime and fifteen cents, but the day will come when we'll ask a half dollar and get it."

And I thought that he was crazy. Even the sale of several scenarios at $25 each did not convince me that motion pictures had come to stay, and I worried for fear Anderson would strand in New Mexico or California, and wire me to send his money back.

Now for an epilogue. Some twenty years later I wrote a series of historical romances for *Collier's,* taking a flaming figure and painting the period through him. The articles were published in book form as *Sons of the Eagle,* and soon after a big motion-picture producer called me up and suggested that one of the stories might do as a successor to *Covered Wagon.* I went down to Hollywood to see him, and after innumerable conferences, shared by countless assistants and a curious breed called "supervisors," Sam Houston was decided on.

Then came the question of price. Not knowing what to ask,

I telephoned a novelist I knew, famous at the time, and begged his advice. "Well, if it was mine," he said, "around fifty or sixty thousand. *You* ought to get twenty-five thousand." That irked me, and I made up my mind to get the higher price if I dropped down dead in the attempt. Back I went, but I couldn't get my upper lip loose from my teeth when I started to say $60,000, and heard myself mumbling $25,000. When the producer said, "O.K.," never batting an eye, my whole insides fell out. While I was still reeling from the shock of losing $35,000, he mentioned casually that it might be well to spend the week end with the director picked for the picture.

This was during prohibition, and the director's palace out in the suburbs—a chaste architectural combination of Moorish, Grand Rapids, and Early Eucalyptus—was packed with people consuming inordinate quantities of bathtub gin. It was two days before I could succeed in getting together with the host for a conference, but when finally cornered, he proved most amiable.

"No question about it, kiddo," he assured me, "you've got something. We'll put a million in the bastard!" he cried, smashing his left hand with his right fist. He kept this up while outlining his grandiose plans, and being worn from lack of sleep, as well as somewhat addled by the gin, I found myself copying the gesture and repeating his words in an idiotic bleat.

"But," he suddenly exclaimed, "you haven't got the old zippo!" Seeing my blank look, he proceeded to explain. "You can't leave out the love note. When Houston walks out of the governor's mansion in Tennessee and goes to Texas, the Little Woman realizes that he is the only man in the world for her. Rushing out to the barn, she puts on boy's clothes and follows him, and at every danger point in his adventurous life, there she is to save him. Maybe we can work in a prologue showing how Houston and Santa Anna met in Texas as young men, and Sam socks the greaser for something or other. That'll show the long-standing enmity between them, and give the reason for Santa Anna invading Texas."

Passionately and at length I set forth the impossibilities involved. When Houston resigned as governor, finding out that his young wife loved another man, he never saw her again. As for Houston socking Santa Anna in a prologue, that was insanity. When Houston went to Texas, it was for the first time, while Santa Anna never crossed the border until he led his army against Goliad and the Alamo. Why, it was all *history*.

"To hell with it." With this end to the argument, the director mentioned from six months to a year as the time it would take to make the picture, and talked of journeys to Tennessee, Texas, and Mexico, in all of which I was to be among those present. Creeping back to Hollywood, the shadow of a once fine figure, I told the producer that he need not bother about the check. At home and in bed, between long talks in which I tried to make my wife understand why I had turned down $25,000, I thought fondly of Broncho Billy, and wondered whether our civilizational advances were all we cracked them up to be.

CHAPTER 19

On Being Married to an Electric-Light Sign

*M*arried life in Colorado, where I loomed large, had all the smoothness of a mill pond, but when we transferred to New York, where my wife resumed the stardom earned in such successes as *Madame Butterfly, The Darling of the Gods,* and *The Girl of the Golden West,* trouble began. I like and admire stage people, but they do get an acclaim out of all proportion to achievement, or rather out of all proportion to the acclaim given accomplishment in other fields. A writer may turn out the greatest book in the world, but his name will never blaze in electric lights or blare forth from billboards, and crowds will not follow him begging for autographs.

Before I had been in New York a month, I had the feeling of a tallow dip engaged in a battle with General Electric. I had no objection to my wife's keeping her identity as Blanche Bates, but it never entered my head that I would cease to be George Creel, and it stung to find myself without other individuality than "Blanche Bates's husband." Minnie Maddern Fiske was my sole comfort, bringing a soothing note into our home, for whether she was addressing my wife in a note or in speech, it was always as "Mrs. Creel." The headwaiter in our favorite restaurant was another who held to Victorian standards, for after the arrival of the first baby he never failed to address Blanche as "Madam Bates."

There is no greater mistake than the fond belief that only women are vain. Like the iceberg, which hides three fourths of its bulk, man's vanity lies deep, close to his self-esteem and as far from his sense of humor as the body permits. Soon after our wedding my wife and I talked plans for the future, and agreed that housekeeping expenses should be shared on a fifty-fifty basis. As a result of being rubbed raw by the "Blanche Bates's husband" business, my imagination drove me to the conclusion that people were thinking me a sort of dependent. Wherever I went on the street, it seemed as if people were whispering, "There goes Man-Cannot-Support-His-Wife." I had always had more than my share of energy, industry, and ambition, but now, under the goad of being the "husband of," I set about money-making with actual ferocity.

An editorial job, of course, was what I would have liked, but various things prevented. The papers with which I agreed had no openings, and the policies of those that offered to take me on were odious, being opposed to every one of my social, economic, and political faiths. Blanche, eager to have me gain the prominence I enjoyed in Denver, failed utterly to understand my point of view, and I could not convince her that only a dishonest hack could dualize himself sufficiently to write against his beliefs.

As a result, I odd-jobbed all over the place. Norman Hapgood was then trying to pulmotor *Harper's Weekly* back to life, and I did a series for him on quacks and quackery, paying particular attention to chiropractic. Radical reforms have since been instituted, but at that time practitioners could get a diploma after a three weeks' mail-order course. There were a lot of laughs in it, although my heart ached to see the gullibility of people. In Chicago, for example, after doing the "colleges," I called on the leading chiropractor and asked for a treatment.

"What seems to be the trouble, friend?" he inquired.

"Pleurisy," I answered, naming the first thing that came into my mind.

"That's swell!" he exclaimed. "I'm good on pleurisy."

"Tell me, Doctor," I inquired after taking off my coat and vest, "just what is the cause of pleurisy?"

"Well," and he wagged his head sagely, "some say one thing and some say another. Maybe it comes from the bronnicals, but I think it's because you're accumulatin' faster than you're eliminatin'."

"And what is your college? The Iowa school?"

"Yes," he nodded, "I'm an alma mater of that institution."

With that he gave me a push in the back that made my spine crack like a bull whip. Sick with pain, and threatening to have his blood if he had maimed me for life, I staggered back to the hotel and spent three days in bed.

Everybody's and the *Century*, then on their last legs, were also profitable markets, and now and then I had the luck to get exciting assignments. Particularly when *Everybody's* sent me out to California to do a study of Hiram Johnson as a presidential possibility. To be honest, I approached the article with a definite bias against Johnson, convinced that he had dealt less than generously with one of my dearest friends.

Mark Sullivan, in a piece for *Collier's* during the war years, wrote that "to Creel there are only two classes of men. There are skunks and the greatest man that ever lived. The greatest man that ever lived is plural, and includes everyone who is on Creel's side in whatever public issue he happens at the moment to be concerned with. In Creel's cosmos there are no shadings and no qualifications. His spectrum contains no mauve, nothing but plain black and plain white."

An exaggeration, of course, but not entirely untrue. Frank Heney, a lawyer with conscience and civic spirit, had uncovered San Francisco's corruption and forced the indictment of Abe Ruef and other rascals in spite of savage opposition from the press and the Best People. Right in the middle of the trials, however, a gangster's bullet put Heney at death's door, and Hiram Johnson took over. From that moment on, Heney's name was never mentioned, and this persistent minimization enabled Johnson to make the graft prosecutions his own single-handed crusade. I watched the shabby business from Denver, and out of my love for Frank Heney, resented it.

At no point in my article did I deny Johnson's brilliant record as governor, for he had broken the power of the Southern Pacific and put many progressive laws on the statute books.

What he had done, however, out of his selfishness and ambition, was to turn a great social movement into a purely personal movement, robbing it of impetus. Among other things I remember mentioning that behind his seemingly open gaze "cold calculation lay coiled like a snake."

A Chicago story, written for the *Century,* plunged me into the American labor movement and brought about my first meeting with Sidney Hillman. He seemed to me to have more promise than any other union leader, and I like to remember that I prophesied his rise. The story had to do with the Hart, Schaffner, and Marx strike, a long and bloody struggle, and the agreement of Joseph Schaffner to set up grievance committees, trade courts, and a permanent board of arbitration, all brand-new and radical departures. Hillman, a young pants cutter who had not come to the United States from Lithuania until his twentieth year, was a leader in the strike and chiefly responsible for the settlement.

From Chicago the dynamic immigrant went on to organize the markets in New York, Rochester, Philadelphia, and other centers, and finally challenged the might of the AFL by launching the Amalgamated Clothing Workers of America. Not only was it the first significant venture in industrial unionism, but Amalgamated was the first important labor body to recognize the mutuality of interest between employer and employee. Although a Socialist, Hillman refused to play up the class struggle and put full emphasis on the fact of partnership. I followed his career through the years, just as I watched the rise of another friend, John L. Lewis.

On the whole, unfortunately, assignments were run-of-the-mill, and as I grew increasingly unhappy with hackwork, my wife and I worked out a financial arrangement. When—and *if*—I made enough money to take care of my share of household expenses for the year, the rest of the time would be my own. As a result, I took joyous part in a Minneapolis campaign for commission government, gave weeks to the Colorado coal strike, and spent happy days in Washington working for the confirmation of Louis D. Brandeis as a member of the Supreme Court. In 1914 I was able to aid Frank Walsh in his job as chairman of the Commission on Industrial Relations, and also found time to turn out a book, *Children in Bondage,* in collaboration with Edwin Markham and Ben Lindsey.

144

The release from hackwork was like heaven, although the research itself sank me lower than I had ever been, for Dante might have been my companion as I toured the sweatshops of New York, the cranberry bogs of New Jersey, the cotton mills of the Carolinas, the coal mines of Pennsylvania, and the shrimp canneries of Louisiana. At the time, I estimated that at least two million children were being fed annually into the steel hoppers of the modern industrial machine. Golden boys and girls—all mangled in mind, body, and soul, and aborted into a maturity robbed of power and promise.

When it came to the writing, I thought to have arguments over my emotionalism, but dear old Edwin Markham made me seem cold to the point of indifference. Every chapter had to be another "Man with the Hoe," and entirely forgetting that our book dealt with the child-labor problem in the United States, he would soar off into consideration of human misery and man's injustice in every part of the world.

Children in Bondage, as a consequence, was more rhetorical than factual—my own contributions, to tell the truth, were anything but objective—and the sale added little to our incomes. But we certainly had a grand time in the writing. However, more magazine assignments came along, and 1915 found me in good enough shape to devote three months to the equal-suffrage campaign in New York.

An old enthusiasm, this, springing from the deep conviction that my mother outweighed any man when it came to brains and character. Curiously enough, she herself held firmly to the Southern insistence that woman's place was in the home. My wife, too, although she had been out in the world since girlhood, earning her living, was a vociferous "anti."

My years in Colorado, where women had been voting since 1893, gave me value as an eyewitness, and a good deal of my time was spent on platforms with Mrs. Carrie Chapman Catt and Dr. Anna Howard Shaw, supporting their arguments with a personal report. What a pair they were! Mrs. Catt, with her gift for debate, and Dr. Shaw, that great orator whose voice had as many stops as an organ. And, something that never ceased to amaze me, a delicious sense of humor.

Once some heckler in the audience yelled out at the top of his voice, "What about women sitting on juries?"

Waiting for the applause to die down, Dr. Shaw smiled and

145

said, "My dear man, there are thousands of poor creatures—scrubwomen in the great office buildings, washerwomen, clerks in department stores on their feet from dawn to dark—who would thank God for the chance to sit *anywhere*."

Others who trouped the state were Mrs. Norman Whitehouse, Mrs. James Lees Laidlaw, Inez Milholland, and Alice Duer Miller. All were lovely, and all took particular pains with their appearance so as to bar the charge of "unwomanliness." On the other hand, many of the antis went in for mannish clothes and "sensible shoes," with the result that there was often confusion. When, for instance, the two groups reached the gates of Grand Central to go to Albany for a legislative hearing, the trainmen always tried to make the antis get on the equal-suffrage Pullman.

Between speeches I wrote articles for the few magazines willing to print them, but my real joy was pamphlets, for in them I could go as far as I liked in dealing with the leaders of the antisuffrage movement. What a sorry lot they were! Senator Tillman of South Carolina moaned that the vote would "mar the beauty and dim the luster of the glorious womanhood with which we have been familiar," giving me opportunity to show that his state permitted women to work sixty hours a week in the cotton mills, and also legitimized the ten-hour day for children of twelve.

Why should women want the ballot, asked Senator Henry Cabot Lodge, when chivalrous men stood ready to grant their slightest wish? I took pleasure in pointing out that it had taken forty years for the mothers of Massachusetts to get a joint-guardianship law, and that while men had the eight-hour day, there was no limit to the hours of women in many employments.

Senator O'Gorman of New York was another whose respect for women made him want to save them from the degrading effects of the ballot. And this, I stressed, in face of the fact that lack of effective factory inspection had just burned 147 girls to death. And when Tammany took a stand against equal suffrage as a "menace to the home," how satisfying to print the criminal records of the leaders.

The end of the campaign—unsuccessful, by the way—found me strapped, but even as I looked around for magazine assignments, I learned that Arthur Brisbane wanted somebody to "ghost" the life story of Jess Willard, the new heavyweight champion. As I was an ardent fight fan and had even done quite a bit of boxing with Tommy Ryan, greatest of all middle-weights, it seemed to be a quick, profitable job right up my alley.

I rushed down at once to Mr. Brisbane's office, and after some dickering he agreed to pay me my magazine rate. "But, Mr. Creel," he continued, and in the same staccato bark that he used for dictation, "you must understand that we have not purchased Willard's story merely for the purpose of glorify-ing the prize ring. Far from it. What we want to do is to inspire the youth of the land with a *love* of clean living by por-traying the life of a man who rose to fistic eminence *through* clean living.

"There must, of course, be no faking. But surely, Mr. Creel, at some period in his life you will find that Willard, strong with strength that comes from never having touched liquor and tobacco, rescued the village drunkard from drowning. And you will also discover, undoubtedly, that this pure-minded young giant, taught by his good mother never to soil his lips by blasphemy, soundly trounced the town bully for using vile oaths in presence of growing lads. But remember, Mr. Creel, there must be no faking. However, here is a point I know you will be able to make: Mention that scientific research has proved positively that one drop of whisky put in the eye of a panther will cut his spring in half."

A dozen or more other things that Willard *must* have done were pointed out, and after he had run down I asked if I would have to see the Big Boy. "Not necessarily," he shrugged.

I did see Willard, however, ashamed not to do so, but when I finally located Jess in Omaha, the big, inarticulate cow-puncher had little to contribute. We talked for an hour or so in the unlighted hotel room where he was "resting his feet," and about all I got from him was his birthplace, the towns where he spent his boyhood, and the fact that he had a dog named Rover.

Not much to go on, but full accounts of his various ring battles were at hand, and I knew all about training camps and conditioning. With proper deference to Mr. Brisbane's wishes, I had Jess whip all sorts of drunken, foul-mouthed ruffians, described at length how and why he came to loathe strong

147

drink and tobacco, and wound up with his judgment that Jack Johnson's defeat was due to his failure to realize the beauties and benefits of clean living. The only thing I left out was any mention of the panther that had the drop of whisky put in his eye.

Like all easy money, it corrupted me, and after Willard had been exhausted I dug up a history of the English prize ring and had the Big Boy describe each famous battle, alleging that the "deep study" of these encounters had done much for him. Brisbane, however, brought the series to an abrupt end by dryly commenting that he too had read Pierce Egan.

CHAPTER 20

The 1916 Campaign

I think I can safely lay claim to being the "original Woodrow Wilson man," for as early as 1905 I boomed him in *The Independent* for the presidency. He had come to Kansas City to speak to high-school students upon the cultivation of the mind and the reading of books, and it was only by accident that I went to hear him. What thrilled me was not merely the clarity of his thought, the beauty of his phrasing, but the shining faith of the man in the *practicality* of ideals. More than any other, it seemed to me that he voiced the true America—not the song that people sing when they remember the words, but the dream of liberty, justice, and fraternity.

From that time on I read everything he had written, and followed his fight for the democratization of Princeton, with growing admiration and belief. During his term as governor of New Jersey I watched his war against the bosses, and everything he said and did strengthened my conviction that he towered above all other public figures.

Early in 1912 I organized a Wilson club in Denver, and dingdonged at Senator Patterson until he quit his liking for Champ Clark and became as ardent a Wilsonian as I was.

When Mr. Wilson came to Denver on his Western tour, I was a guest at the luncheon in his honor and had the privilege of sitting with him for an hour in his private car after the evening meeting. Accustomed to the tricks of the average candidates—the affectation of hearty good fellowship and shirt-sleeve democracy—I was delighted by his simple dignity.

Naturally, then, the 1916 campaign threw me off stride as far as magazine work was concerned, for his re-election loomed as the one thing of overwhelming importance. What moved me was not only his domestic program, with its bold emphasis on progressive laws, but the patience and skill with which he was leading the Allies to higher ground. It seemed plain to me that the President *knew* the United States would be drawn into the war against Germany, and that in his derided notes he was defining the issue between democracy and autocracy so clearly that every American would answer the battle call.

No sooner had the campaign opened than I offered my services to Bob Wooley, in charge of publicity for the Democratic National Committee, and he gave me the job of digging up page features for Democratic dailies and such other papers as would print them. Thomas Edison was my first assignment, as word had been received that he was ready and willing to come out for Wilson. Admiring Mr. Edison as one of the world's great men, I was as nervous as a cat on my way over to the plant in New Jersey, and our meeting did nothing to calm me. Almost stone-deaf, he refused to wear any of his own contrivances, and when I put my lips down to his eardrum and bellowed a question, the noise upset me so that I forgot what I meant to ask.

"Never mind, son," Mr. Edison laughed. "I've got it all written out." Pushing a hand into his pants pocket—the old-fashioned kind that opened at the top—he drew forth crumpled sheets of yellow paper, all scribbled over in pencil but clear as copperplate. There, in simple, homely phrases, he had outlined his reasons for quitting the Republican party, ending up with this classic bit: "They say Wilson has blundered. Well, I reckon he has, but I notice he always blunders *forward*."

Other interviews followed, but my main task, as Wooley put it, was the "rehabilitation" of Josephus Daniels, Secretary of the Navy. For four years he had been abused and lampooned by the press of the country, and not the least of the attacks on

President Wilson was for his refusal to rid the public service of an "unfit, misfit, liar, incompetent, demagogue, and buffoon." Not in our time was an official ever made the target for more savage and sustained assault.

According to the opposition press, "Holy Joe" had made America the laughingstock of the world by abolishing the officers' wine mess on board ship. The Hearst papers in particular carried cartoons showing the cruise of the *Grape Juice* and the voyages of the *Piffle*. It was charged that Secretary Daniels had ordered officers and men to eat together; that he had ridiculed the Navy uniform; that he encouraged insubordination to the point of mutiny; that his proposed plan for the democratization of the Navy was really communization.

I myself had swallowed the stuff, and it was with a sick heart that I went down to Washington for my first meeting with the Secretary. How was it humanly possible to show such a figure in any favorable light? At first sight of his face and eyes, however, I knew that everything was going to be all right, and this feeling was confirmed by hours of questioning. Rarely pausing for answers, revealing the most amazing grasp of his duties, and never evading, he refused to counterattack, although in his heart he must have known that much of the malicious gossip came from venomous men at his side.

The "grape juice" charge was disposed of quickly. As far back as 1899, the sale or issue of liquor to enlisted men on board ship had been forbidden. He had simply extended the rule to officers on the recommendation of the surgeon general of the Navy, who reported an alarming increase in courts-martial for drunkenness. And was it not true, he asked, that the railroads all forbade the use of liquor by trainmen when on duty? Moreover, and he produced the records, within a year the Daniels order had been followed by the navies of Russia, France, and Germany.

By way of supporting data, the Secretary produced the address of the Kaiser to German naval cadets, stressing this paragraph: "The next war and the next sea battle demand sound nerves. Nerves will decide. These become undermined through alcohol. The nation which consumes the least alcohol wins, and that should be you, my gentlemen. Take heed, and provide that indulgence in alcohol not be counted as belonging to your privileges."

The other charges were disproved with equal speed. Never at any time had he ordered officers and men to eat together. Once as some snapshots were being taken on board ship, the Secretary had left his hat below and borrowed an officer's cap. When it fell over his ears he made some laughing remark, and this was twisted into an attack on the naval uniform. The charge of demagoguery was based on a photograph taken with a group of enlisted men. He had spoken at a Navy Y.M.C.A. meeting, and at the close Miss Helen Gould asked him to be photographed with the honor students. This picture was stolen from the club wall by a newspaper and printed as proof of the Secretary's fondness for "grandstand plays."

The only basis for the charge of "fomenting discontent and insubordination" was the establishment of schools on board ship, offering every enlisted man an opportunity for academic and technical education. What, asked the Secretary, was wrong with that? Was he to deny the right of an American boy to rise as high as his abilities would carry him? As for "democratizing" the Navy, since the opening of the schools the percentage of re-enlistment had risen from 52 to 85, and the morale was never higher.

What, then, was responsible for the campaign of calumny? To my amazement and shock, I discovered that a main source of malice was the bitterness of a Navy clique against the Secretary's program of "democratization." As one red-faced, belligerent admiral phrased it, "Daniels is trying to put muckers on a par with gentlemen." In the course of our argument, I brought up a case of which I had personal knowledge. Two brothers—twins, by the way—wanted to go to Annapolis, but as the congressman for their district had only one appointment, the youngsters tossed for it. The winner went to Annapolis, and the loser enlisted. Taking advantage of the ship's school, however, he studied hard, and by dint of industry and ability won a commission.

"How about that, Admiral?" I asked. "Was he still a mucker and unfit to associate with his brother, the *gentleman* by virtue of Annapolis?"

"Yes," he replied, his wattles reddening until I thought he was about to burst. "A mucker stays a mucker."

This bitterness of the "King Charles set," as it was known, played no small part in the campaign of abuse and derision against Secretary Daniels, but the real source was the angers of big business. The powder trust hated him because he manufactured smokeless powder for 34 cents a pound against the 50 to 80 cents asked by the monopoly. The grafters hated him because his economies had effected a saving of $15,000,000 on public work at shore stations. The armor-plate crowd hated him because he cut out more than a million on one bid alone, and was pushing a bill to construct a government plant. Instead of letting an investment of $120,000,000 in navy yards lie idle, he had opened them up to full capacity, and everything produced by them, from dreadnoughts to torpedoes, cost from 20 to 60 per cent less than the private purchase price. And so on and so on.

The interview, widely printed, made a sensation, and resulted in a decided change of attitude toward Secretary Daniels. The shift became even more apparent when I induced Admiral Dewey to back it up. What a handsome old buck he was, his speech as salty as the seven seas! He supported Secretary Daniels at every point, praising his reforms, damning his traducers, and wondering what in the hell got into people to make them willing to join in the hue and cry against an honest, capable official.

After we had finished and were punishing an issue of grog, something one of us said brought up the incident of Dewey's home. On his return from Manila in 1898, staggering under the weight of laurels, a public subscription was started to buy a house for the Admiral, and when a sufficient sum had been raised, the trustees purchased a Washington residence and turned it over to him with a great blare of trumpets. As any other decent husband would have done, he put the title deed in his wife's name.

Nothing was said or thought about it until the opening of the presidential campaign, when Admiral Dewey began to be mentioned as a probable Democratic nominee. He himself gave it no encouragement, but terrified politicians, along with a portion of the press, took the movement seriously, and mean detraction of his naval victories was followed by open attacks. Along with other slanders, the conveyance of the gift home to Mrs. Dewey suffered distortion to a point where the transaction was made to take on the appearance of an abominable crime. The whole disgraceful business had gone out of my mind so completely that it shocked me to see the old sea dog's face darken with pain.

"Surely, sir," I protested, "you can't have been hurt by those infamous lies that nobody believed?"

"Not hurt?" he answered. "Not hurt? Why, if I could take my heart out now, you'd still see the footprints that broke it."

Between interviews and a daily answer to Republican attacks, I turned out *Wilson and the Issues,* a small book that dealt with Mexico, the *Lusitania,* Belgium, "America First," and other subjects of Republican attack. The reviews were flattering, likewise the sale, but with a rush of partisanship to the head, I presented my copyright to the Democratic National Committee. The ten chapters were released to the press, and a paper-bound edition, with a foreword by Secretary of War Baker, was distributed to speakers and state committees.

My prize contribution to the campaign, however, was the organization of a committee of publicists and authors for the issuance of statements and pamphlets; a blue-ribbon list, for these were some of the names: Irvin Cobb, Samuel Hopkins Adams, Ray Stannard Baker, W. L. Chenery, Zona Gale, Fannie Hurst, Peter B. Kyne, Edgar Lee Masters, Kathleen Norris, Harvey O'Higgins, Ernest Poole, Lincoln Steffens, Augustus Thomas, Ida Tarbell, and Harry Leon Wilson.

At the risk of immodesty, I insist that our questions to Mr. Hughes were one of the most effective features of the campaign. Starting off with the flat assertion that President Wilson's beliefs had been expressed in laws and declared policies, providing an open record by which he could be judged, we asked Mr. Hughes for an equally specific statement. "What has he done that you would not have done? What has he failed to do that you would have done or propose to do? What are the exact details of your disagreement with President Wilson?"

With this preamble, we let fly at Mr. Hughes with ten barbed questions. Would you have filed protest against the invasion of Belgium and backed up that protest with the United States Navy? Would you have broken off diplomatic relations with Germany after the sinking of the *Lusitania?* Would you have urged Congress to embargo the shipment of munitions to the Allies? Since you insist that Huerta's morals were of no concern to America, would you have recognized him? As matters stand today, are you in favor of intervening in Mexico? Does your attack on the Wilson shipping bill mean that you are in favor of ship subsidies? Do you endorse the Clayton Antitrust Act and the Seamen's Bill, or will you urge their repeal? As governor of New York, you opposed the income-tax amendment. Does this antagonism still persist? Do you or do you not believe in paying for preparedness out of taxes on income, inheritances, and munitions? Where do you stand on equal suffrage?

These questions, headed "Yes or No, Mr. Hughes?" were printed as full-page advertisements in every city where he spoke, and hecklers shouted them at him. Of course he did not attempt a reply, for every question was packed with dynamite. Whether he answered affirmatively or negatively, thousands of votes were bound to be lost.

Aside from the sheer joy that the campaign held for me, it also had definite educational values. Coming from the West, I looked on Wall Street as a phalanx formation where every man stood shoulder to shoulder in defense of his right to loot and exploit. What, then, was my amazement to find that the two largest contributors to the Wilson cause, and also the most enthusiastic workers, were Wall Street millionaires. It was to Bernard M. Baruch, the "speculator," and Thomas L. Chadbourne, the country's foremost corporation lawyer, that we turned for advice on strategy or to meet deficits.

What a pair they were! Bernie, wiser than a treeful of owls, and studying a proposition from every angle before committing himself to a course; Tom, standing six feet seven, and with a Viking's look as well as build, reaching decisions by a flashing intuition that rarely missed. Both became my dear friends, and I learned more about true liberalism from them than from those who made a profession of it.

At the outset of the campaign I thought the Republicans a push-over, counting confidently on the defection of the Bull Moosers. Why not? In 1912 Theodore Roosevelt had assured his credulous followers—men and women who risked their political lives and fortunes in his cause—that he would stay with the Progressive movement to the last heartbeat. In 1916, when these poor believing souls gathered again, the Colonel exhausted every effort to swing them back into the Republican party, even suggesting the names of such archconservatives as Elihu Root and Henry Cabot Lodge as candidates deserving of support. And when the convention went ahead in blind faith, he rejected the nomination and announced his support of Hughes. Contrary to my expectations, however, there was no mass revolt, the great majority of Bull Moosers seemingly unable to throw off the Roosevelt spell.

With the Republicans again in phalanx formation, and financed by huge contributions from all of the great corporations, our high confidence lessened perceptibly, and the outlook was not brightened by a definite split between Mr. Wilson and the campaign managers. These leaders, convinced that there was an overwhelming sentiment against our involvement in the European conflict, had decided on "He kept us out of war" as a slogan, and Bob Wooley played it up with every force at his command. For a while the President said nothing, but when every billboard in the land began to blaze with the battle cry, he walked into headquarters and blasted all of us for "gross and unforgivable deception."

"You are deliberately giving the impression," he said, white-hot with indignation, "that my policy is one of unchangeable neutrality, no matter what arises. And yet in speech after speech I have made it plain that the day may come when we may be *forced* to fight. Here," and he pulled some papers from his pocket, "are excerpts that I insist upon having emphasized." I quote two:

We are not going to invade any nation's right, but suppose, my fellow countrymen, some nation should invade our right. What then? I have come here to tell you that the difficulties of our foreign policy . . . daily increase in number and intricacy and danger, and I would be derelict in my duty to you if I did not deal with you in these matters with the utmost candor, and tell you what it may be necessary to use the force of the United States to do.

The United States was once in the enjoyment of what we used to call splendid isolation. . . . And now, by circumstances which she did not choose, over which she had no control, she had been thrust out into the great game of mankind, on the stage of the world itself . . . and no nation must doubt that all her forces are gathered and organized in the interest of just, righteous and humane government.

Bob Wooley obeyed the injunction for a while, but when Mr. Wilson's attention seemed safely diverted to other things,

"He kept us out of war" was resurrected as a slogan. How large a part it played in the election is a question, but Bob always insisted that the ballyhoo swung California. During the November days when the election's outcome hung in the balance, but with the victory of Mr. Hughes seemingly assured, the Republicans offered ridiculous odds, and I borrowed heavily to take some of the bets. President Wilson heard about my winnings, and when we met after the final count he beamingly extended congratulations. I beamed back and ventured to remark that I had always understood that Presbyterians frowned on wagers.

"Yes," he laughed, "but in this case it possesses the sanctification of a good cause. Spoiling the Egyptians has Biblical approval."

CHAPTER 21

The Censorship Myth

President Wilson was generous enough to like both my book and my articles, and shortly after the election asked me to come to Washington as a member of his official family, mentioning a post of assistant secretary in one of the departments. I refused with thanks, not only out of dislike for bureaucratic routine, but for financial reasons. Government salaries are higher today, but at the time they came close to being beggarly, and setting up a home in Washington for my wife and children called for more money than I had or could hope to borrow.

In March, 1917, however, with war a certainty, the admirals and generals pressed forward with the demand for a hard and fast censorship law that would have put the press in leg irons and handcuffs. Worse still, word came that the President was inclined to favor it. Believing that the proposed law was criminally stupid and bound to work untold harm, I prepared a brief that set forth the dangers in detail and sent it to Mr. Wilson for his private eye.

I did not deny the need of a large measure of secrecy in connection with the war effort, but insisted that the desired results could be obtained without paying the heavy price of a censorship law. With America's youth sailing to fight in foreign lands, leaving families three thousand miles behind them, nothing was more vital than that the people's confidence in the news should not be impaired. Suspicious enough by reason of natural anxieties, a straight-out censorship would inevitably stir demoralizing fears in the heart of every father and mother and open the door to every variety of rumor.

Freedom of the press, to be sure, was a right that had suffered abuses, but better abuses than the evils of a deadening and autocratic control. I also stressed the narrowness of the military mind—its traditional arrogance in time of war—and pointed out that "information of value to the enemy" was an elastic phrase that could be stretched to cover the whole field of discussion.

In lieu of the suggested law, I urged the superior wisdom of a *voluntary agreement* that would make every newspaper its own censor, putting it up to the common sense of each editor to protect purely military information. But, I argued, what idiocy to assume that the enemy would depend on the indiscretions of newspapers for their information! Where the real danger lay was in the employment of spies, and since speed was the essence, the use of the cables. The intelligent course was a rigid censorship of cable communications, not touching straight news, but solely to block and detect Germany's undercover agents.

Going on from there, I argued that *expression,* not *suppression,* was the real need. During the three and a half years of our neutrality the United States had been torn by a thousand divisive prejudices, with public opinion stunned and muddled by the pull and haul of Allied and German propaganda. The sentiment of the West was still isolationist; the Northwest buzzed with talk of a "rich man's war," waged to salvage Wall Street loans; men and women of Irish stock were "neutral," not caring who whipped England, and in every state demagogues raved against "warmongers," although the Du Ponts and other so-called "merchants of death" did not have enough powder on hand to arm squirrel hunters.

How could the national emergency be met without national

157

unity? The printed word, the spoken word, motion pictures, the telegraph, the wireless, cables, posters, signboards, and every possible media should be used to drive home the justice of America's cause. Not to combat prejudices and disaffection at home was to weaken the firing line.

There was also an even greater task beyond our borders. There were the war-weary peoples of England, France, and Italy that had to be strengthened by a message of encouragement, the peoples of the neutral countries to be won to our support, and the peoples of the Central Powers to be reached with the truth. Not propaganda as the Germans defined it, but propaganda in the true sense of the word, meaning the "propagation of faith."

What I proposed was the creation of an agency that would make the fight for what Wilson himself had called "the verdict of mankind"; an agency that would not only reach deep into every American community, clearing away confusions, but at the same time seek the friendship of neutral nations and break through the barrage of lies that kept the Germans in darkness and delusion.

The President approved the brief, as did Secretary Daniels, and asked me to come to Washington and set up the agency that I had in mind. Acceptance, of course, was compulsory, and on April 14, a week after the war declaration, I took my oath as chairman of the Committee on Public Information, the other members being the Secretary of State, the Secretary of War, and the Secretary of the Navy. My title did not disturb Mr. Baker or Mr. Daniels in the least, but Mr. Lansing was terribly upset for fear that people might think that he was "under" me.

Fortunately, I soon began reporting directly to the President and meeting privately with the War and Navy heads, so that the Secretary of State was shunted off onto a side track. Not that he didn't try to get back on the main line, losing no opportunity to hound me with the petty complaints of a humorless man. For example, there was the occasion when he summoned me before him and in a voice shaken by horror asked if I did not know that no citizen could communicate with the heads of foreign governments except through his office.

"Certainly, sir," I replied.

"Then how," he thundered, "do you explain the effrontery, the insolence, of Rochester, the editor of your *Official Bulletin?*"

Puzzled questioning developed that Rochester had written to European rulers in the most casual manner, even addressing George V and Victor Emmanuel as "Dear King." Back in my office, I called for an explanation, and Rochester gave it with a good deal of indignation. Always resentful of the *Bulletin's* colorlessness, and wanting to give it some "zip," he had cabled messages to Europe asking for five or six hundred words on America's war effort. I ripped him wide open, not only for his obsession with "zip," but for having been guilty of insult.

"Insult, hell!" he shouted. "All of 'em shot back three times as much as I asked for, and I'm still blue-penciling. And that little Italian bird Victor Emmanuel wants to become a regular contributor."

I reported his story to Secretary Lansing, thinking it a great joke, but it was months before he quit his demand that Rochester be boiled in oil. The President, however, loved it, and suggested sending Rochester abroad as a roving ambassador. "His direct methods," he smiled, "might get us somewhere."

Evidently Mr. Lansing nursed a grievance, for in his *Memoirs* he devoted several pages to me. I quote a few choice passages:

Although at first the full committee held several meetings, Mr. Creel soon assumed all authority and ran the Office of Public Information in accordance with his own ideas. I do not think the change to a "one man" office was distasteful to Mr. Wilson, as he had great confidence in Creel's ability and personal loyalty. . . . Creel's Socialistic tendencies, which were well known, and which were evidenced by some of the people he employed, aroused considerable criticism, particularly in Washington. Though this radicalism caused distrust and apprehension among many officials of the Administration, I do not believe that it disturbed Mr. Wilson, who viewed with toleration, if not with a degree of approval, certain Socialistic ideas which he termed "progressive," although they were utterly hostile to the fundamental principles of his party. . . . Creel was hostile to me personally . . . and sought in various way to discredit me as Secretary of State.[1]

---

[1] From *War Memoirs of Robert Lansing,* pp. 322-4. Copyright, 1935. Used by special permission of the publishers, The Bobbs-Merrill Company.

Bosh! After the Rochester incident, I never gave the Secretary another thought, nor did anyone else for that matter. As far as I can remember, the only thing I ever said about him was that he worked at being dull and carried conservatism to the point of medievalism.

Putting the Committee on Public Information together was like asking the Babylonians to build a threshing machine, for there was no chart to go by and I did not even have an office for several weeks. Happily, Secretary Baker lent me Douglas MacArthur, then a handsome young major, and with his help I located a row of old brick houses on Jackson Place, just across from the White House. Arthur Bullard, Ernest Poole, Harvey O'Higgins, Edgar Sisson, W. L. Chenery, and Charles Hart all quit private employment in answer to my despairing call, and by dint of day and night work, things began to take shape.

Starting from scratch seemed a hardship at the time, but on looking back, I see it as my salvation. With the organization put together man by man, I knew it from top to bottom and could keep an eye and hand on every division. By contrast, when Elmer Davis took over the Office of War Information in World War II, he inherited the personnel of three bankrupt concerns—the Office of Government Reports, the Office of Coordinator of Information, and the Office of Facts and Figures. In much the same way, Assistant Secretary of State William Benton started off his postwar Office of International Information and Cultural Affairs with a bureaucratic army dumped on him by the Office of Strategic Services and the Office of War Information.

At the end of a frantic week the Committee was in some sort of operation. A first order of business was the voluntary censorship, and a small card, about ten inches by twelve, went forth under the heading "What the Government Asks of the Press." And what were these requests? Simply to observe secrecy with respect to troop movements, ship sailings, convoys, the number of expeditionary forces abroad, the location of bases, the laying of mine fields, information relating to antiaircraft defenses, shipbuilding, and government experiments in war matériel.

At the end there was this explicit notice: *These requests to the press are without larger authority than the necessities of the war-making branches. Their enforcement is a matter for the press itself.* Not one, I submit, did not have its base in common sense, and yet from the uproar that arose, it might have been thought that I had fitted every reporter with gags, blindfolds, and shackles. This voluntary and self-administered system was the only restraint imposed on the press, yet I was instantly branded as the censor, and never a day passed that the hateful word was not harped on.[2]

After the rules for voluntary censorship, the next step, obviously, was the fight for national unity. Here I proceeded on the theory that before a sound, steadfast public opinion could be formed, it had to be *informed*. Not manipulated, not tricked, and not wheedled, but given every fact in the case. A free people were not children to be humored, cajoled, or lollipopped with half-truths for fear that the whole truth might frighten them. The war was not the war of the administration or the private enterprise of the General Staff, but the grim business of a whole people, and every man, woman, and child had to be given a feeling of partnership. What we did, therefore, was to put trained reporters in the War Department, the Navy, and every other agency connected with the war machine,

---

[2] Even so competent a reporter as Mark Sullivan not only viewed me as a censor, but went on the assumption that press censorship was my *one* duty, for in a *Collier's* article he wrote as follows:

"Creel, temperamental, excitable and emotional to the last degree —Creel in a big and complex administrative job is exceedingly incongruous. Himself the most aggressive and daring of newspaper men, the most insistent on 'pitiless publicity,' the most violent of muckrakers—Creel, summoned by the President to a role of which the very title implies the soft pedal, the suppression of publicity, is exceedingly incongruous. The President did Creel no service when he gave him, of all jobs, this particular job, which includes a kind of administrative supervision over the mails, the telegraph and cable services, and then thousands of newspapers; and entails a repressive function over that most hard-to-be-repressed tribe, the newspaper reporters of the United States.

"For such a job Creel is the most unsuitable of men. President Wilson might just as appropriately have appointed Billy Sunday. Indeed, George Creel and Billy Sunday have much in common. What Sunday is to religion Creel is to politics. Creel is a crusader, a bearer of the fiery cross. His ten years as a newspaper man in Kansas City and five in Denver were devoted to the championship of one form after another of idealism."

and every day saw an honest, unvarnished report of progress to the people.[3]

During World War II, under Mr. Roosevelt's generous, open-handed administration, there was not only the Office of War Information, but every department, board, bureau, and commission had its own high-powered, heavily staffed publicity division, issuing a daily stream of press-agent material. The Army and the Navy, for instance, each maintained between three and five hundred "public relations" officers, and the others averaged between fifty and one hundred. Throughout World War I, the CPI got along with four men in War, three in the Navy, and one in each of the rest.

What followed after the establishment of the Division of News was inspirational rather than planned. One morning, for example, Charles Dana Gibson walked in with a poster that he wanted to contribute. Within the hour he was out again under orders to organize the Division of Pictorial Publicity, recruiting famous artists for the production of paintings and pictures for all departments of government.

That afternoon a rosy-cheeked youth by the name of Donald Ryerson burst in with a plan for putting speakers in Chicago's motion-picture theaters. He left under instructions to form a national organization called the Four Minute Men. Before the year was out, 150,000 trained men were delivering the government's message to the people every week. This "spot speaking" naturally suggested coast-to-coast speaking tours by famous men and groups, so I reached for the telephone and drafted Arthur Bestor, president of Chautauqua.

All in all, some three hundred distinguished and effective speakers—Americans, French, British, and Polish—were sent from coast to coast, addressing mass meetings at key points. The best of the lot were Roald Amundsen, the famous Scandinavian, and Captain Paul Perigord, a French warrior-priest whose breast was covered by decorations won in heroic action. The worst was Sir Frederick Smith, a brilliant creature, but with the true British gift of offensiveness. After a few weeks of con-

---

[3] Of the six thousand releases from the Division of News, only *three* were ever attacked on the score of inaccuracy. In two of these cases the Committee was justified by investigation, while the fault in the third instance was that of a Cabinet officer.

tinual irritation I booted him back to England, where they soothed his hurt by making him Lord Birkenhead.

As usual, lucky accidents figured in the work. One afternoon a very lovely Frenchwoman came into the office and introduced herself as the Marquise de Courtivron. Her father, Prince Polignac, had fought for the South during the Civil War, and a deathbed request was that his sword be returned to Virginia. Very timidly, she asked if it could be arranged without too much trouble. The Marquise was sent not only to Richmond but to every other capital below the Mason and Dixon line, and the whole South cheered her.

After Ryerson and Bestor came Herbert Houston, William H. Rankin, Thomas Cusack, W. H. Johns, and several others, urging the outright purchase of space in newspapers and magazines and on billboards. The outcome was the formation of a Division of Advertising that gave us $2,000,000 in free advertising by the war's end. Not the least of its great jobs was handling all of the publicity for the registration of thirteen million men.

From the first, nothing stood more clear than the confusion and shapelessness of public opinion. The country as a whole accepted the war, but there was no complete understanding of it as a war of self-defense that had to be waged if free institutions were not to go down under the rushing tide of militarism. Big books were not what we wanted, and long, tedious state papers were not what we needed, so the decision was made to go in for pamphleteering.

Out of the mass of stuff that came in by every mail, I chanced on a patriotic address by Guy Stanton Ford, head of the history department of the University of Minnesota and dean of the Graduate School. I had rarely read anything that made more instant appeal, for it had beauty without sacrifice of force; simplicity, sequence, and obvious knowledge of every detail in America's material and spiritual progress. I wired him to come on without delay, and when he reported, sketched an outline and gave him a desk.

To his side Dr. Ford called every distinguished historian in the country, and then worked out a method of preparation that was foolproof. When a pamphlet was decided on, the next question was the proper man or men for the job. Perhaps a professor at Princeton or Cornell or Harvard or some state

163

university, or maybe all of them. Brought to Washington, they were given one simple direction: "Do it so that you will not be ashamed of it twenty years later." When finished, the pamphlet was submitted to a review board and then referred to the various divisions of government for checking.

Although distribution was entirely by requests from individuals and organizations, more than seventy-five million pamphlets were circulated by the war's end. *How the War Came to America* alone ran up to seven million. Used in schools, published as supplements by newspapers, the pamphlets became an arsenal from which speakers, officials, and editors drew their ammunition. Taken as a whole, they were the clearest expositions of American policy ever presented, and the most sober and terrific indictment ever drawn by one government against the political and military system of another. And it was Dr. Ford's pride that of all the mass of matter issued, dealing with thousands of facts, not one statement was ever challenged as to accuracy.

So it went on from day to day. When the motion-picture people came forward with a commercial proposition for handling our films, Charlie Hart was told to put the CPI in business as a producer and distributor. Most of the material came from the photographers of the Signal Corps, so why turn it over to private companies for their profit? *Pershing's Crusaders*, *America's Answer*, and *Under Four Flags*—great seven-reel feature films—played every theater in the country, as did our *Official War Review*, a weekly release. Aside from reaching the entire population, they netted us a profit of $900,000.

The accidental quality that marked many of our ideas was never more marked than in the war expositions that came to be a principal activity. One day some state fair people came in with a request for guns, gas masks, hand grenades, depth bombs, mines, etc., so as to show people how their money was being spent. The exhibits proved successful, and it was decided to put them on in every large city, enlisting the co-operation of the British, French, and Italians. Chicago was selected for the first big show, and we boldly took over the lake front, erecting buildings and digging trenches for the sham battles that the Army wanted to put on.

It was at this moment that Congress called me to explain what I was doing with my money. Every item was a quarrel,

164

but when it came to the war expositions, the committee damned it as a "silly idea," and only after long argument was I granted $5,000 for them. Naturally, my insides turned to jelly, for we had already spent $200,000 on the Chicago venture. However, there was nothing to do but go ahead.

The gates opened in a downpour of rain, killing attendance, and when Charlie Hart telephoned the bad news, I barely made the bathroom in time. Then, thank heaven, the sun came out, and at the end of the two weeks two million people had attended and the books showed a clear profit of $318,000. Better still, we went on to fifteen other cities and finished up with a net gain of $1,438,000.

In connection with these profits from the expositions and motion pictures, let me give the cost of the CPI without waiting to finish the full story. From April 14, 1917, to December 30, 1918, the Committee covered the world, making the fight for "the verdict of mankind" both at home and abroad, and at the end accountants set down these figures:

From the President's fund	$5,600,000
From Congress	1,250,000
Total working capital	$6,850,000
Returned to Treasury from earnings	2,937,447
Cost of CPI to taxpayers	$3,912,553

Not bad when compared to the hundreds of millions spent for the same purpose in World War II.

CHAPTER 22

Telling the World

*W*hen the Committee turned away from the United States to the world beyond our borders, a triple task confronted us. First, we had to carry the facts of our case to the neutral nations, all poisoned by German lies; second, we had to make the tired peoples of England, France, and Italy know that effective aid was on the way; third, we had to get our war aims and peace terms into the Central Powers, together with proof of America's invincibility.

At the outset it was a task that looked to be hopeless. For years Germany had been building a vast publicity machine, designed to convince foreign peoples of her military power and her overwhelming pre-eminence in industry, commerce, science, and the arts. By 1917 it operated in every corner of the earth. Both England and France, through the ownership of certain great cable arteries or by liberal subsidies, had long been able to direct currents of public opinion favorable to themselves. Moreover, Great Britain conducted direct governmental propaganda through the Reuters news agency, and France exercised a similar control over Havas, also an international news agency.

The United States alone neither owned nor subsidized any cables, and had no tie-up whatsoever with the Associated Press, the United Press, or the International News. The volume of information that went from our shores was small enough in the beginning, and grew smaller and smaller after it had been filtered in London, Paris, and Berlin. Moreover, the news dealt almost entirely with the violent and unusual in our national life: strikes, graft scandals, sensational divorce suits, murders and riots, lynchings, and the bizarre extravagances of the newly rich and addlepated heirs to huge fortunes.

The Germans had taken advantage of this situation with vigor and skill. Russians competent to judge assured us that the agents of Berlin spent $500,000,000 in that country alone in their work of corruption and destruction, and German expenditures in Spain were estimated at $60,000,000. Close to $5,000,000 went to Bolo Pasha for the corruption of the Paris press, and the sums spent in Mexico ran high into the millions. I know that they owned or subsidized dailies in most of the important cities of Spain, South America, the Orient, Scandinavia, and Holland; that their publications, issued in every language, ran from costly brochures to the most expensive books and albums; that they thought nothing of paying $25,000 for a hole-in-the-wall picture house, and that in every large city in every country their blackmailers and bribe givers swarmed like carrion crows.

166

Their propaganda, while playing upon different points of prejudice in various countries, was much the same everywhere. As an initial proposition America's military strength was derided. By no possibility could the United States raise or train an army, and if by some miracle this did happen, the army could not be transported. America was a fat, loblolly nation, lacking courage, equipment, ships, etc. Working away from this pleasing premise, they described America as a nation of dollar grabbers, devoid of ideals and inordinate in their ambitions.

Our war with Mexico in 1847 was played up as a cold-blooded, evil conquest, and our struggle with Spain was painted as an effort of our financial masters to enter upon dreams of world imperialism; Cuba, the Philippines, and Puerto Rico were pitied as "America's slave nations"; the Colorado coal strike and other industrial conflicts were all treated in the utmost detail to prove America's "system of wage slavery"; pictures were drawn of tremendous wealth on the one hand and peonage on the other; and lynchings were exaggerated until it was made to appear that almost every tree in America was used for that purpose.

In Spain every effort was made to revive the bitternesses of 1898; in Switzerland we were accused of withholding grain in order to starve the Swiss into alliance with us; in South and Central America the Germans moaned about the "Panama Canal rape" and the "conquest and annexation" of Haiti and Santo Domingo; in France they blamed Americans for high prices, and Italians were asked to believe that we had "deserted" them; in Russia they played up the case of Tom Mooney, the California labor leader then under sentence of death. When the Bolsheviks threw rocks at his windows, poor Ambassador Francis sent a plaintive cable asking, "Who *is* Mooney?"

Looking about for a way to remedy this evil situation, we saw the wireless stations of the country, taken over by the Navy some time before. All were lying idle, and Secretary Daniels immediately granted our request for their use. But where was the man able to blaze a brand-new trail? Just at that minute, as if in answer to prayer, in walked Walter S. Rogers, a gangling, youngish man whose hobby was "world communication."

Under Rogers' competent direction, "Compub" opened offices in every capital of the world outside of the Central

167

Powers. A daily service went out from Tuckerton, Long Island, to the Eiffel Tower for use in France, and was then relayed to Bern, Rome, Madrid, and Lisbon. From Tuckerton the service was also flashed to England and on to Holland, the Scandinavian countries, and Russia. The Orient was served by telegraph to San Diego, thence by wireless to Cavite and Shanghai, Tokyo, Peking, and Vladivostok; Austria, India, Egypt, and the Balkans were also reached. We went into Mexico by cable and land wires, and from Darien sent a service to Central and South American countries, thus completing a world chain.

For the first time in history, the speeches of a national executive were given universal circulation. The official addresses of President Wilson, setting forth America's position, were put on the wireless at the moment of delivery, and in twenty-four hours were in every language in every country. Our war progress, our tremendous resources, the acts of Congress, proofs of our unity and determination, etc., all went forth for the information of the world.

President Wilson himself was pressed into service, for his famous Fourteen Points were laid down as the result of this cable from Edgar Sisson, the CPI representative in Russia: "If President will restate anti-imperialistic war aims and democratic peace requisites of America, thousand words or less, short almost placard paragraphs, I can get it fed into Germany in great quantities in German translation, and can use Russian version potently in army and everywhere."

I took the request to the President, who met it with the dry comment that he had never tried his hand at slogans and advertising copy. Two or three days later, he called me to the White House and let me read the address in which he did restate America's war aims and peace terms in "placard paragraphs." Not only did we use the Fourteen Points in Russia and Germany, but we plastered them on billboards in every Allied and neutral country.

Before we had gone far, it was seen that the wireless and the cables could not entirely meet our foreign needs. It was not enough to give the world daily news and daily answers to German lies. There were misconceptions of long standing that had to be met and defeated. What the other countries needed were descriptions of our development as a nation and a people; our social and industrial progress; our schools, our labor unions, and our labor laws; everything, in fact, that had bearing on the American way of life.

The wireless and cables, therefore, were supplemented by a mail service. As always, our emphasis was on volunteer effort, and Ernest Poole gathered together a group of famous authors that money could not have hired. Booth Tarkington, Owen Wister, Gertrude Atherton, William Dean Howells, Ida Tarbell, Fannie Hurst, Edna Ferber, William Allen White, and scores of others turned out weekly articles on American life that were welcomed by newspapers and periodicals in every country.

To our representatives in foreign capitals also went the feature films that showed our military effort—cantonments, shipyards, training stations, warships, marching thousands— all retitled in the language of the land. In addition, we flooded every country with films that showed America "at home"— pictures dealing with factories and farms, urban and rural life, education, athletics, health, etc. Here again we bought nothing, begging industrial films from such great corporations as Ford, Corn Products, International Harvester, United States Steel, and lumber and coal companies.

An export licensing system that gave the Committee control over every foot of commercial film that left the country was what enabled us to force acceptance of CPI programs in neutral countries. In order to get their movies abroad, Hollywood producers had to agree that no American entertainment films would be sold to any foreign exhibitor who refused to show the Committee's war pictures, and that none would be sold to houses where any sort of German film was being used. As exhibitors simply had to have our comedies and dramas, for the German output was rotten, we soon had sole possession of the field. Much as they may have disliked our propaganda features, Douglas Fairbanks, Mary Pickford, and the Keystone Cops were a necessity. Even more important, our licensing system stopped the export of the gangster and underworld movies that had done so much to give a false impression of American life.

Our approach to the neutral countries was simple and direct. Instead of prattling about "cultural relations," sending Hollywood stars on good-will missions, pouring out millions in largess, and begging an exchange of singers and dancers, we went straight to the governments with a plain statement of purpose:

"It is desired to establish offices for the distribution of a wireless, cable, and mail service to the press; for the exhibition of motion pictures expressive of America's aims and energies; for the assignment of speakers, for pamphlet distribution and other open activities. Our purpose is not the coercion of public opinion, but its information, and every activity will be open and aboveboard."

An effective feature of our fight for public opinion in neutral countries was the bringing of their leading newspapermen to the United States that they might see with their own eyes. Delegations of editors from Mexico, Switzerland, and the Scandinavian countries were toured from coast to coast, and shipyards, cantonments, and factories were opened for their inspection. These trips were of incalculable value, for not only did the visitors send home daily reports by cable and mail, but upon their return they wrote pages and even went on the lecture platform. Each delegation, at the end of the tour, was taken to the White House, where President Wilson set forth our war aims and peace terms.

Before the flood of our publicity, German lies were swept away. The Latin-American countries became our allies, and other countries were won to friendship. From being the most misunderstood nation, the United States became the most popular. A world that was either inimical or indifferent was changed into a world of well-wishers.

The maintenance of British, French, and Italian morale, of course, was of supreme importance. It was not that either soldiers or civilians had lost courage or determination, but simply that war weariness had slowed them down. "Can America come in time?" was a question on every lip. In order to answer it, the CPI worked no less actively in Allied countries than among neutrals. The emphasis, naturally, was different, for what we stressed was the magnitude and speed of the American war effort and the certainty of immediate aid.

Strangely enough, China was one of our gravest problems. Reuters, the British news agency, and Kokusai, the official Japanese news agency, supplied world reports to the press of China, and as each played the game of its own country, the Chinese did not even know that the United States was in the war.

Inasmuch as China feared England and hated Japan, a door was opened wide for German propaganda, and a daily cable service from Berlin poured poison into the wells of Chinese opinion. The tide was turned, of course, when the Committee opened offices and let China know the extent of America's war effort, along with our war aims and peace terms.

From the first, unhappily, our work in the foreign field was complicated by wrangles with the State Department. In the beginning Secretary Lansing demanded that CPI representatives should be subordinate to ambassadors and ministers, and when he lost this battle, he quarreled with the "kind of people" we selected. The State Department wanted us to send "diplomatic types," charming gentlemen who knew just what to wear and how to kiss a hand and handle a teacup. We wanted plain Americans who thought regularly and enthusiastically in terms of America, and who would worry over doing the job, not whether they had on the right coat.

The row came out into the open when an ambassador sent back a sneering letter in which he said that "Creel's man" in Italy was a "yokel from the Illinois cornfields," and that the appointment had made us a "laughingstock." The Secretary of State sent the letter to the White House, and President Wilson called on me for an explanation. I gave it gladly, saying that the "yokel" was none other than Professor Charles E. Merriam of the University of Chicago, not only a famous scholar but a man with wide and varied experience in public life.

Proceeding blithely, I mentioned other "yokels" with whom the State Department was not pleased. In London, Harry Rickey, a high executive of the Scripps newspaper chain; in Mexico, Robert Hammond Murray, for years the correspondent of the New York *World* in that country; in China, Carl Crow; long resident in the Orient as editor and correspondent; and in France—this with heavy emphasis—James Kerney, owner and publisher of the Trenton *Times,* New Jersey's most progressive newspaper. Interrupting at this point, the President grimly stated that I need not fear any further interference. Some days later I learned that he had sent a note to Mr. Lansing telling him that in the future his ambassadors and ministers were to mind their own business and keep their noses out of CPI affairs.

Getting the truth into Germany and Austria-Hungary, while

of primary importance, was no simple task, for a rigid censorship guarded every frontier and crushed every internal attempt to speak or write honestly. Both the armies and the civilian population were drugged with lies about Germany's "defensive war," the "cruel purposes" of the enemy, the "collapse" of the Allies, and the "utter failure" of America's war effort. These lies had the force of divisions, and it was necessary to destroy them as though each were a machine-gun nest.

France and Italy, of course, were principally used for the direct drive into the Central Powers, and in the beginning efforts were made to bring about a single Allied propaganda command. Lord Northcliffe called many conferences, but I did not like the ideas or the methods of either the British or the French, convinced that the voice of America was the only one that counted. When President Wilson approved, I ordered CPI representatives to go it alone.

Professor Merriam set up an office in Padua for an attack on the morale of Austria, and in France the closest relations were established with the Intelligence Section of the American Expeditionary Force, headed by General Dennis Nolan. At first army planes were used for raining down literature into enemy territory, but with every plane imperatively needed for military purposes, other means had to be devised. Guns and rockets loaded with leaflets were used for close work on the front lines, and balloons filled with coal gas for deeper penetration into Germany. All paper was chemically treated so as to be weatherproof.

An American invention that promised to supplant all others was a balloon that carried a tin container holding about ten thousand leaflets. A clock attachment governed the climb, the balloon had a sailing radius of eight hundred miles, and the mechanism could be set in such a manner that it dropped the leaflets one at a time at regular intervals. Unfortunately, the invention was perfected only a short time before the Armistice.

The first proof of the effectiveness of our drive was an order issued by the German General Staff decreeing the death penalty for all those found with American material in their possession. Austria-Hungary followed with a similar ukase, threatening soldiers and citizens with firing squads if they picked up any of our "printed lies."

172

The real job of reaching the civilians of the Central Powers, however, was principally done through the CPI offices in Switzerland, Denmark, Holland, and Russia. Switzerland in particular was a "first-line trench," for its newspapers were printed in the German language and had a large circulation in Austria and Germany. There was also heavy travel back and forth between Switzerland and the enemy countries.

Mrs. Norman de R. Whitehouse had charge of the work, picked by reason of her brilliant conduct of the successful equal-suffrage campaign in New York. Placing a woman in a position of international importance brought considerable criticism, but she more than demonstrated the wisdom of her appointment. Mrs. Whitehouse soon won over the Swiss press, and by her clever employment of the German radical groups in Switzerland developed a regular messenger service into Germany. More than that, she herself slipped across the frontier time and again, placing our material in the proper channels for thorough circulation.

To Denmark we sent George Edward Riis, an able newspaperman who possessed added values by being the son of that great Danish-American, George Edward Riis. Henry Suydam, long a distinguished European correspondent, was the CPI man in Holland. Like Mrs. Whitehouse, they captured the newspapers and motion-picture houses and also took the same advantage of the free movement between their countries and Germany.

Once Riis got a huge bundle of pamphlets into Germany through a trick that succeeded by its very boldness. Picking an agent who spoke German and had the look of a Prussian, he had him stop the German courier just as he was leaving the legation for Hamburg. "Here," the agent commanded, pushing forward his bundle. "Deliver these on arrival." Handing him the names of several newspapers and the addresses of certain socialist groups, he rasped, "By order of the Minister." And the courier *did*, paying for it with a prison term.

Valuable aid was also given to CPI representatives at key points by the European agents of the Congress of Oppressed Peoples of Austria-Hungary. This was an organization that we formed in 1918 with Ignace Paderewski and Dr. Tomáš Masaryk at its head, and along with Poles and Czechs included Lithuanians, Ukrainians, Hungarians, and Yugoslavs. The first meeting was very near the last, for Mr. Paderewski recognized the Ukrainian representative as the gentleman who had once shot a Polish ambassador right through the stomach. He calmed down eventually, and the Congress became a powerful propaganda instrument, proving particularly helpful in putting CPI representatives in touch with the undergrounds operating in Middle Europe.

The organization of the Congress, of course, committed the United States to the dismemberment of the Austro-Hungarian Empire, and President Wilson gave the matter much thought before letting me bring in Mr. Paderewski and Dr. Masaryk to receive his authorization. What he feared, and with reason, was the outbreak of revolution, attended by bloodshed and riot. However, he realized that militaristic and autocratic governments had to be overthrown, and comforted himself with the thought that changes could and would be effected by purely political processes.

The first conclusive proof that CPI material was getting into the Central Powers came about as the result of a bitter clash with the War Department in March, 1918. Without consultation or even the courtesy of a warning, Benedict Crowell, acting secretary in Newton Baker's absence, sent me a curt note saying that in the future all casualty lists must be issued to the press without the home address or the name of the next of kin. For example, instead of "Wounded: Private John Jones, S. J. Jones (father), 2 Yale St., Brooklyn, N.Y.," we were to adopt this form: "Wounded: Private John Jones."

I took the matter up at once with the War Department, pointing out the stupidity and cruelty of the order. Merely to announce that John Jones or Patrick Kelly had been killed or wounded meant that the parents, relatives, and friends of the countless John Joneses and Patrick Kellys would be given over to grief, since there was nothing to indicate exact identity. The answer returned was this: German spies, reading the casualty lists, would go to the home and find out the unit to which the soldier belonged. The information would then be transmitted to Berlin, and Berlin would send it to the front, thus acquainting German generals with the character of the American troops before them.

Branding the explanation as utterly asinine, I carried the

174

dispute to the President, and he called a meeting at which I faced Secretary Baker and the Chief of Staff. Why, I asked, would the Germans use such a crazy, roundabout method when a trench raid would give them the information in a night? Granting the absurd contention that there were enough German spies to visit homes in every city from coast to coast, how would they communicate with Germany?

"Aha!" they answered. "We have proof that Berlin receives American news within twenty-four hours of publication."

"Let's see the proof," I demanded.

When a sheaf of papers was triumphantly produced, I burst into a loud laugh. All of the stuff was CPI material that we had filtered into Germany through Bern, Copenhagen, and the eastern front. Not troubling to hide his smile at their discomfiture, the President peremptorily ordered a return to the former method that gave the home address and the next of kin.

CHAPTER 23

The German-Bolshevik Conspiracy

*F*rom the very outset Russia was a separate problem requiring specialized treatment. Shortly after our entrance into the war, President Wilson sent a mission headed by Elihu Root to St. Petersburg, both as an expression of friendship for the new Kerenski regime and to ascertain Russian needs. Unfortunately, it fell far short of its purpose, for the Bolsheviks, not yet in power but already conspiring against the Kerenski government, attacked Mr. Root as the representative of "dollar diplomacy," and never abated their campaign of falsehood and abuse.

The mission, on its return, handed in a huge sheaf of recommendations, and the President passed it on to me for analysis. I endorsed the dispatch of railroad experts and a Red Cross medical and welfare unit, but reported strongly against the allotment of $5,512,000 as a year's budget for propaganda. A half million, for example, was to be spent on the employment

175

of Russian speakers, and an equal sum for the subsidizing of newspapers.

Still another disturbing note was contributed by William Boyce Thompson, a multimillionaire copper magnate serving in Russia as a Red Cross colonel. Although a rock-bound conservative at home, warring continually on labor unions, the Colonel was a roaring radical in St. Petersburg, and among other activities had contributed $1,000,000 to Madame Breshkovskaya, the "grandmother of the revolution." It did not seem to me that he was quite the man we wanted to preach American gospel.

Going to the President, I suggested the sending of a CPI representative to Russia for the earliest possible installation of an information service after thorough study. Mr. Wilson agreed, and the man selected for the errand was Edgar G. Sisson. Editor of the *Cosmopolitan,* he had resigned his high-salaried post to serve the Committee with its much lower government pay. In a few weeks, pleased with his sound judgment and executive ability, I made him associate chairman, a rank he later shared with Harvey O'Higgins, the author and playwright.

The President, after a searching interview with Mr. Sisson, approved my choice and gave him a letter that contained these explicit instructions: "We want nothing for ourselves, and this very unselfishness carries with it the obligation of open dealing. Wherever the fundamental principles of Russian freedom are at stake, we stand ready to render such aid as lies in our power, but I want this helpfulness based upon request and not upon offer. Guard particularly against any effect of officious intrusion or meddling, and try to express the disinterested friendship that is our sole impulse."

When Mr. Sisson sailed on October 27, 1917, he journeyed to a supposed ally, for Kerenski's government was being patterned along democratic lines and stood pledged to continue war against the Central Powers. Reaching St. Petersburg on November 25, however, he found Kerenski overthrown and Lenin and Trotsky wielding autocratic power. To my mind there is no greater proof of Communist impudence and dishonesty than the claim that the revolution was against the Czar, blandly ignoring the fact that the government overthrown was democratic and anticzarist.

In his first cables Mr. Sisson reported that the Bolsheviks were cool to the point of antagonism, and mentioned the common gossip that the Germans had conveyed Lenin from Switzerland through Germany in a sealed car and then brought him into Russia by way of Sweden. Nevertheless, it was his opinion that we should assume the friendship of the Bolsheviks and go full steam ahead without regard for the whisper of German control. He also made happy mention of the fact that Colonel Thompson, having bet his million on the wrong horse, was sailing for home.

By a stroke of luck, Arthur Bullard, the author, publicist, and sociologist, was then in Moscow, having gone over to study Kerenski's experiment in self-government, and Sisson drafted him at once. With this as a start at organization, he called on me for the wireless and mail services, films and pamphlet material, and filed a list of needed helpers.

I still wonder at his courage and resourcefulness, for Lenin and Trotsky leaned heavily on killings to consolidate their power. As late as January 20, Kokoshkin and Shingarev, former Kerenski officials, were shot in their sickbeds, and General Dukhonin, deposed Russian commander in chief, was tossed on the bayonets of laughing soldiers. Street killings increased, and homes gave no protection.[1]

Russia's blight of grinding poverty, of course, proved a help to Sisson in his work, for he was able to make arrangements with controllers of printing plants and billboards; and hungry

---

[1] In his book *The Making of a State,* Dr. Tomáš Masaryk gives this eyewitness account: "The word Bolshevism recalls to my mind one scene among many horrible and inhuman sights I saw during the Bolshevist revolution. After the street fighting at Petersburg and elsewhere, the bodies of the fallen were sent to their families in the well-known Russian isvostchiks (2-wheel carts). The stiffened bodies were thrown like logs into the little carts, the legs sticking out on one side and the head or sometimes a hand on the other. Often the corpse was placed on its feet and bound fast with a piece of rope or a rag. I even saw one standing head downwards with the legs sticking up in the air. When I think of those gruesome sights, the barbaric, senseless killing of human beings by the Bolsheviks always returns to my mind." By permission of G. Allen & Unwin, Ltd., London, and Frederick A. Stokes Co., Philadelphia. (Published in U.S.A. under title *Memories and Observations.*)

and idle soldiers from the teeming barracks were willing to earn money by pasting up posters of Wilson speeches and distributing Wilson leaflets and pamphlets. In Petrograd and Moscow it was commonplace to put up fifty thousand posters at a whack, and quickly to get a street distribution of three hundred thousand leaflets. Soldier "package men" were also glad, at small hire, to shovel America's messages across the disintegrating front into the German lines, and eastward in the Russian interior to German prison camps, where the inmates already were elated with the hope of an early return to Germany. Whenever they went they would be carrying Wilson literature with them.

Trotsky was always inimical to any American activity, but Lenin, in the beginning, alternated between hostility and tolerance. The nation-wide circulation of Woodrow Wilson's Fourteen Points speech, for instance, was due to Lenin's personal order. Sisson took it to him on the moment of receipt, and after careful reading, the Bolshevik boss declared that it was a very fine document to come from a "class opponent," and ordered its publication in *Izvestia* the official newspaper, thus enabling Sisson to put the *Izvestia* credit line on leaflets, ensuring their widest distribution everywhere.

At no time had we ever fooled ourselves by thinking that Lenin and Trotsky would continue their armies in active combat, and we were sympathetic to this attitude, knowing what the Russian people had suffered at the hands of corrupt and stupid leadership. We did, however, assume that the Bolsheviks would favor the Allies rather than the Germans, for certainly the ideals of Wilson offered greater hope than the brutal militarism of the Kaiser. This belief continued even when Sisson sent me the following transcript of a conversation with a high official in the Commissariat for Foreign Affairs:

"You know," said this commissar, "that we regard all established governments as enemies, for we aim at a world-wide revolution that will overthrow every capitalistic state."

"Do you mean to tell me," exclaimed Sisson, "that you make no distinction between a democracy like the United States and an absolutism like Germany?"

"Yes. America is a financial empire and so is Germany. Both exploit the working class, although the United States is slyer, covering up its capitalistic oppressions with a lot of smooth phrases. As far as we are concerned, they are one and the same, and it is our hope that each will destroy the other."

More and more, as time went on, Sisson became convinced that the Bolsheviks were taking orders from the German General Staff, and urged authorization for an undercover search for facts. I gave him the permission, but with explicit instructions that the utmost secrecy must be observed, and that nothing must be made public as long as there was the least hope of continuing relations with the Soviets.

The infamous treaty of Brest-Litovsk brought the hope to an abrupt end. Throwing off all masquerade, the Bolsheviks first subjected Sisson's work to sabotage and suppression, and then in March, 1918, raided our offices and forced the staffs into flight. Some got out through Finland, while others had to make the long trek home by way of Siberia and Mongolia and then across the Gobi Desert to Peking. Sisson escaped by the Finnish route, and he did not come back empty-handed, for with him he brought complete documentary evidence of the German-Bolshevik conspiracy.

The "Sisson documents," as they came to be called, still have a heavy content of interest despite the years that have passed. Not only do they throw light on the methods by which Lenin and Trotsky rose to supreme power, but their publication brought about the first direct interference in our domestic affairs by Communist agents. The technique used then is much the same as that employed ever since: bold attack on whatever is said or done against them and the unceasing repetition of lies until they take on the look of truth.

Aside from the fact that Lenin had been brought into Russia by the Germans for revolutionary purposes, Sisson's suspicions were first stirred by certain documents that were placed in his hands by anti-Bolshevik groups, purporting to show how Lenin, Trotsky, Zinoviev, and others were financed by the Germans. While plausible enough, they lacked substantiation, and he used them, very properly and wisely, only as a starting point. After receiving authorization to make a full investigation, he got in touch with these groups again and succeeded eventually in establishing intimate relations with Eugene Semenov, well-known Russian writer and the head of a compact anti-German organization that had its representatives in the Smolny Institute, then Bolshevik headquarters. Many of these men were clever and brave enough to hold positions on naval and military staffs, and even in the Commissariat for Foreign Affairs, with access to all files.

The procedure worked out was both simple and practical. Each day Sisson was to be furnished with a list of the communications passing between the Bolsheviks and the German General Staff, and he would then indicate the ones worth taking from the files and photographing. Usually the documents were slipped out to another room for photographing, but on more than one occasion they were snapped on the spot, the men explaining that it was urgent work for the higher-ups.

For our purposes, however, *original documents* were needed, and this word was sent to Sisson. His answer, while stressing the many grave difficulties, stated that he would do his best. What gave him his opportunity was a curious turn of the wheel in the German-Bolshevik relations. With the Russian people embittered by increasing evidence of German control, Lenin was forced to a show of independence; and when he rejected certain extortionate demands, the Germans advanced on Petrograd.

For a brief moment the defense of the city was decided on, and orders were given for the removal of the archives to Moscow. The panic and confusion that ensued gave Semenov's men the chance for which they had been waiting. On the night of March 3, as German planes dropped bombs, the conspirators ransacked the files they had marked, lifting out the papers of principal importance. The job completed, the documents were hurried to Sisson and Bullard, and two hours were spent in listing and checking.

Not daring to run the risk of capture, Sisson wrapped the documents in one package, sealed it with embassy seals, and directed it to the American minister in Christiania (Oslo) with instructions to hold. The Norwegian minister, strongly pro-Ally, then placed the package in his diplomatic pouch and sent it off at once by courier.

Slipping out of Russia into Finland on March 4, Sisson reached Stockholm after an arduous journey of twenty-six days, for Finnish reds, armed by Russia, were waging a bloody civil war. A large part of the travel was across long stretches of ice in sledges. Proceeding to Christiania, he recovered his packet of papers and finally reached Washington in May. The docu-

180

ments that he brought with him were sixty-eight in number. Along with the originals, annotated by Bolshevik officials, there also were photographs of originals showing annotations, and the circulars that had initiated his investigation.

Taken as a whole, they proved conclusively that Lenin and Trotsky had been, and were, German agents, taking their orders from the German General Staff and receiving their funds from the German Imperial Bank. Stockholm was the banking center used, and in one lump fifty million rubles in gold were transferred to the people's commissars. Four days later another five million rubles were provided for the dispatch of Bolshevik agents to Vladivostok "to get possession of the Japanese and American war materials at that port." In this connection a report to Bolshevik leaders informed them that, in accordance with instructions, "all the books of the Nia bank at Stockholm" had been "audited" to conceal the payment of money to Lenin, Trotsky, and others for the peace propaganda in Russia.

One document, dated November 19, 1917, advised the Council of People's Commissars that "the following officers have been put at the disposal of the Russian Government as military advisers," and after naming them, concluded with this statement: "These officers will choose a cadre of the most suitable officers from the list of our prisoners, who will likewise be at the disposal of the Russian Government, as was agreed at the conference in Stockholm when Lenin and Zinoviev were traveling through to Russia." Other documents proved that German officers were not only accepted as military advisers but also as spies in the embassies of Russia's allies and as directors of Bolshevik foreign and domestic policies.

An original protocol revealed that two incriminating German documents were taken out of the Russian files under orders from Lenin and Trotsky and handed over to the German General Staff. The reason for it was that one of the papers proved that Germany had decided on war in June, 1914, while the other was the order for incendiarism in the United States. Small wonder that the Germans wanted the evidence destroyed.

Spread as plain as language could make it was the whole shameful story of the Brest-Litovsk "slave treaty," and no less shameful was the manner in which Bolshevik leaders suppressed their own socialist revolution in provinces where their activities interfered with German annexation. An original letter from the Germans to the Bolshevik Commissar of Foreign Affairs contained these stern orders:

"According to instructions of the representatives of our General Staff, I have the honor once more to insist that you recall from Estonia, Lithuania and Courland all agitators of the Central Executive Committee of the Council of Workmen's and Soldiers' Deputies." Another ordered the Bolsheviks to cease the agitation in Estonia that had "finally led to the local German landlords' being declared outlawed," and to "take immediate steps for the restoring of the rights of the above-mentioned German landlords."

Documents also gave a complete synopsis of the terms on which Russia intended to control all Russian industries. For five years from the signing of peace, English, French, and American capital was to be "banished," and coal, oil, and metallurgical branches of industry were to be developed under the control of a "supreme advisory organ consisting of ten Russian specialists, ten from the German industrial organizations and the German and Austrian banks." Germany and Austria were "to enjoy the unlimited privilege of sending into Russia mechanics and qualified workmen," and private banks in Russia were to arise "only with the consent of the union of German and Austrian banks."

In November, 1917, when Russia was still regarded as the ally of the United States, France, and Great Britain, the German General Staff was ordering Bolshevik leaders to inform it concerning the "quantity and storage place of the supplies which have been received from America, England and France, and also the units which are keeping guard over the military stores."

In December the Germans and Bolsheviks were arranging to send "agents-agitators and agents-destructors" out of Vladivostok to ports of the United States, Japan, and British colonies, and were also arranging for the issuance of fraudulent passports for Germans who were going to England, France, and America as spies and enemy agents.

A parade of letters showed how Bolshevik leaders and German officers arranged for the assassination of Russian nationalists, for the destruction of Polish legionnaires in the Russian army, for the disorganization of the Rumanian army and the deposing of the king, for the suppression of patriotic agitation among Russian soldiers, and for complete German

182

control of all Russian industries. A shabby business throughout, for at every turn one partner was trying to double-cross the other.

For three months the documents were submitted to every known test by various agencies of government, experts on ink, paper, and typewriter type faces being called in. Even when authenticity had been proved to the satisfaction of all, publication was still postponed out of the hope that the Bolsheviks would yet break away from their treacherous alliance. Instead of that, the partnership intensified, reaching the point where the Germans felt it safe to transfer divisions from the eastern front to the western front for the drive through France. Convinced, therefore, of the situation's hopelessness from the Allied standpoint, the President ordered publication, and the full story of the German-Bolshevik conspiracy began in the press on Sunday, September 15, 1918, and ran in daily installments through the week.

On Monday, when only one installment had been printed, the New York *Evening Post,* then in process of a change in ownership, came out with an editorial attack on the authenticity of the documents. Without the slightest knowledge of the remaining installments, one Alsberg, the editor, flatly charged that "some of the most important charges brought forward by Mr. Sisson were published in Paris months ago, and have, on the whole, been discredited."

On September 17 the *Post* carried another editorial, using its own manufactured confusion between the Russian calendar and the German calendar as the ground for a second attack upon the Committee's honesty. Nevertheless, an editorial on September 18 contained this surprising admission: "It [the *Post*] is ready to be convinced that all of the papers, originals, photographs and circulars are genuine."

Nevertheless, on the twenty-first the *Post* front-paged a statement by one Santeri Nuorteva, described as head of the Finnish Information Bureau, branding the documents as "brazen forgeries." Nowhere in the interview did Nuorteva make a single charge based on his own personal knowledge, but claimed that he received his assertions from Raymond Robins, Colonel William B. Thompson, and Thomas Thacher, all of the Red Cross organization in Russia. The *Post* printed Nuorteva's unsupported statement without the slightest effort to obtain corroboration, and also without any attempt to ascertain the true identity of the man.

Brought to Washington and put under examination, Nuorteva made a pitiful showing. At the very outset he confessed that he was on the Bolshevik pay roll, sent to the United States as a propagandist, and went on to admit that he had never spoken to Colonel Thompson or Mr. Thacher, and had never even seen them. As for Robins, he had met him briefly in New York in August. At a later date Nuorteva came out openly as a Bolshevik official, but becoming involved in the factional battles of New York Communists, was recalled to Russia. After a period of service in the Foreign Office, however, he was sent to prison for some offense and disappeared from view.

While no other daily echoed the charges of the *Post* or supported them even remotely, one or two professors of some standing voiced the view that the documents should be submitted to an authoritative historical body. I accepted the suggestion as an effective answer to the Communist attack, and asked the National Board for Historical Service to appoint a committee. The request was approved and these two scholars named: Dr. J. Franklin Jamieson, director of the Department of Historical Research of the Carnegie Institute, and Dr. Samuel N. Harper, professor of Russian Language and Institutions in the University of Chicago. It was also stated that other historians would be called in for consultation. On the appointment of the committee, every document was turned over, and Mr. Sisson himself was placed at its disposal.

In our release to the press we divided the documents into three groups: (1) originals, (2) photographs of documents believed still to be in the file rooms at Smolny, (3) typewritten circulars not traced to their originals. The first and second group—fifty-three in number—constituted the body of the report, and the circulars of the third group were printed merely as appendices, together with the plain statement that they were included for their interlacing and therefore corroborative value.

The committee went to work at once, and reported on October 26. With respect to the fifty-three documents on which we rested our charge of the German-Bolshevik conspiracy. this was the finding: "We have no hesitation in declaring that we see no reason to doubt the genuineness or authenticity of these fifty-three documents." Coming to the material in the ap-

184

pendices, about which we had made no claim of authenticity, the report refused to make any "confident declaration," but said: "We can only say that we see in these texts nothing that positively excludes the notion of their being genuine, little in them that makes it doubtful, though guarantees of their having been accurately copied, and accurately translated into Russian from the German, are obviously lacking." (Later on, Professor Paul Miliukov, minister in Kerenski's cabinet and well known as a prewar lecturer at our universities, vouched publicly for the authenticity of the appendix group.)

The report considered the specific criticisms of the *Post* in detail, and dismissed them almost contemptuously. After mentioning that the majority was largely concerned with dates, the historians said: "Most of them [the criticisms] fall away when it is known that the main series of documents, Nos. 1 to 53, are written in Russian, and dated in accordance with the calendar currently used in Petrograd."

By the time of the report, however, the fellow travelers had rallied their forces; led by *The Nation*, they denounced the whole proceeding as a "sham investigation."

CHAPTER 24

The Plague of Partisanship

*I*n nothing did World War II differ more radically from World War I than in the attitude of the Congress. It was not only that Franklin Roosevelt had the good fortune to find a Vandenberg and an Austin in the Senate, men big enough to put country above party and with a statesman's outlook. Both the people and a major part of the press had come to see isolation as a myth, and realized the necessity of a world order. Woodrow Wilson, on the other hand, faced a people who still thought in terms of Washington's Farewell Address, while in the Senate stood politicians who thought only in terms of office seeking and officeholding, the sordid habits of their lives blinding them to America's desperate necessities. From first to last a bushwhacking group, led by Henry Cabot Lodge, Boies Penrose, Hiram Johnson, Jim Reed, Lawrence Sherman, and Jim Watson, tore at public confidence with daily lies, hampered war activities by their obstructions, and broke many a spirit by mean persecutions.

Bernard Baruch and his associates on the War Industries Board were accused of using their positions to get inside information for stock-market deals; Julius Rosenwald, the selfless head of the Council of National Defense, was bedaubed regularly; Clarence Wooley was charged with manipulating the War Trade Board for the benefit of the American Radiator Company, and Howard Coffin and Colonel Edward A. Deeds, dynamic directors of the Aircraft Board, were shamed as men who put personal profit above public service. I myself escaped with no greater damage than being called a "licensed liar," a "depraved hack," a pro-German, and a Bolshevik.

There was no way in which an effective reply could be made, for members of Congress could not be called to account for any utterance on the floor of the House or Senate. Under the provisions of the Constitution, their mouths were above the law, and speech was not only free but privileged. The heavens might fall, the earth be consumed, but the right of a senator or a representative to defame remained inviolate.

Never very patient under attack, particularly when unjust, I made the blunder of fighting back. During the first year every Congressional blast met with vigorous reply, and on one occasion I changed over from pen to tongue. While I was answering questions after a speech before a New York forum, somebody asked, "What do you think of Congress?" Stupidly, but out of the heart, I replied, "Oh, it has been years since I went slumming."

A reporter for the *World* pounced on the answer, and the next morning saw it spread across the front page. A senator, looking up the definition in the dictionary, found that slums were a place where "low, abandoned and dissolute" creatures gathered, and straightway the scream arose that I had branded congressmen as low, abandoned, and dissolute. The debate raged for days, and a committee even waited on the President to demand my discharge. I handed in my resignation, but while

Mr. Wilson refused to accept it, he did insist that I "put a padlock on my lips."

The worst thing about partisanship was the shock and surprise, for with America at war, all of us were confident that politics would be adjourned. Our disillusionment was not long in coming, for before the President's war message had ceased to echo, Theodore Roosevelt pressed forward with the request that he be permitted to recruit volunteers for service in France. At the time the administration was seeking the enactment of a selective-service act, and the controversy came close to killing this vital measure. The depth of prejudice that it stirred at the time—and the persistence of that prejudice—may be judged by the following excerpt from William Allen White's recent autobiography:

> In those days, when I was supporting Wilson and the war, I came to dislike him—this man who was President—for his cold, mean, selfish policy toward those whom he liked to segregate and hate as his enemies, those who he probably fancied had forced him into preparedness, notably Roosevelt. I can still in my mind's eye recall the picture that I had from that day's press reports when Roosevelt, who more than any other thing on earth desired to fight for his country, walked up the curved path to the White House, swallowing his pride—and it was certainly a bitter mouthful—and asked the President to be allowed, under any terms, to recruit a regiment for France. The frigid malevolence with which Wilson denied this strong man's plea, made in what Wilson, being sensitive and wise, knew was excruciating abasement, carved deeply in my heart a picture of Woodrow Wilson that I could not erase when I wrote a book about him. His salving over his humiliation of Roosevelt with the oily pretext that it was in the interest of military discipline was, for me, worse than his real reason, wicked as I felt it to be.[1]

Never was anything more cruel and false, and the only possible explanation lies in the fact that Mr. White always held T.R. in an admiration that bordered on worship. Instead of a "regiment," the request was for a division of infantry and a divisional brigade of cavalry, and also included the services of scores of key men in the high command of the regular army. At no time, according to the record, did Mr. Roosevelt say that he would

---

[1] From the *Autobiography* of William Allen White, p. 534. By permission of The Macmillan Company, New York, publishers.

be willing to recruit "under any terms." Nor was the petition presented to the President until after it had been definitely rejected by the Secretary of War on the recommendation of the General Staff.

It was on February 2, two months before the declaration of war, that Mr. Roosevelt asked permission to raise his divisions. Secretary Baker, replying under date of February 9, pointed out the wastes and inefficiencies of the volunteer system, and stated flatly that the General Staff had decided that universal service was a military necessity. It was not until April 11, five days after the declaration of war, that Mr. Roosevelt reached Washington and asked the President to make an exception in his case.

It happened that I saw Mr. Wilson directly after the interview, going in as T.R. went out, and took the liberty of asking him about it. As he told it, the conversation was marked by both frankness and friendliness, and his own tone was warm as he spoke of the former President. Mr. Roosevelt's first remark was to the effect that he would "promise not to come back," and with that as a jocular opening, he made a strong case for his volunteer divisions, stressing the enthusiasm that would be aroused and the necessity for convincing the Allies that America was in the war with men as well as money.

The President agreed, but pointed out that even one exception would weaken his appeal to Congress for a selective-service law. His desk, he said, was piled high with petitions from senators, representatives, Indian fighters, Texas rangers, and Southern colonels, all eager to raise a company, a regiment, or a division for service in France. The war, he urged, was no Charge of the Light Brigade, but the grim subordination of human valor to the cold-blooded science of killing as developed by modern methods. Moreover, it was a "young man's war." The middle-aged must realize that the strain of the trenches was not for them.

Mr. Roosevelt admitted that his divisions might not prove a material contribution to the struggle, but stood firm on their "moral value." The President replied that the situation called for more than a gesture, and went on to discuss the imposing list of officers that Mr. Roosevelt wanted to take with him, asserting that it would rob the new army of the very men that would be needed for training.

His principal objection, however, was that any exception would imperil the enactment of the selective-service act and open the door to every public man with a yearning for military glory. At the last, he begged the former President to put his powerful influence behind the draft bill, and Mr. Roosevelt consented. When he left the White House it was in high good humor, and correspondents were told that Mr. Wilson had received him with the "utmost courtesy and consideration."

Mr. Roosevelt kept his word, seeing senators and congressmen, but also continued the drive for his volunteer divisions. Not even Secretary Baker's definite rejection, based on the recommendation of the General Staff, had power to move him. The fight was carried to the Senate floor, and for two weeks the Republican leaders held up the Selective Service Bill with an amendment that would have given permission to recruit Mr. Roosevelt's four volunteer divisions. In the end, by way of compromise, the mandatory feature of the amendment was withdrawn, making it optional for the President to accept or reject the Roosevelt proposal.

Straightway Mr. Wilson was faced with this consideration: to refuse was to give an impression of ungenerousness, an effect of partisan narrowness; to authorize the enlistment of volunteer divisions was to upset the whole machinery of the draft, and would serve notice on the General Staff that its recommendations were subject at all times to political pressure. In his public statement the President made no attempt to dodge the issue. After expressing a very real desire to have paid the Allies "the compliment of sending to their aid one of our most distinguished public men, an ex-President who has rendered many conspicuous public services and proved his gallantry in many striking ways," he said:

But this is not the time or the occasion for compliment or for any action not calculated to contribute to the immediate success of the war. The business now in hand is undramatic, practical and of scientific definiteness and precision. I shall act with regard to it at every step and in every particular under expert advice from both sides of the water. That advice is that the men most needed are men of the ages contemplated in the draft provisions of the present bill, not men of the age and sort contemplated in the section which authorizes the formation of volunteer units, and that for the preliminary training of the men who are to be drafted, we shall need

189

all of our experienced officers. Mr. Roosevelt told me, when I had the pleasure of seeing him a few weeks ago, that he would wish to have associated with him some of the most effective officers of the regular army. He named many of these, and they were men who cannot possibly be spared from the too small force of officers at our command for the much more pressing and necessary duty of training regular troops to be put in the field in France and Belgium as fast as they can be got ready. The first troops to be sent to France will be taken from the present forces of the regular army, and will be under the command of trained soldiers only.

Another hullaballoo was in connection with General Leonard Wood. When he was not sent to France, the Republicans raised the cry of politics and attacked the President and Secretary Baker for their "mean partisanship." The facts in the case were these: All of the generals in charge of training camps were sent to France in the summer of 1917, not only that they might see and study the new styles of fighting, but that General Pershing might pass on their character and abilities. After a time they were sent home, and in due course Pershing gave the Chief of Staff a list of the commanders that he wanted. *The name of General Wood was not on the list.* As General Pershing had been given fullest powers, and assured that his decisions would be final, the President and Secretary Baker approved the list without question. Nevertheless, the uproar continued for weeks.

Another lie that struck hard at America's morale had to do with the sailing of our first troop transports for France. It was charged that I had deliberately invented a submarine attack, issuing the lurid account of an ocean battle that never took place. Day after day the press and the Senate denounced me for the "Fourth of July hoax" and demanded my discharge for having perpetrated a "shameful fake." It was also the lie that hurt the most, for it carried beyond me and struck down a people's pride in their navy at a time when that pride was a military necessity.

Here are the facts in the case: The transports, leaving in June, 1917, sailed in four separate groups to minimize the dangers of the crossing. The precaution did not avail, for Admiral Gleaves, in command, cabled in code that two groups had been attacked by submarines. The news, of course, could not be released until the arrival in France of all four groups, but when this word came on July 3, the press was informed instantly. A wave of joyful enthusiasm swept the country, and for a moment the meannesses of partisanship were subordinated to the exaltations of patriotism.

Three days later, however, the Associated Press published a dispatch from its London correspondent stating that officers at the American flotilla base in English waters had declared that the transports were *not* attacked by submarines, and that the supposed U-boats were merely "floating spars or blackfish." The dispatch was anonymous in that it did not give the name of a single American officer responsible for the statement.

The partisan press accepted the A.P. cable as truth, and even friendly papers, unwilling to lose a good story, joined in the hue and cry. Demanding an immediate investigation of the "fake," Senator Boies Penrose trumpeted that I had "regaled the American people with the bombastic account of a battle that never occurred, and relating to a squadron which crossed the ocean in placid seas, and arrived on the other side without an important event."

Incredibly enough, while the attack was at its height corroborative reports poured in from independent sources. The New York *Times* carried an account of the attack on the transports written by its Paris correspondent. The New York *World* printed an interview with the "captain of an American ship," telling of the battle in detail, and even the Associated Press came out with statements from British sailors on ships near the encounter, substantiating our story in every particular.

We ourselves, unhappily, had to wait for Admiral Gleaves to file his full report, and owing to Navy red tape, it did not arrive until late July. Not only did the report sustain our release, but went beyond it, for the Admiral specifically stated that *three* of the four groups had been attacked. The flagship, in the first group, sighted one submarine; and the vessel *B* reported "strong indications of the presence of two submarines." One torpedo crossed the bow of the flagship, and another passed ahead of the *D*, "leaving a distinct wake."

The second group was also attacked, and Admiral Gleaves claimed that one U-boat was sunk. To quote:

The *H*, leading the second group, encountered two submarines ... about a hundred miles off the coast of France. The *I* investigated the wake of the first without further discovery. The *J* sighted the bow wave of the second at a distance of 1500 yards and headed for it at a speed of 25 knots ... the *J* passed about 25 yards ahead of a mass of bubbles which were coming up from the wake, and let go a depth charge just ahead. Several pieces of timber, quantities of oil, bubbles and debris came to the surface. Nothing more was seen of the submarine.

The *K* of the third group was made the target for torpedoes and opened fire from the port guns. "Lieutenant V., in personal charge of the firing, reports that he saw, with all the gun crews and look-outs aft, the submarine fire two torpedoes toward the direction of the convoy, which sheered off from base course to right 90 degrees when alarm was sounded."

Here at last was the ultimate word, the conclusive proof that the Secretary of the Navy had not lied. And what happened? The Senate ignored the report, and the press, without exception, either chopped it to pieces or printed it inconspicuously. Such editors as took notice of it dismissed the report as "the last chapter in an unfortunate incident." What happened next was an inquiry into the sending of the Associated Press dispatch, and on August 3 these findings were forwarded to Washington by Commander J. R. Pringle:

Frank America, the A.P. correspondent at Queenstown, had received a wire from his London office telling of the submarine attack and asking for a "follow-up" story. Permission was refused. The report said that:

He sent to the London office a wire intended for the private information of his superiors, and not intended for publication, and that since the wire was private, he did not consider it necessary to submit it to censorship ... that the information contained in this wire represented his general impression formed as the result of casual conversations held with a couple of officers and some men. That he did not know any one of the officers or men, but had met them on the pier, in the streets or at the hotel.

It appears to me [continued Pringle's report] that so far as the publication of the dispatch is concerned, Mr. America is more sinned against than sinning. He felt that his dispatch would not be published, and if he was justified in his belief, his superiors have put him in a very embarrassing position. ... I doubt very much whether any of the persons from whom Mr. America got his information were aware of the fact that the Secretary had given out a statement.

There is a general tendency among officers and men of the Force to attribute many cases of supposed torpedo attack to the sighting of blackfish or porpoise, while spars are sometimes mistaken for periscopes, and any statements made are much more likely to have been intended to express a belief that the reports were exaggerated at the source than to express anything else.

What a record! The word of an admiral of the Navy, the authorized statement of the Secretary of the Navy, both set aside and publicly shamed on the strength of gossip by men "met on the pier, in the streets or at the hotel," and whose names were not even known to the correspondent! And the wire sent as *private*, and *not* intended for publication. Did the newspapers print these findings? *Not one!*

By the summer of 1918 things had reached the point of unbearability. Up to that time the Committee had been supported by money from an appropriation of $50,000,000 that Congress had voted the President as an emergency fund for the "national security and defense." Going to the President, I asked Mr. Wilson to cut me loose from this private purse, as far as the domestic work of the CPI was concerned, and let me go to Congress for an appropriation. This, I urged, would give me my day in court, and bring lies out into the open. "Anything," I told him, "is better than being nibbled to death by ducks."

He agreed, and so for three days, eight hours a day, every activity of the Committee and every dollar of expenditure were subjected to hostile examination by a House committee. Not only that, but every charge of dishonesty, inaccuracy, and partisanship, and also my "temperamental qualifications." I found that agents had even been sent to Kansas City and Denver to find out what I had written or said. Much of it sounded pretty high-pitched as congressmen intoned it, and I expressed regret for certain extravagances of expression, explaining that they were due to the "emotionalism of the moment."

"Just what do you mean by that?" barked Uncle Joe Cannon.

"Well, sir," I answered, "let me illustrate. When Theodore Roosevelt and his Bull Moosers referred to you and other members of the Old Guard as second-story men and burglars, he didn't really mean that you robbed homes and stores. Political feeling ran strong in 1912, and the statement proceeded from what I call the emotionalism of the moment."

193

The press, on the morning after this colloquy, carried the story that I had "recanted," but nothing was further from the truth. What I said was this: "Every single thing for which I have fought is today *law,* in either federal statutes, state statutes, or municipal ordinances. There is not an advocacy of mine that has not been approved by American majorities. My crime is that I fought for these reforms before they were fashionable. It is true that I have urged constitutional changes, but I refuse to admit that this was sacrilege. Times change, new needs arise, and it is the inalienable right of citizens to keep pace with these changes and these needs."

At the end of the three days I was given $1,250,000 to carry on the domestic work of the Committee. Pitifully small compared to World War II appropriations, but big money in 1918. Moreover, in reporting to the House as a whole, Republicans joined with Democrats in the statement that the work of the CPI had great importance and had been marked by honesty, competence, and patriotism. The press, with only a few exceptions, ignored the result of the hearings, and after a lapse of time sufficient to dull memory, Reed, Penrose, Johnson, and Lodge brought forth the same old lies and put them through their spavined paces.

CHAPTER 25

High Priests of Hate

*N*ot the least of the fears that agitated the country in the first days of war was with respect to the attitude of our foreign born. From every section came gloomy predictions of wholesale disloyalty that would manifest itself in armed uprisings, sabotage, incendiarism, and domestic riot, making monster internment camps a stern necessity. Even actual revolutions were predicted in such German centers as Milwaukee, St. Louis, and Cincinnati.

Why not? For years the United States had discharged its

194

duty to the immigrant by glib reference to the melting pot, and yet nowhere in the land was there any evidence that the pot had done any melting. Hopeful thousands, coming to America with their hearts in their hands, met with only indifference and neglect, and were denied the bright promises of democracy. Cheated by employers, loan sharks, and employment agencies; excluded from American life as "wops," "hunkies," "dagoes," and "sheenies"; able to learn English only at night schools after drudging days of toil; herded in ghettos and foreign quarters by their poverty and ignorance—what more natural than to assume their disloyalty?

To meet this troubling situation, I called in Josephine Roche, a strong right hand in my Colorado days, and established a Division of Work among the Foreign Born. Getting under way with her usual certainty, she established close relations with some twenty racial groups, utilizing existing organizations wherever possible, and began a drive that carried down from cities to remote hamlets. It was not only that their own speakers, their own writers, and their own newspapers were used to make for full understanding, but through volunteer helpers Miss Roche went into homes and aided bewildered thousands to solve the problems presented by draft regulations, income-tax provisions, and other laws that confused them.

Here was a vital work that commanded the co-operation of every American, yet from the start Miss Roche met with the ugly antagonism of the countless "patriotic" bodies that sprang up all over the land. It was not that these groups were bloodthirsty, or that they did not want to be helpful, but simply that chauvinism was forced upon them by the necessities of their organization. As they were dependent for existence upon cash donations, it was essential that they "make a showing" in order that contributions might continue to be attracted. As they were outside the regular war machinery, and especially as they were not organized for fixed service, it was inevitable that these "societies" and "leagues" should turn to the emotions as a field of activity, and try to create an effect by noise, attack, and hysteria.

In the first days the Committee tried faithfully to establish working relations with such organizations, but it soon developed that they did not want to put their emotionalism in harness, but preferred to keep it free for exhibition purposes.

For a time they filled the air with all sorts of sensational charges with regard to "spies" and "intrigues," but after one high official was called before a New York grand jury and forced to admit sheer recklessness of statement, they confined themselves to general thundering.

Not the least of their complaints was our refusal to preach a gospel of hate. From the first we held that undocumented "atrocity stories" were bound to have bad reactions, for if the Germans could manage to refute one single charge, they would use it to discredit our entire indictment. This view was shared by the President and the War Department, and once on the authority of General Pershing, and again by direction of General March, we issued denials of "horror stuff" unsupported by date and place.

The chauvinists, however, managed to figure largely in the Liberty Loan drives, over which the Committee had no control, and flooded the country with posters showing "bloody boots," trampled children, and mutilated women. Unfortunately, many worthy people held the CPI responsible, and to this day I am reproached for having manufactured hysteria.

The National Security League and the American Defense Society, officered by prominent citizens, were easily the most active and obnoxious. At all times their patriotism was a thing of screams, violence, and extremes, and their savage intolerances had the burn of acid. From the first they leveled attacks against the foreign-language groups, and were chiefly responsible for the development of a mob spirit in many sections. They worked, of course, in fertile ground, for there is a simplicity about hate that makes it attractive to a certain type of mind. It makes no demand on the mental processes, it does not require reading, estimate, or analysis, and by reason of its removal of doubt gives an effect of decision, a sense of well-being.

A principal demand of the chauvinists was for a prohibition against every other language but English. No effort at distinction was made, for along with their attacks on German they also clamored for a ban against Italian, French, Czech, Spanish, Russian, Danish, Norse, and Swedish, the languages of our allies and the neutrals. Several states yielded to this vicious pressure, an example being this proclamation by the governor of Iowa:

First, English should and must be the only medium of instruction in public, private, denominational or other similar schools;

Second, conversation in public places, on trains or over the telephone must be in the English language;

Third, all public addresses should be in the English language; and

Fourth, let those who cannot speak or understand English conduct their religious worship in their homes.

The Council of Defense for Seward County, Nebraska, requested all the churches in the district to conduct their services in English, except one for old people who could not understand English. The minister of the Danish Lutheran church of Staplehurst, one Hansen, asked the Council's permission to continue preaching in Danish because he was not young when he came to America, and because his bad ears had prevented him from learning English sufficiently well to preach in it. The Council denied his request and also refused him a year's grace while he found other work to support himself and his family.

In other states similar prohibitions were put into effect, compelling many sudden changes in schools, churches, and the press. The Committee did not deny the evil that these efforts were attempting to cure, but we did insist that it was criminally stupid to ignore plain facts. If there were thousands of foreigners who could neither speak nor read any language but their own, where was the fault but in America's own failure? The drive against the use of their native tongues merely pushed them further into aloofness, and robbed us of the opportunity to reach them with our speakers and literature.

The sweep of mean intolerance, of course, developed a mob spirit, and in some states loyalty meetings of the foreign groups were actually stoned. In one Texas town, virtually all of the young men of the Czechoslovak colony volunteered, and their departure was made the occasion of a great demonstration. Many old people were there, and the speeches were made in Czech. Without any attempt to inquire into the nature of the meeting, "native patriots" smashed the windows with rocks, attacked the audience, and drove them from the building as though they had been Huns caught in some atrocity.

In the Northwest, where Germans and Scandinavians figured largely, there was not only a pro-German sentiment in the be-

197

ginning, but people had been fed the lie that it was a "rich man's war," without other purpose than to protect the loans of Wall Street bankers. What more important than to preach the gospel of Americanism? Yet when the Committee tried to send its speakers in, the chauvinists barred them. Even when we persisted, and arranged Liberty Loan rallies and patriotic meetings, they had to be held in the fields or in barns. Parades were stopped by home guards, automobiles were overturned, and on one wretched occasion a baby of six months was torn from its mother's arms by the powerful stream from a fire hose. "Tar and feather parties" were common, and even deportations took place.

The state councils of defense did splendid work as a rule, but there were some infamous exceptions, for many of these councils conducted themselves in a manner that would have been lawless in any other than a "patriotic" body. During Liberty Loan drives, for example, it became a habit in certain sections to compel a regular income-tax return from the foreign born. Men claiming authority would insist on a statement of earnings and expenditures, and then calmly announce the amount of the contribution that the dazed victims were expected to make. Anything in the nature of resistance was set down as "disloyalty," and some of the penalties visited were expulsion from the community, personal ill treatment, or some pleasant little attention like painting the house yellow.

"Americanization" was another pet activity of the chauvinists. The technique consisted of a group descent on homes in foreign quarters and bawled demands that the inmates learn English overnight, cancel subscriptions to foreign-language newspapers, and make the Constitution and the Declaration of Independence instant studies for their children. Miss Roche came in one day with the delightful story about some ladies who descended on the tenement home of a Bohemian family in Chicago during the first summer of the war.

"We are here," the spokesman announced impressively, "in the interests of Americanization."

"I'm sorry," faltered the woman of the house, "but you'll have to come back next week."

"What!" The cry was a choice compound of protest and reproach. "You mean that you have no *time* for our message! That you want to put *off* your entrance into American life?"

"No, no!" The poor Bohemian woman fell straightway into a panic, for not even a policeman has the austere authoritativeness of those who elect themselves to be light-bringers. "We're *perfectly* willing to be Americanized. Why, we never turn *any* of them away. But there's nobody home but me. The boys volunteered, my man's working on munitions, and all the rest are out selling Liberty bonds. I don't want you to get mad, but *can't* you come back next week?"

The press, from which we had the right to expect help, failed us miserably. One alien speaking disrespectfully of the flag could be sure of front-page notice, but ten thousand aliens could gather in a great patriotic demonstration without earning an agate line. Paderewski told me that nothing depressed his people more than the manner in which the newspapers ignored Polish loyalty meetings, and Dr. Masaryk had the same story to tell about the Czechoslovaks. Hungarian-Americans, Yugoslavs, the National Croatian Society, Scandinavian organizations, and Dutch groups staged spectacular parades and voted thousands for Liberty bonds, all without getting more than a line or two.

As a consequence, the chauvinists had the field to themselves, singing their hymns of hate and damning officials for inefficiency and spinelessness when they failed to produce traitors to be put before a firing squad. Not until the Praeger lynching did the madness show signs of abatement. This poor devil, absolutely innocent as proved afterward, was lynched by a mob that refused to grant his pleas for an interpreter. I went to President Wilson at once, and his public denunciation of the mob spirit sobered the people as a whole, if not the super-patriots.[1]

Through it all, Miss Roche and her helpers worked with a patience that never failed, nor was it only pamphlets and spoken appeals that they employed. In every city and town

---

[1] German propaganda paid particular attention to the Negro, stressing racial discrimination in both military and civil life. At no time, however, was this a cause of concern for the Committee. Newton Baker appointed Dr. Emmet Scott, Booker Washington's secretary, as an Assistant Secretary of War, and this able, understanding man handled the problems of his people. Some 2,900,000 Negroes answered their country's call, and whether as combat troops or in labor battalions, served loyally.

there were devoted groups who gave days and nights to straightening out the difficulties of the poor, bewildered, bedeviled thousands whose ignorance of English and American ways made them the prey of rascals and superpatriots alike. Bags of mail, pouring in from unhappy men and women, were answered either by letter or in person. In the end, when final tallies were made, it was found that those communities where revolutions had been feared led all others in volunteer enlistments and Liberty Loan subscriptions.

The record of North Dakota, branded by the chauvinists as a "nest of disloyalty," owing to the large number of foreign born, may be cited as typical. Despite three successive crop failures, the farmers of that state oversubscribed the first Liberty Loan 140 per cent; the second 70 per cent; and the third 76 per cent. With only one regiment at the outset, North Dakota promptly recruited a second, and prior to enactment of the Selective Service Bill 3,887 men entered the service as volunteers. The cost per certified conscript in North Dakota was $1.83 against an average of $4.23 for all other states. In one Red Cross drive, North Dakota's allotment was $200,000, and it subscribed $575,000. Its Y.M.C.A. allotment was $100,000, and it subscribed $175,000.

In 1918 North Dakota increased its wheat acreage over 630,000 acres at the request of the government; it was one of the first states to decree that all persons between the ages of eighteen and fifty must be employed in essential industry; also to provide a moratorium protecting soldiers from foreclosure of loans.

As for the disloyalty of the foreign born, never was a fear more thoroughly disproved. A scientific system of registration, prescribed by law, revealed that there were about five hundred thousand German enemy aliens living in the United States, and between three and four million Austro-Hungarian enemy aliens. These figures, as a matter of course, did not include the millions of naturalized citizens, or the sons and daughters of such millions. Out of this large number just *six thousand* were adjudged sufficiently disaffected to be detained under Presidential warrants! Even a large percentage of these, as a matter of common sense and justice, were eventually released from the Army internment camps under a strict parole system.

As for criminal prosecutions, 1,532 persons were arrested

under the provisions of the Espionage Act prohibiting disloyal utterance, propaganda, etc.; 65 persons for threats against the President; 10 persons for sabotage; and under the penal code, with relation to conspiracy, 908 indictments were returned, the last group including the I.W.W. cases. Even this does not spell guilt in every instance, for there were acquittals as well as convictions.

Opposed to this small percentage were the millions of foreign birth or descent who sacrificed to buy Liberty bonds, and the other millions who fought in France for their adopted country. Nothing was more significant than the list of those cited for distinguished service by General Pershing, for on it were hundreds of names betokening other than native origin—Schulteis, Mickiewicz, Amato, Ceglinski, Olson, Tvrzicka, Rosenstein, Hinkovic, and so on.

The climax of Miss Roche's work came on July 4, 1918, when the representatives of thirty-three foreign-language groups journeyed to Mount Vernon to reaffirm their devotion to America and American ideals. As John McCormack sang "The Battle Hymn of the Republic," they walked one by one up to the tomb of Washington and offered a prayer as they laid wreaths on the grave. Then, easily and naturally, they gathered about President Wilson, who stood on a grassy mound to the right of the vault, while their spokesman read an address of which this was a part:

"One hundred and forty-two years ago today a group of men, animated with the same spirit as that of the man who lives here, founded the United States of America on the theory of free government with the consent of the governed. That was the beginning of America. As the years went on, and one century blended with another, men and women came even from the uttermost ends of the earth to join them. We have called them alien, but they were never alien. Though they spoke not a word of the language of this country, though they groped only dimly toward its institutions, they were already Americans in soul, or they never would have come. We are the latest manifestations of the American soul."

If I have devoted a chapter to the Division of Work among the Foreign Born, it is because the problem remains unsolved. There are still ghettos and foreign colonies walled off from their communities and viewed with either indifference or dislike. Signs are not lacking to show that intolerance is far from dead in the land. Every day witnesses hundreds of naturalizations, but at best it is a purely political procedure, barren of all true meaning.

In the second World War, as in the first, the millions of foreign born rallied to the colors with no less enthusiasm and bravery than the native stock. Hope, however, has a way of festering when turned back on itself year after year, and there is a death of the spirit infinitely more tragic than any death of the body.

Unless we abandon the great American tradition of the Open Door, large numbers of Europe's homeless and despairing will be coming to the United States, and if the melting pot does not melt, better for them and for us if they do not come. And the pot will not melt unless the fire of democracy is kindled under it. How can that be done? Why, through slum clearance, stricter enforcement of child-labor laws, and greater emphasis on education. More schools and better schools; more teachers and better-paid teachers. What so shocking as the fact that the pay of a public school teacher, and even the salary of a college professor, is less than that of an unskilled laborer?

And why not some governmental control of the thousand and one organizations that have as their professed objective the promotion of "patriotism" in one form or another? No man is permitted to drive an automobile until he has passed an examination, and yet it is the right of every Tom, Dick, and Harry to put together a league, a society, or a committee without the slightest inquiry into fitness or honesty of purpose.

CHAPTER 26

President Wilson Saves My Face

Of the many American elections that have cast discredit on the democratic process, that of November, 1918, was the most inexplicable and disheartening. The war's end was in plain sight, with Allied victory due in no small part to Woodrow Wilson's leadership and moral offensives, and yet the vote indicated popular rejection of both the man and his policies. Every day witnessed further disintegration of the Central Powers, enemy after enemy surrendering on the basis of the Fourteen Points, and still Republican repudiation of these points was endorsed by the election returns. Nor was there the excuse of confusion, for Theodore Roosevelt and other spokesmen made them the principal point of attack.

The chief target was Point 3: "The removal, as far as possible, of all economic barriers, and the establishment of equality of trade conditions among all the nations consenting to the peace, and associating themselves for its maintenance." This, declared Will Hays, chairman of the Republican National Committee, was an "absolute commitment to free trade with all the world, thus giving Germany out of hand the fruits of a victory greater than she could win by fighting a hundred years."

In the main, however, the Republican quarrel was with Mr. Wilson's "arrogance" in daring to "dictate" peace terms. His Fourteen Points were an "insult to our noble Allies," and should be repudiated, for what to do with the Central Powers was something for the victors to decide in the hour of Germany's defeat. Who did Woodrow Wilson think he was, laying down the law to Britain, France, and Italy?

When the election is analyzed, however, certain extenuating circumstances stand clear. Out of overconfidence, Democratic leaders had not been on their jobs, and the party went into the campaign without funds or organization. The Republicans, on the other hand, had perfected a machinery that worked with smooth precision, and were in even better shape financially.

Proof of this was furnished one year later when Truman Newberry, who had defeated Henry Ford for the Senate in Michigan, was indicted for violation of the state's corrupt-practices act. The trial developed that more than a million had been spent, and Newberry, along with sixteen others, was found guilty. An obliging Supreme Court, however, saved him from prison by ruling that the Michigan act was unconstitutional.

For another thing, President Wilson let the politicians persuade him to make an appeal for the return of a Democratic majority to both Senate and House. In it, to be sure, he tried to guard against the charge of narrow partisanship by inclusion of this paragraph: "I have no thought of suggesting that any particular party is paramount in matters of patriotism. I feel too deeply the sacrifices which have been made in this war by all our citizens, irrespective of party affiliations, to harbor any such idea. I mean only that the difficulties and delicacies of our present task are of a sort that makes it imperatively necessary that a nation should give its undivided support to the government under unified leadership."

It was a blunder, nevertheless, and the Republicans took quick and unscrupulous advantage of it. Every medium was used to brand the appeal as an "ungenerous, unjust, wanton and mendacious attack" on their patriotism, and "an insult to every loyal Republican in the land." As if Democratic lack of money and organization were not enough, the flu epidemic came along to prevent the meetings at which the charges might have been answered.

The margin of victory was small, for it was only the vote of Truman Newberry that made possible the reorganization of the Senate by the Republicans. Coming to the chairmanship of the Committee on Foreign Affairs, Henry Cabot Lodge was lifted from mediocrity to evil power, and enabled to translate his personal hatreds into national policies. At Lodge's back stood Theodore Roosevelt, through with Bull Moose heresies and again a party man.

One week after the election came the Armistice, and in the joy of it the election returns, and their meaning, were lost to sight. Not one of the administration forces but looked on the denunciation of the Fourteen Points as "campaign stuff," a political play to the bitterness of certain minorities. The Republicans would not dare to continue their repudiation.

Within twenty-four hours of the signing of the Armistice, orders were issued for the immediate cessation of every activity of the CPI. Many of the divisions had a continuing value, but I believed that a Committee on Public Information had no proper governmental function in time of peace. No matter how honest its intent, how scrupulously impartial its administration, such an agency was bound to be caught in the net of political controversy and could not possibly escape the charge of favoring the party in power.

On November 14 the press was released from all obligations imposed by the voluntary censorship, and on November 15 the censorship of cables came to an end. At the same time I stated publicly that the Paris conference would be wide open as far as the United States was concerned, and that every effort would be made to have France and Britain adopt a similar policy. In the interest of full coverage, any accredited correspondent would be given a passport.

While I was deep in the liquidation of the CPI, President Wilson was kind enough to ask me to go with him to the conference in a personal capacity. The honor, of course, lifted me to the skies, but my stay in the clouds was tragically short. Some months before, Postmaster General Burleson had been given authority to take over the cables if and when the need arose, and in late November he suddenly decided to exercise his power. Just why was never explained. Going to the President, I urged him to overrule Burleson, but in his preoccupation with other things he dismissed the matter as unimportant.

As I had foreseen, the press and Congress went raving mad. The President and I had *lied,* for now it stood plain that correspondents were to be "gagged, muzzled, stifled, and throttled." Senator Hiram Johnson moaned, "What a sad thing it is that Creel should ration the news which is to be received by the American people," and New of Indiana declared that I had already decided "to limit the press to 28,000 words a day." When I tried to stem the flow of falsehood by denials, Sherman of Illinois stated that I was about as worthy of trust as a "drunkard in a wine cellar."

I went to the President at once and released him from his offer, pointing out that any service I might be able to render would be more than offset by the harm of my presence at his side. "The Senate group," I explained, "will seize on it as support for their charge of news suppression and distortion. But, sir," I added, "since it has been published that I am to be a member of your party on the *George Washington,* I've *got* to go. These last two years have been pretty hard for me, and if it is made to appear that I have lost your confidence, I'm sunk. All I want is a chance to save my face. As soon as possible after arrival, we can work out some mission that will take me away from Paris and out of the picture."

With his usual generous understanding, the President agreed. I talked with him often on the *George Washington,* and one evening as we walked the deck I spoke of the tremendous help

205

that his addresses had been to us in our work, and how the peoples of the world had rejoiced in his words. He stood silent for a while, and then answered slowly and soberly: "It is a great thing that you have done, but I am wondering if you have not unconsciously spun a net for me from which there is no escape. It is to America that the whole world turns today, not only with its wrongs, but with its hopes and grievances. The hungry expect us to feed them, the roofless look to us for shelter, the sick of heart and body depend upon us for cure. All of these expectations have in them the quality of terrible urgency. There must be no delay. It has been so always. People will endure their tyrants for years, but they tear their deliverers to pieces if a millennium is not created immediately. Yet you know, and I know, that these ancient wrongs, these present unhappinesses, are not to be remedied in a day or with a wave of the hand. What I seem to see—with all my heart I hope that I am wrong—is a tragedy of disappointment."

Brest brimmed with flower-bearing children, and on the way to Paris the train passed through a veritable lane of women and little ones crying: *"Vive l'Amérique! Vive le Président!"* They crowded the stations, they lined the fields, and their shrill pipings were the last thing we heard at night, the first thing in the early dawn.

Before I had been in Paris a day, the correspondents waited on me and demanded that I come to their rescue. Only four transatlantic cables were available for their use, a totally inadequate service, and the men who had been most hysterical in demanding that I get out were loudest in insisting that I stay on. The necessities of the situation left me no alternative. As a first measure to lighten the cable load, I agreed to keep the Navy's wireless in operation and transmit each day all official statements, major speeches, etc., making simultaneous delivery in New York to the three press associations. After further study, we also consented to send a daily total of 3,500 words of textual matter under the same terms.

It had been the President's expectation that the conference would convene on his arrival, but Lloyd George, Clemenceau, and Orlando had no such intent. What they wanted was time for the people to forget Wilson's "ideals," and start to thinking in terms of annexations and indemnities. The President chafed under the delay, but while resisting all efforts to have him visit the devastated areas, he could not well refuse to accept the invitations of the English and the Italians. I did not go with him to London, as arrangements for the trip to Rome had been placed in my lap.

In Paris the government had been at pains to keep the President from talking to the people, and Italy's statesmen adopted the same tactics. When I reached Rome a delegation informed me that no arrangements had been made for any public appearance, and that the masses simply *must* see and hear Woodrow Wilson. With the consent of the President I organized a meeting, and cleared the time and place with the proper authorities. As early as one o'clock more than fifty thousand people packed and jammed the Piazza Venezia. When word finally came at six that Mr. Wilson was not coming, a riot broke out. That evening the President told me how Baron Sonnino had kept him away by saying that the meeting had been canceled.

As the Italian visit neared its end, I went to the President and asked for some European mission that would take me away from the peace conference and at the same time save my face. After we had talked things over, he suggested a journey to Czechoslovakia and Poland, for the two new states were disputing over the Teschen coal fields; after that a swing through Hungary, where Count Károlyi was teetering insecurely as president of an infant republic.

There was no passenger service of any kind between Italy and Bohemia, and we traveled to Prague with a troop train of Czechoslovak legionaries. There were about one thousand of them—veterans who had seen fighting on many fronts—and with their horses and guns and baggage they filled thirty-five freight cars. For our own accommodation we managed to secure a battered passenger coach, stripped of all upholstery and indescribably dirty. To add to congestion our party of fourteen was asked to share this car with Colonel Phillippe, the French officer in charge of the legionaries, his aides, and the newly appointed British chargé d'affaires, who was trying to reach Prague at the earliest possible moment.

The journey to Prague from Padua took almost four days, a weary crawl through the devastated Piave Plain and over the Alps, with never a chance to get the bitter cold out of one's marrow. We took off nothing but our hats when we slept on the narrow seats, and aside from hot coffee made over char-

207

coal braziers, we ate out of mail sacks that we had filled with dried apricots, Italian bread, bully beef, and canned stuff. Heaven only knows what would have happened to us but for the blankets lent in Padua by the American Red Cross. The stations in Austria were closed as we passed, owing to fear of trouble, and all that we saw of the people were sullen faces peering at us through railings or from the hills. They looked well fed and fat, the villages were whole, and the land was unravaged—all in sharp contrast to the hunger and devastation of France and Italy. I knew, of course, that the peace of the world depended upon just treatment of these defeated enemies, but I could not help thinking that justice took much of the joy out of life.

The one thrill of the dreary journey came to us on the night we reached the border of what had once been the ancient kingdom of Bohemia, the new boundary line of the free republic of Czechoslovakia. For an hour the whole train had hummed to a vast excitement, for among the legionaries were many men who had gone into exile as youths, and others who had been fighting abroad for four years, out of touch entirely with their homes and people. No sooner had we stopped at the little station across the border than every legionary was off the train, kissing the sacred soil that had been won at last from the Austrian. Officers and men embraced with tears running down their cheeks; then the entire thousand grouped reverently and, lifting their faces to the hills and the stars, sang the national hymn of Bohemia. A song in minor key for the most part, like the songs of all oppressed peoples, but rising at the end to a tremendous challenge that rang like a trumpet. After that a great cheering for America, "the hope of the world."

If any of those legionaries are alive today, I wonder what they think about the vassalage of their country to Russia. A republic in name only, with President Beneš a Moscow marionette, and a once proud people compelled to swallow every known humiliation.

CHAPTER 27

The Ruins of Empire

Prague, after the confusions of Paris, was a delight. Woodrow Wilson was no less an idol than President Masaryk, and the people were a unit, putting country above parties and political feuds. In the coalition cabinet that worked as a team were Socialists and Agrarians, and even a Catholic priest who served as director of railroads. Our association in Washington had given me a high regard for Dr. Masaryk, and it deepened immeasurably as I sat with him in the Hradčany, Bohemia's national palace, and listened to his plans and hopes.

Not the least of Woodrow Wilson's tragedy was that the smallness of the new state prevented the great Czech from playing a larger part in the peace conference, for he had infinitely more breadth and vision than Lloyd George, Clemenceau, or Orlando. With his broad forehead, deep-set thinker's eyes, and general suggestion of the university, Dr. Masaryk gave little hint of the revolutionary, and yet he had known what it was to be proscribed and hunted.

In the course of one conversation, I mentioned to the President that I had been reading Palacký, Bohemia's famous historian, and commented on his statement that "if the great state of Austria had not been long in existence, it would be necessary and urgent to create it for the sake of Europe, nay, of mankind."

"Yes," Dr. Masaryk replied, "it is true that the Austro-Hungarian empire had value, doing away with trade barriers and rivalries between component states. But we can do democratically what the empire did autocratically. What I have in mind is a Danubian association that will give Middle Europe all the benefits of federation without its servitudes." His death, unfortunately, prevented the fulfillment of the dream, and Eduard Beneš, his successor, lacked the character and ability to make it come true.

When the talk turned to Russia, President Masaryk made no secret of his apprehensions, seeing no difference between the despotism of Lenin and Trotsky and the autocracy of the czars. "Bolshevism," he said, "will not stop short of absolute dictatorship, and with its aggressions, hatreds, and intolerances, it is bound to be a threat to the peace of Europe."

As an example of Bolshevik ill faith, the President went on to tell of his experiences during the time he led 200,000 Czechoslovaks from the Ukraine to Vladivostok. These men, deserting to the Russians, had fought valiantly against the Germans, Austrians, and Hungarians and refused to lay down their arms when Lenin and Trotsky made peace with the Central Powers. Rather than surrender to ancient enemies they would march across the whole of Russia to the Pacific, hopeful of ships that would take them halfway around the world to join the Allies on the Western front. There was no quarrel with the Russians for quitting, but until their country won freedom, Czechoslovaks must continue the fight.

After prolonged negotiations Dr. Masaryk gained permission for a peaceful departure, the agreement being signed by Leon Trotsky himself. In return the Czechoslovaks handed over the vast stores of artillery and munitions that they had captured from the Germans, so that they set forth without other arms than machine guns and rifles. Before the legions had gone a hundred miles, however, the Bolsheviks broke faith, issuing orders for the arrest and imprisonment of every Czechoslovak.

There was no plume in Dr. Masaryk's straw hat, and his baton was a cotton umbrella, but at his command the exiles swarmed from their cars and gave battle against overwhelming odds in numbers and equipment. The first engagement proved the superiority of the disciplined Czechoslovaks, for the red troops were more of a mob than an army, but defeat only enraged Lenin and Trotsky. Every station on the Trans-Siberian Railroad witnessed bloody fighting; tunnels were blocked, rails torn up, ambuscades prepared, but at last the long, weary stretches lay behind, and Dr. Masaryk led his "children" to the gates of Vladivostok and captured the port after a brief but savage struggle.

What a story! Even now I thrill to the memory of that evening in the ancient Hradčany when the aging statesman, peering shortsightedly through his spectacles, told of treachery, blood, and battle as quietly and detachedly as though he himself had not been the central figure. And what a tragedy that the years could not have been rolled back, returning him to youth and strength!

On making inquiry into the Teschen situation, I found that the Poles had marched in and that the Czechs were massing to repel what they termed an invasion. Eager in his desire for a peaceful settlement of the controversy, President Masaryk approved the suggestion that I visit the coal fields and then proceed to Cracow for a conference with the Poles. The Catholic priest who was head of the railroads put the private car of Emperor Franz Josef at my disposal and I set forth for Teschen in state.

At the time, incredible as it may seem today, the regard of Europeans for America was actually religious in its devotion. No matter what the American or where the place, crowds followed him as though he had come down from Sinai. In many towns and hamlets, young second lieutenants were called on to render all manner of decisions, the people having no doubt whatsoever as to their possession of infallibility. In Teschen, therefore, I found myself playing Moses, a role somewhat difficult to sustain without the aid of knee-length whiskers. Talking with the Czech commanders in Ostrava, I pointed out the disastrous effects of a border war and insisted that the dispute be solved by peaceful conference. Proceeding to Cracow, I made the same speeches to the Poles, and out of the conversations came a truce and eventual agreement on a plebiscite.

Speaking neither Czech nor Polish, and dependent upon interpreters, I never spoke without thinking of a story told me by Mary Roberts Rinehart. A government agent, meeting with the Blackfeet tribe for the settlement of some difference, sat for an hour while the chief delivered an address in praise of his people and their courage. Whether it was in battle with the foe outnumbering them a thousand to one, or amid storm when the lightning crashed down the giants of the forest, or face to face with savage beasts, their jaws agape, the Blackfeet had never known fear. On and on he went, citing innumerable examples of bravery and fortitude, and sat down at the end fairly bathed in sweat. Then the interpreter rose to his feet, and flipping a thumb in the direction of the chief, laconically remarked, "This guy he say he not afraid of nobody."

After finishing up in Czechoslovakia I set off for Budapest, breaking the journey in Vienna. My brief stay in the Austrian capital had all the quality of a nightmare, for gone was the laughter and the music that I remembered, and there was the smell of death in the air. A republic, replacing the Hapsburg dynasty, had consented to very heavy cessions of territory, and where once the proud city had queened it over an empire, now the starving, broken people stood in lines to beg the bitter bread of charity. But for the splendid work of Herbert Hoover's relief commission, the place would have been a mortuary.

The trip from Vienna to Budapest did nothing to relieve my depression. Where once a dozen fine express trains plied daily between the two capitals, there was now but one, and that as battered a collection of cars as were ever coupled together. The station was packed to suffocation with expectant passengers, and it took a guard of soldiers to get me and my interpreter through milling hundreds to the compartment that had been assigned. Finally gaining possession, we locked the door and prepared to stretch out on the two long seats for a good night's sleep.

In the corridor, however, were women facing the prospect of standing on their feet for twelve long hours, and after a struggle with my baser nature I finally told the interpreter to open the door and let six come in. We drew a Czech, two Austrians, two Magyars, and a Turkish lady of enormous proportions. Warmth fairly poured from her as she sat beside me, and as the wretched night wore on I squirmed around until my stockinged feet were buried to the ankles in the small of her back. She bucked like a broncho at first, but finding it impossible to dislodge me, eventually accepted and subsided.

Hungary, like Austria, had been proclaimed a sovereign republic, but this democratic gesture was characterized by the same lack of meaning. Count Mihály Károlyi, a disciple of Karl Marx despite his aristocratic background, had signalized his ascension to the presidency by wholesale expropriations, but instead of satisfying the Communists, his concessions encouraged them to bid for complete power. Béla Kun, a former real-estate agent, suddenly returned from exile in Russia, and at the time of my arrival had his "revolution" well under way.

Moreover, the Rumanians, in utter disregard of plain armistice provisions, were ravaging with all the thoroughness of locusts. Factories, stores, and even homes were looted, and but for General Harry Bandholtz, the thievish crew would have stolen the art treasures and historic relics stored in the National Museum. Taking his stand before the door, the chief of the American Military Mission in Hungary beat off the Rumanians with his riding crop, a brave deed that later earned him a statue in Budapest's principal square.

Nothing was more obvious than that Károlyi, weak, demagogic, and fundamentally stupid, could not be saved even if he had been worth saving. The one helpful thing to be done was to get rid of the Rumanians, and I so reported by letter to President Wilson. The Big Four responded with a declaration that the armistice terms must be respected, but as no steps were taken to give force to the order, the pitiful republic rushed to its fall. In March, Béla Kun took over, ushering in the Red Terror that sent hundreds of Hungary's best and finest to their death.

Never once throughout the war did I have a doubt as to the wisdom and justice of our propaganda, preaching the Fourteen Points in particular with gospel fervor. True, we had said that it was the right of every people to choose the kind of government under which they wished to live, but all the same there was plain implication that the republican form was far and away the best. Why not? What more conclusive proof than the United States?

This complacence was jarred into small pieces by my closeup of Europe. "Self-determination" did not have the old rich, satisfying sound when seen in action. Instead of seventeen countries, twenty-six had come into being, and the growth of an intense and aggressive nationalism added mean hates to the tragedy of chaos precipitated by the utter lack of any sound economic basis.

Whatever the faults of the Hapsburg dynasty, at least it assured the unity of the Danube basin, the indispensable keystone of European equilibrium. With this unity shattered, and free movement and free trade shackled by the creation of new frontiers, Europe's progressive pauperization looked to be inevitable. Only Germany, the real criminal, had hope of finding profit in the muddled situation.

Today I have the implicit belief that a United States of

Europe is the one chance for world peace; a Europe welded into a working whole by a common currency, a customs union, free use of waterways, etc. I will not say that this idea was clear in my mind back there in the early months of 1919, but I did have the sense to see that there was no possibility of health or hope in a Europe divided, and even fragmentized, by the insistences of nationalism.

I returned to Paris in late January, and at luncheon with the President in the Palais Murat told him in detail where I had been and what I had seen. In particular I emphasized the passport difficulties at every frontier, and the trade barriers that cut through Europe's life lines. Rather naïvely, I had thought to open up a brand-new field of discussion, but soon found that the President had long been a believer in the necessity of a federated Europe.

"However," he said, "now is not the time to advance it or even suggest it. Preoccupation with present miseries leaves no room for long-term planning or thinking. But the Covenant of the League of Nations will contain a clause permitting Europe's reconstruction on sane lines, and when the rage for revenge, indemnities, and annexations has passed, perhaps people will see the wisdom of collective effort."

The long, lean face was scarred by deep furrows, and except when animated by conversation, the eyes held a weary look. I told him of the feeling that I had found in Middle Europe— the faith in America and in him—and while he smiled, the smile had in it a touch of cynicism.

"Let us hope," he said, "that I will not be called on to combat any of their nationalistic aspirations. It might help if I could get to the people, but I am being shut off completely. Only a few days ago Clemenceau canceled a meeting at the Trocadero where I was scheduled to address the women of France. And have you been following the papers? Every day the Republicans tell Lloyd George, Orlando, and Clemenceau that I do not and cannot speak for my America, and that my one function is to act as their rubber stamp."

It was my wish to sail for home at once, but the President asked that I go to England and Ireland for a look at the Irish situation. "I have noticed several ill-natured reports," he added, "that you are no longer in my good graces, and I do

214

not mean to let the impression gain ground. As you said in Washington, your face must be saved, and faces like ours," he laughed, "take a lot of saving."

CHAPTER 28

Ireland and the Irish

I did not need to have the importance of the Irish errand explained to me. In Paris the most clamorous of all the nationalist groups was a Sinn Fein delegation from Dublin, pressing a demand that Ireland's case be judged by the peace conference. Side by side with them stood a highly vocal committee from the United States, claiming to speak for the fifteen million Americans of Irish birth or descent, and no less insistent than the Sinn Feiners that Erin's revolt against British rule was a proper subject for consideration by the Big Four.

President Wilson, of course, was the target for their arguments and appeals, and the spokesmen went so far as to threaten him unless he made recognition of the Irish Republic a first order of business, putting it ahead of the peace. This demand was unreasonable, and even preposterous on the face of it, and yet the bitterness of the Irish and the Irish-Americans was not without good and sufficient cause, for not in all history had any people been subjected to crueler or more continuous oppression.

From that tragic day in 1169 when the Earl of Pembroke landed his Anglo-Norman host on Irish soil, there was never a year in the whole of five centuries that did not witness invasion and bloody attempts at subjugation and even actual extermination. King after king was beaten back, however, for there was that in the soul of the Gael that could not bear a chain.

Elizabeth spent lives and money without stint in a sixteen-year struggle to make her sovereignty over Ireland more than a "mere phantom of rule," and at the end Hugh O'Neill and Hugh O'Donnell compelled her to confess defeat. James I

215

seized the whole of Ulster and parceled out the land to English and Scotch Protestants, who were not allowed to have an Irish tenant. Countless thousands died of cold and hunger, lips stained with the nettles that were their food, and yet resistance continued.

The Roundheads, hating Catholicism, then came with fire and sword, and to this day the "curse of Cromwell" is the worst threat that the Irish can throw at an enemy. How many were slaughtered and how many shipped to Barbados as slaves will never be known. Even little children were not spared, Cromwell brutally commenting that "nits make lice." Such of the wretched population as remained were herded into the waste places of Connaught, where they were made to paint black spots on their faces as a "mark of the beast."

Once again, incredibly enough, the Irish climbed up from the pit, and under Patrick Sarsfield, the great Earl of Lucan, gave successful battle to William of Orange and his horde of English, Dutch, and Huguenots. Crushed at last by overwhelming odds and starvation, Sarsfield surrendered on honorable terms, only to have every pledge repudiated. Following the broken treaty of Limerick came the Flight of the Wild Geese, thousands of Irishmen enriching other lands with their genius and courage, all of whom would have known degradation or death had they remained in the house of bondage.

Five centuries of actual war were succeeded by two hundred years of unceasing revolt—an unbroken record of protest, disorder, and bloody uprisings, all met by barbarous reprisals. Again there is no record of the number that followed Robert Emmet to the scaffold or that died in torture chambers. Not until 1870, decimated by war, famine, and pestilence, did the Irish turn away from the futility of force and beg of the English Parliament some measure of home rule. Not independence, but merely the poor right to have a voice in their own government.

Isaac Butt started the campaign, but Charles Stewart Parnell, the Protestant, carried on, turning Parliament into a bedlam by his obstructive tactics. In time Mr. Gladstone recognized the justice of Ireland's cause and made home rule an integral part of the Liberal platform, but the House of Lords was no less adamant than Elizabeth and Cromwell. Finally, however, the veto power of the Lords was taken away by the Liberals under Mr. Asquith, and when the Irish bill came up for the third time in 1914, home rule seemed assured.

What defeated it was the bold threat of rebellion by Unionists, who shouted, "If the blow falls, German aid will be sought and welcomed." Sir Edward Carson, galloping to Ulster, organized training camps, and without pretense of secrecy, rifles and ammunition were shipped in from Hamburg and distributed by motor trucks. Ulster Volunteers sprang up in cities and towns, and when it was announced that these armed bodies meant to seize all government arsenals, the War Office in London ordered the army in Ireland to "take special precautions for safeguarding depots and other places where arms or stores are kept."

The answer was mutiny. General Gough, commanding the Third Cavalry Brigade, handed in his resignation, and fifty-seven of his fellow officers did likewise, flatly refusing to proceed to Ulster for the enforcement of law and order. Mr. Asquith denounced it as a "deadly blow," a "grave and unprecedented outrage," but not only did the mutineers go unpunished, but the Home Rule Bill was amended to the point of worthlessness.

What wonder that Germany struck on August 2! With the most powerful voices in England hailing the Kaiser as "that great Protestant prince and deliverer," with Ulster armed and the army in mutiny, what more natural than for the Germans to assume that they would be welcomed even as William of Orange and his Dutch were once welcomed?

It was not only that home rule was shelved on the outbreak of war. The heads of the Ulster rebellion—Balfour, Carson, Curzon, Bonar Law, Milner—were put in places of power, and when a wave of passionate resentment swept Ireland, scores of leaders were arrested and sent to England to be confined "during the King's pleasure."

Rage grew and marched automatically to that tragic Easter Monday of 1916 when a handful of Dublin men pitted themselves against the might of England in one of those futile uprisings that have ever been the glory and despair of Ireland. The mad venture was doomed to defeat from the first, as every man knew, and British reprisals took many more lives than the pitiful "revolution." Some two thousand suspects were imprisoned, and all of the leaders met death before firing squads in Kilmainham jail. Connolly, too badly wounded to stand, was propped in a chair so that his shattered body might be filled with new bullets.

Up to 1916 the Sinn Fein—For Ourselves—had been without political power, but as the people saw home rule derided and rejected, and contrasted the treatment of the Ulster mutineers with the execution and quicklime burials of the Dublin rebels, they turned away from the Nationalists definitely and forever. John Redmond died of a broken heart, and John Dillon and T. P. O'Connor, idols through the years, now sat in loneliness.

At the elections in December, 1918, Sinn Fein went before the people with the demand for an Irish republic and won a victory so overwhelming that no room was left for doubt as to popular feeling. Most surprising result of all was the outcome of the election in Ulster, where all nine counties had been claimed as solidly Protestant and Unionist. When the votes were counted, it was found that Sinn Fein had won 100 per cent in Donegal, Monaghan, and Cavan and carried Fermanagh and Tyrone by majorities as high as 75 per cent. Only Down, Derry, Armagh, and Antrim were lost. In Leinster, Munster, and Connaught, the other three provinces, the vote for Sinn Fein was unanimous.

It was against the background of seven centuries of struggle, and armed with the results of the election, that the Dublin delegation and the Irish-Americans presented themselves in Paris, slashing at President Wilson with questions that had a cutting edge. What about the right of a people to self-determination? Had not the war been fought to free enslaved people from their chains, and to end forever the oppression of the strong? What, then, more just than that the case of Ireland be heard and judged? If Poles and Czechs were to have their chains struck off, why not Ireland?

Before leaving for Rome I had talked with the leaders of both groups, and found their minds padlocked. The conference, I pointed out, was not a world court with power to hear and judge any and all complaints, but a council of victors to impose terms on the vanquished. Was it their contention that President Wilson should tell his associates that he could not and would not discuss peace terms until the claims of Ireland were allowed? When they admitted that that was exactly what

218

they did contend, I asked their idea as to the President's course in event of England's refusal to consider his demand.

"Simple enough," they answered. "Let him walk out of the conference and sail home."

On many occasions during the war I had discussed the Irish question with the President, and never once had he left any doubt as to his position. Believing sincerely in the simple justice of home rule, he could not understand England's persistent failure to redeem explicit pledges. With his express approval, I had also made the matter a subject of conversation with Lord Reading, the British ambassador, stressing the fifteen million Americans of Irish blood and pointing out the disastrous effect of his government's policy on our morale.

In Paris I told the Irish-Americans of these conversations and stressed the President's interest in the Irish question, but none of it softened their truculence. Throughout the month of my absence in Middle Europe they had continued to bombard the President with their demands, not stopping at threats of political reprisal in the United States. It was because of this intransigence that Mr. Wilson asked me to go to Ireland for a firsthand study of the situation.

In London I had luncheon with Lloyd George, but trying to pin him down to any detailed consideration of the Irish question was like trying to hold quicksilver in the hand. The Irish, he shrugged, were an impossible people, loving nothing so much as disagreement. The reason for his attitude, of course, was not hard to find. When the Welshman joined with Northcliffe in 1915 to overthrow Asquith, the bulk of the Liberal party would not follow him, and this compelled an alliance with the Tories. The price that he paid for their support was the complete abandonment of home rule, for years his most strenuous advocacy, and these masters were still insistent that he keep to his bargain.

Dear old "Tay Pay" O'Connor gave me letters to friends in Dublin, and on arrival I went at once to the home of John Dillon. Like Redmond and all other Nationalists who had given their lives to the home-rule fight, he had been swept aside by the Sinn Feiners, a heartbroken old man. He was able, however, to put me in touch with the leaders of the new movement, and a few nights later I met with them at a secret rendezvous, for many were being hunted by the English.

Of the twenty-odd men that stood before me, the two that stay clearest in my memory were Mike Collins and Harry Boland, then like brothers, but later to divide in hate and each meet death in fratricidal strife. The men were young for the most part, but with faces black and hard from inherited hates. Eamon de Valera, having escaped from prison with Collins' help, was hiding out in the hills, and only my excited protests kept them from bringing him in to meet with me.

For all their implacability, the Sinn Feiners were far more reasonable than the Irish-American group in Paris. Even while contending that it was President Wilson's right to urge consideration of Ireland's case by the peace conference, they listened without interruption to my insistence that it was a meaningless gesture that could have only dangerous consequences.

It was not Ireland alone, I argued, that pleaded for justice and the right of self-determination. There was not a corner of the world in which some body of people did not raise a similar demand. What more plain, however, than that the peace conference did not have the power to hear and adjudicate these appeals? It was merely an association of states, victorious in war, and assembled to decide and present peace terms to the Central Powers. It had, however, a second purpose, and one rich in hope for the oppressed of the world. Not the least important of President Wilson's Fourteen Points, and one approved by America's allies, was this: "A general association of nations must be formed under specific covenants for the purpose of affording mutual guarantees of political independence and territorial integrity to great and small nations alike."

Moreover, it was the fixed determination of the President that the Covenant of the League of Nations should contain a provision explicitly providing that each member state would have the right to bring to the attention of the Assembly or of the Council "any circumstances whatever affecting international relations which threatened to disturb either the peace or the good understanding between nations." This, I maintained, would give the United States the right to put the case of Ireland before the League of Nations, or the case of any other people whose bitternesses and revolts menaced "good understanding between nations." Not only was it the orderly process for the redress of wrongs, but the only possible process. Surely even the most ardent Sinn Feiner must see that the American people, even though overwhelmingly sympathetic with the Irish people, would not go to war with Britain on account of it.

The disappointment in every face was plain to be seen, but except for one or two hotheads, there was general admission of the argument's force and logic. But was it not possible, they urged, for President Wilson to bring personal and private pressure on Lloyd George that would force him to some regard for English pledges? In view of America's enormous contributions to England's war effort, where was there any impropriety?

I gave this promise, and kept it, omitting nothing in my report to the President. Unfortunately, I had no chance to present it in person, for when I got back to Paris he had sailed for the United States, carrying with him the first draft of the League Covenant for discussion with the Senate Committee on Foreign Affairs. That he read it carefully, however, was proved by the letter that he wrote me under date of March 20, soon after his return to France. I print the whole of it out of my pride in the closing paragraphs.

My dear Creel:

I was very glad to find your letter of the first of March awaiting me here in Paris, and heartily sorry that I did not have another chance to see you before you left this side of the water. The suggestions of your letter are very valuable indeed, and you may be sure will remain in my mind.

I wanted to tell you in person, but I find I must now tell you by letter, how deeply I have appreciated the work you have done as Chairman of the Committee on Public Information. The work has been well done, admirably well done, and your inspiration and guidance have been the chief motive power in it all. I have followed what you have done throughout and have approved it, and I want you to know how truly grateful I am.

Your personal consideration of myself and your constant thoughtfulness have been a source of pleasure to me all the way through, and I feel that I now know beyond peradventure the high motives by which you are governed. It is with real emotion, therefore, that I sign myself,

Your sincere friend,
WOODROW WILSON

Events also proved that some of the report's recommendations were adopted by the President, for the Lloyd George government began releasing the Irish prisoners who had been held in jails, and without arraignment, since May, 1918. Aside from this, however, nothing was done, and the bitterness of Irish-Americans found full expression during the League of Nations fight in the Senate. More than anything else, perhaps, it was responsible for the treaty's rejection.

CHAPTER 29

Woodrow Wilson's Last Years

I sailed from France shortly after March 1 and reached Washington to find the job of CPI demobilization nearing its end. The domestic divisions had finished their audits, and nothing remained except to wind up the cable and wireless offices in Paris and New York and wait for the foreign commissioners who were straggling back from far points. With everything well in hand, I cut the organization down to a small clerical force, housed in one building, and handed in my resignation. Even so, I continued to make weekly trips from New York to Washington, directing the liquidation at my own expense.

On June 30, however, Congress peremptorily wiped the Committee out of existence, leaving no one with authority to indorse checks, transfer bank balances, sign a pay roll, or rent quarters. Borrowing trucks from the Army, I moved the records of two years into vacant space in the Fuel Administration building, riding with each load to see that nothing was spilled. As the offices were unfurnished, files and ledgers were dumped on the floors, and after hiring a watchman out of my own pocket, I began a round of departments in search of some agency willing to take over the job of liquidation.

There was no secret as to my plight, and Washington correspondents looked on it as a great joke, sending out word that

"Congress has the laugh on Creel." Not until August 21, when the President designated the Council of National Defense as a liquidating agency, did the mangled remains of the CPI find a resting place. Once again the records were loaded into trucks, carted to the Council's building, and scattered over three floors.

Bad enough, but worse was to come. Even as I begged the Council to employ a competent accounting force, Senator Reed Smoot charged that I had "deserted" soon after the Armistice, leaving everything "in grossest disorder, premeditatedly designed to cover reckless waste and probable corruption." For days I was pictured as one who had spent a "few delightful months wallowing in public funds, and then went away, leaving the whole mess to be cleaned up by others." Many papers followed up by editorial speculation as to how much money had "stuck to my fingers."

Not until November did my repeated visits force the Council to employ accountants and permit CPI executives to appear for explanation and report. In the end Senator Smoot's charges were disproved in detail, for the "gross disorder" and "planned confusion" were found to be no more than the displacements of two hurried movings. Every dollar had its proper voucher, and the Council made public admission that honesty and competence had marked the expenditure of every single cent.

Hope that the report on the Committee's liquidation would end my troubles was soon dispelled. Senator Smoot, returning to the attack, charged that I had joined with Roger Babson to "loot the government of a property worth $600,000 a year," bellowing that "a gang of safeblowers could hardly have created greater havoc to a country bank than did these government employees in the office of the *Official Bulletin* [CPI publication] when the final word was given that Uncle Sam had refused to continue as their benevolent paymaster."

Patiently and laboriously I compiled a statement of the facts in the case. At the time of the Committee's demobilization, I tried to sell the *Official Bulletin* to save the expense of returning small amounts due on unexpired subscriptions, but the Attorney General ruled against it. Clinging fondly to red tape, he ordered me to pay back all balances to subscribers down to the last penny, after which I was to make the mailing lists available to any citizen. This I did, and Babson merely copied it as anyone else could have done, starting a similar publication of his own. So far from earning $600,000 a year, he lost his shirt and soon quit throwing good money after bad. Neither Smoot nor the press took any cognizance of my statement.

Next came the Republican National Committee with a loud shout that I was the prime mover in a conspiracy to steal the government's $14,000,000 nitrate plant at Perryville, Maryland. This accusation was contained in their Speaker Series No. 11 as an example of the "orgy of corruption" that marked the Wilson administration. Never having heard of the nitrate plant, and not even knowing where Perryville was, I had to content myself with a blanket denial.

All of these charges, however, were no more than pinpricks, for concern over the fate of the League of Nations made all else seem small. From the time that the Senate began its consideration of the treaty, I wore a path between New York and Washington, doing what I could to help in the fight. What alarmed me was President Wilson's confidence in the outcome. He admitted frankly that there was much in the treaty that he did not like, and to which he had agreed only under the threats of Britain, France, Italy, and Japan, backed as they were by the Republican majority in the Senate. "But we have the League," he argued, "and in its powers and machinery there is the cure for every injustice." It was a passion of faith that burned away all doubt.

His confidence was not shaken until debate developed the full implacability of Lodge's hate, and even then the President felt that his personal appeal to the people would shatter the flimsy structure of Republican lies. I saw him in September, just before he left for his tour of the country, and was shocked to note the alteration in his appearance. The thinning hair had gone white, and the blaze of his eyes only made clearer the signs of exhaustion. He confessed to being far from well, but neither the pleas of friends nor the implorations of Dr. Grayson could dissuade him from his purpose. An appeal to the people was a vital necessity.

It is a wonder that Woodrow Wilson lasted as long as he did. In Paris he had labored night and day, and the strain told heavily on a constitution already impaired by the drudgeries and anxieties of war. Even so, his speeches were among the best he ever made, and as he drove himself from coast to coast, from city to city, addressing great audiences without the aid of a loud-speaker, neither word nor sign showed that he was balanced on the grave's edge. In the very hour of his collapse he begged not to be taken home, insisting that he could find the strength to go on.

I did not visit him again until November, and then went to Washington in sickness of heart, for not only had the Senate group been broadcasting his absolute incapacity, but every channel of gossip ran full with rumors that he had lost his mind. At sight of me he gestured pathetically, a tragic sweep of the hand that took in the whole of his wasted, helpless body. Illness had ended the iron control that distinguished him in health and strength, but aside from a new and quick-springing emotionalism, he was in possession of every faculty, for when our talk turned on the Senate fight, he spoke with all of his old vigor and clarity. What stirred him most was the sneer of the opposition that his "stubbornness" stood in the way of the treaty's "Americanization."

"Americanization indeed!" he exclaimed. "The Covenant exempts the Monroe Doctrine; acknowledges that it is the sole right of Congress to declare war and to authorize the employment of the naval and military forces of the United States, and while disclaiming all intent to interfere with the domestic affairs of any other nation, flatly states that no nation may interfere with ours. We can withdraw at any time by giving due notice, and there is the plain provision that each nation is to be the judge as to whether its international obligations have been fulfilled. The League Council can take no action without a unanimous vote, so that we can never be forced to do anything that we ourselves do not vote for.

"I have said time and again," he continued, "that there is no objection, and can be no objection, to the fullest restatement of our understandings of these matters, for while meanings are clear, I have no quarrel with any attempt to make the obvious more obvious. My one and only 'stubbornness,' as they call it, is in connection with Article Ten, guaranteeing the political independence and integrity of member nations and specifically renouncing force and aggression."

One must go back to the "bloody shirt" era after Lincoln's assassination to find any parallel for the Senate debates during the treaty's consideration. Sherman of Illinois shouted that "history would forget the reign of Caligula in the excesses and follies of the American government operated under the League of Nations by President Wilson and Colonel House." As an appeal to bigotry, he also insisted that "twenty-four of the forty equal votes of the Christian nations are spiritually dominated by the Vatican." Reed of Missouri, on the other hand, screamed that the black races would rule the world through the League, while Johnson of California held unshakably to the conviction that "greedy, conscienceless England would control the habitable parts of the globe."

It was actually charged that Congress would not have the power to pass an appropriation bill without specific authorization by the League, that the League had usurped the right of Congress to declare war, and that one million Americans would be required to serve as soldiers in foreign lands.

Out of the madness that possessed the Senate, even the very foundations of American unity were weakened. Forces of hyphenation were called on, and no effort was spared to revive and intensify the divisive prejudices of American life. "Professional" Germans, silent throughout the war, were brought out of retirement, and "professional" Irishmen incited to bellow their hate of England. Day after day delegations of Italians, Egyptians, Hindus, Armenians, etc., flooded Washington, and were given elaborate hearings on the dishonest assumption that the Senate had power to redress their grievances.

What aided this campaign of hate and falsity was a spreading wave of reaction from the emotionalism of war. With people picking up old threads and finding them sadly tangled, irritability had replaced enthusiasm. The extent of the revulsion was brought home to me when I published *The War, the World and Wilson* in June. Written as a campaign document, designed to answer Republican attack, it considered every controversial matter in detail—the war itself, how the League came to be conceived, the Paris battle, the Fourteen Points, the Senate fight, etc.

I wrote it with my heart's blood, and party leaders were good enough to praise it as conclusive and irrefutable, but as far as effect was concerned, I might as well have committed it to the wind. Many booksellers refused to order, and such as did make purchases put the books on back shelves. At that, some fifty thousand copies were sold, mostly through orders sent to the publisher by ardent Wilsonians.

A year or so later I spoke in Salt Lake and sat next to a high dignitary in the Mormon church. When the attention of those near us was centered elsewhere, he leaned close and whispered that he had bought one hundred copies of my Wilson book for private distribution.

"Ah!" I murmured brightly. "A booklegger."

It was my belief then, and still is, that Lodge and his wolf pack did not start their fight with fixed intent to kill the League. It was the purpose, rather, to make certain changes, cutting out this comma and adding that semicolon, all in the interests of "Americanization," and then claim the League as their own, *not* Woodrow Wilson's. What happened was that they could not control the forces unleashed by reckless demagoguery, and a tidal wave of hyphenated Americanism swept them before it.

Even Republicans who had been strong in support of the League turned tail and recanted. Mr. Root, swallowing his explicit approval of Article X, solemnly urged the "Americanization" of the treaty. Mr. Taft, after offering a compromise reservation that was accepted by the Democrats and as promptly rejected by the Lodge group, subsided and soon began to purr against the party's knee. On March 19 the treaty, with the Lodge knife deep in its heart, came up for final vote, and was rejected a second time.

This was not the finish. The final act in the drama of treachery remained to be played. In early May the Republican majority in the House passed a resolution declaring an end to the state of war with Germany. On May 15 the Republican majority in the Senate approved a peace resolution by Senator Knox ending the state of war with Austria-Hungary as well as with Germany. And yet only six months before—in December, 1918—Senator Lodge had shouted these words: "We cannot make peace in the ordinary way. We cannot, in the first place, make peace except in company with our allies. It would brand us with everlasting dishonor and bring ruin to us if we undertook to make a separate peace."

Until the very last, President Wilson refused to consider the possibility of the treaty's rejection, and when the blow fell it found his heart unguarded. I saw him soon afterward, and the pallor of death lay on his face. I sat with him miserably, fumbling for words of comfort, but it was as though I had not been in the room. All the while his bloodless lips moved continuously, as if framing new arguments and forming new appeals. Only as I was leaving did he look at me seeingly, his eyes filled with an anguish such as I trust never to see again. "If only I were not helpless," he whispered.

About it was none of the self-pity of a sick man, only the despair of a stricken soldier watching his banners driven backward and straining with sweat of soul to lift himself for another blow that might change the tide of battle. Even though stunned by the treaty's defeat, he soon rallied under the call of his own indomitable spirit and his Covenanter's faith that God is not mocked. And so he went about the business of office as efficiently as ever, though less swiftly, making decisions with the old certainty. Never at any time, even in the first terrible days, was his mind affected.

In October, 1920, for example, I went to him with a suggestion for the settlement of the Mexican question. Roberto Pesqueira, Mexico's special envoy and a dear friend of mine, had come to me with President Adolfo de la Huerta's hope of recognition by the United States, and carrying full assurance of Mexico's desire for an early resumption of fraternal relations. It looked like a good opportunity to crown the President's Mexican policy with success, and in Washington I explained the offer and expressed a willingness to go to Mexico unofficially and at my own expense.

The President approved without a single dissent, and I then asked for a categorical statement of the terms on which recognition would be granted. In reply he spoke for a full thirty minutes, covering every detail of our controversies with Mexico, quoting the substance of this speech and that speech, and never hesitating for a name, a date, or a fact. Not even when he was at the peak of his power was he more the master of his mental processes.

The story that Mrs. Wilson spoke and acted for him was pure fiction. Never once was she present at the interviews I had with the President, and I have the same report from others. Her pride in him was as great as her love for him, and I felt always that she absented herself purposely from conferences to guard against any assumption that the President was not able to make his own decisions. True, she was always a hovering presence, never far away at any time, but her one purpose was to guard him against overdoing.

Down to the very day of the 1920 election, the President counted confidently on a vast tidal wave of public opinion that would vindicate the League and sweep its enemies out of public life. Not even the desertion of Mr. Taft, Mr. Hoover, and Mr. Root had power to shake this faith, and such was the force of his belief that hardheaded James M. Cox, the Democratic nominee, caught fire. After the last rally of the campaign in New York, I rode back to his hotel with Mr. Cox and nearly fell out of the seat when he told me that his victory was certain.

"I had very little hope at first," he said, "but now the country understands. Lies and hates have lost their power to confuse, and fathers and mothers are remembering that the war we fought was a war to end war."

Governor Cox's overwhelming defeat fell on Mr. Wilson even more crushingly than the treaty's rejection. That had been the work of politicians, while now it was the *people* who had turned away from sacred pledges. He had been so sure of their verdict, so certain that they would repudiate Lodge and his crew of wreckers. Down beneath his hurt and bewilderment, I caught a note of isolation, much as though he felt himself suddenly excluded from popular affection and shut out from the heart and mind of America. There was an afternoon that I went driving with him, and when we came to the gate, where quite a crowd stood waiting, I saw him shrink back into the the car, just as though he were avoiding a blow.

"Why, what is the matter, Mr. President?" I asked.

"Didn't you see them?" he answered.

"Of course, sir. But what about it? I saw only respect and devotion."

"No." And his voice was low and sad. "Just curiosity."

There was no letdown while in the White House, but behind the walls of the S Street home there were frequent surrenders to the tragedy of his thoughts. One visit saw him cheerful and composed, and then the next would find him silent, his eyes staring into space. I thought for a time that he was putting himself on the rack of the past, torturing himself with speculations as to what could or should have been done, but when I mentioned this, he shook his head.

"No," he said, "I am not brooding over what might have been. It is only the future that concerns me. What is going to happen now? Something *must* happen, or else a second World War is inevitable."

More and more the purely personal ceased to interest him. In August of 1920 he had turned the management of his literary affairs over to me, and I had great ideas of what he could do after being released from the cares of the presidential office. One offer in particular, running high into the thousands, was for additional volumes that would bring his *History of the American People* up to date. He refused even to consider it.

"I am not a historian," he shrugged, "nor do I wish to be considered as one. I only wrote the history in order to learn it myself."

On the *George Washington*, going to Europe in 1918, he had mentioned to me in the course of a casual conversation that his deepest interest was in education, and that someday he hoped to write a real work on the American school system. During his professorial years it had been his habit to drop into class-rooms whenever occasion offered and put questions to the pupils.

"All of them," he laughed, "could tell me how many inches there were in a foot, how many feet in a yard, and how many yards in a mile, but when I placed my hand on a table and asked them how high it was from the floor, not one had any idea. Education is fast losing all relation to life."

I recalled the discussion and asked him if he still retained his interest, but he shook his head. Magazines deluged him with requests for anything he chose to write, and syndicates offered huge amounts for articles on current topics, but he would have none of them. Sunshine poured into the room where he sat, the walls were bright with books, and loving care wrapped him close; yet I never left him without a sense of his inner loneliness. Only a few short years before he had com-panioned with the peoples of the world in a great crusade, and now he seemed to feel that he walked alone, the shattered evangel of a lost cause.

A change, thank God, came before the end. At sight of Woodrow Wilson in the procession to dedicate the Tomb of the Unknown Soldier, a cheer rose from the gathered thousands, a great cheer that spread and swelled and never died until the gaunt, crippled figure disappeared behind the door of his home. As he heard that mighty chorus, tears rolled down his wasted cheeks and washed away his loneliness forever. He refused to believe that it was a personal tribute in any sense, holding that it was the cause they cheered, and that it meant a people's return to faith. It was this warming belief that he took to his heart, holding it ever closer and closer. There were days of depression, to be sure, due to the march of his illness, but his eyes never lost the serenity of a deeply religious conviction.

"It will come," he said over and over. "Yes, it will come."

CHAPTER 30

Woodrow Wilson the Man

*O*f all our presidents, not one was ever more the victim of legend than Woodrow Wilson. As a result, there is today a continuing belief that he was a "thinking machine," cold, selfish, and egotistical, devoid of human warmth and without capacity for friendship; an autocrat who played a lone hand instead of inviting counsel; an ingrate who took but never gave, possessed of a cruel, mean streak precluding loyalty.

From the first days of war in 1917 down to his death, it was my privilege to enjoy close association with Mr. Wilson, and continued misrepresentation of the *man* distressed me even more than attacks on the President. It was not only that I myself found him unfailingly generous, courteous, and considerate, possessing wit, humor, and winning geniality. As a student he played baseball and sang on the glee club, and collegemates held him in warm affection. During his professorial years at Princeton he was voted the most popular member of the faculty four times in succession, and his daughters adored him as a gay and delightful companion.

More than once I ventured to suggest that this side of him be put on public view, but he would not hear of it. It was not only that Woodrow Wilson loathed the handshaking, back-slapping, time-wasting technique of professional office seekers—he called it "campaign mummery"—but there was his clear understanding of the presidency as a *job*. In 1908, long before he had thought of filling the office, he had written of it as one that demanded an "inexhaustible vitality. . . . Men of ordinary physique and discretion cannot be presidents and live, if the strain be not somehow relieved. We shall be obliged always to be picking our Chief Magistrates from among wise and prudent athletes."

Not being the iron type, he knew from the first that he would have to choose between popularity and service. Either he could consider the office politically, disregarding duty in the interests of personal acclaim, or he could assume it as a task to be discharged in honor and high faith, thereby surrendering all hope of applause. He made his decision as an American, not as a politician. After estimating the job in terms of routine and national needs, and measuring the demand against his strength, he saw plainly that the one chance was a careful, systematic, scientific conservation of every ounce of energy. Taking up the study of his problem with the cool detachment of an engineer in charge of a plant, the President and Dr. Cary Grayson worked out an iron regimen, a fixed daily program that ordered every minute of his life with machine-like exactitude.

There were certain hours for work, sleep, and exercise, a rigid diet, and stern caution against waste effort. Mental habits as well as physical were brought under discipline. Instead of the "open door," interviews were confined to those of official importance, and personal approaches increasingly gave way to the submission of memoranda. In the quiet of his study at night, every suggestion received the painstaking attention of the President, but even this larger efficiency failed to soothe wounded vanities.

It is also to be remembered that those were the frugal years, when the lavish expenditures of the New Deal were not yet even dreamed of. Franklin Roosevelt had ten secretaries, but Woodrow Wilson was forced to get along with one. After a crowded day he gave his evenings to the papers that stacked his desk, typing off comments, suggestions, or instructions on his own battered little machine. Oftentimes it took weeks to get a reply from the State Department, but the President answered at once with a dictated letter or else on the morning of the second day there came a small page, either penciled or typed, signed W.W.

I saw him many times when his face had the gray of ashes, but the only complaint that I ever heard was on the score of drowsiness. "I'm getting to be like Dickens' fat boy," he laughed. "I could go to sleep at an angle of ninety-five degrees." The importance of husbanding his energies, however, made him less and less willing to spend them upon the trivial, and the immaterial and irrelevant became increasingly unbearable. There was so much to do, and always the fear of being hampered in the doing by some rebellion of the body.

More and more, as pressure increased, his decisions were reached by a process of incubation, assisted at every point by the most painstaking study and thorough investigation. Instead of an "impatience of counsel and failure to subject himself to the corrective process of association," the very reverse was true. To use his own favorite phrase, he "borrowed brains" wherever he found them, and many important matters were delayed unwisely while he waited to see persons assumed to have certain special knowledge. Complete information was a passion with him, but once in possession of every fact in the case, the President withdrew, commenced the business of consideration, comparison, and assessment, and then emerged with a decision.

This habit of thought was by no means a short cut to popularity. There is a certain vanity in all of us that makes us like to feel that our views carry weight, that our conclusions have the ability to convince, and a certain chill is bound to come when we see our views and conclusions carted away to be sorted over with a lot of others. Also, in politics, advice usually means control. The charge that the President "disliked advice" was simply that he preferred to form his own decisions instead of letting others form them for him.

Tourist groups, delegations of every sort, and "visiting firemen," naturally enough, were irritated by the President's refusal to quit work and join them on the lawn for group photographs. Politicians of the feet-on-the-desk school were resentful because they were not permitted to use the White House as a parking lot, and city bosses were angered by his open dislike for them and their methods. Tammany was then at the height of its power, but Mr. Wilson indignantly refused to be photographed with Murphy, Tammany's overlord. Even the better type of Democratic leader complained about his lack of interest in party affairs.

As a young professor writing an article on Grover Cleveland, Woodrow Wilson defined him as "the sort of President the makers of the Constitution had vaguely in mind: more man than partisan, with an independent will of his own: hardly a colleague of the Houses so much as an individual servant of the country: exercising his powers like a Chief Magistrate rather than like a party leader." With great questions to be decided, questions that concerned the lives and hopes of millions, the President evidenced a growing dislike for the long-winded visiting that had no larger object than the discussion of a postmastership, the party outlook in a district, or the necessity of placating this or that boss.

The thing that chiefly contributed to the manufacture of the "aloofness" legend, however, was the President's failure to establish cordial relations with the Washington correspondents. They wanted drama and he refused to furnish it. They wanted something that would lend itself to "scareheads," and he responded with an exposition. In the first years of his administration the President received the correspondents regularly, talking to them freely, and the discontinuance of the interviews was not based upon any violation of confidence, but upon his conviction of their futility. Soon after I took office, newspapermen came to me and urged that the conferences be resumed. Believing them to be highly important, I promised to do what I could, but the President proved adamant.

"It is a waste of time," he said. "In the beginning I believed that close relations with the press would be my greatest aid. I prepared for the conferences as carefully as for a Cabinet meeting, and discussed questions of the day frankly and fully. Many men of brilliant ability were in the group, but I soon discovered that the interest of the majority was in the trivial and personal. In the middle of an exposition of policy I would be asked about the sheep on the White House lawn, what we ate for dinner, and even about intimate family affairs."

The principal distaste of the President, however, was based upon what he termed "conjectural journalism." He felt that the press was not interested in what had happened, or what would happen, but only in what *might* happen. As he phrased it, their idea of news was "the satisfaction of a vulgar curiosity."

234

What more plain, he argued, than the folly of taking eggs from under a hen every few minutes in order to note the progress of hatching? Yet when great questions of national and international import were under discussion, the press insisted upon the right to examine every stage of the negotiations.

Mental habits have a clutch as strong as the physical. As time went by, with increasing necessity for husbanding hours and energy, it was easy to see the growing dominance of the intellectual factor in the President's equation. He came more and more to view every problem mentally, to look into the minds of men rather than into the hearts of men. America possessed him to the exclusion of Americans, and in increasing degree he gave his thought to the people as a whole rather than to individuals.

One of the fixed traditions of American political life is that the way to success is through compromise, and as a consequence those have been most admired and most elevated who have managed to slither their way through opposed ideas and irreconcilable ideals without commitment. In sharp contradiction, a fundamental of the Wilson philosophy was that truces were dangerous when they were not discreditable. Where disputes were personal he was willing to search for the basis of concession, but when a vital issue was at stake he did not know the meaning of compromise. With all his soul he believed that principles had to be fought out.

A revolt against the charlatanism of politics, with its emphasis on palliatives, gave intensity to his search for causes and cures. On every side he saw politicians and papers trying to content people with thrills, and his determination grew to make people *think*. With his mastery of language, his rare ability to give words poignancy as well as point, it would have been easy for him to dramatize himself, but he shrank from this usual political trick as cheap and unworthy. On his trip in support of the League of Nations he was urged to "warm up a bit," and his answer was an indignant refusal to "capitalize the dead."

Any standing possessed by me with the President was due to the fact that I divined his sense of urgency. Before an interview I would prepare for it just as a lawyer prepares a brief, putting each subject down in its proper order, heading and subheading, and working up the manner of presentation in order to strip away every vestige of the nonessential. Within ten seconds after shaking hands I had commenced my memorandum and followed it through without pause or change.

So few did this. During the war I took scores of visitors to the White House, many of them men of large affairs, and it was seldom indeed that any of them drove hard and straight to the point. One banker that I took to him had twenty minutes to present his matter, and did not even touch upon it until after eighteen minutes had passed. When he still fumbled, the President interrupted without effort to conceal his impatience.

"Mr. So-and-so," he said, putting the man's ramblings into a succinct phrase, "is that what you are trying to propose?" When the banker nodded gratefully, Mr. Wilson answered, "I see nothing in it."

The financier left in a huff, of course, and was one of those who did most to spread the report that Wilson did not want advice or counsel. After his departure I let out a moan over the manufacture of another enemy, but the President shut me off.

"I'm sorry," he said, "but these ignorant specialists try one's very soul."

Seeing Woodrow Wilson's mind work was like watching the drive of a perfectly tuned engine. Intellectual discipline, supplementing natural ability, placed every faculty at his immediate call, and there was no waste or delay. What often passed for "peremptoriness" with him was nothing more than his habit of thinking straight and thinking *through*. Having certainties of his own, he paid people the compliment of assuming that they had equally definite opinions, and invited the clash of ideas. Instead of disliking argument, he welcomed it. What he did *not* like was the blithe custom of substituting mere assertions for facts.

As chairman of the Committee on Public Information, I was brought into contact with the head of every department, bureau, and board, and I can say truthfully that of all those assembled minds the President's was the most open. This does not mean the usual catch-basin type of mind into which any passer-by may throw his mental trash, but a mind receptive to suggestions, one with a welcome for new ideas. He came to his conclusions too carefully to give them up quickly, but once his facts were disputed successfully, he surrendered without question.

The war interrupted Woodrow Wilson's domestic program

before completion, but what he did accomplish was monumental. Tariff revision, the Federal Reserve Act, rural credits, the Federal Trade Commission, workmen's compensation, the Clayton Antitrust Law, the Child Labor Law, the Seaman's Act, the Shipping Bill, the development of natural resources—all of these and more were put through in the face of bitter opposition from the class that had come to look on special privileges as a right.

It did not seem possible that human strength could stand additional strain, yet when war came he redoubled effort. He had his hand on the pulse of each department, and his knowledge of detail was as amazing as it was often disconcerting in the hour of report. It was a heartbreaking drive, taking heavy toll of his strength, yet when those about him urged a slowing down, he merely smiled and said, "I'd like to, but the boss won't let me." We thought for a while that Mrs. Wilson was meant, but it developed that the boss was his Presbyterian conscience.

The charge that Woodrow Wilson had no capacity for friendship was true only as it applied to the public service, for the same stern conscience made him look on his oath of office as an eleventh commandment. As a historian he knew that personal affection had led many an honest official into byways of broken faith and virtual dishonor.

As long as he felt that a job was being done well, he championed warmly and unwaveringly, but once convinced of unfitness or failure, he turned away irrevocably, regardless of personal feeling. Once I went to him with the newspaper story that a very popular Cabinet member was being excluded from all important war work. Knowing that the President admired and loved the man, I asked why he was being shoved into the background.

"For a very good reason," the President answered. "He dines out every night and is the life of the party. As a result, his mind has been given over to anecdotes and chitchat, and it takes him an hour to come to the matter in hand. In peace he would be a delight, but in time of war he's a headache."

Even family affections were repressed. Frank Sayre, a son-in-law, was selected on his merits as one of a group of specialists to attend the Paris conference, but the President, finding it out at the last moment, ordered him to surrender the assignment.

He had the highest regard for Frank's abilities, but the least suggestion of favoritism was abhorrent.

I myself had many proofs of his loyalty and willingness to make last-ditch stands for those to whom he gave trust. On one occasion, for example, a member of the House claimed that the boys in France were not able to get mail from home because the Creel committee loaded down the ships with tons of pamphlets. The charge was taken up by others, and when finally called on to render full report, I made irritated answer that I had never sent a pamphlet of any kind to France, and that the absurdity of the attack could have been ascertained by a mere telephone inquiry, thus saving a lot of valuable time.

That touched off the fireworks, and after prolonged debate the House rejected my communication as "insulting." Then followed several more days of feverish argument as to whether I should be called before the august body on a charge of contempt. Just when the uproar was at its loudest, my telephone rang and I found the President on the wire.

"I trust that you are not worrying over the antics of the people up on the Hill?" he asked.

"Well, sir," I answered, "I'm not feeling very happy."

"I was afraid you might be taking it to heart," he continued, "and I called up to say that if they do cite you for contempt, I'll be very glad to act as your counsel."

And did I pray that the House would summon me! Unhappily, the teapot tempest died down and nothing more was heard of it.

Then there was the New York speech during which I mentioned "slumming" in connection with Congress. I knew at the time that a Senate committee headed by Henry Cabot Lodge waited on the President to demand my discharge, but it was not until months later that I learned the details.

According to Senator Pat Harrison of Mississippi, Mr. Wilson entered the room where the committee waited and listened politely enough to the recital of the complaint against me. When the last speaker had finished, he stood up, his face set and cold, and declared: "Gentlemen, Mr. Creel's comment is to be regretted, of course, but when I think of the manner in which he has been subjected to misrepresentation and actual abuse by members of your body, I think that what he said was very human. Good morning."

Many others had the same story of loyalty to tell, particularly Newton Baker, Josephus Daniels, and Bernard Baruch. All three were made the victims of savage attack, but because of his conviction of their high competence, the President sustained them unflinchingly.

A habit of emphasizing the Scotch strain in Wilson's blood curiously obscured the fact that on the paternal side his grandfather and grandmother were both Irish. Never in anyone were two strains more apparent or more evenly balanced. The result was the very unusual combination of strength and sensibility, but the mixture was likewise responsible for a very definite cross pull. He himself was aware of it, for in talk one day he made this confidence: "The Irish is the first to react and yells to go ahead. But the Scotch is never more than a second behind, and always catches me by the coattail with the warning to wait a minute and think it over."

Nevertheless, the Irish strain took command when the decision had been reached, and he brought to his advocacies a fighting spirit that took no account of odds. Slow to take fire, he burned inextinguishably when once alight. Only the Taft-Hartley labor act of 1947 furnishes a parallel for the bitter controversy that raged over the Adamson eight-hour law for railroad workers. Employers as a whole, backed by a majority of the nation's newspapers, fought the bill as a radical measure that would cripple industry, and Democratic leaders, frightened by the clamor, begged Mr. Wilson to quit the fight. Instead of that, he took the field in person, championing the measure as just, and forced its enactment. By comparison with the opportunism and pliability of the average politician, the Wilson tenacity of purpose inevitably took on the look and feel of granite.

The Irish also showed itself in as hot a temper as ever burned in any breast. An iron discipline had banked it down, but every now and then it burst out. There was the day, for example, when he berated the correspondents for printing reports of his daughter's engagement, and ended up with this promise: "If these stories appear again, I'll thrash the guilty man."

At another time I entered his office while he was talking over the telephone. Miss Margaret Wilson, in testifying before a Congressional committee, had been treated rudely by one of the members, and the President was getting a report on her second appearance. "Go back," he ordered, "and stay there until the hearing is over. And if that blackguard repeats his discourtesy, I'm going up there and punch his head."

Determinedly detached where the public service was concerned, when it came to ideas and ideals he glowed to white heat. I remember the time I took representatives of the oppressed nationalities of Austria-Hungary to the White House for a call on the President. It was not a long interview—only twenty-five or thirty minutes—but as we came away there were tears on Paderewski's cheeks, and Dr. Masaryk's weary old face fairly shone.

"And they told me that he was cold!" the great Czech suddenly exclaimed. "Why, your president is the most intensely human man I have ever met. He's actually incandescent with feeling."

The constant charge of egotism was another that never failed to anger me, for one of the things that most marked the President was an invincible modesty. Not once in two years of fairly intimate association did I hear a word from him that had a touch of vainglory. As a matter of fact, he rarely spoke of himself, and when he did so it was always with a deprecatory note. No man was ever more generous in his estimation of the worth of others, and in making the appraisal his voice invariably took on a wistful note. Dr. Charles W. Eliot, president of Harvard University, was one of the objects of his admiration, and once after an enthusiastic enumeration of the scholar's splendid qualities he murmured, almost sadly, "How I wish I could be like him!"

No convention ever gathered but that it wanted a telegram or letter from the President, and as a means of lightening his load, it was my habit to take these requests and write the necessary words of welcome or commendation. When I took the finished product to Mr. Wilson for his signature, he would look up with the most disarming smile and ask if I minded a few corrections. After striking out a good many of my beloved adjectives and changing words that missed the right shade of meaning, he would hand back the copy saying apologetically, "I do hope I haven't ruined it."

In 1918, by way of featuring Josephine Roche's work, we decided to have the representatives of every foreign-language group make a pilgrimage to Mount Vernon on the Fourth of

240

July and offer new pledges of love and devotion to the United States at the tomb of Washington. When all arrangements were completed, I asked the President to make the address of the day. He shrank back as though I had suggested some gross impropriety.

"At the grave of Washington and on the Fourth of July! Why, my dear fellow, I would be crushed under a weight of presumption."

It took a week to gain his consent, but when he did surrender it was with his usual completeness and generosity. A few days before the Fourth the President telephoned me and said that if I had no objection to urge, he and Mrs. Wilson would be very glad to have the representatives as their guests on the *Mayflower*. Needless to say, I had no objections, and on the yacht piled Albanians, Armenians, Belgians, Bulgarians, Chinese, Czechoslovaks, Costa Ricans, Danes, Dutch, Ecuadorians, Finns, French, French Canadians, Germans, Greeks, Hungarians, Italians, Japanese, Lithuanians, Mexicans, Norwegians, Poles, Filipinos, Russians, Venezuelans, Rumanians, Spaniards, Serbs, Swedes, Swiss, Syrians, and Ukrainians—a group as motley as impressive.

It was a day of burning heat, and the great majority of the representatives were incased in heavy frock coats and smothered under silk hats of every vintage. I saw the President's keen eyes noting their sweat and discomfort, and no sooner were we under way than he went from group to group, gaily insisting that everybody "peel off the funeral wrappings," and set the example by shedding his own coat.

"Where on earth did all the Prince Alberts spring from?" he whispered to me in passing. "I thought they disappeared along with the beaver, wild pigeons, and horsehair furniture."

It was one of the few occasions when Woodrow Wilson the President gave way to Woodrow Wilson the man. About him were plain, simple men and women gathered for an affirmation of selfless devotion—a group, moreover, that was in itself a living, breathing demonstration of the practicability of the League of Nations. He loved it, and such was his own warm friendliness and compelling charm that formality and constraint quickly disappeared, and by the time we reached Mount Vernon it was a family party.

The pictures of that day—the President, happy, laughing,

surrounded by America's adopted sons and daughters; the President speaking from the top of a wooded slope, the simple brick tomb of Washington at his side, purple wistaria over his head, and silent, enraptured thousands listening, their faces illumined as he declared the ideals of America—these pictures remain to me as my dearest and clearest memories of a great man.

CHAPTER 31

Why Wilson Broke with House

*T*o this day it is a fairly general belief that Woodrow Wilson was guilty of cold-blooded, brutal ingratitude in his treatment of Colonel Edward M. House, kicking him into the outer darkness after eight years of closest association with never a word of thanks for unremitting and devoted service. More than anything else, perhaps, this lie has contributed to the myth that the President was selfish and self-centered, without capacity for friendship and utterly lacking in every generous impulse.

It is true enough that there was a break in the Damon and Pythias relation of the two men, and that the Little Gray Man was suddenly barred from intimacy and even excluded from the funeral train that followed Woodrow Wilson to his last rest. To find the reason, however, it is necessary to go back to 1911, in the reign of William Howard Taft, and start with a gay spring morning when Colonel House left his Texas home and fared eastward with set determination to become a Warwick.

On the face of things it was so absurd as to be pathetic. Here was no ardent young D'Artagnan, but a middle-aged wisp of a man, oozing deprecation at every pore, and remarkable only for a pair of steadfast blue eyes that mirrored an invincible belief in fairies. Even his political experience had been confined to gubernatorial campaigns in Texas, yet with an abiding

242

faith in Oberon and Titania, he journeyed to the Atlantic seaboard to pick a president of the United States.

The Colonel's first thought was to hitch his wagon to the star of William J. Gaynor, the mayor of New York, but when the Gaynor boom collapsed, he crossed the Hudson River and offered his services to Woodrow Wilson, then governor of New Jersey, but growing in prominence as a presidential candidate. There is no question that a whimsical fate directed the Texan's steps, for he fitted the Wilson needs as skin fits the hand.

New to politics, the former president of Princeton loathed the details of the game even as he disliked professional politicians. Whispering men who insisted on putting their lips far down his Eustachian tubes before releasing the simplest announcement irritated him profoundly, and at their very first meeting the Governor was enchanted with the little man so agreeably lacking in annoying, nerve-racking habits.

What added to delight was the discovery that the Colonel wanted nothing and asked nothing but the chance to be of service. Blessed with an independent fortune, he neither needed nor wished for office, and as he became more and more convinced of this absolute selflessness, Woodrow Wilson grappled the Texan to his heart with hooks of steel. The need for such a friend increased after the Baltimore convention, when the nominee found himself faced by personal contacts with Toms, Dicks, and Harrys, endless conferences, and the quarrels of leaders and subleaders.

Into this situation the Colonel insinuated himself, unobtrusively and even humbly, and with a cry of thanksgiving the harassed candidate seized upon him and made him "contact man." Overnight the unknown Texan was above all other party heads as far as real power was concerned, for it was he who collected the information on which Mr. Wilson based his decisions, and he who guarded the door.

With the election won, the necessity for these helpful services increased, for there was the vast and ever growing army of office seekers to be confronted. To the President the whole business was a distasteful squabble over jobs, robbing him of time and strength that could be devoted to larger things. So what more natural than that he should turn to Colonel House, the Man Who Wanted Nothing? As a consequence, he who had left Texas but two short years before, with nothing but wistful

243

yearnings to build on, was lifted to the seats of the mighty, his study a threshing floor where he winnowed the applicants for both high place and low.

A blunder of magnitude, as it proved, for not only was the Colonel without exact knowledge of the progressive movement that elected Wilson, but his intimates, without exception, were Texas reactionaries. A moan went up from true Wilsonians when Burleson and Gregory were named to the important posts of postmaster general and attorney general, and it changed to actual anguish when medieval McReynolds received his appointment to the Supreme Court. Every one a House selection.

As great tasks beckoned, the President became increasingly impatient with personal contacts, so many of them time-wasting, and used the Colonel more and more for seeing people and the collection and sifting of information. Had he not proved selfless and discreet, ever subordinating his mouth to his ears? In such fashion was the Little Gray Man raised to one of the most remarkable positions ever occupied by a private citizen.

There was never any question as to his value among those that knew. Like a sponge he went from man to man, place to place, soaking up opinion and points of view, and in the quiet of his study the President squeezed him dry and sent him forth again. He was soon accepted as the one quick approach to the preoccupied master of the White House, and the leaders of politics and industry crowded his waiting room, grateful for an interview; when he crossed the Atlantic on various errands, kings and statesmen dined him and lords and ladies spread red carpets for him.

Through it all, the Colonel seemed to remain exactly the same—meek, mild, and unassertive—never presuming or arguing, always ready to drop his own position if it aroused dissent, and elevating listening to the level of an art. In conversation with a hard-boiled politician I commented on it as a phenomenon, and expressed my real admiration for one who could be lifted to such high place almost overnight and yet retain his native simplicity with never a sign of cranial enlargement.

"It isn't natural," he answered. "Vanity is a perfectly human trait, and someday the Colonel's going to bust with an explosion that'll be heard around the world."

As time went on, however, and honors heaped higher upon

244

the humble, almost shrinking figure, there were no indications of any such untoward happening. Loyally, patiently, indefatigably, the Colonel continued to serve as listening post, courier, contact man, and companion, seemingly dedicated to self-effacement. Because of this gift of abnegation, the President held him nearer and dearer, proclaiming himself blessed in the service of one who was not as other men.

So it might have gone on to the end of their days but for the Colonel's development of a secret vice. *He began keeping a diary.* Why diaries have never been brought under the Narcotic Act is one of life's mysteries, for not even opium, heroin, or cocaine is more insidious in its disintegration of character. Soon after I took office as chairman of the Committee on Public Information, a very wise old bird gave me a piece of advice:

"Don't start a diary," he warned. "When you sit down at night to record the events of the day, in spite of honest resolves you'll soon be giving yourself the best of it in every conversation and every incident, and before you know it you'll have a hell of a case of big head. When you feel the craving, my boy, yell for friends and have them tie your hands behind you."

There can be no question, I am sure, that the Colonel struggled manfully against the habit, having been brought up in a Southern school that placed emphasis on the sanctity of confidences. Undoubtedly his soul was swept by many misgivings as he jotted down intimate conversations, particularly those with the President that were held under the assumed protection of faith and friendship. Elemental forces, however, were too strong for him, and his vanity, denied normal outlet, created a backwash that swept all before it.

It is also probable that the Colonel had no thought of publication when he first became a diary addict, and his ultimate change of mind may well be attributed to a general lowering of ethical standards. In the postwar twenties, it may be remembered, the decencies of reticence began to be set aside; violations of confidence brought a horde of gossip columnists into action, and spiritual nakedness became so much the order of the day that even fig leaves invited the accusation of Victorianism. Reaching 1926 with his large bundle of manuscript, Colonel House merely fell a victim to the spirit of the age.

It is in his diary that the real reasons for the break with President Wilson are to be found. In its first years the tone is naïve and juvenile, no more offensive than the vanity of the boy who locks himself in his room and postures before the looking glass in fond imitation of Gary Cooper or Clark Gable. There is actually a sort of wistful charm in the picture of the Colonel hurrying to his room of an evening, pulling down the blinds, divesting himself of his meekness as though it were a mask that had served its purpose, and then standing forth as the man of his daydreams—tall, strong, iron-jawed, and masterful. As his trusty pen raced along, statesmen, politicians, and captains of industry became marionettes that danced to his will, and by listening closely one could almost hear the low, sardonic laugh that escaped the Colonel as he thought of what the world would say if it but knew his power and realized him as the Puller of Strings. Mark this passage:

"The life I am leading transcends in interest and excitement any romance. I cannot begin to outline what happens from day to day; how information from every quarter pours into this little unobtrusive study." [1] Vanity, to be sure, but rather appealing in its innocence. And again, after learning of the President's decision with respect to the Panama Canal tolls controversy: "I am glad to find that he took the same view I have." [2] What is there in that to arouse more than an indulgent smile?

In such fashion, sweetly and ingenuously, the diary flows along until the Colonel's first trip to Europe. Here again we find Woodrow Wilson's temperamental distastes figuring strongly in the fortunes of the little Texan. At no time did the President ever attempt to conceal his bitterness at the ease with which English diplomats captured our representatives, flattering, befuddling, and cajoling them into abandonment of the American point of view. During the war the newspapers made much of a report that Mr. Wilson did not read the reports of Walter Hines Page, our ambassador to the Court of St. James's, and I took occasion to mention the matter to him.

"The rumor happens to be true," he said. "If I want the British point of view, I can get it far more succinctly from the

---

[1] From *Intimate Papers of Colonel House,* II, 339, edited by Charles Seymour, by permission of Houghton Mifflin Company, publishers.

[2] *Ibid.,* I, 193.

British Ambassador. How I wish," and his voice rose, "that we could find a man to represent us in London who would stay American for more than a month."

In Colonel House he thought he had the man, and it was in pride and confidence that he sent the Texan to England to obtain certain vital information. Unhappily, the Colonel proved no more immune to captivation than Mr. Page. From the moment of his arrival in London, the whole spirit of the diary changes, and it is this change that marks the beginning of the break. The note of appealing juvenility disappears suddenly and permanently, just as though the Colonel had said to himself, "When I was a child I thought as a child. After my English experiences, I must put away childish things." Note the entry on return from his first voyage:

"I find the President singularly lacking in appreciation of the European crisis." [3] A second trip added to this austere judgment, for in the entry of May 30, 1915, he wrote, "I have concluded that war with Germany is inevitable." [4] And one week later: "I told Plunkett I was leaving for America, and my reasons for doing so. I said it was my purpose to persuade the President not to conduct a milk and water war." [5]

This, mark you, was two years before our war declaration, and at a time when Woodrow Wilson was trying desperately to find some formula that would bring peace before America's involvement. Failing in his effort to make the President draw the sword, the Colonel returned to the more congenial atmosphere of London in December, and shortly afterward there is the record of a visit with Ambassador Page: "We dined at the embassy in order that Page and I might have a quiet talk. My entire evening was spent listening to his denunciation of the President and Lansing, and the Administration in general. I did not argue with him. 'The President has no policy. He has lost the respect of Great Britain and the world.' " [6]

"I did not argue with him!" Had he shouted the change in his feeling for Woodrow Wilson, he could not have been plainer. What else but cold indifference can be gained from his

[3] *Ibid.*, I, 296.
[4] *Ibid.*, I, 453.
[5] *Ibid.*, I, 454.
[6] *Ibid.*, II, 177-8.

own admission that he listened to the vilification of the President and said no word? Never at any time, as proved by the diary, did Colonel House have any appreciation of the fact that his position in Europe was entirely due to the generous friendship and unbounded favor of the man he refused to defend; that if he was wined and dined, consulted and flattered, it was only because of the knowledge that the President held him in love and trust.

On March 24, 1916, the *Sussex* was torpedoed, and the Colonel made this confidence to his diary: "I am hardly well enough to make the trip to Washington, but I feel I ought to be there to advise the President during these trying hours. I am afraid he will delay and write further notes." [7] Refusing to plunge his country into war until every hope of peace had been struck down, Mr. Wilson *did* write further notes.

What also irked the Colonel was the President's continued interest in purely American affairs. As the diary records, domestic matters had come to seem "so insignificant [to me] compared with the vital questions now on the boards, that I find myself not caring what he does." [8] What is this but plain evidence that Woodrow Wilson was not only a disappointment to the Colonel, but was actually on the way to becoming a positive bore?

Doubtless out of sentimental regard for an old association, Colonel House said nothing about his change in feeling, and the war declaration also put him in a better mood. The President, entirely unconscious of having given offense, added to honors already bestowed, making the Little Gray Man a member of the Supreme War Council, and then, after the Armistice, selecting him to serve on the Peace Commission.

Any good effect that might have been worked by these proofs of devoted friendship was nullified by the President's decision to go to France. Was not Colonel House himself in Paris on the ground? And did it not stand to reason that he was far better equipped to deal with the delicate questions of the peace than one who had not enjoyed the advantages of intimate association with kings and premiers? Mr. Wilson persisted in his determination, however, and from that time on the proof is plain that

---

[7] *Ibid.*, II, 226.
[8] *Ibid.*, II, 340.

the Colonel regarded his "discovery" of Woodrow Wilson as one of his mistakes.

In February, 1919, I returned to Paris from Poland, Czechoslovakia, and Hungary, and ran into Herbert Bayard Swope, then covering the conference for the New York *World*. "Have you seen House?" was one of his first questions, and when I shook my head, he assured me that I could count on the surprise of my life. "Believe it or not," Herbert went on, "but he's swelled up like a poisoned pup."

And so he had! Gone was the old unassertiveness, the deprecatory air, and the effect of humility. When he walked, his feet hit the floor with the noise of pistol shots; his chest was on a level with his eyes, and an austere disapproval darkened his brow. The diary had done its deadly work. And as I talked with his office staff, from each and every one came the moan, "Oh, if Woody had only stayed away and left things to the Colonel!"

There was no truth in the whisper that this changed attitude stirred the irritation of the President. Always blind where the Colonel was concerned, he saw nothing himself, nor did he hear anything, for he never listened to ill-natured gossip. Moreover, proof is furnished by the fact that when he left for the United States to report on progress, his last act was to appoint Colonel House to represent him in his absence. Fighting single-handed, Woodrow Wilson had forced agreement on the League of Nations as an integral part of the peace treaty, defeating the advocates of "blood and iron," and it was to stand guard over this victory that he chose the Colonel above all others.

It was while on his return trip that the President received the well-nigh unbelievable news that his confreres had repudiated their solemn pledges, kicking the League out of the treaty. The new program, as dictated by Lloyd George, Clemenceau, and Marshal Foch, and agreed to by Colonel House, was to defer demobilization, invade Russia, and jam boundary questions, reparations, colonies, etc., into a preliminary treaty with Germany to be imposed by force. The Colonel met the President at Brest and admitted that the action had been taken, and with his approval.[9]

___

[9] Mrs. Woodrow Wilson, in *My Memoir*, quotes these expressions of the President after the conversation: "House has given away everything I had won before we left Paris. He has compromised on

Mr. Wilson, reaching Paris on March 14, took immediate steps to repair the damage, and issued this statement: "The decision made at the Peace Conference in its plenary session, January 25, 1919, to the effect that the establishment of the League of Nations should be made an integral part of the Treaty of Peace is of final force, and there is no basis whatever for the reports that a change in this decision was contemplated."

Stabbed in the back by his associates, and under daily attack by the Republican majority in the Senate, the President could rely only on truth and logic, and under the rain of his merciless reasoning the plotters repudiated their repudiation.

The record held Colonel House in a vise, proving that he had voted with Lloyd George, Clemenceau, and Orlando in junking a solemn covenant. Nevertheless, there were no reproaches, for although hurt to his heart, the President still believed that it was an error of judgment, an unconscious betrayal induced by adroit flatteries. As a result, the Colonel remained in undisturbed possession of his peacock feather and yellow jacket.

Next to the League, the President's great battle was against the theory of indemnities, his insistence being that only reparations should be exacted, and these based on Germany's "capacity to pay." Such a position was poison to others of the Big Four, for they had excited their people with expectations of billions for war damage, and dared not face realities. Woodrow Wilson won, but worn out by the incessant strain, he fell ill and took to his bed. In his absence a new draft was drawn and signed, omitting all mention of Germany's capacity to pay, and Colonel House approved.

Again the President forced reconsideration, and after an interval the Colonel was sent to London on some vague mission, and there marooned. The two never met again, for in the years

---

every side, and so I have to start all over again and this time it will be harder, as he has given the impression that my delegates are not in sympathy with me. His own explanation of his compromises is that, with a hostile press in the United States expressing disapproval of the League of Nations as a part of the Treaty, he thought it best to yield some other points lest the Conference withdraw its approval altogether. So he has yielded until there is nothing left." (From *My Memoir*, by Edith Bolling Wilson. Copyright, 1939. Used by special permission of the publishers, The Bobbs-Merrill Company.)

that followed, White House rugs waited vainly for the soft caress of the little Texan's velvet tread. To the day of his death, however, Woodrow Wilson would permit no slurring reference to the man he had loved. In talk with me, he confirmed my understanding of the facts in the case, but when I made them the subject of critical comment, he silenced me with a wave of his hand.

CHAPTER 32

Woodrow Wilson's Blunders

For some years now, ever since his death in fact, the politicians, pundits, and cloistered pedants of the universities have been arraigning Woodrow Wilson for his sins of omission and commission, putting full blame on him for the "tragic failure" of the peace conference and the subsequent rejection of the treaty by the Senate. Few of them knew him, or ever took the trouble to talk with those who did know him, all spinning their judgments out of themselves like so many silkworms.

If only the President had stayed in Washington instead of going to Paris! If only the President had taken Senator Lodge, Mr. Taft, Mr. Root, Mr. Hughes, or Theodore Roosevelt with him, not just a few stooges. If only the President had stood firm against Clemenceau and Lloyd George instead of being bamboozled into abandonment of the Fourteen Points and meek acceptance of the "infamous treaty of Versailles."

In considering the truth or falsity of these charges, I offer myself as a fairly competent witness, for I discussed the Paris trip with him at length; I walked and talked with him on the deck of the ship that carried us to Europe; in Paris, on various occasions, he explained the tortuous progress of the conference, and while the treaty was being debated by the Senate I sat with him and heard from his own lips the reasons for his alleged stubbornness.

On the day of the Armistice, Woodrow Wilson was the

world's best-loved figure. In foreign lands they burned candles before his picture, named squares and streets in his honor, and hailed him as the invincible champion of human rights. Better than anyone else, the President knew that he risked this universal popularity by going to Paris in person. Why, then, did he take the gamble? Because he foresaw the tragedy of reaction and intrigue that would stage itself at the Peace Conference!

What the statesmen of Europe had promised when American men and materials were their salvation was bound to lose importance when a merciless enemy lay at their feet. For close to five years, French, English, Italians, Belgians, Serbians, and Czechs had suffered every horror of invasion, and the future that stretched before them was gray with the smoke of burning homes. A League of Nations, a peace of justice, were fine faiths when issues hung in the balance, but with victory won, what more certain than that natural and understandable bitternesses would have the sweep of a flood?

Moreover, the surrender of Germany was in every sense *unconditional,* for the terms of the Armistice placed no limit on the demands of the Allies. The one restraint was the Fourteen Points, accepted by all as the basis of settlement. Mr. Wilson well knew, however, that these points did not constitute an enforceable contract, but were articles of faith. If dealt with in a mean, legalistic spirit, every one could be denied without large loss of face.

For the President to have stayed in Washington would have been the easy way. Enthroned in the White House, high above the jangles of Paris, he could have placed entire responsibility on others, reserving an Olympian detachment for himself. But even as he knew that this would save him his popularity, just as surely did he know that it would lose the peace. The one chance for the League of Nations, for a just and permanent settlement, was for him to go to Paris in person, to sit at the peace table himself, fighting face to face for the pledges that he had framed. To remain in Washington was to invite defeat, for with a situation that would change with every word, it was idle to assume that intelligent communication could be maintained by cable and wireless. These, then, were the reasons behind Woodrow Wilson's decision to head the American Commission to Negotiate Peace.

At the time he told me of his purpose, I took the liberty of discussing the Commission's personnel. The number decided upon was four, exclusive of the President, and two of the places were filled from the first. The Secretary of State was compelled to be chosen by virtue of his position, and Colonel House was equally inevitable, owing to the President's continuous use of his services in European affairs. What I suggested was that the other two posts be given to Republican leaders so as to take off the curse of partisanship.

"But who?" the President demanded. "Tell me that. The Fourteen Points, accepted by the Allies, embody the terms on which Germany surrendered, and are therefore the basis for negotiations. Yet the entire Republican party is on record in flat opposition to every single point. Not a day passes that Mr. Roosevelt and Senator Lodge do not repudiate them. Mr. Hays, chairman of the Republican National Committee, foams at the mere thought of a 'negotiated peace,' and goes on to insist that America must and will 'uphold her allies in whatever reparation they may exact for the frightful outrages inflicted upon them by the accursed Huns.'

"Mr. Taft?" He shrugged his shoulders wearily. "A fine, honest man, but the very amiability that constitutes his charm makes it impossible for him to stand hitched. An ardent champion of the League throughout the war, he now wobbles all over the place.

"Mr. Root? Unfortunately, the peoples of Europe look on him as a representative of big business and advocate of dollar diplomacy. I sent him to Russia at the head of an important mission, and its failure was largely due to Russian distrust of Mr. Root."

In the end the President filled the two places with General Tasker H. Bliss, a wise old soldier and brilliant scholar, and Henry White, a veteran diplomat who knew the European mind as a fox knows its burrow. More than that, he had been our ambassador to Italy and France by appointment of Republican presidents, and had served as the head of many American delegations to international conferences.

The Commission, however, was not an important body in any true sense. When one thought of England, France, and Italy, it was in terms of Lloyd George, Clemenceau, and Orlando, each his country's authoritative voice and picked champion. Woodrow Wilson, no less, would stand as America's voice and picked champion. The Paris meeting plainly forecast itself as a grapple of *four* wills, a test of strength confined to *four* leaders. What the President needed on the Commission was not men who would share his power and responsibility, but counselors who would guard his back.

Realizing this, he spent weeks in combing the country for the foremost specialists in finance, history, economics, international law, colonial questions, map making, ethnic distinctions, and all other matters bound to come up at the conference. Compared to the Wilson group, the men that Mr. Roosevelt and Mr. Truman took to Yalta and Potsdam look like pygmies.

Among the economists, financiers, and industrialists were such men as Herbert Hoover; Bernard M. Baruch; Thomas Lamont; Frank Taussig, head of the Tariff Commission; Alex Legg, of the International Harvester company; Frederick Neilson and Chandler Anderson, authorities on international law; and Norman Davis.

Dr. Sidney Mezes, president of the College of the City of New York, headed a brilliant group of specialists, all of whom had been working for a year or more on the problems that would be presented at the peace conference. Among them were: Professor Charles H. Haskins of Harvard, specialist on Alsace-Lorraine and Belgium; Dr. Isaiah Bowman of the American Geographical Society; Charles Seymour, professor of history at Yale, specialist on Austria-Hungary; James T. Shotwell, professor of history at Columbia; George Louis Beer, an authority on colonial matters; Clive Day of Yale, specialist on the Balkans; R. H. Lord of Harvard, specialist on Russia and Poland; and a score of others. The President's dependence on them was made clear at the very first discussion on the *George Washington*.

"You are, in truth, my advisers," he said, "for when I ask information, I will have no way of checking it, and must act on it unquestioningly. We shall be deluged with claims plausibly presented, and it will be your job to establish the justice or injustice of these claims, so that my position may be taken intelligently."

The President was well aware of the risks that he ran, the dangers that he faced. The joy of the Armistice, which caught everyone in its tidal sweep, was perhaps his last experience with unalloyed happiness. His fears were confirmed even while we were on the water, for from England came word that Lloyd George was campaigning on a platform of "Hang the Kaiser" and "Make Germany pay the whole cost of the war." Worse still, we were barely settled in Paris before Clemenceau shouted his defiance of the League of Nations, making this speech before the Chamber of Deputies: "There is an old system which appears condemned today, and to which I do not fear to say that I remain faithful at this moment. Countries have organized the defense of their frontiers with the necessary elements for the *balance of power.*"

Why not? From the United States Theodore Roosevelt was crying this message to Europe, carrying a specific promise that the Republican majority in the Senate would support any and every repudiation of the League of Nations and the Fourteen Points:

Our allies and our enemies and Mr. Wilson himself should all understand that Mr. Wilson has no authority whatever to speak for the American people at this time. His leadership has been emphatically repudiated by them. The newly elected Congress comes far nearer than Mr. Wilson to having a right to speak the purposes of the American people at this moment. Mr. Wilson and his Fourteen Points and his four supplementary points and his five complementary points, and all of his utterances every which way, have ceased to have any shadow of right to be accepted as expressive of the will of the American people.

Not content with this desertion of the President and his grant of power of attorney to Lloyd George and Clemenceau, Mr. Roosevelt then went on to slur America's war effort in these words:

America played in the closing months of the war a gallant part, but not in any way the leading part, and she played this part only by acting in strictest agreement with our allies, and under the joint high command. She should take precisely the same attitude at the Peace Conference. . . . Of the terrible sacrifice which has enabled the Allies to win the victory, America has contributed just about two per cent.

This, then, was the situation when Woodrow Wilson took his place at the conference table. Instead of support from the American people, there came only the daily shrilling of the Senate, vile in its abuse and treacherous in its desertion of war aims. Facing him were men who jeered at him in their souls and whose minds were set on the repudiation of pledges. Not for them "Utopian theories" and "emotional experiments," but flat assertion that to the victor belongs the spoils.

For Woodrow Wilson to have thrown up his hands and returned to the United States as a protest would have been not merely desertion but actual betrayal. Left to themselves, with every restraint removed, the Allies would have given themselves over entirely to their fears and hates, finally deciding on a treaty holding no promise of the world peace that had been pledged. The one honorable course was to stay and *fight it out,* and this was Woodrow Wilson's decision.

From the very first the Allies stood like iron against having the League of Nations as an integral part of the treaty. Equally intransigent was their attitude with respect to indemnities, for Lloyd George, Clemenceau, and Orlando had led their peoples to believe that as much as $40,000,000,000 could be squeezed out of Germany. Even more disturbing was the disclosure of secret arrangements that provided for territorial grabs. The Rhine valley and the Saar Basin were to be annexed by France; Italy was to have Fiume and the Dalmatian coast; the whole of East Prussia was to be Poland's share, and Rumania, that jackal nation, had been promised large chunks of Austria-Hungary.

As for the German colonies, their disposition had been arranged in advance. Japan was to hold the Chinese province of Shantung in fee simple and take over the Marshalls and the Carolines; Australia and New Zealand were to divide South Pacific possessions; the Cameroons and Togoland were to go to the French, and even South Africa was to be given former German territory. Nothing was further from Allied thought than any idea of mandates as laid down by the Fourteen Points.

The President, as a matter of course, refused to be bound by the secret treaties, and urged that the League be taken up as a first order of business. He won, but only after weeks of bitter debate, and when the first draft of the Covenant was confirmed unanimously on February 14, Mr. Wilson took it back to the United States for the information of the Senate.

What followed will always stand as a singularly shameful chapter in American history. Instead of welcoming the opportunity for conference, Senator Lodge and his crew refused to advance objections or to make any recommendations, sullenly

256

announcing that they would defer action until the treaty came before them for confirmation or rejection. Going still further, on March 4, the day before the President's return to France, thirty-seven Republican senators signed a round robin declaring unalterable hostility to the League as part of the peace treaty. When this news was cabled to Paris, Clemenceau, Lloyd George, and Orlando repudiated sworn agreements, and after discarding the League, returned to their plan for a "hard peace" enforced by armies.

Back in France, the President faced his associates in another test of strength. Logically, convincingly, he ripped their plan to pieces, showing that it was not only unjust but unworkable. Did they not have sense enough to see that their greedy imperialism would lead to the manufacture of new wars? What stood more plain than the need of a civil machinery to administer the terms of the peace treaty? Were they fools enough to dream that this administration could be furnished by the Allied high command, backed by armies drawn from the youth of America, England, Italy, and Japan? Did they not have the vision to perceive that the peoples of these nations were sick of militarism, and that they would not stand for a military dictatorship any more than would the people of Germany?

Were they so blind as not to see that the League of Nations provided the very machinery that was needed? That the whole peace treaty would fall to pieces without a fair, independent civil body to live on through the years that would be necessary to carry out the treaty's provisions? What madness possessed them that they imagined for one moment that the United States would furnish the money for a Russian invasion or the maintenance of a military dictatorship in Germany?

Under this merciless rain of logic Lloyd George curled up and Clemenceau writhed. There was no answer to it, either from the gay insouciance of the one or the insolence of the other. On March 26 it was announced, grudgingly enough, that there *would* be a League of Nations as an integral part of the peace treaty.

The victory won, the President plunged at once into another battle. While in the United States, and after his insolent rebuff by the Senate Committee on Foreign Relations, he submitted the draft of the Covenant to various Republican leaders with a request for suggestions. Mr. Taft, as a result of study, submitted four amendments: (1) that the vote of the Council should be unanimous in order to safeguard the United States against any combination of other powers; (2) exclusion of all domestic questions from the purview of the League; (3) explicit provision for withdrawal from the League by giving a two-year notice; and (4) revision of the armament schedule every five or ten years.

Judge Charles E. Hughes endorsed Mr. Taft's recommendations and added two of his own: that there should be specific exemption of the Monroe Doctrine, and that a nation would not have to accept a mandate without its consent. Mr. Root, after supporting the suggestions of Mr. Taft and Judge Hughes, urged that subjects suitable for arbitration should be clearly defined; that a permanent court of international justice should be created; and that the guarantee of territorial integrity in Article X should run for five years only. All three leaders were explicit in stating that if these amendments were adopted, every honest objection would be removed.

There was not a single suggested change that had honesty back of it. The League was an association of sovereigns, and as a matter of course any sovereign possessed the right of withdrawal. The League, as an international advisory body, could not possibly deal with domestic questions under any construction of the Covenant. No power of Congress was abridged, and necessarily Congress would have to act before war could be declared or a single soldier sent out of the country. Instead of recognizing the Monroe Doctrine as an American policy, the League legitimized it as a world policy. The President, however, was bound to propose that these plain propositions be put in kindergarten language for the satisfaction of his enemies, and it was this proposal that gave Clemenceau, Lloyd George, and their associates a new chance for resistance.

All of the suggested changes were made without great demur until the question of the Monroe Doctrine was reached, and then French and English bitterness broke all restraints. Why were they expected to make every concession to American prejudices when the President would make none to European traditions? They had gone to the length of accepting the doctrine of Monroe for the whole of the earth, but now, because American pride demanded it, they must make public confession of America's right to give orders. No! A thousand times no! It was high time for the President to give a little consideration to French and English and Italian prejudices—time for him to realize that the lives of these governments were at stake as well as his own. France, Italy, and Japan renewed their claims, and Clemenceau demanded that England and the United States enter into a tripartite pact that would pledge them to France's aid in event of another invasion by Germany.

Rising from his sickbed, the President faced the Council and stated flatly that there must be an end to the dreary business of making engagements only to break them. If a peace of justice could be framed, he would stay; if a peace of greed, then he would leave. At all times he had recognized the grievances of the Allies, and stood firmly for a treaty that would drive home their guilt to the Germans; but he could not and would not consent to the repudiation of every war aim or to territorial grabs that would leave the world worse off than before.

The gesture was conclusive with respect to France and Britain. Straightway Lloyd George swung over to the President's side, and Clemenceau issued an official statement explicitly denying that his government had any annexationist pretensions. Many bitternesses, however, still persisted. The French demanded the tripartite agreement. Belgium announced intent to withdraw from the Conference unless given a larger share of reparations, and Orlando had already quit the Conference on account of Fiume. Japan also threatened withdrawal out of her anger over Shantung.

None knew better than the President that if the Conference dissolved in anger and confusion, nothing but another World War would restore the League of Nations to the realm of practical politics. None knew better than the President that the constitution of the League contained every power of remedy for the evils of the treaty, and that these powers would be exercised wisely and effectively in the day when the rule of reason should prevail again. These were the considerations that impelled the President to certain measures of compromise.

Facing the Japanese anew, he told them that he would support their claim to the German rights in Shantung if Japan, in return, would agree to recognize the sovereignty of China and rest content with the mere role of an economic concessionaire. While standing firm against Italy's grab of Fiume, he did consent to the internationalization of the seaport. Although rejecting Poland's demand for East Prussia, he agreed to the internationalization of Danzig. Neither was he shaken as to the continuance of German sovereignty in the Rhine valley and over the Saar Basin, but he saw only justice in Clemenceau's insistence on the tripartite alliance that would guarantee France against German invasion.

Against these compromises, later to be attacked as shameful, what were Woodrow Wilson's gains? The German indemnity was fixed at $14,000,000,000 instead of $40,000,000,000, and placed under the direction of a reparations commission that had the power to adjust payments to the needs and abilities of the German people.

The German colonies were withdrawn from conquest and annexation, and put under the supervision and protection of the League by a system of mandates. The territorial integrity of weak and small nations was explicitly guaranteed.

The French claim to the Rhine valley and the Saar Basin was denied, likewise Italy's claim to Fiume. Japan, instead of grabbing Shantung as a prize of war, was forced to accept the role of economic concessionaire, and under pledge to evacuate within a given period.

The League of Nations was adopted as a primary and integral part of the treaty, the very keystone in the arch. The establishment of an international court of justice opened the way for the reign of law throughout the world, and an international labor office held the promise of social justice.

The Republican Senate may have felt that Woodrow Wilson was "bamboozled," but no crow of self-congratulation came from any Allied country. In England both Parliament and the press snarled at Lloyd George as "Wilson's puppy dog"; in Italy Orlando was denounced for his "servility," and France's Chamber of Deputies pilloried Clemenceau for permitting the "autocratic Wilson" to bully him into the surrender of French rights.

There is still another significant fact that Woodrow Wilson's critics are at pains to overlook. From the first day of the Conference to the last, the insistence of the Senate was on speed, and the President worked under the strain of daily denunciation for his "dilatory tactics" and "criminal delay." The Senate received the treaty on June 10, 1919, and killed it on March 19,

1920. Less than four months for construction and a full ten months for destruction.

In this connection there is a deadly parallel to be drawn. In February, 1945, President Roosevelt, Prime Minister Churchill, and Marshal Stalin held an eight-day conference in Yalta and laid down definite decisions with respect to the peace that was then in sight. "It is not our purpose to destroy Germany," said the final statement, "but to restore hope for a decent life for Germans, and a place for them in the comity of nations." Continuing, it said that "the establishment of order in Europe, and the rebuilding of economic life, must be achieved by processes which will enable the liberated peoples . . . to create democratic institutions of their own choice." Then came a reiteration of the principles of the Atlantic Charter— "the right of all peoples to choose the form of government under which they will live; the restoration of sovereign rights and self-government to those peoples who have been forcibly deprived of them by aggressor nations." This was followed by a specific pledge to guarantee free elections.

In April of 1945, at San Francisco, the United Nations Conference on International Organization added the capsheaf to a great world structure, rendered obeisance to the Four Freedoms, and reiterated the explicit provisions of the Atlantic Charter. At this writing, two years since the cessation of hostilities, not a single pledge has been redeemed, and true world peace is not even a prospect.

Poland, Rumania, Bulgaria, and Yugoslavia are puppet states, ruled autocratically by Moscow stooges, many of them with criminal records; Czechoslovakia maintains a shadow of independence by servile fawning on Russia; Italy cowers under a treaty that puts her at Tito's mercy; Hungary and Austria and Germany, mutilated, ravaged, and famine-stricken, have given up any hope of escape from their pit.

Yet the outcry against Woodrow Wilson's "blunders" and the "infamous treaty of Versailles" still continues.

CHAPTER 33

Harding, Coolidge, and Hoover

*T*he years between 1920 and 1932 were "blackouts" as far as the progressive movement was concerned. Exhausted by the high emotionalism of war, sick of sacrifice, and gasping from the upper air that Woodrow Wilson had made them breathe, people turned to Warren Harding's "normalcy" with all the glad alacrity of a Lazarus reaching for balmy oils with which to soothe his sores. As if at a given signal, the League of Nations, the World Court, and even disarmament became subjects that bored. Industry and thrift were tossed into the discard along with other basic concepts on which the national life had been built. Financiers and economists openly encouraged a madness of speculation by the lie that earnings had nothing to do with the value of a stock, and counting paper profits superseded baseball as the national game. Instead of being laughed out of the country, M. Coué was hailed as the prophet of a new order, and thousands gibbered his formula for happiness and prosperity: "Day by day, in every way, I am getting better and better."

Prohibition also played its part in the drop from the heights, for the "noble experiment" worked an almost instant loosening in the moral fiber of the nation. Law, as Brand Whitlock once observed, is what the people *back up,* and no statute was ever more rejected by public opinion. Thousands drank who had never before touched liquor, risking blindness in their eagerness to "strike a blow for liberty," and the youth of the land followed the example of their elders. Out of it came the organized gangs that still remain an integral part of our social order, switching over to the labor movement after prohibition's repeal. Big business, no less quick to take advantage of the general letdown, again rattled the loaded dice that Wilson had taken away.

Even if Warren Harding had been a man of ability, courage, and ideals, it is to be doubted whether he could have bucked the reaction. As it was, his easy amiability, lack of standards, and mental sloth fitted the mood of the times as if made to measure. I met him first in Ohio when I was doing the story on George B. Cox, Cincinnati's iron boss. The hulking former saloonkeeper, shrewd for all his grossness, had seen the possibilities of the small-town editor as a "front," and at the time of my visit Harding was lieutenant governor.

Every gang, from Tweed on down, has had keen appreciation of the value of "window dressing," rarely failing to put forward respectable figureheads as a screen for the skulduggery that goes on behind. In Warren Harding the Cincinnati boss found a "natural," for behind the noble façade of a Roman senator lolled the soul of a born henchman. Personally honest, in that he did not graft himself, the country editor sat silent during the years that Cox debauched a city and the state, lifting his pen and voice only to praise.

In the Senate, where I knew him next, he was the unasking, unquestioning rubber stamp for Lodge, Penrose, and other Republican leaders, taking their orders even as he had obeyed the profane bellows of George Cox. He had not wanted the presidency, acutely aware of his incapacity for the high office, and it was to lessen this feeling of inferiority that he surrounded himself with as cheap and venal a crew as ever grimed the White House.

There can be no doubt that he was shocked by the scandals that rocked his administration, just as he must have been shocked by the corruptions of Cox and his gang, but the henchman habit of a lifetime stilled any public expression. Instead of cleaning house, he tried to cover up, and like every other "front," attempted to disguise his servility by calling it loyalty.

This, then, was the man that the people chose to succeed Woodrow Wilson. And in 1924, when opportunity offered to lift the country back to a high plane, Calvin Coolidge was elected by an overwhelming majority. True, the Democratic party had been split into warring halves by the bitter struggle between Alfred Smith and William G. McAdoo, but John W. Davis stood out as a man of character and pre-eminent ability, his quality proved in both private life and public office.

The accidental factor in American politics was never better

exemplified than by the case of Calvin Coolidge. After the nomination of Harding, party leaders spent sweating hours in vain search for some outstanding figure to take second place on the ticket. Hiram Johnson was one of those who turned down the vice-presidency, a blunder that he lived to regret with tears and curses. And what finally attracted attention to Coolidge? Just one incident that colored the commonplace of his career, and which had no more base in fact than the story about George Washington and the Cherry tree.

During Mr. Coolidge's term as governor of Massachusetts, there was a police strike in Boston and he was given the credit for breaking it. According to press report, he faced the strikers with dauntless front and cowed them into submission by declaring that there was no right superior to the public welfare. A later and more truthful account proved that the Governor had to be dragged into the controversy by the hair of his head, and only after the police commissioner had smashed the backbone of the strike. By that time, however, the original version was firmly fixed in the public mind.

President Coolidge, although in a different way, fitted the mood of the times no less snugly than President Harding. Sitting in the White House as immovably as a rabbit in its form, and distinguishable from the furniture only when he moved, he said nothing and did nothing that stirred thought or ruffled the general complacence with things as they were. More than half tight between bathtub gin and a stock market that seemed to have no ceiling, people joined in a Gadarene gallop to the abyss.

Whatever else may be said about the Coolidge administration, it had dignity and decency. When the President took an automobile ride into the country, for example, the First Lady did not have to hide empty bottles under the lap robe for deposit in some remote ravine. Nor were White House visitors called on to wade through spittoons and cigar butts, or wait in the outer chamber until the President had been regaled with the latest story.

There is not much question but that Mr. Coolidge could have had the nomination again in 1928, for he met every need of Wall Street, and bosses were still in control of the Republican organization. With true New England shrewdness, however, he appraised the future more accurately than any of the great financiers and industrialists. Undoubtedly convinced that the madness of speculation had pushed high above the safety gauge, he announced that he did not choose to run, and stepped out to let another feel the full force of the deluge.

Writing about Herbert Hoover is like trying to describe the interior of a citadel where every drawbridge is up and every portcullis down, thus leaving nothing for inspection but a stretch of blank wall. When he came to Washington to head the Food Administration, it was with the prestige so richly deserved by his brilliant handling of European relief, and all of us rushed forward with open arms to greet our coworker. If we had been carrying tin cups and wearing the blue glasses of mendicancy, our reception could not have been colder. Chin firmly tucked against his breastbone, he talked to us through his hair, and then only in chill monosyllables.

We worked side by side throughout the war, but never once was there a suggestion of intimacy or even an approach to friendship. Once when President Wilson asked me how I got along with Mr. Hoover, I answered that he always gave me the feeling of a cockroach sliding around in a porcelain bathtub. "It must be," I added, "that he looks on all of us as politicians, and therefore not to be trusted."

Nevertheless, Herbert Hoover did a great job with the Food Administration, and as he was outside all controversy, enjoyed enormous popularity. So much, in fact, that party leaders considered him seriously for the Democratic nomination in 1920, for while no one knew his politics, he was strong in support of the League of Nations. At the last minute, however, he decided that he was, or would be, a Republican.

Ignored by the convention in favor of Harding, Mr. Hoover not only campaigned for the ticket, but joined with Mr. Taft and others in the declaration that Republican victory would ensure both League and World Court. In the hour of repudiation, no word of protest came from him, nor as President Harding's Secretary of Commerce did he ever lift his voice against the corruptions of the regime. All the while, however, devoted Hooverites spread the whisper that only the Chief could restore the party to good standing.

The campaign continued throughout the Coolidge administration, and that the President was not unaware is fairly well attested. Asked by a friend for his opinion of Mr. Hoover, the shrewd New Englander answered crisply, "How can you like a man who's always trying to get your job?"

When he attained the ambition nursed for a full decade, it might have been thought that Herbert Hoover would have burst into flower, or at least into bud, showing some of the warm, human qualities—the vision and decision—that made his relief work a masterpiece of administration. Instead of that, he seemed to draw still more deeply within himself, raising new barriers against popular contact, and even against those assumed to be his counselors. His public appearances were not only infrequent but actually painful, for he read his uninspired speeches monotonously, rarely lifting his eyes from the manuscript.

In retrospect, his approach to the problems of the day are seen to have been sound. As an engineer, putting facts before action, he appointed commission after commission for the study of causes and cures, refusing to plunge forward until he knew where he was going. Only recently I went over the reports of these bodies, and there was not one that failed to make sense. At no time, however, did he go before the people with the findings, explaining and persuading, but he dumped them into the Congressional hopper without any clarifying public appeal.

Out in San Francisco the Bohemian Club owns several thousand acres up on the Russian River, and every summer sees the entire membership leaving the city for a month or two in the redwoods. Along with the Grove play, the Low Jinks, concerts, etc., a feature of the encampment is the noonday talk at the lakeside by some member or guest. It was in 1945, if I remember correctly, that Mr. Hoover made one of these informal addresses, reporting on his survey of the European situation.

I nearly rolled off the bank into the water as I listened to him. Head high, gaze direct, he spoke for an hour with a choice of words, a vigor of phrase, and a lucidity that would not have shamed Woodrow Wilson. I have heard him many times since then, both from the platform and over the radio, and there is no public figure today speaking more convincingly, more courageously, or more sanely. Governor Dewey may be the titular head of the Republican party, but Herbert Hoover is its spiritual leader. It is interesting to speculate what would

266

have happened had this new Hoover, or the *real* Hoover, been shown to the people during his presidential term.

As a matter of truth, I have no business speaking disrespectfully of the Harding, Coolidge, and Hoover administrations, for the swing back to reaction and isolationism gave me the chance to go about the chore of money earning. With Washington a forbidden city to Wilsonians, and people interested only in home brews and the stock market, I turned again to magazine assignments after the 1920 election.

Both *Everybody's* and the *Saturday Evening Post* opened their pages to me, but when *Collier's* offered a staff job, I leaped at the prospect of steady employment. Now, at last, I cashed in on my years of drudgery with *The Independent*, where I turned out sixteen pages of editorial, sport, fiction, fashions, and humor every week. As a sort of handy man on *Collier's*, I did leaders, historical romances, and articles on every known subject. In 1922, however, the editors had the bright idea of a series along the lines of Mr. Dooley, discontinued by Finley Peter Dunne some years before, and after much travail of spirit I invented a homespun character called Uncle Henry. Heaven knows the pieces were miles removed from the brilliance of Mr. Dooley, but they proved popular, and I ground them out week by week for a full ten years.

In 1926, restored to solvency and thoroughly sick of New York's summers and winters, my wife and I decided to move to San Francisco. Why not? Our two children—Frances Virginia and Bates—would flourish in California's sunshine, and whenever the need arose, I could fly east for a month or so. Moreover, with three thousand miles between me and Washington, I would run no risk of being drawn back into politics.

It is a decision that has never been regretted, for at the risk of controversy I am willing to go on record with the flat statement that San Francisco offers more to its people than any other American city. Set on a score of hills above the shining bay, and rimmed by mountain ranges, it yields to no other city, not even Naples, in beauty; all the world streams through this gateway to the Orient at one time or another, making for a cosmopolitanism that leaves no room for parochialism; intensely communal without sacrifice of individuality, treasuring pioneer traditions while alive to progress, and proud without bumptiousness, San Francisco is outstanding for its superb *balance*.

267

Unfortunately, my idea did not work out as planned. The stock-market crash of 1929 put my nose back against the grindstone, compelling more frequent and longer stays in the east, and then came the presidential campaign.

CHAPTER 34

Franklin Roosevelt Takes Over

*W*ith the country sinking deeper and deeper into the pit of depression, nothing was more certain than the election of a Democrat in 1932. Franklin Roosevelt, quick to realize it, sent Jim Farley on a coast-to-coast scout for state delegations, and Al Smith, attracted by the outlook, soon changed his mind about not being a candidate. Along with many others who had worked with him during the war, I was for Newton Baker, and when the party in California split into Smith and Roosevelt factions, it looked like a good chance to slip through a Baker delegation. With this idea in mind, I ran down to Los Angeles for a talk with my old friend William G. McAdoo, then a resident of California and beginning to interest himself in local politics.

It may be that affection colors my judgment, but I hold that in the matter of administrative genius, only Alexander Hamilton offers a parallel to Woodrow Wilson's Secretary of the Treasury. At every point in McAdoo's career there is ample evidence of the same gifts that distinguished George Washington's strong right hand.

Entering New York as a young man, poor and unknown, he took up a project that famous engineers had abandoned as hopeless, and drove tubes under the Hudson River. This and other undertakings lifted him to high place among the great industrialists of America, bringing him wealth and power, yet when asked to accept the Treasury post, he quit his $50,000-a-year position and sold all of his holdings at a loss.

No less bold, dynamic, and assured than Hamilton, McAdoo

268

was not only Secretary of the Treasury but also chairman of the Federal Reserve Board, chairman of the Farm Loan Board, chairman of the War Finance Corporation, director general of railroads, administrator of the War Risk Insurance Bureau, and director of the Liberty Loan drives. To all of these duties he brought not only supreme competence but a courage that won him enduring hates.

Among other reforms, he ended Wall Street's control of the Treasury; demanded 2-per-cent interest on all government deposits, a ruling that gained millions; he warred against exorbitant interest rates, and by threatening to withdraw government funds from offending banks, put a stop to usury; and further angered the great bankers by refusing to let them sell Liberty bonds on a commission basis.

When McAdoo became director general of the railroads, what he took over was a junk heap, for almost every system had been gutted by upscrupulous financiers. What he had to do, and what he did do, was to create a brand-new transportation machinery. Worthless executives, drawing down hundreds of thousands in salaries and bonuses, were kicked out; railroad workers were granted the right to organize and bargain collectively; he ended discriminations against women and Negroes, establishing the principle of equal pay for equal work, and by way of creating new enmities, went on to advocate the Child Labor Law, the Workmen's Compensation Law, and other measures designed to take the cruelty and unfairness out of industry. These were some of the reasons behind the enmity with which big business pursued him to the day of his death.

I knew Mac did not like either Smith or Roosevelt, and with good reason. In the 1924 convention he had had a clear majority of the delegates, just missing the necessary two thirds, and the deadlock that beat him out of the nomination was due to the Smith lie that McAdoo was the candidate of the Ku Klux Klan. This in face of the fact that Mac's two principal supporters were Bernard M. Baruch, the Jew, and Senator James Phelan, the Catholic. As for Franklin Roosevelt, he was Al Smith's most ardent supporter, although he owed his appointment as Assistant Secretary of the Navy to McAdoo. As vice-chairman of the Democratic National Committee, Mac had a potent voice in patronage matters, and he picked young Roosevelt on the strength of his courageous anti-Tammany fight while a state senator.

A talk with Mac developed that he also disliked Baker, because of differences while in Wilson's cabinet. No two men were ever more dissimilar, for the Secretary of War was scholarly, philosophical, and contemplative, while the Secretary of the Treasury shot ahead with the speed and directness of a bullet. Dynamic and intuitive, with supreme confidence in his abilities, Mac raged against Baker's cautious approach to problems, and the two were in continual dispute.

Not liking any of the three principal candidates—Roosevelt, Smith, or Baker—Mac entered into a deal with William R. Hearst and put a delegation in the field committed to Congressman Jack Garner of Texas. As he had foreseen, the Smith and Roosevelt forces engaged in a knockdown fight, letting the McAdoo-Hearst ticket slip through. Garner, of course had no chance whatsoever for the nomination, but the California and Texas delegations constituted a balance of power in the convention.

I went with Mac to Chicago, still hopeful for Baker; but when Garner finally released his delegates, the California caucus decided to go for Franklin Roosevelt. The Texans reached a similar decision, but only after a struggle, for the vote was 54 to 51. These switches gave Roosevelt the nomination, but instead of the expected enthusiasm, McAdoo was booed for half an hour when he mounted the platform to cast California's vote.

The Roosevelt that flew to Chicago to make his acceptance speech in person was a vastly different Roosevelt from the gay, volatile Prince Charming I had known during the war years. There was vision, courage, and certainty in both his words and his voice as he outlined the policies of the New Deal, and as he spoke in the rich, assured tone that was to prove such a radio asset, it was as though clean air blew through a sickroom. Stirred to real enthusiasm, I told the people at *Collier's* that they would have to stagger along without me for a while, and hurried back to San Francisco to take part in the campaign.

With Roosevelt's election in the bag, however, it was McAdoo's candidacy for the Senate that took the larger part of my time, for notwithstanding his national stature, native sons opposed him as a "carpetbagger." Roosevelt, incredibly enough,

270

refused to say a word in Mac's behalf, and not until long afterward did I learn the reason. With infinite capacity for holding grudges, F.D.R. never forgave the men who had been against his nomination, and not even McAdoo's switch had power to make the President forget the Garner campaign. At that, McAdoo won easily in the primary, and went on to pile up a huge majority in the general election.

When the count showed a Roosevelt landslide I returned to *Collier's,* and was at once assigned to do a story on the President-elect that would deal with his purposes and plans in the greatest possible detail. The day that I spent with him in Albany, just before his departure for Washington, confirmed the Chicago impression that as a result of his illness, with its time for thought and study, Franklin Roosevelt was one who had experienced a spiritual rebirth. Rapidly, brilliantly, never hesitating for a word, he set forth his reasons for believing that the debacle of 1929 was no mere financial panic, but the *end of an era.*

The old order, as he called it, was based on a predominantly agricultural civilization. Rugged individualism and unrestricted competition were the rules of the day, because there was no great need of co-operation, and very little opportunity for it. Great public-service monopolies were unknown, for springs, wells, and cisterns furnished water, and elbow grease the power. There were, in fact, no corporations of any kind until 1840 or thereabouts, and with industry open to all eyes, greed and cruelty were held in check by a forceful public opinion.

After praising it as a kindly, gracious order, Mr. Roosevelt then proceeded to discuss the fundamental changes that had taken place: the switch from an agricultural civilization to industrialization, with science and industry controlling the destinies of millions; the change from individual ownership to corporate ownership, eliminating any close relation between labor and management, and virtually inviting industrial war; the growth of cities with their slums; the replacement of free and helpful competition by wolfish competition. No longer was industry ruled by a decent majority. Ninety per cent of employers might agree on a code of honor and fairness, but a lawless, rapacious 10 per cent had the power to destroy the code, forcing the honorable 90 per cent to choose between

271

lowered standards and bankruptcy. Hence child labor, sweat-shops, and like industrial cancers.

Interdependence was now the rule of the day. With the income of city workers creating the market for farm products, their disemployment resulted inevitably in the collapse of agriculture. No longer were there vacant lands or frontiers offering the promise of escape. No longer was the head of a family able to care for his women and shelter his elders. Age had become a thing of terror just as involuntary idleness had become a thing of despair.

A new economic order, recognizing these changes, was compelled by common sense and every instinct of self-preservation. A government that could not care for its old and sick, that could not provide work for the strong, that fed its young into the hopper of industry, and that let the black shadow of insecurity rest on every home was not a government that could endure or should endure.

While professing a sincere respect for states' rights, he pointed out the existence of many twilight zones, and insisted that there were needed standards in many social and economic areas that must be *national*. Unless great unitary systems, such as mining, milling, manufacture, and agriculture, were brought under one central policy control, instead of being left to the favoritism or prejudice of forty-eight different states, how could anarchy be avoided?

Was it necessarily an attack on enterprise and initiative to say that fraud, bribery, cruelty, and rapacity must quit masquerading as enterprise and initiative? What more plain than that all business had come to be vested with a public use, and that any business unable to make a fair return except by child labor, long hours, dog's wages, lying, and cheating was not a business that the country wanted?

With this as a background, he set forth the reforms that he had in mind: a blue-sky law; the right of workers to organize and bargain collectively; a drive against monopoly; the development of our natural resources; a far-flung social-security program; the protection of bank deposits; a federal works program to fill in the valleys of unemployment; soil conservation; taxation based on ability to pay and benefits received, etc. A new order, in fact, that would raise consumption to a level with our highest possible production; an order that would banish the

272

terrors of present-day existence, so that a man might go to sleep at night without fearing that the morrow would drag him down from security to despair; an order that would make for true individualism by restoring and safeguarding independence and self-respect.

It was plain, of course, that much of what he said came from the "policy board" that he had gathered about him at the very outset of the campaign, but the very composition of the group supported my theory of a spiritual rebirth. In it were none of the inheritors of wealth and position with whom Franklin Roosevelt had been associated from boyhood, nor yet any of the purely political type that thought in terms of precincts, trades, and chicane. All were students of government, more idealistic than practical, perhaps, but every one altruistic rather than self-serving.

Raymond Moley, a professor without a hint of the cloister and its narrownesses, was as authentic a liberal as I ever knew. Best of all, his enthusiasms were held in check by an orderly habit of mind that made him precede action by inquiry and research. The one blunder that marred his record for sound judgment was when he let himself be cajoled into accepting the post of Assistant Secretary of State, responsible to the President and not to Mr. Hull. The impossibility of the situation, as he had foreseen, led to his resignation, and I have always believed that it robbed the administration of a highly necessary balance wheel.

For all of his cocksureness—a fault that militated against his political career—Adolf Berle, Jr., was able far beyond the average, being one of the few "infant prodigies" who carried early promise over into adult life. I doubt if any man in the country knew more about credit and corporate finance, and in the field of his specialized knowledge he contributed powerfully to the formation of Franklin Roosevelt's thought. Rexford Guy Tugwell's later aberrations dimmed his luster considerably, but he had made the economics of agriculture a life study.

General Hugh Johnson was no less the genuine liberal than Ray Moley, but with radical differences in approach. Ardent and excitable, the broad sweep of his mind induced a high degree of tangentalism, to coin a word, but notwithstanding his love of pyrotechnics, no man had a better understanding of democracy's ills or a more burning desire to cure them. As I listened to the President-elect, it was easy to detect the influence of Hugh's enveloping humanity.

It was not only that Franklin Roosevelt had chosen these men, and others of similar type, as his aides and counselors. What impressed me most was that he did not rattle off his views as though he had merely memorized the memoranda submitted to him. Every tone of his voice, every flash of his eye, conveyed sincerity, and forced the feeling that his acceptance had its base in the *rightness* of their findings. It is an opinion that has never changed, for to this day I hold the conviction that when Franklin Roosevelt first entered the White House, it was with noble resolves and high purpose.

I left the President-elect with an enthusiasm I had not known since the days of Woodrow Wilson, and when he took office I made an instant offer of my services as a volunteer in the field. Doubtless as a result, General Hugh Johnson wired me in July, saying that he wanted me to help administer the National Recovery Act on the Pacific Coast. No letter followed, and the next I knew about it was a newspaper story announcing that I was one of a district board of nine for California, Utah, Nevada, Alaska, and the Hawaiian Islands. Along with this district board, however, a hodgepodge of other boards was also set up. I accepted the appointment, but days passed without a word from Washington as to the powers and duties of the new bodies, or even an inkling as to who would head them.

Flying to Washington to get some exact information, I had my first experience with the headlong, haphazard methods that were to make a mess of the New Deal. On every hand there was the confusion of activity with action, and the firm conviction that the mere announcement of a plan automatically created the machinery for its completion. The Cotton Textile Code—first of six hundred—was put in operation before the proper constitution of a code authority had been decided upon, and there was only vague surmise as to the workings of 7-A, the all-important section having to do with labor's right to organize and bargain collectively.

I had known Hugh Johnson in World War I, when he served under Bernard Baruch on the War Industries Board, and loved and admired him for his brilliance and warm, human qualities. Away from Baruch's wise guidance, however, his sanguine temperament had no leash, and leaping enthusiasm took the place

274

of deliberated decisions. Every second saw the creation of a new board, every minute heard a new order, and not even on the seventh day did he rest.

A visit with the President did nothing to allay my fears or clear up my confusions. Neither in word nor tone was there any resemblance to the man with whom I had talked in Albany, grave in the face of great tasks and overwhelming responsibilities, and with high resolves tempered by full appreciation of difficulties. Instead of being alarmed by the spirit of improvisation, he seemed delighted by it, whooping on the improvisers with the excitement of one riding to hounds. Throughout the talk, all emphasis was on ideas, administration being pushed aside as something that would take care of itself.

There was an infectious quality in his enthusiasm that persuaded even if it did not convince. Perhaps, after all, exuberance was a natural consequence of such a victory and would soon give way to a more sober approach. I held to the hope even as I fought a way through the NRA bedlam, where hundreds of young collegians translated their commencement addresses into economic policies and entered the office where General Johnson searched his soul for new screams.

Although Hugh embraced me affectionately, I could get no word from him as to the California setup, and after several days took my stunned eardrums back to San Francisco. On my return I walked into the customhouse, picked myself an office, and calmly announced that I was the head of NRA for the Coast, and the sole source of authority. Fortunately, nobody had the wit to challenge my right, and before any embarrassing questions could be asked I had an organization going full speed ahead. From the start there was no lack of co-operation, from either business or labor, for out of their bewilderment and unhappiness both were eager to adopt any suggestion or order that was put forward authoritatively.

Section 7-A, naturally, was the high hurdle; for Los Angeles, in particular, boasted of its open-shop policy, and even in strongly unionized San Francisco, management and labor were at swords' points. Similar conditions obtained in Nevada and Utah, and as for Hawaii, unionization came under the head of unavailable rights. I gave a lot of thought to this controversial business, and finally worked out a clarifying statement that I still think made sense:

275

The right of employees to organize and bargain collectively through representatives of their own choosing is something that does not permit of compromise or dispute. Where satisfactory employment relations exist, they will not be disrupted. If it can be shown that a union, unaffiliated with any national or international body, operates along democratic lines, free from coercion, it will be accepted as representative. If it is dominated by the employer, it will not be accepted.

What the law aims to bring about is a co-operative order, as opposed to an unlimited competitive order, with the public interest enforced as against the selfish interests of any group. This policy applies to labor unions as well as employers. Just as management is called on to change their outlook, so must organized labor prepare for radical departures from old habit. The day of "wildcat strikes," sympathetic strikes, and jurisdictional disputes is over. When employers are robbed of the power to crush workers, unions cannot expect to retain the right to bedevil industry with a babel of demands. Labor, therefore, must develop a code of collective practice which will not appear to reflect the temporary benefit of separate groups, but which will be recognized instantly as part of the more rational organization of the various forces in industry to achieve the end of greater stability, more regular employment, and the attainment of the highest possible standard of living.

Both management and labor quarreled with some parts of the statement, but public opinion backed it up. Scores of strikes were averted, and those that could not be mediated successfully were settled quickly, fairly, and even amicably. Public opinion was also a force in gaining compliance with the provisions of the various codes, and at no time were we called on to bellow threats and go to court. In August a National Labor Board was set up in Washington, and Senator Robert Wagner, the chairman, named me as regional head for California, Utah, and Nevada; but we paid small attention to the rules and regulations that flooded in, and pursued our own simple, effective way.

Before long, however, all but the cockeyed could see that the NRA was headed hell-bent for a bust. Going back to Washington was like a journey into bedlam, for all touch with the sane and simple had been lost. Each visit found scores of new agencies, boards, and commissions, headed by campus experts and pink-pill theorists; and the spread of the bureaucratic mania had the sweep of a pestilence. Instead of holding to a

276

comparatively small number of basic codes, the administration went crazy, and soon some six hundred were in active operation with more in process of preparation. As one instance out of scores, the manufacturers of egg beaters and bird cages were not put under the Wire Code, but had separate codes of their own.

Henry Wallace, putting his muddled economics on view for the first time, came forward with the theory that the depression was caused by overproduction; yet while he paid millions to farmers for crop curtailment, another agency of the Department of Agriculture provided huge sums for irrigation and other aids to crop increase. Nothing stood more plain than that the trouble came from underconsumption, not overproduction; yet no voice was raised to drive home this truth.

Owing to San Francisco's distance from Washington, I managed to get away with my independent administration of Pacific Coast affairs for the first few months, handling code violations and labor disputes as purely local problems. In September, however, the bureaucrats cracked down, and I received orders to regard myself as no more than a chief clerk without other power than to refer everything to NRA headquarters in Washington.

I dissented violently, as a matter of course, pointing out the number of strikes we had averted and stressing the fact that 100-per-cent compliance had been procured without man hunts and jail threats. How, I asked Hugh Johnson, could a Washington group deal swiftly and intelligently with problems three thousand miles away? How could codes and labor regulations framed to meet the needs of the Atlantic seaboard possibly have application to conditions on the Pacific Coast? My protest went unheeded, for by this time the administration was firmly committed to a policy of centralization, and so I telegraphed my resignation.

Their undoubted pleasure in getting rid of me was short-lived. California, Nevada, and Utah let loose a scream of protest, trade associations and labor unions joining in telegrams to the President that demanded my retention. Very little of it was personal, to be sure, but rather an expression of the resentment at having the Pacific Coast treated as an outlying province, and not as a vital and integral part of the United States. The uproar kept up for weeks, and at the end President

Roosevelt himself sent me a telegram asking that my resignation be withdrawn, and Hugh Johnson assured me that my idea of regional controls was sound and would be respected.

A victory, but hollow to the core; for every day saw new and complicating agencies brought into being, all without other purpose than putting additional thousands on the federal pay roll. One morning would bring me a bundle of orders, interpretations, and rulings, and the next morning would find all of them set aside by a fresh batch of instructions. Particularly was this true with respect to Section 7-A; and as confusion grew, both employers and workers changed from friendly negotiation to ugly belligerence. What was no less than industrial war broke out in October, for strikes involved 10,000 cotton pickers, 2,300 workers in the lettuce fields, and some 7,500 longshoremen.

Faced with this situation, Senator Wagner, chairman of the National Labor Board, cut loose from red tape and bureaucracy and gave me full authority. Calling all of the contending elements together, I threatened them with the lash of public opinion and succeeded in winning their consent to have the disputes submitted to arbitration. More than that, the foremost figures in California's public life consented to serve on the boards—the Catholic archbishop, for example, was one of those that handled the cotton strike—and their awards were so just as to meet with immediate acceptance.

Now, however, came a body blow in the shape of the Civil Works Administration, that bumptious, feckless organization that was to take four million off the relief rolls and put them on federal, state, and local public projects. The idea was a good one, for there were any number of worth-while things to be done, but from the outset millions were squandered on trivial undertakings of every sort, with the result that "boondoggling" was incorporated into the language as a term of contempt and derision.

Then, in late December, came the notice of a brand-new organization—the National Emergency Council—that was to "coordinate" the activities of the NRA, the CWA, the Federal Emergency Relief Administration, and every other New Deal agency. According to the wire, I was to assume the administration of the California division, along with my other duties as NRA chairman for the coast and director of the San Francisco Labor Board. It was, of course, the last word in absurdity, for each board, bureau, and commission claimed independent power, and thumbed its nose at any suggestion of control. All that it did was to create fresh angers and confusions.

Nor was that the finish. In March, 1934, the National Recovery Review Board came into being, headed by Clarence Darrow, and empowered to investigate the "growth of monopolistic practices" as a result of the six hundred codes. This body turned at once into a prosecuting agency, going on the assumption that the employers were not playing the game in good faith, and instituting regular man hunts. No "monopolistic practices" were discovered, but the smear campaign killed the co-operative spirit of the industrialists and excited the unions to denunciation and attack. One by one the old leaders were pushed aside by "direct actionists" who spat on arbitration and clamored for strikes. It was this change in attitude that first gave prominence to Harry Bridges, the Australian long-shoreman.

By late March things had worsened to the point of hopelessness. There was also the consideration that after eight months of unpaid drudgery I was at the end of my financial rope. Even the collection of my traveling expenses entailed struggles, for the General Accounting Office in Washington seemed never to have heard of planes, and quarreled with me for not going from San Francisco to Washington by oxcart. At the time of resigning, my keenest pleasure was a letter to the Comptroller General in which I congratulated him on his efficiency, for owing to his administrative genius, it now cost only five dollars to save five cents.

Just as I was writing *Collier's,* asking Bill Chenery if he could find a place on his staff for a New Deal casualty, what should blaze up but a "Creel for Governor" boom. As soon as my shattered nerves recovered from the shock, I stated publicly that I was not and would not be a candidate, and followed the declaration by private appeals to Democratic leaders to "lay off." It was not only that I hated the routine of public office, vastly preferring the excitements of my profession as a writer, but even greater was my loathing of the political techniques to win office.

The laborious trek from town to town; the back-slapping and handshaking; the careful weighing of each word so as to guard against distortion; the long-winded conferences with local politicians; the ever pressing problem of campaign funds; the settling of factional quarrels; the fawning approach to powerful groups; the cap-in-hand visits to editors—all of it was foreign to my temperament, taste, and training. Granted that I *might* make a good governor if elected, every habit of my life made it certain that I would be a poor candidate.

All of my objections were swept aside. Upton Sinclair, the Socialist turned Democrat overnight, was campaigning for the nomination on a "crazy platform that meant the ruin of the party and the state." The man who had been groomed to run against him had dropped out of the race for some reason known only to himself, and I stood forth as the "one hope."

Maurice Harrison, who had kept the Democratic party alive in the lean years before Roosevelt, assured me that the north would be a unit in my support. Thomas M. Storke, the Santa Barbara newspaper owner and publisher, and Hamilton Cotton, a power in Los Angeles politics, promised to organize Southern California. Weeks of pressure, and suddenly I was stunned at hearing myself mumble, "All right." As I look back, the only possible explanation is that I was tired out and off balance after eight months of toil and controversy.

CHAPTER 35

Utopia Unlimited

*U*ntil 1933, the climate of California completely satisfied every physical, mental, and emotional need of the state's inmates. With 360 days of sunshine in each calendar year specifically guaranteed by chambers of commerce, only the captious felt that life had anything more to offer. As a result of the depression, however, swarms of self-annointed "saviors" poured out of every pecan grove, each with a large pink pill for the cure of every social and economic ill.

Upton Sinclair, suddenly quitting the Socialist party, announced his candidacy for the Democratic gubernatorial nomination and published a pamphlet in which he set forth a plan to End Poverty in California. EPIC was the program's shorter name, but scoffers soon twisted it into EPICAC and even EPILEPTIC. No political program was ever more free from doubt, for at the beginning the author went on record with this flat statement:

"I say positively and without qualification we can end poverty in California. I know exactly how to do it, and if you elect me governor, with a legislature to support me, I will put the job through, and it won't take more than one or two of my four years."

Almost overnight the climate lost its fixed place in California conversation, and when EPIC was followed by another promise of millennial dawn, sunshine and citrus fruit were driven entirely out of public consciousness. The Utopians, going further than Sinclair, proposed to end poverty in *all* forty-eight states by the direct and simple expedient of destroying capitalism, uprooting the profit system, and "producing for use." In Los Angeles alone, converts rushed forward at the rate of five thousand a day.

Catching the fever, a certain Dr. Francis Everett Townsend, down in Long Beach, cleared his throat authoritatively and proclaimed a national plan for old-age revolving pensions. Every man and woman over the age of sixty was to be given the sum of $200 a month without other obligation than that the entire amount be spent down to the last penny between the first day and the last day of each month.

With the same speed that marked the growth of EPIC and the Utopians, Townsend Clubs sprang up in every community, propagandists flying from county to county in such numbers as to break down the branches of trees with their weight. A vast happiness permeated all of Southern California, with elderly people crowding stores, real-estate offices, and automobile agencies, joyfully picking out furniture, homes, and cars in full confidence that the national treasury would soon gush forth a golden stream.

Notwithstanding fierce competition, EPIC more than held its own; for, in addition to being first in the field, Mr. Sinclair's pledges had a broader sweep. The California Authority for Land, to illustrate, would take over all idle acreage, all land sold for taxes and at foreclosure sales, and then proceed to the establishment of agricultural colonies where workers would till the soil and live in handsome, air-conditioned homes.

Each colony would have its community dining hall, a community kitchen with electric gadgets for cooking and dishwashing, a community laundry, a model hospital, a great assembly hall for lectures, concerts, and ennobling motion pictures; a newspaper devoted to culture rather than crime, and best of all, a community nursery where babies would be cared for while the mothers were working at some pleasant task, "or learning in library, concert hall, or theater."

A second public body, the California Authority for Production, would take over idle factories, where the unemployed would produce the necessities required for themselves and the land colonies. Bakeries, canneries, clothing and shoe factories, cement plants, brickyards, etc., would be taken over, all serviced by a great fleet of trucks and by a chain of stores in which would be sold the goods and foodstuffs produced by CAL and CAP.

The California Authority for Money would put out a bond issue of $300,000,000 with which to finance the land colonies and the factories, and also have the power to print script as a medium of exchange. In the matter of a tax program, EPIC proposed immediate repeal of the sales tax; a tax of 10 per cent on unimproved land; a state income tax beginning with incomes of $5,000, and tax exemption for homes and ranches where the assessed value was less than $3,000.

It was with respect to the great Central Valley Water Project, however, that Mr. Sinclair really went to town. Fifty thousand men would be put on the job, although competent engineers estimated that not more than fifteen thousand could possibly be used; and, while vague as to how these workers were to be paid, he was precise as to how they should be fed. The farmers were to act as a commissary, taking warehouse receipts, which, after the five years necessary for the completion of the project, would be accepted by the state in payment of irrigation charges.

The worst of it was that I could not attack Sinclair's sincerity, branding him as a cheap demagogue playing on credulity for political profit. Starry-eyed and ecstatic, he believed as implicitly in his nostrums as Peter the Hermit in the validity of the Children's Crusade. Facts and figures were a disturbing and even irreligious noise to which he closed his ears.

As an example of his blithe disregard for even elementary arithmetic, one of his proposals was to repeal the sales tax and substitute a tax on stock transfers, and he claimed that an equal revenue would be derived. This in face of the fact that the sales tax yielded more than $46,000,000 annually, while a 4-per-cent tax on stock transfers could not possibly produce more than $2,000,000. Soon afterward an EPIC spokesman came around and asked me to believe that no dishonesty had been intended. Upton had simply confused monthly averages with daily averages and made a mistake of several ciphers in his figuring.

The Utopians were the creation of a former investment banker, a promoter, and a gasoline salesman, all jobless. The original idea was a fraternal order with insurance features; but, on seeing the success of EPIC, the trio decided to offer a brand-new social order based on Bellamy's *Looking Backward,* Plato's *Republic,* and More's *Utopia.* An end to private ownership, the establishment of a priceless, profitless system, production for use, and the evolvement of a vast co-operative commonwealth.

As all three were broke, the organization started in private homes, with groups of ten agreeing to bring ten others to the next meeting. This endless chain worked with amazing success, and since the initiation fee was $3 and dues ten cents a month, there was soon no lack of money. Resolving on expansion, the promoters rented an auditorium with seven thousand seats and began swearing in new members wholesale, delighting and exciting huge audiences with crude shows on the lines of the Elizabethan morality plays. The whole business was supposed to be very hush-hush, but where such large numbers were concerned, secrecy proved a joke.

After a mumbo-jumbo ritual, the curtain would go up, revealing a counter piled high with loaves of bread, presided over by a fat, oily creature exuding avarice from every pore. Before him appears a mob of men and women and children, dripping rags and begging that he save them from starvation. When it develops that they have no money, the Food Merchant bids them begone, screaming that nothing matters to him but Profit.

A blackout, and then a second cycle showing a Cloth Merchant sitting before shelves packed to overflowing with every variety of wearing apparel.

"Give us clothes to cover our nakedness," cry the Mendicants, "or we freeze."

Like the Food Merchant, the Cloth Merchant makes it clear that he cares nothing about human suffering, living only for profit, and drives them off.

The third cycle is the office of the Moneylender, a revolting figure crouched greedily over his gold. When the naked, starving people appeal to him, he bursts out into fiendish cackles and tells them that to borrow money they must become his slaves, paying interest "each year tenfold." Desperate, hopeless, sobbing, they accept his terms and are loaded down with chains.

As the unhappy wretches turn away, rattling their shackles, they are joined by the Cloth Merchant and the Food Merchant, no longer arrogant and prosperous but as destitute as any member of the Mendicants. They too, out of their greed, have fallen into the clutches of the Moneylender, and are picked to the bone. Interest, as the loud-speaker is at pains to make clear, spares no one, eventually destroying the high as well as the low.

Suddenly the darkness is shot through with a blaze of light, and out bobs a benevolent old gentleman with long white whiskers who identifies himself as the Hermit Reason. If, he intones solemnly, they are ready and willing to "co-operate collectively toward universal abundance," he promises to lead them to the Land of Plenty for All, where everybody "produces what he uses and uses what he produces."

All accept with shouts of joy, and the fourth cycle shows the workings of government in this land of production for use. Prices and profits, banks and interest rates, all are unknown; and every citizen is assured of a constant supply of necessaries and luxuries by making a proper contribution to the service of society. For the purpose of establishing distribution quotas, all persons under twenty-five were regarded as minors; all between twenty-five and forty-five are set down as "available productive people," and those over forty-five are "retired," being considered to have already rendered their share of productive effort.

The fifth cycle was simply the communication of signs,

symbols, and passwords, that would permit Utopians to know one another. For example, the question "Have you a knife?" would be met by the answer "Yes, I have a knife with which to sharpen my wits." The left hand on the heart carried the message "I bear no malice to anyone," and when the hand was extended palm upward, the thought conveyed was "I am my brother's keeper."

Packed auditoriums worked themselves up to camp-meeting frenzy over these primitive spectacles, and the summer months found the Utopians numbering 600,000 in the Los Angeles area alone. With converts fairly fighting to get in, the leaders of the movement seemed to have good ground for the boast that another year would witness an enrollment of 30,000,000, covering every state in the Union.

Undaunted by the sweep of EPIC and the Utopians, Dr. Townsend drove forward with his own campaign for followers, a somewhat impressive figure with his gray hair and ascetic face. Asking himself the causes of the depression, he gave this explanation: unemployment and lack of purchasing power. Going on from there, he cited census figures to show that there were around ten million men and women in the United States more than sixty years of age. Give them each $200 a month, under pledge to spend it, and what would happen? The ten million would withdraw from industrial competition at once, thus creating a labor shortage, and the expenditure of their pensions would revive purchasing power immediately.

Figure it out for yourself, shrugged the good doctor. With $2,000,000,000 pouring into the channels of trade each month, every factory would be compelled to run day and night shifts; every farmer would have to till every available inch of soil; stores would multiply, and every business would know an astounding leap in revenue. Lacking the labor of "senior citizens," employers would have to fight for workers, so that wages might well treble and quadruple. The government, of course, would have to put up $2,000,000,000 for the first month, but a transaction tax of 2 per cent would take care of pensions after that.

This, then, was the opposition I had to go up against in my candidacy for the Democratic gubernatorial nomination. Northern California offered no problem, for hardheaded, hard-working native sons and daughters were in a majority, but when

I crossed the Tehachapi into Southern California, it was like plunging into darkest Africa without gun bearers. Epics, Utopians, and Townsendites might have their points of difference, but all turned faces of hatred to me when I attacked the validity of their creeds.

Rupert Hughes, Irvin Cobb, Kathleen Norris, and Eleanor Banning Macfarland were the only gleams of light in my darkness. Despite the frank confession that he was "an old maid in politics, and hoped to die a virgin," Rupert took the stump in my behalf. "Being somewhat deaf," he told me, "has its advantages. I can't hear them hiss me." Irv had better luck, for his humor was irresistible, but enthusiasm always chilled when he denounced "self-appointed messiahs who undertook to restore prosperity by promising money they didn't have, to people who hadn't earned it."

Kathleen Norris, the best-loved woman in the state, risked her popularity by writing a pamphlet *My Friend—George Creel*, for the cultists did everything but burn it in the plazas. As for Eleanor Macfarland, the brilliant daughter of a pioneer family, she was told to "go back where she came from" by people so newly arrived that they spelled California with a K.

With California already $30,000,000 in the red, and facing enormous deficits unless drastic economies were instituted, where did Mr. Sinclair expect to get his money? His pension plan alone would cost $300,000,000 a year. Who would buy his bonds, and what about a redemption fund? Did he not know that property was assessed on a 40-per-cent valuation, and that his exemption of homes taxed at $3,000 would strip 55 of California's 58 counties of almost every cent of revenue? As for idle land, where was there any in California with water on it? And where were there any idle factories except those with worn-out, obsolete equipment?

Audiences did everything but lynch me, and it was the same way when I argued against Utopianism as a return to the barter system of primitive times. Taking on the Townsendites, I made the point that total retail sales in the United States amounted to only $32,000,000,000, and that a 2-per-cent tax would not pay even one month's pensions. I also showed that the entire income of the nation had been less than $40,000,000,000 in 1933, and that if we handed out $24,000,000,000 a year to all

286

persons over sixty, it meant that 10 per cent of the population would receive more than half of the national income.

I might as well have been talking through my lower lip to my chin. When the primaries came around in August, the Utopians and a large number of Townsendites joined the Epics and I was badly beaten. The north gave me a flattering majority, and I even carried South Pasadena, but the votes of Los Angeles county buried me under a landslide.

Straightway, of course, I was confronted with a decision with respect to the general election in November. Merriam, who had won the Republican nomination, was reactionary to the point of medievalism, but how was it possible to swallow EPIC? Finally going to Sinclair, I told him flatly that I could not and would not support him if he continued to advance his plan, inasmuch as I had denounced it daily as utterly unrealizable and even dishonest in many of its features. If, however, he would junk his crack-brained, unworkable hodgepodge and accept a sanely progressive platform, I would support him.

He and his "economists" agreed, and as chairman of the Democratic State Convention I was able to state honestly that our declaration of purpose was one to which every true Democrat could subscribe without sacrifice of principle. This done, I went east, hoping for magazine assignments that would replenish a purse badly depleted by my unpaid months with NRA and the Labor Board.

On reaching Washington I saw President Roosevelt and Jim Farley, and both praised the bargain and hoped that it would be kept. For a few weeks it seemed that this would be done; but when Sinclair found that his followers were dropping down from hysteria pitch, he went back to his original plan with only minor changes. Receiving Immediate EPIC, as he called it, on October 5, I sat down at once and wrote him a letter in which I repeated the criticisms made during my primary campaign, and ended with these paragraphs:

Let me say again that I do not question your honesty, but you have the most amazing faculty of making yourself believe the things you want to believe. As an example, take your repeated statement that you can and will end poverty in California, and that in one or two years. This is an optimism carried to the point of delirium. Your dream of creating an economic island, alien and antagonistic to its immediate environment, and to the rest of the country as well, has been damned by every economist, and yet you persist in it.

Immediate EPIC, I am sorry to confess, puts me back exactly where I was in the primary campaign. In its essence it is the original EPIC that I attacked as unsound, unworkable, and un-American, designed to appeal to credulities, ignorance, and despair, and immeasurably hurtful in its effect on true progressivism. It is, therefore, with the very real regret that must always be stirred by lost opportunities that I withdraw my offer to campaign in your behalf.

I debated for some time as to whether I should make the letter public, but when party leaders insisted that it be given to the press, I did so on October 26. At the same time I stated frankly that I was now a man without a vote, for between the epilepsy of Sinclair and the catalepsy of Merriam there was no choice.

Sinclair was defeated in the November election, and now followed the most incredible feature of the whole incredible performance. Within a year EPIC had vanished completely, except for a few vestigial remnants, and a similar fate befell the Utopians, the leaders engaging in a disgraceful dog-eat-dog fight over the loot. Only the Townsendites retained any semblance of organization, and there is this to say for the good old doctor: While his plan had about as much soundness as a worm-eaten nut, it did stir the country to a belated interest in the aged.

CHAPTER 36

On the Steps of the Throne

*T*he outcome of the gubernatorial campaign not only left me at a loose end, but also found me neck deep in unpaid bills as the result of two nonearning years. Not a rosy outlook; but, as I sat amid ashes, Bill Chenery, the editor of *Collier's*, telephoned from New York. If, he said, I felt reasonably certain that the political bug was out of my system, the job of Washington correspondent was mine for the taking. It was only by a powerful effort of will that I waited long enough to pack.

I had thought that Southern California was the world's closest approach to bedlam and babel, but Washington made the Epics, the Utopians, and the Townsendites seem staid and conservative. Under Coolidge and Hoover the White House had held the solemn hush of a mortuary establishment, but now it lacked nothing but a merry-go-round and a roller coaster to be a Coney Island. High-domed "planners," home-grown economists, overnight sociologists, magic-money nuts, social workers, and campus experts elbowed and shouted, and even the minstrel touch was provided by Tommy Corcoran's accordion and George Allen's anecdotes.

Even so, there was health in it and hope. Once again, as in the days of Theodore Roosevelt and Woodrow Wilson, the progressive forces of the nation were massed in phalanx formation, and everywhere people had thrown off apathy and were aflame with enthusiasm for the New Deal and its drive against every evil that menaced the democratic process. Despite the President's almost juvenile joy in the ferment, it was still the case that he drove with a firm hand, and out of seeming confusion had already come many sound laws.

The insurance of bank deposits; the Securities and Exchange Act that put an end to blue-sky swindles; the Civilian Conservation Corps, with its dual purpose as a reforestation agency and a body and character builder for America's youth; the soil conservation program; Section 7-A in the National Recovery Act, giving workers the right to organize and bargain collectively—all constituted a firm foundation for the building of a better social order.

By reason of my New Deal services on the Pacific Coast, and also because I represented *Collier's,* the doors of the White House were opened to me, affording the privilege of a fairly intimate relationship with the President. At the very outset of the association I noted definite changes. Along with an almost adolescent exuberance that found delight in hurly-burlies, there was a supreme self-assurance that had a touch of royalty. Nevertheless, he still retained a certain measure of the politician's cautious approach to objectives, and made a habit of sending up trial balloons, studying popular reactions with a good deal of care and shrewdness.

289

Time after time, for example, he used my articles in *Collier's* to test out public opinion. Under such titles as "Roosevelt's Plans and Purposes" and "Looking Ahead with Roosevelt," he would outline the laws and policies that he had in mind, and then sit back to see what happened. Although every article was preceded by an editorial blurb that boasted of its authoritativeness, "due to Mr. Creel's long and close association with the President," it was still in his power to repudiate me if the reaction proved less than favorable.

Oftentimes he would actually dictate whole paragraphs, and have me read them back to him. As an instance, I have before me his exact words about his so-called "soak the rich" program. "Taxes," he said, "should and must be levied in proportion to *ability to pay* and in proportion to *benefits received.*" (He himself ordered the italicization.) "Wealth does not come from individual effort alone, but through the co-operation of the entire community, from people in the mass. Income is the one true measure of benefits received and ability to pay."

I had thought, as many still think, that a great majority of the President's speeches were "ghosted," but that idea was soon dispelled. Many persons contributed suggestions and provided material, but when the first draft was placed in his hands, their connection ceased. It was common for him to go over a "fireside chat" six or seven times; and although he was no Woodrow Wilson, he had a nice feeling for words and a very exact appreciation of shadings. His love of phrases, I think, came from Theodore Roosevelt; for a volume of T.R.'s addresses had a fixed place on the President's desk, and almost every page was heavily marked. Quotations from "Uncle Ted" also figured frequently in his conversation.

As time went on, the change in the President became increasingly apparent. Trial balloons were less frequent, and "must" bills were rushed up to the floor leaders in the Senate and House by messenger. Instead of attempting to placate opposition, he met it with resentment, and every Congressional debate on one of his proposals was regarded as an encroachment on the powers of the Executive. What stirred him the most, however, was the Supreme Court's assertion of a right to pass on the constitutionality of all legislation.

I first became aware of his deep and even bitter feeling in

August, 1935, when we were preparing the article entitled "Looking Ahead with Roosevelt." In June the Supreme Court had wiped out all of the codes set up under the NRA, and the President made no effort to hide his anger as he spoke of the decision. While admitting that there had been extremes and absurdities, he insisted that the fundamentals of the act were sound and vital, and that the Court had gone out of its way to place a stone in the way of progress. After considering NRA accomplishments in some detail, he set his jaw and dictated the following as his idea of how the article should start off:

It is the deep conviction of Franklin D. Roosevelt that the Constitution of the United States was never meant to be a "dead hand," chilling human aspiration and blocking humanity's advance, but that the founding fathers conceived it as a living force for the expression of the national will with respect to national needs. Sincerely, steadfastly, the President refuses to believe that the framers meant to tie the hands of posterity until the end of time, denying future generations freedom of action in meeting the problems presented by one hundred and fifty years of change. The thing that has come to be called the New Deal is Franklin Roosevelt's conscientious, deliberated effort to continue the Constitution as a truth and a hope, not as a mere collection of obsolete phrases. The laws that he has proposed are frank attempts to gain new objectives in human relations, and nothing is more certain than that he will keep up the drive with all the force of his being and all the power of his office.

Then followed a discussion of the measures that he had in mind for rounding out the New Deal's legislative program, but at the end he returned to the NRA decision and again dictated:

In the next few months, the Supreme Court will hand down fresh pronouncements with respect to New Deal laws, and it is possible the President will get another "licking." If so, much will depend on the language of the licking. In event that unconstitutionality is found, perhaps the decisions will point the way to statutory amendments. If, however, the Constitution is construed technically; if it is held that one hundred and fifty years have no bearing on the case, and that the present generation is powerless to meet social and economic problems that were not within the knowledge of the founding fathers, and therefore not made the subject of their specific consideration, then the President will have no other alternative than to go to the country with a Constitutional amendment that will lift the Dead Hand, giving the people of today the right to deal with today's vital issues.

291

"Fire that," he said grimly, "as an opening gun."

Contrary to his expectation, the press did not make the statement a subject of comment; and although a certain number of letters praised his stand, nothing was more plain than the lack of public interest. Some sixteen months passed without further mention of the Supreme Court, but in December, 1936, he let me know that the matter had never left his thought. As we sat, nothing was more plain than that the President regarded the election as a purely *personal* victory. And why not? Throughout the entire campaign, the one and only issue was Franklin Roosevelt, and every state in the union, save Maine and Vermont, had attested faith in his leadership. What was it, if not a mandate to take and wield supreme power?

What he suggested was an article to be called "Roosevelt's Plans and Purposes," and we gave an afternoon and evening to its preparation. After summing up what he called "social gains," he switched to immediate and long-range objectives. Child-labor laws, social security from "the cradle to the grave," minimum wages and maximum hours, crop insurance, farm tenancy, etc., all, he pointed out, would have to run the gantlet of a hostile Supreme Court.

"But," he continued, his face alight, "I've thought of a better way than a constitutional amendment stripping the Court of its power to nullify acts of Congress. The time element makes that method useless. Granted that Congress could agree on such an amendment for submission to the several states, it would be two, three, or four years before the legislatures could or would act. What do you think of this?"

Reaching into a drawer of his desk, he pulled out a copy of the Constitution, issued by the State Department, and ruffled the pages to show me passages that had been heavily marked. These he read off one by one, emphasizing each wih a big forefinger. First the Preamble:

"We, the people of the United States, in order to form a more perfect Union, establish Justice, insure domestic tranquility, provide for the common defense, promote the *general welfare . . .*"

Then Article I, Section 1, providing that "all legislative powers herein granted shall be vested in a Congress of the United States," and Section 8, setting forth that "the Congress shall have power to lay and collect taxes, duties, imposts and

Excises, to pay the debts and provide for the common defense and *General Welfare* of the United States . . . To make all laws which shall be necessary and proper for carrying into execution the foregoing Powers, and *all other powers vested* by this Constitution in the Government of the United States or in any officer or department thereof."

"What plainer," declared the President, "than that 'all other powers vested by this Constitution' carries with it explicit authorization to enact laws to 'promote the general welfare,' so specifically mentioned in the Preamble, and again in Article One? And listen to Article Three, Section One: 'The Judicial Power of the United States shall be vested in one Supreme Court, and in such inferior courts as the Congress may from time to time ordain and establish. Where," he asked, "is there anything in that which gives the Supreme Court the right to override the legislative branch?"

As our talk went on, I was amazed by his reading on the subject and by the grip of his mind on what he conceived to be essential facts. For example, he quoted at length from Madison's *Journal* and Elliot's *Debates,* citing them as his authority for the statement that the framers of the Constitution had voted on four separate occasions against giving judges the power to pass upon the constitutionality of acts of Congress.

"Not until 1803," he declared, "did Chief Justice Marshall assert the right, and then for purely political reasons. A passionate Federalist, he hated Jefferson and the Democrats; and his opinion in the case of Marbury versus Madison was to block the progress of a new order that he resented and distrusted."

The thing to do, then, was for Congress to reclaim the powers that had been filched from it by a steady process of usurpation. And how could this be done? Very simply. If the coming session should witness the adoption of a housing bill, or a bill providing maximum hours and minimum wages, or a bill relating to sweatshops and child labor, each of these acts could carry a rider *charging* the Supreme Court to bear in mind that the law was enacted pursuant to the Constitutional provision vesting *all* legislative power in the Congress, and explicitly authorizing it "to provide for the general welfare of the United States."

And what if this proved ineffective? "Then," said the President, his face like a fist, "Congress can *enlarge* the Supreme

293

Court, increasing the number of justices so as to permit the appointment of men in tune with the spirit of the age. And what is there radical about it? The country started out with six justices and has had as many as ten."

The article appeared in the December 26 issue of *Collier's,* and as a full three columns was devoted to the Supreme Court discussion, I fully expected an explosion both in the press and in Congressional debate. Incredibly enough, not a newspaper in the country caught the significance of the statement, although dealing at length with other things in the article. Senators also passed it over. When, therefore, he asked Congress some three months later to enlarge the Supreme Court, it came as a bombshell. Our discussions about the Court plan, prior to its introduction in the Senate, were most revealing. It was not only his belief in himself—a confidence in his decisions that was not shaken by a single doubt—but the very evident assumption that he did not need to support his wishes by argument or appeal. Enough for him just to state the wish or give the order. For example, when I asked him if he meant to discuss the Court bill with members of Congress and party leaders before its introduction, he shrugged off the question as if it dealt with an unimportance.

The President's failure to make the matter a subject of conference stirred resentments that were not abated by his subsequent course. Tommy Corcoran was designated as a "royal messenger" to whip recalcitrants into line; and when this failed, the White House let it be known that "disloyal senators" would not receive any patronage favors in the future.

Right while the struggle was at its height, a White House friend telephoned that the Boss wanted me to put my work aside for a while and sit on the "board of strategy." I told him that my contract with *Collier's* forbade, but that even were this not the case, I saw no point in waging a battle that was already lost. Shortly afterward I said the same thing to the President, and he produced Tommy Corcoran's poll of the Senate to prove that I was wrong. Looking it over, I found on the list of supporters at least ten senators I knew to be against the bill, but he again insisted that I did not know what I was talking about.

For a moment he almost had me agreeing. With only his huge torso showing above the desk, and waving his cigarette holder like a marshal's baton, he exuded the confidence that had its base in a conviction of indisputable power. I cannot remember whether I was responsible for his holder habit, but I did wean him away from the short kind, for after watching him squint his eyes against smoke curls, I sent him three long ivory ones. At our next meeting, when he insisted that something was due me in return, I said that I would be more than repaid by an autographed copy of *On Our Way,* his last book.

"My tome," he laughed, "isn't worth three holders, but glad to do it. Bring in a copy the next time you come."

On the face of things the President seemed to accept defeat with good grace, but in private conversation he took no pains to hide his anger. The tenacity of his resentments against all who dared to question his orders or infallibility was made manifest by the attempted "purge" of 1938. Over the protests of Jim Farley and the pleas of other party leaders, he campaigned against the Democratic senators who had incurred his displeasure by voting against the Court bill. All were re-elected; but instead of working any change in the President, defeat only heightened his implacability and strengthened his cold determination to crush all who conspired against the throne. I do not think there is any question that Vice-President Garner's lukewarm attitude during the Court fight was entirely responsible for his elimination in 1940.

Out of a long-standing conviction that no judge or set of judges had the right to nullify a law passed by the legislative branch and approved by the executive, I liked the Court plan although I was dismayed by the manner in which the fight was handled. The whole Roosevelt program, for that matter, stirred my enthusiasm, as it did *Collier's;* for Tom Beck, the president, and Bill Chenery and Charlie Colebaugh, the editors, were all inheritors of the Wilson tradition.

Not that there were no chilling notes. This was particularly true of the growing influence of the campus experts with their glee-club approach to problems. Another thing that brought out the cold sweat was the enormous increase in the federal pay roll and the reckless expenditure of public money. Every day saw the creation of new boards and commissions; and after a modest start with five or ten people, the end of the month saw them with hundreds. The Works Progress Administration was the Abou ben Adhem that led all the rest, both in size and squandering; and as I had been sharply critical, it came as a

295

surprise to have Harry Hopkins offer me the chairmanship of a National Advisory Board.

Harry, however, insisted that intelligent faultfinding was exactly what he wanted. Paul McNutt, governor of Indiana, and Edward O'Neal, head of the American Farm Bureau Federation, were also named as board members; and at the initial conference we were told that our job was to get an "unbiased perspective."

The idea was sound enough fundamentally; but, like so many other New Deal inspirations, it failed to work out. Owing to the speed and bewildering variety of Harry's operations, any effort at analysis was about as futile as trying to pass judgment on the colors in a kaleidoscope. When we reported on one set of policies, it was to find that they had been discarded weeks before in favor of brand-new activities, all involving the expenditure of more millions. As a consequence, the National Advisory Board faded out of the picture in five or six months, and the funeral was strictly private. On handing in my resignation, I told Harry quite frankly that the pace was too hot for me, and I can still recall his derisive grin.

"You're horse and buggy," he said. "A five-dollar man in a billion-dollar town. Raise your sights, boy. Raise your sights."

The trouble with Harry, as with so many others that Franklin Roosevelt gathered around him, and even with the President himself, was that he had never spent his own money. A social worker throughout his adult life, he had obtained his funds from municipal treasuries or foundations, so that dollars were never associated in his mind with work and thrift. Just figures in a budget. At that, the record of the WPA, gone over fairly, shows a lot of real accomplishment. Thousands of miles of roads were built; rural sanitation was lifted to a high level; hundreds of cities were supplied with schools, playgrounds, and airports. If much of the credit was due to Colonel Lawrence Westbrook, the fact remains that Harry Hopkins borrowed him from the Army and gave the hard-driving man a free hand.

Aside from administrative incompetency, headlong extravagance, and the alarming growth of an irresponsible bureaucracy, there were other things that flew danger signals. Essentially an aristocrat, both by birth and environment, Franklin Roosevelt had the British squire's attitude to "people in trade," and as the great industrialists and financiers persisted in their antagonism to the New Deal, dislike deepened into prejudice and distrust. Out of the feeling came the introduction of a sharply divisive note into American life, a deliberate accentuation of the stresses and strains inherent in the relations of labor and management.

In 1932 he had done no more than to promise a proper balance of power between employer and employed, but by 1936 he was committed to courses that gave organized labor the status of a privileged class. Ruling after ruling by his National Labor Relations Board compelled collective bargaining on a nationwide scale, rather than locally, thus creating a union hierarchy despotic in its powers. In return, the President demanded absolute loyalty and equally unquestioning obedience, outlawing such leaders as dared to refuse.

CHAPTER 37

The Roosevelt-Lewis Feud

*T*he big Washington story, both in 1935 and in 1936, was not concerned with Roosevelt and the New Deal, but centered around the activities of John L. Lewis, head of the United Mine Workers of America. His sponsorship of the Committee on Industrial Organization as a rival of the American Federation of Labor split the workers of the country into two warring camps and gave the labor movement a new and disturbing militancy. The sit-down strike was only one of the many original techniques developed by the secessionists.

The front pages of the press were also given over to the large amounts that Mr. Lewis poured into the Democratic campaign fund in 1936 for the re-election of Franklin Roosevelt. Aside from the controversy stirred by these donations, the gifts led to a spectacular feud between the President of the United Mine Workers and the President of the United States.

At the time, the reporting of both events was clouded by charges and countercharges. According to AFL chieftains, John

Lewis had plotted to make himself president of the Federation, ousting William Green, and seceded when his conspiracy failed. With respect to the campaign contributions, it became a general belief that Mr. Lewis had raided the treasury of his union without a shadow of warrant, shoveling hundreds of thousands into Democratic hands for his own political profit. A curious feature of the clamor was that while people and press thought it shameful for John Lewis to have *given*, no paper or person made mention that it was equally shameful for Mr. Roosevelt to have *taken*.

My interest in both stories—the organization of the CIO and the campaign contributions—was personal as well as professional. Along with my job as *Collier's* Washington correspondent, years of friendship with John Lewis also entered into it. I first met him during the Colorado coal strike, and as our friendly relations continued, came to have a high regard for his character and abilities. Columnists sneer at him now as a strutting actor, the Great Ham, but he had every mannerism in 1914 that he has today, and all were as much a part of him as his shaggy mane and bushy eyebrows.

The son of a Welsh miner, and a miner himself throughout his youth, John Lewis worked in gold, copper, and hard and soft coal mines. Poor and nomadic, he had no chance for formal schooling, and as one way to get an education, chose the classics for his textbooks. If today he has a love of long words, it is because he read and even memorized Shakespeare, Hugo, Montaigne, and the poets rather than the potboilers of the period. Together with his Johnsonian style of speech, a natural dignity also makes the man seem somewhat stilted in comparison with the rough-and-tumble type of labor leader.

It was in the early months of 1935 that word first came to me that John Lewis was planning to take his Mine Workers out of the American Federation of Labor and start a new organization. I went to him at once, and quite frankly, although confidentially, he admitted the truth of the report. The AFL, he declared, had failed in its most essential function, for after a quarter of a century it had a membership of less than 4,000,000 out of a working population of 40,000,000. "A record of incompetency," to use his own words, "without parallel."

The reason, contended Mr. Lewis, was that Green and his associates were either too blind or too selfish to see that mass-production industries could not possibly be organized on a craft basis. In the steel and oil and automobile industries, for example, a craft setup would mean from twenty to thirty different unions in a single plant. Not only would the incessant quarrels over jurisdiction weaken the labor movement itself, but they would provide employers with a sound excuse for antagonism. For years, in convention after convention, he had pleaded with the AFL hierarchy to realize conditions, and he was now weary of lies and evasions.

The open break came on November 9, 1935. These powerful labor chieftains joined John Lewis in the creation of the Committee for Industrial Organization: Sidney Hillman, president of the Amalgamated Clothing Workers; David Dubinsky, president of the International Ladies' Garment Workers Union; Harvey Fremming, president of the Oil Field, Gas Well and Refinery Workers; M. Zaritsky, president of the Cap and Millinery Department of the United Hatters, Cap and Millinery Workers; Thomas Brown, president of the International Union of Mine, Mill and Smelter Workers; and Charles P. Howard, president of the International Typographical Union.

It was, of course, a plain declaration of war, and by way of removing any doubt, John Lewis resigned as vice-president of the AFL when ordered to discontinue his activities. Few more dramatic scenes were ever staged than William Green's appearance before the convention of the United Mine Workers in February, 1936, imploring the delegates to repudiate their leader. In a voice that broke repeatedly, the head of the AFL painted the tragedy of division and begged the miners to maintain their relation with the parent body.

Lewis sat throughout like a Buddha, his eyes cold and unwinking. At the end of the appeal he arose, with precise courtesy presented Green's arguments one by one, and then asked if any delegate had been persuaded to change his attitude. With a shout that shook the building, the convention rejected William Green and upheld John Lewis. His face grim and menacing, but still in the same level tone, the President of the United Mine Workers turned to the President of the American Federation of Labor and said, "Sir, you have your answer."

Proof of the justice of John Lewis's contentions was not long delayed. Mass-production industries, either untouched by the AFL or else feebly and ineffectually, were organized under his direction, and within three years the CIO not only matched membership with the parent body but outstripped it in point of energy and aggressiveness.

Today Philip Murray and other CIO leaders have only hate and abuse for John Lewis; yet but for his leadership and the money of the Mine Workers, the organization would have died aborning. During 1936 and 1937, when the CIO was without internal revenue, the Mine Workers contributed 88.37 per cent of the total expended. The services of executives, field directors, trained organizers, attorneys, clerical help, etc., paid for by the Mine Workers at a cost of $3,904,303, were contributed, and in addition the sum of $1,685,000 was loaned. These figures do not include the $200,000 donated to Sidney Hillman for the conduct of the organizing drive in the textile industry, or the salary of Philip Murray, detached from his duties as vice-president of the UMW to direct the organizational drive in the steel industry. Loans of $601,000 were also made to the Steel Workers, but these were repaid eventually.

In the matter of the contributions to the Democratic campaign fund in 1936, John Lewis has maintained, and still maintains, a vast silence. Others, however, have proved less reticent, and the account given to me is backed up at many points by a written record. The subject was first brought up at the convention of the United Mine Workers in Washington in January, 1936. Knowing that it was the unbroken rule of the AFL never to endorse any candidate, the Policy Committee decided that it would be good strategy to come out for the President's re-election, thus putting the UMWA in a favored position in event of victory. Lewis approved, and the following resolution was adopted by acclamation:

The United Mine Workers of America, in this convention, pledge their wholehearted support to bring about the continuance of the work of Franklin D. Roosevelt as President of the United States for another term. . . . We are for Roosevelt, the greatest humanitarian of our time . . . We urge united action on the part of all our officers and members, and the labor movement in general, to join together in this great battle for political freedom, social security and economic justice. As evidence of our sincerity, your committee further recommends that the International Executive Officers be authorized to make such contributions, subject to authorization by the International Executive Board, as may be necessary in support of this program.

The high command of the UMWA met soon afterward and decided that a contribution of $250,000 would be more than generous in view of the fact that F.D.R. was a hundred-to-one choice over Alf Landon. In due course, therefore, President Lewis called at the White House, flanked by Vice-President Philip Murray and Thomas Kennedy, the treasurer. The resolution was read, and after a brief exchange of speeches the UMW officials presented the check and asked President Roosevelt if he would be kind enough to let a photographer record the historic scene.

"No, John," the President replied, beaming affectionately. "I don't want your check, much as I appreciate the thought. Just keep it, and I'll call on you if and when any small need arises."

As the group left the White House, Mr. Lewis remarked, somewhat gloomily, that they had been "outsmarted," for now there was no limit to the amount that could be asked. The others took a more cheerful view, holding that Democratic victory was so sure that a large part of the $250,000 might be saved. "You don't know politicians," was the Lewis retort. "They stay under the golden drip from the honey barrel until no drop is left."

Time confirmed his fears. The first request was from Jim Farley asking $50,000 for the expenses of the headquarters in New York. A second call begged $92,000 for the purchase of radio time, and a third came from Senator La Follette and Frank Walsh, who were organizing Progressives in support of Roosevelt. Cannily enough, John Lewis adopted a fixed pattern of procedure at the start. As each petitioner presented himself, he intoned this ritual: "Sir, I know you well and favorably, of course, and have no doubt as to your authority. My arrangement, however, was with the President, and I must ask that you bring me his written order."

This was the procedure followed invariably before the disbursement of a dollar. In some cases the order was procured, but in others Mr. Roosevelt confirmed the request by telephone to Mr. Lewis. Slowly at first, but then faster and faster the appeals poured in, and eventually this steady suction exhausted the $250,000. Mr. Lewis then called his Policy Committee together and asked for instructions. All of the members, while unhappy, insisted that since their good money was on the board, the bet must be protected. Surely, they argued, not many more contributions would be asked, as everybody conceded Roosevelt's re-election.

For a second time Mr. Lewis expressed doubt, and again had the poor satisfaction of saying, "I told you so." Requests continued to pour in, each backed by an order or telephone call from the President, and when election day came around at last, the treasury of the UMW had been nicked for $469,668.91. To this amount was added the sum of $14,119.64 turned in by local unions, and $2,500 worth of tickets for the inaugural parade, making a total of $486,288.55. A large part of this huge sum was plainly earmarked as loans, but only $50,000, secured by the Democratic National Committee's note, was ever repaid.

For a while it looked as if the great gamble had been a winning one. The White House doors swung wide for John Lewis, and in the first glow of his re-election the President lost no opportunity to declare affection for the generous head of the UMWA. Soon, however, correspondents noted that the Lewis visits were increasingly rare, and the whisper spread that a beautiful friendship had come to an end.

What was rumor soon became established as fact, for out of the White House began to seep explanations. According to anonymous spokesmen, Mr. Lewis, grown arrogant by reason of his campaign contributions, had tried to claim the powers of an assistant president. When the President indignantly refused to be blackmailed, the miners' chieftain had gone off in a sulk. At a later date this explanation was embellished by the sly circulation of a statement that Mr. Lewis had actually gone so far as to demand that he be chosen as Roosevelt's running mate in 1940.

I have never known a public man more indifferent to personal attack than John Lewis. Where his miners are concerned, he flames into speech or print on the instant, but if it is something directed against him, he shrugs it off as unimportant. When I asked him about the reports, he merely answered that at no time had he ever sought a meeting with the President, going to the White House only when invited. If these interviews had become less frequent, doubtless it was for the good reason that Mr. Roosevelt's attention was engrossed by larger matters.

"But what about the demands you are alleged to have made?" I persisted. "The White House charge that you tried to climb into the driver's seat as a sort of assistant president."

"If I remember correctly," he said, "and my memory has never failed me, only once did I ever present a petition of any kind to the President. When the Wagner Act was enacted by the Congress and signed by the Chief Executive, I looked on it as the law of the land. As a result, I felt strongly that the government should quit giving contracts to the large-scale employers who were open in their defiance of the Act. Mr. Roosevelt saw fit to ignore the request, and I said no more."

I have always been of the opinion that the real explanation of the break lies in the contrasting personalities of the two men. Proud and independent, utterly lacking in the pliability that makes the successful courtier, John Lewis grated on the President, accustomed as he was to the Corcorans and the Rosenmans. Franklin Roosevelt, in his turn, rasped John Lewis by his assumption that it was both an honor and a reward for a coal miner, and the son of a coal miner, to be received.

As the feud became an established fact, the President set to work, shrewdly and deliberately, to detach Philip Murray and Sidney Hillman from their allegiance to John Lewis. There was no secret about it, for the favors that he heaped on them were too open to escape comment. The two bobbed in and out of the White House with increasing frequency, and before long Sidney and Phil were proudly whispering to their friends that the President not only called them by their first names, but even massaged their shoulder blades with his caressing touch. It came under the head of unfair competition, of course, for how could the head of a miners' union expect to win in a rivalry with the President of the United States? Particularly when both Murray and Hillman were immigrants, the one a Scot and the other a Lithuanian. Lacking John Lewis's fierce independence, the handclasp of Franklin Roosevelt was as the sword of the king that makes a knight.

This was the situation in 1939 when Hitler invaded Poland and plunged all Europe into war. From the first John Lewis was an ardent advocate of America's neutrality, and came out in full support of Bernard Baruch's "cash and carry" policy. If and when the Allies wanted our matériel, then let them send their ships for it and put money on the barrelhead. It was because of his conviction that the President, by sheer force of his own will, meant to carry the United States into the war as a belligerent that John Lewis came out for Wendell Willkie.

Though Murray and Hillman refused to follow him into the Willkie camp, snuggling closer to Franklin Roosevelt, nevertheless both still professed friendship for John Lewis. That he believed in their good faith stands proved by the fact that in 1942, when he resigned the presidency of the CIO, he engineered the election of Philip Murray as his successor. Then, and not until then, was the mask thrown off, for one of Murray's first acts was to repudiate the debt to the United Mine Workers. After paying $20,000 on the notes that aggregated $1,685,000, he welshed on the balance. Nor did Sidney Hillman ever make even incidental mention of the $200,000 advanced to him by the UMWA for the organization of the textile industry.

Steadily, inexorably, the President widened the breach. Even as he took advantage of every occasion to minimize John Lewis, so did he honor Murray and Hillman, building them up as the real leaders of organized labor. The former took his place as a presidential adviser, and the latter received appointment as associate general director of the Office of Production Management. When this weird hodgepodge fell of its own dead weight, Sidney was made a member of the Supply Priorities and Allocation Board, and after the collapse of SPAB became director of the Labor Division of the War Production Board. Through all of it, John Lewis's picture was not only turned to the wall, but nailed there.

In 1943, when John Lewis sat down with the operators to negotiate a new contract, the feud reached the shooting stage. What he demanded was a raise in the daily wage from $7 to $9, pointing out that unskilled boys were earning twice that money in defense factories. In the very middle of the conferences, however, the matter was taken away from collective bargaining and put in the hands of the War Labor Board. John Lewis attacked the transfer as a breach of faith, and charged that the Board was a "hodgepodge body whose decisions went by favor." The President replied by intimating that the head of the United Mine Workers was now entitled to be regarded as Public Enemy Number One.

Bitterness increased as the 1944 campaign opened up, for Murray and Hillman formed the Political Action Committee and levied contributions from every member of the CIO. In a piece that John Lewis gave me for *Collier's*, he minced no words in assailing the "sinister partnership" between the CIO and the White House.

Today [he thundered] we witness the ever-widening spread of what can only be called *company unions,* as much under the control of a party as the industrial company union is under the control of the employer. It is an alarming approach to the situation in Russia, where unions are an integral part of the Communist state, without independent function, and purchasing the right of existence by abject servility. The labor movement in the United States cannot hope for health until there is an end to this sordid alliance.

As President Roosevelt continued to single him out for attack, John Lewis again took his pen in hand at my request.

For a year and more [he declared in *Collier's*] I have been branded Public Enemy Number One, and the 600,000 members of the United Mine Workers have been stigmatized as malcontents who put mean greeds above the welfare of their country. Political malignity, springing from a determination to destroy all who cannot be controlled, has conducted an organized campaign to stir a fury of rage against us, both at home and on the firing lines abroad. No other labor executive or union has been subjected to any such bitter, cruel and sustained attack.

Countless strikes, many for reasons shocking in their essential triviality, have disrupted and are disrupting the nation's war effort, but neither leaders nor strikers have been named and pilloried. No clarion from the White House starts the hue and cry against them by accusations of disloyalty and sabotage. Miners alone, for pressing just demands, have been singled out for hate and obloquy.

In this record may be found the explanation of John Lewis's seeming intransigence in later years. His treasury looted by a trick, his friends seduced, and his union the object of steady governmental attack, he turned to the economic strength of the UMWA as his one reliance.

CHAPTER 38

The Third Term

*P*resident Roosevelt, at a press conference in 1943, let drop that the New Deal had served its purpose as an energizing force, and intimated that future activities would be concerned with the consolidation of gains. As a matter of truth, the New Deal began to lose impetus as early as 1936, and slowed almost to a full stop after the defeat of the Court plan in 1937. No longer was Congress deluged by White House bills, all labeled "must," and even projects under way, such as slum clearance, housing, and reclamation, were permitted to bog down in morasses of confusion.

Administrative neglects were responsible in some degree, for the innumerable boards, bureaus, and commissions were more concerned with size and power than accomplishment, but the real reason was the President's own increasing preoccupation with politics. Angers carried over from the Court fight had much to do with the attempted purge of ten Democratic senators in 1938, but the real purpose was to bring the party under his direct personal control. Always impatient with opposition, he was convinced by two overwhelming victories that he alone had a mandate from the people.

As a consequence, new ideas ceased to be welcomed, and even planned projects went into the discard. Among these was the blueprint for a scientific, co-ordinated campaign that would view the country as a whole, studying all natural resources, but with particular emphasis on every drop of running water and every inch of soil. It was one of the President's enthusiasms in the early days of the New Deal, and he talked long and largely of "not just one TVA, but eight, ten, or even a dozen." Great all-purpose dams were to be raised at the headwaters of every principal river for flood control, hydroelectric power, irrigation, reclamation, drainage, low water control, and rural water supply.

Instead of the pulls and hauls of the past, geographers, engineers, foresters, sanitarians, and erosion experts would be organized for team play. Barren earth would be restored to its former fertility and the owners taught intelligent use; arid stretches would be made to blossom, and planned rural communities, with the development of local trades, arts, and crafts, would bring about a better balance between agriculture and industry, so that superfluous city workers might be drawn back to the land.

Aside from its broad sweep, the plan held a personal interest for me, as my own state of California faced catastrophe. Owing to lowered water tables, orchards and vineyards were dying in the Sacramento and San Joaquin valleys—California's heart land—and thousands of fertile acres were rapidly reverting to desert. By no means was it a purely local problem, for unless ravages were checked, the nation's income was threatened by an annual loss of $150,000,000.

Unfortunately, by the time our delegation reached the President the great plan had ceased to excite his imagination. With Herbert Hoover's Boulder Dam completed and the Grand Coulee, Bonneville, and Fort Peck projects well under way, his interest in further undertakings had sagged perceptibly. Gone from his mind was an estimated appropriation of $500,-000,000 over a long term of years for the campaign against floods, droughts, and soil erosion.

Another road block was Secretary Ickes' theory that public money should be allocated geographically rather than on the basis of need, and his contention that California had already had "more than its fair share." Only after weeks of persuasion and appeal were we able to wangle an appropriation of $20,000,000 for initiation of the Central Valley project.

On the heels of this chore for California, another presented itself. San Francisco, my home town, suddenly conceived the idea of a Golden Gate International Exposition, and as there was no available land for the site, it was gaily decided to build a four-hundred-acre island in the shallow waters of Yerba Buena shoals. The huge undertaking called for federal aid, of course, and Leland Cutler and a picked crew of native sons descended on Washington with a bland request for millions.

The President was not any too enthusiastic at the outset, for New York was also begging funds for an exposition in 1939, but he softened considerably when we pointed out the benefits that would accrue. Aside from providing employment for five thousand men and pouring large sums into the federal treasury by a tax on admissions, there was the added inducement that the island would be turned over to the Navy at the Exposition's end. A wonderful and necessary base! Under the spell of Lee Cutler's oratory, the President approved allocations in the amount of $8,545,000, and along with the grants came the suggestion that I take the post of United States Commissioner.

While I was ashamed to tell Bill Chenery and Charlie Colebaugh that I was quitting *Collier's* again, two reasons led me to accept. Not only was the New Deal in the doldrums, but Senator McAdoo was up for re-election in 1938, and with more than an off chance that he might be defeated. What he faced, in fact, was the same sort of popular madness that I had to buck in 1934. EPIC had vanished from memory, but Dr. Townsend was still going strong, and a brand-new pension plan also made even larger appeal. "Thirty dollars every Thursday" for everybody over fifty, and with this slogan: "Ham and Eggs for California."

Harangued by some smart salesmen with an initial capital of only $200, the denizens of Southern California fairly fought for the privilege of swallowing the latest thing in pink pills. And, too, another mahatma had risen to take the place left vacant by Upton Sinclair. Sheridan Downey was an even more perfect specimen of cultism, for he had a very real oratorical gift and contemporaneous sincerities that enabled him to change positions in mid-air with all the easy grace of the daring young man on the flying trapeze.

A Republican up to 1932, he ran for Congress that year only to meet with a humiliating defeat. No whit deterred, Sheridan announced his candidacy for the Democratic gubernatorial nomination in 1934, but soon switched over and became the EPIC candidate for lieutenant governor. He made quite a race of it, too, leading Sinclair by 125,000 votes. With EPIC dead on the vine, the daring young man made another leap, landing in the Townsend party, where he earned instant acclaim by coining "senior citizens" as a more pleasing way to refer to would-be pensioners. Retained as Dr. Townsend's personal attorney while at the same time acting as the movement's mouthpiece, Mr. Downey figured prominently in the Cleveland convention where the good doctor, Father Coughlin, William Lemke, and Gerald K. Smith wrestled mightily with the problem of a third party. No man was more loudly cheered by the delegates, and doubtless excited by the baying, Mr. Downey ran for Congress as a Townsendite in 1936, and again went down to defeat.

On the face of things, his candidacy for the Senate against a man of McAdoo's stature looked to be hopeless, but various causes made Mac's strength more apparent than real. Powerful politicians in the South who owed prominence and fortune to his friendship turned against him, and the party was torn by factional quarrels. With "Ham and Eggs" sweeping the state, it was also the case that his conscience would not let him cater to mob sentiment.

At that, the outcome of the campaign was fifty-fifty until a derelict in San Diego took poison and left behind him on the park bench a note that read, "Too young for pension, and too old for work." Racing to the potter's field where the pauper was buried, the Ham and Eggers placed him in a bronze coffin and carried him in solemn state to a plot in Los Angeles' expensive Glen Abbey Memorial Cemetery. There, in the presence of seven thousand sobbing, hysterical men and women, Sheridan Downey delivered a funeral oration built around the "message from the dead." That did it!

With the election out of the way, there was the job of putting up a federal building on Treasure Island and deciding what to have in it. Congress gave me $1,500,000, less than a fourth of what New York received, and it did not require much thought to see that our dependence must be placed on originality. A first decision was to go in for simple one-story redwood construction rather than marbles and bronzes, and with plenty of courts where the park and forestry services could show what they were doing even while adding to beauty.

A second decision was to have all exhibits functional in character rather than departmental. Instead of allotting each federal agency a certain amount to do with as it liked, such as had a close relation would be grouped together so that citizens might see the whole picture and not a part. All of the depart-

309

ment heads howled like wolves, but I held to my plan, and the result was a sequential showing of the government's activities.

Mrs. Roosevelt came to San Francisco in March, 1938, to deliver a lecture on peace, and was kind enough to consent to break ground for the federal building on Treasure Island. Her one condition was that she would not be asked to pull any levers or "ride in anything," and I gave the promise with hand on my heart. What I did not count on was the owner of a big steam shovel and his pride in it. No sooner was Mrs. Roosevelt installed in the flower-garlanded seat than he started off hell-bent, plowing through puddles and plunging into ditches. I raced after him, ruining a perfectly good pair of striped trousers, but the proud gent had gone a full three hundred yards over rough terrain before I could bring him to a halt. Mrs. Roosevelt's famous smile was conspicuously absent as we helped her down, and the rest of the program was abruptly suspended.

The President himself came to Treasure Island in July for a look-see at progress, and the visit, while a great boost for the Exposition, left bitternesses that never healed. Only one thousand guests could be crowded into the room where the luncheon was to be given, and ten thousand Democrats demanded invitations; particularly the candidates, for everyone was hanging to Roosevelt's coattails and felt that his chances would be ruined if he was not seen in the company of the Great White Father. As the favored thousand sat down, the rage of those outside had the roar and beat of a tidal wave.

The luncheon itself was a very gay affair, for the President was in rare form, bantering Senator Hiram Johnson about his vote against the Court plan and exchanging quips with Governor Merriam, the Republican who had defeated Sinclair in 1934. Catching his spirit, I threw formal introductions to one side and presented the Governor as the sole survivor of a once mighty tribe that ruled the region, and who still practiced the mysterious rites of his weird sect. At the time Mayor Angelo Rossi was having a raucous quarrel with the Secretary of the Interior, and I introduced him as one who suffered from "the seven-year Ickes."

Because of unavoidable delays, the Exposition did not open until 1939, thus putting us into competition with New York.

At that, we held our own—so successfully, in fact, that it was decided to carry on into 1940. This decision on the part of the directors came as something of a blow, for marching events had put me in a sweat to get back to Washington. Not only did Germany's invasion of Poland bring the shadow of a second World War, but a presidential campaign was in the offing.

In preparing the article on "Roosevelt's Plans and Purposes," published December 26, 1936, in *Collier's,* I asked the President point-blank if he entertained, or would entertain, the idea of a third term, for his two overwhelming victories made it a fair question. As a result of the discussion that followed, I started off my article with this statement:

Not the least cause of laughter in these post-election days is the growing whisper that the idea of a third term has taken fixed shape in the President's mind. Aside from the precedent established by George Washington, and the humiliation suffered by U. S. Grant when he sought to break that precedent, it happens to be the case that Franklin Roosevelt looks forward to private life with the keenest expectation. More than any other Chief Executive, perhaps, he has loved the presidential years, his bold spirit rejoicing in the challenge of great problems, but the hour of his retirement will be shadowed by no regrets. Quite recently, in conversation with an intimate, he said: "On January 21, when a new President takes over, I will be in Hyde Park having the time of my life."

I was that "intimate." The matter came up again in 1939, and not only did he reiterate his determination to retire, but told me of his plans. There was a history of the New Deal that he wanted to write, and it was also his purpose to deal with current problems in signed articles from time to time. *Collier's* had asked him to become a contributing editor, and as the salary and terms were most satisfactory, he was about ready to sign the contract. In 1940, when I went to Washington to get additional funds for the Exposition's second year, the President was even more explicit in respect to his retirement.

What he did bring up, however, was the question of his successor. Where was the man to take over the load? I mentioned the fact that there was much talk of a Hull-Farley ticket, and ventured the comment that it looked like a winning combination. The Secretary of State was then at the peak of his popularity as a tried public servant, and I did not think there

311

was a man in the country more liked and trusted than Jim Farley. Paul McNutt, I continued, was already campaigning as Indiana's favorite son. The President showed no enthusiasm over McNutt, but nodded agreement as to Hull and Farley. I think that Jack Garner's name figured in the discussion, but I am not sure.

Several days later I talked with members of the White House secretariat, and their comment on the various candidacies was most illuminating. Secretary Hull was a splendid man but barred by reason of his poor health. Jim Farley was a standout, but the time had not yet arrived when the people would send an Irish Catholic to the White House. Paul McNutt had nothing but his Hollywood glamour, and Jack Garner, while the finest American type, had swung so far to the right that liberals would not accept him. Much as they regretted it, the Boss would have to be "drafted."

When Paul McNutt's campaign showed promise, sly innuendo changed to direct action, for a rumor spread that he had been guilty of skulduggery in connection with his income tax. The Treasury professed profound ignorance; nevertheless, its agents flooded Indiana, every possible organization being asked if Mr. McNutt had been paid for his speeches, and if so, in what amount. Every interview left the plain inference that the former governor was suspected of fraud and his candidacy went into eclipse.

The convention, and all that led up to it, left a bad taste in many mouths. Harry Hopkins, taking full charge of the so-called "draft," insisted that he was acting independently, although everybody knew that his every move was directed by the White House. The Massachusetts delegation had been instructed for Farley, but instead of letting the members vote as in honor bound, Hopkins brought pressure to make them switch so that the President could be renominated by acclamation.

Senator Carter Glass was booed when he placed Farley's name in nomination, and so were those who nominated Senator Millard Tydings and Vice-President Garner. "We want Roosevelt" was a cry that bellowed from every loud-speaker on the floor, and the din ceased only when it was discovered to be a one-man uproar, staged by Mayor Ed Kelly's superintendent of sewers, hidden away in a basement room. Chicago's Democratic boss also contributed the hundreds of ward workers who rose at a given signal, waving "Roosevelt and Humanity" banners.

The nose-led delegates were not even permitted a voice in the selection of a vice-president, for a telephone message from the White House gave the order that votes should be cast for Henry Wallace. There was a brief moment when revolt threatened, for Wallace's name was greeted by boos and catcalls, and when an Oklahoman suddenly nominated Paul McNutt, the convention staged a demonstration without precedent. When McNutt tried to disclaim the honor he was drowned out by cries of "No, no!" and Chairman Barkley's efforts to calm the tumult were rewarded by the largest raspberry ever grown in any Democratic gathering.

Unless the President put names in a hat and shut his eyes as he drew one out, there is no explanation of his choice of Henry Wallace. At the time he had not formed his alliance with the left wing, and even as he was not known to the Hillmans and the Murrays, Democratic regulars viewed him with alarm as a "screwball." It was not only that he surrounded himself in the Department of Agriculture with a weird collection of nuts that even included cultists, but there was the open accusation that he consulted astrologers and sought guidance from the stars. Fumbling in speech to the point of being inarticulate, when he did speak to party leaders, all confessed that they didn't know what in hell he was talking about. As one hard-boiled old politician once confided to me, "Henry's the sort that keeps you guessing as to whether he's going to deliver a sermon or wet the bed."

Even with the convention an evil odor, there was never a doubt in my mind as to the outcome of the election. A world war was in plain sight, impressing people with the danger of changing horses in mid-stream, and back of this feeling was an army of three million federal jobholders fighting in phalanx formation. These factors, taken in conjunction with the Republican party's lack of a sound precinct organization, made Willkie's defeat inevitable.

The Golden Gate Exposition ended triumphantly—a financial success as well as artistic—and it was my purpose to hurry east after the final settlement. Suddenly and tragically, however, my wife fell ill, and Pearl Harbor found me still at her bedside. Her gallant spirit gave hope to the last, but on Christmas Day she passed away in her sleep.

CHAPTER 39

Mad Hatters and March Hares

*W*ith the war call sounding, I flew to Washington after the New Year, eager for a chance to serve in any capacity. As my failure to show enthusiasm for the third term had lost me the favor of the White House, I trudged from office to office, patiently recalling the part I had played in World War I. The young men to whom I talked, many of them looking as if they had just come from commencement exercises, were very courteous, but seemed to have difficulty in differentiating between the 1917 conflict and the Punic Wars. By the time I gave up in despair, they almost had me believing that I was a veteran of Caesar's campaigns.

What afforded some comfort was the sight of Bernie Baruch sitting lonely on a bench in the leafy solitudes of La Fayette Park. He too had been making the rounds, hopeful of a place in the war machine, and while somewhat downcast, professed pride in the fact that there was no denial of his abilities. All admitted that he had been a good man in his day, but that day, unfortunately, was in the dust-covered past. What *they* planned were brand-new approaches to brand-new conditions, so what did experience have to offer?

There was an embarrassing moment when Winston Churchill made his first visit to the White House, for he asked at once about "my old and dear friend Baruch." There was nothing to do, of course, but to pluck the Gray Man from his bench, but back he went at the Prime Minister's departure. Patience and perseverance, however, had their reward ultimately, for as the "brand-new approaches" cracked up one after the other, a

314

White House window was raised, and a finger beckoned to the lonely figure on the park bench.

For my part, I returned to my old job as Washington correspondent for *Collier's* and watched out the war from that vantage point. From the very first, blunder piled on blunder, and the miracle of our war effort stands, and will ever stand, as proof positive that some higher power has America in its keeping. What made the stumbling and the fumbling so inexplicable was the absence of any excuse, for at hand was the chart left behind by Woodrow Wilson showing every rock, shoal, and reef encountered in World War I, and particularly clear in warning where *not* to go and what *not* to do.

One look at that chart would have shown that the very first necessity was the creation of a single, all-powerful board for the mobilization of industry; a body that would have entire charge of the country's raw and unfinished materials, making allocations on the basis of actual and immediate requirements, and able to compel plant conversions, subcontracting, and the skeletonization of nonessential industry. A War Industries Board, in fact, such as Woodrow Wilson finally empowered after a year of false starts, putting Baruch at its head.

Equally important was price control. Not piecemeal stuff, but an over-all ceiling for everything, with wages, salaries, rents, interest rates, agricultural prices, and commodity prices all stabilized as of a set date. Next in order was the building up of stock piles of rubber, tin, mica, chrome, tungsten, and other strategic materials so as to end our dependence on overseas supplies.

Plain directions, but instead of heeding them, the administration began to pour forth a stream of alphabetical agencies that might have been devised by Lewis Carroll. The first of these was the Office of Emergency Management, supposedly created to co-ordinate everybody and everything, but which had as its real purpose the concentration of all authority in the hands of the President. After that, with much flourish of trumpets, came the Office of Production Management with "Big Bill" Knudsen and Sidney Hillman as its codirectors.

The executive powers of OPM could have been written on the head of a pin. This made no difference to Hillman, happy as a lark over his elevation, but Knudsen had neither the temperament nor the training to endure the Mad Hatter setup.

Like a bull in the ring, he pawed the earth and rumbled distressful sounds, not knowing when or where to charge. OPM's failure soon stood so clear that the Great Magician reached down into his hat for another white rabbit.

What the President now drew forth was the Supply Priorities and Allocations Board, with none other than Vice-President Wallace as its head. Why Wallace? It was a riddle to which even ouija boards could return no answer. More weird than OPM, ill-fated SPAB crashed to ruin within six months, giving way to a War Production Board with Donald Nelson as the chairman. Here again, however, there was responsibility without power.

The one consolation afforded by SPAB was that Henry Wallace lay buried under the ruins. But no! Suddenly, and without the mercy of warning so that people could brace themselves, Henry emerged as the directing genius of the Board of Economic Warfare. The importance of the job may be measured by the fact that it was his duty to "advise, develop and coordinate all policies, plans and programs for the protection and stengthening of America's economic relations in the interest of the national defense."

The incredible appointment was followed by an equally incredible performance. Not only did BEW mushroom into gigantic proportions, employing every nut still at large, but Mr. Wallace announced that the acquisition of strategic materials was not the sole function. All Latin America was to be given a New Deal, for through the medium of BEW contracts the standard of living was to be raised for the oppressed masses in each and every country.

The Great Adventure struck a snag at the outset, for while Wallace could draw up the contracts, approval and payment were up to Jesse Jones, head of the Reconstruction Finance Corporation. Looking over BEW activities with a cold, hard eye, Jesse informed Henry that he could find nothing in the law that justified the expenditure of millions for social uplift.

Erupting with Vesuvian violence, the Vice-President attacked Mr. Jones for a "timid, business-as-usual approach to great moral problems," and left no doubt that he considered the Keeper of the Purse a hateful combination of small-town banker and East Side pawnbroker. Jesse answered that the charges were "falsehoods out of whole cloth," called Henry hysterical, and alleged

316

that BEW had flooded Latin America with social workers ignorant of business practices and concerned only with grandiose plans for a Richer Life. Compelled to intervene, the President curtailed Jesse's powers and cast Henry into the outer darkness.

Price control in many ways was the prize mess of all for barrel-chested, bull-voiced Leon Henderson was handed a toothless bill. When both the AFL and the CIO thundered that the just demands of workers must not be curbed, the White House meekly agreed to the exclusion of wages from the price-control law. Straightway the farm bloc swung into action and forced the incorporation of a provision that farm prices should not be brought under restraint.

Hamstrung from the start, harassed Leon soon gave way to former Senator Prentiss Brown, and when he too threw up his hands, in came Chester Bowles, an advertising man. Convinced that the inadequacies of the law could be cured by expansion, Mr. Bowles quadrupled the size of the OPA organization, and to his side rushed briefless lawyers, social planners, theorists, crystal-gazers, and congenital unemployables, pushing and jamming until shoehorns had to be used to get them in. Headless and footless, the jitterbug crew shouted, "Good hunting!" and plunged into an orgy of directives and questionnaires that turned the country into a shambles. One book of regulations had 300,000,000 words, and I remember one questionnaire on vitamins that measured four feet wide and twenty feet long after being filled out.

What happened on the food front was no less fantastic. The United States Employment Service ballyhooed the higher wages and shorter hours in industry until 500,000 agricultural workers were lured into war plants and defense projects. By way of making the situation worse, draft boards raided the farms of the country for another half million, ignoring the plain intent of the Selective Service Act, whereupon an alarmed Congress voted the deferment of all men engaged in essential farm labor.

The Manpower Commission, however, asserted the right to decide what constituted essentiality, and draft boards were informed that a farmer would be entitled to the deferment of one worker for every sixteen "war units." Under this Alice in Blunderland scheme, a milch cow and a calf counted for a whole unit; a sow expected to farrow twice in the year two

317

thirds of a unit; each beef-type cow one tenth of a unit; a laying hen one seventy-fifth; a ewe one thirtieth; each acre of corn one fifteenth, and each acre of wheat one twentieth.

An arrangement for the importation of Mexican farm workers held promise of relief, but a snarl of red tape ended that hope. First the Farm Placement Bureau of the Employment Service certified the need of labor to its regional office in San Francisco. The request was then transmitted to the War Manpower Commission in Washington, and if approved went to the Bureau of Naturalization and Immigration in Philadelphia. After that the papers were returned to the War Manpower Commission in Washington, then forwarded to the regional office of WMC in San Francisco, then to the regional office of the Farm Security Administration, then to the state director of FSA in Phoenix, and then back to the FSA regional director in San Francisco. Only then were agents given the right to go to Mexico and start recruiting.

Scattered here and there in the confusion, as a relief, were little gaieties. Generous sentimental Aubrey Williams did some fine things with his National Youth Administration, but now and then a Lewis Carroll note crept in. One summer while I was back in San Francisco on a vacation, Melvyn Douglas and Helen Gahagan sent me a telegram asking that I come to Los Angeles to hear an important message from Mrs. Roosevelt. I flew down, of course, and on reaching their lovely home in the Senalda hills found the terrace occupied by some fifty or sixty boys and girls, tuning up all sorts of instruments.

"What's this?" I demanded. "Where's the message?"

"That will come later," Helen explained. "First we are going to hear the NYA orchestra play Grieg's *Peer Gynt* suite. They have been working on it for five or six months."

After quite a wait, the conductor gave the word to go, but a high wind soon swept the music off the stands. Clothespins finally corrected the situation, and the orchestra attacked the composition with all the energy and zest of healthy teen-agers. Right in the middle, unfortunately, the house shook to a small shock and I turned to the man next me and remarked, "Quite a temblor."

"Temblor, hell!" he growled. "That's *Grieg* turning over."

Many of the alphabetical agencies, however, seemed to have no other point than the provision of an emotional experience

318

for the New Deal's sophomore class. The executive order creating the Office of Civilian Defense, for example, was so vaguely drawn that it gave room for everything from parlor games to a voyage on the *Walloping Window-blind*. Instead of concentrating on advice and assistance to the several states with respect to programs for the protection of life and property in emergencies, the Office went so far afield that its outposts could not be reached by radar.

The start, of course, was the appointment of a host of inspector generals, and then came a Survey Section "to collect all available data relating to the social and economic life of the community, and collate such material so as to present an overall picture of problems associated with war activities which are arising; to note the steps being taken to meet them, and to appraise the social and economic gaps that such a picture presents in terms of norms established by the Civilian Participation Division in consultation with other interested government and private agencies."

A Volunteer Participation Committee had as its duty the "utilization of human energy," and a Know Your Government Division employed two hundred clerks "to handle inquiries developed by radio programs." A Press Division not only prepared and released daily bulletins and brochures, but sent high-salaried men and women out over the country to dig up human-interest stories for processing in Washington by information specialists and senior and junior analysts.

A Physical Fitness Section justified itself on the ground that people could not possibly hope to escape bombs unless they had the muscular co-ordination of a roebuck. One activity of the Section was the employment of a Director of Industrial Recreation to go about the country teaching factory workers to play, making talks in praise of deep breathing, and particularly urging Sunday picnics so as to avoid the heavy noonday meal that makes for torpidity. As a capsheaf to the Mad Hatter pyramid, "co-ordinators" were appointed for sixty-one sports, including archery, badminton, yachting, and horseshoe pitching, and a protégée of Mrs. Roosevelt was employed to teach eurhythmic dancing to children in air-raid shelters.

Along with this sort of squandering there were also criminal wastes of millions, notably the famous Canol project, undertaken to supply oil to the Alaskan area from a field in the vicinity of Normal Wells, in Canada, and only seventy-five miles from the Arctic Circle. Harry Truman, a senator then, considered the case very fully in an article that he wrote for *Collier's* at my suggestion and with my help.

Lieutenant General Brehon B. Somervell [declared Truman] authorized the project on April 30, 1942, estimating the cost at $34,000,000, and directing that it be completed by October 1, 1942. All hopes with no base in reality. Canol did not even come into partial operation until May, 1944, and then with only limited quantities of truck gasoline produced at excessive cost. And instead of $34,000,000, the bill on that date had amounted to $134,000,000, not counting the pay of officers and enlisted men for months, and the cost of air transport.

General Somervell, called to the witness stand, admitted that no other department of government had ever been consulted. The Navy had as great an interest in oil for Alaska as the Army, but the Navy was ignored. So were the Petroleum Administrator, the War Production Board, the War Shipping Administration and Lend-lease. . . . Had these war agencies been consulted, there is small doubt that Canol would have died aborning. On learning about the project after it was under way, the Secretary of the Navy, the Petroleum Administrator and the War Production Board united in urging its abandonment. Secretary Ickes went so far as to brand the undertaking as "fantastic," and the WPB damned it as a "huge and useless program . . . which will never serve a useful purpose." Testimony was offered that four tankers, at any time after April 30, 1942, could have carried in one trip more 100-octane gasoline, motor gasoline and fuel oil than would be produced by the entire Canol project by January 1, 1945.

Worse than the squandering of millions was the waste of manpower and vital equipment. Some 200,000 tons of scarce materials and transportation equipment, urgently needed elsewhere, was diverted to Canol's use. Taken from the war effort were a host of Army officers, 4,000 enlisted men and 12,000 civilians.

Equally shameless in its waste of millions and materials was the War Department's project for linking the United States and the Panama Canal with an all-weather highway. In the beginning the cost was estimated at $20,000,000 and completion was promised by May, 1943. At this writing only 347 miles of road have been finished at a cost of $36,000,000—much of it absolutely unusable—and the Senate's Special War Investigating Committee finds that the undertaking, if pushed through, will tap the Treasury for $139,000,000. Along with brazen grafting by contractors, the White House approved a detour of forty-two miles in Nicaragua so that the highway would pass by the property of a former president.

My keenest interest, of course, was in the agencies that dealt in information and propaganda, and my brain reeled as I watched organization succeed organization. The first was the Office of Government Reports, and when that folded up, Archibald MacLeish burst upon the scene with the Office of Facts and Figures. When it developed that Archibald had neither, Wild Bill Donovan entered the confused picture as a coordinator of information. A shrewd man at bottom, Master Donovan soon saw that the setup held no promise, and received White House approval for a mysterious organization that he called the Office of Strategic Services. Supposedly charged with the duty of reporting on mass psychology both at home and abroad, he quickly changed it into a cloak-and-dagger affair that entered into competition with the intelligence branches of the Army and the Navy.

Next came the Office of War Information, with brilliant, likable Elmer Davis as its head. After all the blundering, I assumed that OWI, like the Committee on Public Information, would bring everything together under one tent, but this was not the case. The Army, the Navy, and every one of the war-making branches of government set up a public relations division of its own, each employing hundreds. Byron Price took over the administration of the voluntary censorship, surrounding himself with a large staff, but the Army and the Navy claimed the right to censor, and scores of lieutenants, majors, colonels, and even generals, brought in from civil life, read every article and book that had to do with the war effort.

One division of the Committee on Public Information handled propaganda in all neutral countries, besides bucking up the morale of Italy, France, and England and tearing down the morale of the Central Powers. Out of the blue the approach to South America, Central America, and Mexico was made a special undertaking, and given over to an Office for the Coordinator of Inter-American Affairs, with Nelson Rockefeller as its head. In its first year the Office spent $3,332,000, and in the second year asked for $7,331,000 with the right to contract for an additional $3,000,000—a sum almost twice as large as the amount spent by the Committee on Public Information during the two years in which it covered the whole world.

Mr. Rockefeller, to be sure, worked in fields that the CPI never dreamed of entering. Our one aim was to acquaint Latin America with the facts in the case—our war aims, our peace terms, and the certainty of our victory—a program designed to *earn* good will rather than attempting to *buy* it. That it sufficed stood proved when South America and Central America pledged friendship and aid, and even Mexico abated its distrusts and suspicions.

The Rockefeller organization, on the other hand, went in heavily for art, literature, music, drama, and the dance. The novels and poetry of Latin America were translated into English, likewise scientific articles, and there was a brisk exchange of composers, choreographers, singers, authors, and artists. Large amounts were spent on the promotion of athletic competitions, and $357,000 allotted for a Pan-American Institute to be a "center for higher studies of Latin America."

Administrative blundering persisted to the very end, and yet out of chaos came the mightiest war machine ever developed by any nation. I still insist that a higher power had much to do with it, but credit cannot be taken away from what can only be termed the genius of America—the energy, initiative, high resolve, and unity that have ever been developed by crises.

CHAPTER 40

The Road to Yalta

*T*he Washington muddle proceeded in some degree from Franklin Roosevelt's inability to delegate authority, but the main cause was his intensity of interest in the international situation that left no room for domestic affairs. It was not a concern first stirred by the Munich pact or the invasion of Poland, but one that went back to an earlier day when Adolf

Hitler was generally regarded as a crackpot demagogue, cheaply imitative of Benito Mussolini.

I think it was in 1938, or maybe 1937, that he made *Mein Kampf* the subject of several conversations. Instead of dismissing the Führer as a ranting buffoon, the President viewed him as a psychopathic case who would and could put his program into effect, and believed implicitly that the program could have no other end than world war. In this event, he believed, the United States, despite every effort to maintain neutrality, would be drawn into the conflict on the side of Britain and France, just as in 1917. This statement, fortunately, does not rest on my unsupported assertion, for in 1946, when I collaborated with Vice-Admiral Ross McIntire in writing *White House Physician,* he furnished this report of the President's attitude:

There was a night during the debate [on the repeal of the embargo provisions in the Neutrality Act] after a small and informal dinner at the White House, when the President talked frankly about his own feelings with respect to England and the English. A great people, brought up in a great tradition . . . but often an irritating people by reason of a conviction of superiority so ingrained and perfected by time as to transcend mere egotism. Likewise a shrewd, hard-bargaining people, aggressive territorially and in every trade relation . . . nevertheless a steadfast people, a people kin to us by blood, holding to the same ideals, and an assured ally of the United States in event of international discord. A conquered England, her lands and shores in the possession of Germany, meant the end of America's security, therefore England *had* to be saved.

This belief was translated into action when Germany invaded Poland. America's neutrality was proclaimed, of course, but under cover the President worked steadily, and even autocratically, to "save" England. The handing over of fifty destroyers in exchange for leases on British island bases was a personal arrangement that by-passed Congress, and with similar adroitness he put across Lend-Lease as an "aid-to-democracies" measure that would keep war away from our shores.

The Atlantic Charter was no less personal. Not until its publication was it known that the President had met with Prime Minister Churchill in the waters off Newfoundland. While the Charter itself bore on its face no larger significance than a Roosevelt-Churchill agreement on a postwar program in the interests of world peace, in effect it joined the United States and Britain in a hard and fast alliance.

Germany invaded Russia in June, 1941, and the President's dispatch of Harry Hopkins to Moscow was attended by the same secrecy that surrounded the Newfoundland rendezvous. An hour or two with Marshal Stalin surcharged Harry with enthusiasm over Russia as a loyal and effective ally, and it was on the strength of his report that Franklin Roosevelt and Winston Churchill addressed a joint letter to the Marshal, pledging military and economic aid without stint, and also without the exaction of a single promise in return.

Utterly ignored was the Hitler-Stalin pact that gave the signal for war. Pushed to one side, as though it had never happened, was Russia's invasion of Poland in violation of solemn treaties, and the enslavement of the Baltic States. Also thrust into the background was the Communist gospel that preached undying enmity to all capitalist countries, and justified falsehood and treachery as proper weapons in the struggle for their overthrow.

With the White House clamping down on all but innocuous news, the various embassies became sources of information, for all watched every move in the game both tirelessly and intelligently. Jan Ciechanowski, the Polish ambassador, Constantin Fotich, the Yugoslav ambassador, and Wei Tao-ming, the Chinese ambassador, were not only men of extraordinary ability, but statesmen in the true sense of the word. Dr. Wei and his brilliant wife, having been educated at the Sorbonne, knew Europe as well as the Orient. Another source was Tibor Eckhardt, head of the Small Holders party in Hungary until his bitterly anti-Nazi stand forced him into exile. Dr. Eckhardt came to me with a letter from John F. Montgomery,[1] our former minister in Budapest, and lived up to his endorsement as an "authority on Hitler and Stalin."

The outcome of the Hopkins-Stalin conversations turned both Poles and Yugoslavs pale with apprehension. Wladyslaw Besterman, the gay and able press attaché of the Polish Embassy, tried to calm them by explaining that the lavish promises to Stalin proceeded entirely from Harry Hopkins' WPA training.

---

[1] After eight years of distinguished service, Mr. Montgomery was abruptly displaced in 1941 to make way for a Long Island friend of the Roosevelt family.

"After years of giving," he laughed, "poor Harry is as much the victim of habit as any dope fiend."

The others, however, persisted in their gloomy views. Why had the pledges of aid to Russia not been conditioned on the return of Polish territory, and an end to Communist terrorism in Yugoslavia? Both Jan Ciechanowski and Dr. Fotich took their fears to the President, and were somewhat soothed by his assurances that such matters would be ironed out at a meeting with Marshal Stalin in the near future. Meanwhile they were not to doubt his unchanging support of a free Poland and a sovereign Yugoslavia.

Michal Zwapiszewski, the Polish minister, who had both studied and served in Russia, prophesied that Stalin would meet the President and the Prime Minister in his own good time and on his own ground. "Where Mr. Roosevelt makes his mistake," commented Tibor Eckhardt, "is in forgetting that Stalin is not only a Marxian but also an Asiatic. Having parted with all of his bargaining power, what can the President hope?"

Wise Michal Zwapiszewski predicted truly, for after refusing to attend the Casablanca conference, Marshal Stalin curtly rejected an invitation to sit with the President and the Prime Minister in Quebec. In the end the meeting was held in Teheran, and by way of driving home his control of the situation, Stalin had Mr. Roosevelt quit the American Legation for a house in the Russian compound.

On his return the President changed his mind about reporting to Congress, and also failed to give any detailed information to the newspapermen. From friends who had attended the conference, Ambassador Ciechanowski soon learned that the President and the Prime Minister had agreed to the so-called Curzon line, thus handing the whole of eastern Poland over to Russia. From his sources. Dr. Fotich received the disturbing news that Stalin had persuaded the President and Mr. Churchill into abandoning General Draja Mihailovich and transferring all Allied support to Tito and his Communists. On being questioned about these reports, Mr. Roosevelt denied that there was a word of truth in them.

The Chinese were also on the anxious seat throughout this period, for an anti-Nationalist bias had developed in the State Department, and certain members of our armed forces in China were openly pro-Communist. Added to these worries, promises of aid to the Generalissimo were not being kept in full measure. These pledges had been won by Madame Chiang Kai-shek during her White House stay in the spring of 1943. As it happened, I had a chance to see China's First Lady at work, for the President and Mrs. Roosevelt invited the new Mrs. Creel and me to meet her at an informal dinner.

In March, I had married Alice May Rosseter in New York at the home of our dear friends John and Hedwig Montgomery. She was the widow of John H. Rosseter, and we had known each other since the first World War when John was Director of Operations in the Emergency Fleet Corporation. I took the invitation, therefore, as Mrs. Roosevelt's gracious gesture to Mrs. Creel.

Nevertheless, it came as something of a surprise, for I had followed up my defection in 1940 by bolting California's Democratic nominee for governor in 1942. Not only was Earl Warren, the Republican, a vastly superior person in every way, but I had sickened of the crackpot demagoguery that passed for liberalism. Marvin McIntyre, the President's secretary, called on three occasions, urging me to withdraw my endorsement of Warren, and my refusals left a distinct chill in the air.

I judged that Madame Chiang had been driving hard at the President with her urgencies, for as we sat down Mrs. Roosevelt remarked gaily, but still pointedly, that business would be adjourned. Without even the flicker of an eyelash to show that she had heard, the Madame continued to hold the President's ear with her recitation of China's desperate needs, neglecting course after course. Later on, as we watched a motion picture, I could hear her taking advantage of every pause.

In talk with Madame Chiang before dinner I mentioned my puzzlement at hearing her speak English with a distinctly Southern accent. "Why not?" she smiled. "I went to school in Macon, Georgia."

Mrs. Creel also had a chat with her that can be told without offense to good taste. When she said that it must be a help to the Generalissimo to have a wife able to share the burdens of state, Madame Chiang shook her head.

"I don't know about that," she shrugged. "Maybe it would be better if my tired businessman did not find a tired businesswoman when he came home in the evening."

The presidential campaign of 1944 offered a startling con-

326

trast to that of 1940. Then even the most ardent New Dealers were fearful of the third-term tradition, while now they were fairly begging Franklin Roosevelt to run again. The retirement of Jim Farley and Jack Garner had removed every voice of dissent, and the President dominated the national scene so completely that no other name could be considered. Nor was it the case that pleas were necessary. By this time he was not only convinced of his indispensability, but he saw himself as the founder of a "world family of democratic nations," going down in history as one who had succeeded where Woodrow Wilson failed. What other explanation is there for the decision of an aging, failing man to face the strain of a campaign and the killing load of a fourth term? How else explain the repudiation of sworn pledges in return for signatures to a United Nations pact?

It was a worn, sick man who went to Bernard Baruch's South Carolina plantation in the spring of 1944. Nothing organic, to be sure, but plain evidence of physical deterioration. The month of rest worked improvement, but a shrunken neck and loosened facial muscles still attested inner processes of disintegration, and additional proof of his condition was soon furnished by his handling of the vice-presidential nomination.

There was never any question as to the jettisoning of Henry Wallace. Not only had SPAB and BEW shown his dismal lack of administrative capacity, but on a speechmaking tour under the auspices of the CIO the tousled Iowan had taken violent issue with Mr. Roosevelt, and even gone so far as to threaten a "bloody revolution." Ed Flynn, speaking for the Democratic bosses, turned thumbs down on Wallace's renomination, and also rejected the candidacies of Justice Byrnes and Senator Barkley on the ground that the choice of a Southerner might alienate the Negro vote. The outcome of this preconvention conference was Harry Truman's selection as Roosevelt's running mate, and at the Chicago convention Bob Hannegan made large use of a White House letter endorsing the Missourian.

Had the President been hitting on every cylinder he would have called in Jimmie Byrnes and Alben Barkley and told them of his decision. Instead of that he let them believe that the field was open, exposing them to useless and undeserved humiliation. Sidney Hillman publicly kicked Mr. Byrnes out of the

327

running, and Senator Barkley polled no more than the votes of the Kentucky delegation.

The President's journey to the Pacific on the eve of the convention was attacked at the time as a political maneuver, shrewdly designed to center attention on him as the commander-in-chief rather than as the presidential nominee of a political party. Undoubtedly that angle figured in the decision, but the real reason was the hope of his physicians that the sea voyage would have beneficial effects.

In his speech of acceptance the President had said, "I shall not campaign in the usual sense for the office. In these days of tragic sorrow I do not consider it fitting. Besides, in these days of global warfare, I shall not be able to find the time." [2] Governor Dewey's aggressive campaign compelled a change in program, and the choice of an audience for the President's opening speech did little to support his somber allusion to "days of tragic sorrow." No more rowdy affair was ever staged than the dinner given by Dan Tobin's teamsters, for along with continuous bellowings, the "boys" smashed glasses and chinaware.

Only the indomitable will of the man carried him through the rest of his tour. In New York and Philadelphia he rode through the driving rain, and in both Chicago and Boston the weather had a chill that bit at the marrow. There were times when his voice broke, with here and there an incoherency, but still he managed to give an over-all effect of fitness that kept the newspapermen from making critical comment.

From the outset of the campaign, the attitude of Polish-Americans was the deep concern of Democratic leaders, for of the six million, the great majority voted in such pivotal states as New York, Pennsylvania, Michigan, and New Jersey. In June, therefore, it was suddenly announced that Stanislaw Mikolajczyk had been invited to meet with the President, and on his arrival the White House red carpet was spread for him. No honor was omitted, and as a crowning favor the Prime

---

[2] "This was in accordance with my urgent request. While admitting that he [the President] *could* travel and make speeches, I pointed out the danger of overexertion and the necessity of guarding his reserves."—Vice-Admiral Ross McIntire in *White House Physician.*

Minister was allowed to give me an interview for *Collier's* in which he set out the Polish position in grim detail. Nothing was left out with respect to Russia's aggressions, brutalities, and treacheries, and the article ended on this strong note:

"A wronged Poland, suffering from a deep conviction of injustice, may be counted on as a continuing source of instability and unrest. This is not a threat in any sense but a plain statement of fact. Look back over history and you will find that while Poland has been swallowed many times, never once has she been *digested.*"

On leaving, the Prime Minister told me that he was proceeding to Moscow, the President having urged the visit, and at the same time expressing confidence that Stalin would be in a mood to "arrange things." Things *were* arranged, but not in the manner expected. While Mikolajczyk and Stalin sat in conversation on August 1, the Red Army reached the gates of Warsaw and called on the beleaguered city to rise. General Bor-Komorosky, in command of the Polish underground, gave the word, confident of the Russian advance, but instead of that the Red troops moved back and left Warsaw to its fate.

Even more incredibly, Stalin refused to allow the British to use Russian airfields, forcing the RAF to fly supplies from Mediterranean bases. For two months the doomed city held out, but daily bombardment by the Germans, coupled with famine and disease, finally forced surrender. On the heels of this tragic news, Ambassador Ciechanowski received a cable from Mikolajczyk asking him to get either confirmation or denial of Stalin's flat statement that President Roosevelt, at Teheran, had agreed to Russia's grab of eastern Poland.

The President refused to see the Ambassador, pleading a press of engagements, and made the same excuse for delaying his answer to the question contained in the Mikolajczyk cable. On October 28, however, he found the time to meet in Chicago with Charles Rozmarek, head of the Polish-American Congress, and on being assured by the President that he would take active steps to ensure Poland's independence, Mr. Rozmarek endorsed the entire Democratic ticket. On November 17, thirteen days after the election, Mr. Roosevelt sent Ambassador Ciechanowski a letter for Prime Minister Mikolajczyk in which he made no mention of Teheran, but by plain inference urged Poland to grant Stalin's territorial demands.

Any doubt as to who sat in the driver's seat was dissipated by Yalta. First, the President, old, tired, and sick, was forced to travel halfway across the world because Stalin refused to leave the security provided by his soldiers and secret police. Second, no newspapermen were permitted to go with the American delegation, for Stalin had ruled against it. Not until the end of the conference was anything connected with the deliberations allowed to leak out, and then a carefully edited statement dealt in half-truths.

There was, of course, a ringing reaffirmation of the Atlantic Charter with particular emphasis on the right of all liberated peoples to sovereignty and self-government. Then followed the acceptance of Poland's puppet government and Tito's totalitarian regime in Yugoslavia, glossed over by assurances that both would be "reorganized on a broader democratic base." There was triumphant announcement of Russia's agreement to come into the United Nations, but less emphasis on the fact that Stalin had been given two additional votes in the UN organization. In return for a pledge to enter the war against Japan at some later date, Russia was also promised the Kuriles and the southern half of Sakhalin.

Even his enemies must have felt the pathos of the President's appearance when he went before Congress with his Yalta report. As he sat in a chair, where once it had been his habit to stand radiant and erect on the speaker's dais, his face deeply lined and his voice sagging, not even perceptible effort could recapture an effect of vitality. Admitting that the Polish settlement was an unhappy compromise, he defended the other actions of the conference, but without his customary force and plausibility.

Proof of the President's unsatisfactory physical condition was soon furnished, for Admiral McIntire ordered him to Warm Springs for a complete rest. After the first week, reports as to his improvement began to be issued, and Dr. Bruenn, the heart specialist, was even optimistic on the morning of April 12. The President had gained eight pounds in weight and planned to attend a barbecue in the afternoon. At 3:35 he was dead, never recovering consciousness after a massive cerebral hemorrhage. The suddenness of it held mercy, for he was not only spared the anguish of hopeless invalidism, but also the shame of seeing appeasement's price.

CHAPTER 41

Roosevelt as I Saw Him

*O*nly two kinds of books and articles have been written about Franklin D. Roosevelt. Those who fell under the spell of his famous "charm," or followed him ideologically, are unable to find a single flaw, and those who disliked him, or hated his policies, can see no good. As always where clashing extremes are concerned, the truth lies in between. Even then the task of analysis is far from simple, for in the whole of American public life there is no record of a more baffling personality or one with such a quicksilver quality.

As I look back over an association that covered thirty years, it seems to me that the man's elements of greatness were no less obvious than his weaknesses. As an inspirational leader, a dynamic and propulsive force, a clarion call to courage, Franklin Roosevelt was in a class by himself. Only Winston Churchill deserves to be ranked with him. As an administrator, however, handling the fortunes and future of a nation and its people, and as a statesman planning a new world order, he was subject to temperamental ardors that robbed him of prudence and hurried him into momentous decisions without study or the benefit of counsel.

No man ever dreamed more nobly or had less skill in making his dreams come true. Like Michelangelo, he could see the statue in the unhewn block, but unlike the great Florentine, he all too often turned aside before he had even chipped the marble. Go back over the road traveled by the New Deal, and it will be found littered by ideas and schemes that were forgotten after the first burst of enthusiasm. Follow his international conferences—Casablanca, Teheran, and Yalta—and it will be seen that he made no effort to gain the guarantees without which agreements are so much waste paper, his interest flagging when signatures were appended.

331

The very gifts that gave Franklin Roosevelt his vision and certainties, his eager mind and fine flame of the spirit, unfitted him for the sober and drudging tasks of execution. It was his tragedy, and the tragedy of America for that matter, that he was either unable or unwilling to sit in judgment on his own temperament, or to have men about him with sufficient independence of thought to file vigorous dissents.

The great majority of his supposed advisers were really listeners, a mere collection of eardrums. I do not say this on my own authority, but on that of a member of the President's secretariat, devoted to him but grown somewhat cynical through the years. When I asked him once if F.D.R. had ever had a "no" man since the death of Louis Howe, this man shook his head, but added that he himself came the closest to being one.

"You see," he explained, "I'm a *super*-yes man. When the Boss comes out with one of his big ideas, everybody gives a gasp of awed admiration except me. I come back with a violent dissent, saying that the idea is no good and won't work. Then suddenly I stop short and beg him to go over it again. When he does, I gasp, throw up my hands, and exclaim, 'God! It's so tremendous I didn't get it at first!' "

Louis Howe himself, queried about his relations with the Boss, is said to have made this remark: "Franklin has to have a new interest every day, and I supply it." Had the President's familiar gone on to the extent of volumes, he could not have been more revealing, for it was his adolescent quality—the amazing manner in which he carried over the enthusiasms of his teens into adult life—that furnishes one answer to the Roosevelt riddle.

Protracted adolescence was at once his strength and his weakness. For example, it furnished the bravery to blaze new trails, the gay disregard for outworn traditions, the never failing optimism that refused to admit either depression or defeat, and a vision not held back by immoderate reverence for decrepit institutions. On the other hand, it precluded contemplation, reflection, and detachment; put all emphasis on daring and dash rather than steadfastness; led to a passion for short cuts; and all too often confused activity with action.

Study the record of his administration with any degree of care, and it will be seen that the President's concern was with the end and not the means. Always it was the idea that stirred

332

his interest, and rarely the methods of making the idea work. It irked him to burden his soaring conception with the details of execution, and not only did he leap before looking, but it was rare indeed for him to take a look after the leap. Why bother with the wreck of a plan when a brand-new one was at hand? All of which furnishes a partial explanation of his enormous popularity, for the mass mind is anything but adult. Woodrow Wilson not only asked people to think but called on them for sustained thought. Franklin Roosevelt exploited the emotion of the moment and dropped it for another before it became tiresome or irritating.

All of which might have been stripped of hurtful consequences had he been able to delegate power, turning the idea over to men skilled in the somewhat exact science of thinking things through and getting them done. Because he never made any such delegations, his enemies argued a vainglorious egotism, but the real cause was his adolescent quality.

When Woodrow Wilson appointed a man, not only did the appointment carry authority, but duties were explained in minute detail. After that the appointee was on his own. If the work went badly, you heard from him, but as long as things went well, he did not want to hear from you. Nothing irritated him more or forfeited his confidence more quickly than to have officials popping back to the White House with their problems. "Man Afraid of His Job" was his characterization of such persons.

Franklin Roosevelt was absolutely incapable of pursuing such a course. Not because he was petty or egotistical, but out of a youthful eagerness to know everything that was going on and to have a finger in every pie, whether that pie was some grave international crisis, the expenditure of billions, or putting a comfort station in a public park. Instead of being vexed by appointees returning for advice and consultation, he *loved* it. Huddles and "bull sessions" were the delight of his soul, and he was at pains to compel them.

Examine the executive orders that he issued in a constant stream, and in almost every instance it will be found that nothing could be done without the approval of the President. Supposedly executive boards and commissions were not long in discovering that all major decisions had to be taken up with the White House. As a consequence his desk became a bottle-

333

neck, and it was common for high officials to twiddle thumbs for weeks before they got the green light.

No matter what importance pressed for decision, it was pushed aside if something touched off the adolescent note. I saw him one day at a time of crisis and found him tremendously excited by a "perpetual motion" scheme presented by a group of nuts. For a full hour, while senators and Cabinet members waited, he enthused over the idea's possibilities, littering the floor with diagrams. On another occasion, when we were working on an article that had to do with his plans and purposes, he spent the allotted time talking about a "solution" of the automobile-tire shortage that had been given him by a WPA worker at Hyde Park. First you wound rope about the rim, then poured on tar, then more rope, then more tar, and so on and so on.

Or take passages from the diary of Henry Morgenthau that have been allowed to leak out. The former Secretary of the Treasury tells how the President fixed the price of gold at twenty-one for no other reason than that he thought it a "lucky number." Having decided, he chuckled gleefully as he thought of "the hairs on the heads of foreign bankers standing on end" on learning of our foreign-exchange operations. A matter affecting world stability, and yet approached in the spirit of a lark.

As nothing else, the Roosevelt nonage is illustrated by the higgledy-piggledy manner in which the war machine was put together—the headless, footless bodies that followed one another in an endless stream after May 28, 1940, when we set out to be the "great arsenal of democracy." There was no possible excuse for blundering, since Woodrow Wilson had left behind a great volume of experience tested by trial and error. A prudent man called on to sail the same course would have hailed the records of World War I as a master chart set down by a master mariner and rejoiced in it.

No more attention was paid to it than if the chart had been left behind by the Phoenicians or Leif Ericson, for following it would have entailed the delegation of authority, thus robbing the President of the excitement of keeping a large forefinger, and sometimes the whole hand, in every pie. The Office of Emergency Management, a catchall containing more than a score of important agencies, was actually set up as part of the executive office under the President's personal direction.

No human being could possibly have done well the thousand and one things that Franklin Roosevelt piled on himself, and as a result, there was none of that careful designation of function that marked the Wilson way. Excited by a suggestion, he made appointments and created new agencies without ever stopping to learn if the job had been done or was being done. It was common for zealous souls to rush out of the White House on fire with enthusiasm, only to find a half dozen others in the field that they thought had been assigned to them. One executive order, signed in the usual rush, actually transferred control over foreign policy from the State Department to Henry Wallace's Board of Economic Warfare.

There can be no question that this adolescent quality had its values, for out of it came the ardors that gave people hope and courage in the black depression years. Unhappily, it did not stand alone as a determinant of thought and policy, but tied in with other factors. Not even Andrew Jackson had more of the democratic manner, and yet Franklin Roosevelt was an aristocrat to his finger tips; so much so, in fact, that it came close to being a "royalty complex."

Why not? The descendant of Dutch patroons, the only child of wealthy parents, as handsome as a young Alcibiades, he had lived always in the confines of his class, with the world of workers and tradesmen entirely outside his purview. Once in conversation Woodrow Wilson commented on the fact that the average American confused graciousness with democracy, and the observation always came back to me as I watched Franklin Roosevelt.

No man could be more charming when he wished. He liked laughter, and court jesters were not the least important members of the inner circle. He himself joked and joshed and gibed, but what a change occurred when anyone took a liberty with him! The atmosphere chilled instantly to the freezing point. When a reporter offended at a press conference, invariably the President, with darkening face, told him to put on a dunce cap and stand in the corner.

As with royalty, his decisions were often reached without consultation, and Joe Robinson and Alben Barkley, his Senate floor leaders, often complained that they learned what they were expected to do from the morning papers. While we were putting together the piece for *Collier's* in which he outlined his Court-packing plan, I ventured to suggest that such a breath-taking proposal ought to be taken up well in advance with Democratic leaders in the Senate and House. "Oh, if they kick up," he shrugged, "I'll send for them." While he was economical enough in his personal expenditures, no Stuart was ever more lavish when it came to spending public money, and not the least of Congress's irritations was his incessant demand for blank checks.

Jim Farley, in his *Collier's* series, quotes Mrs. Roosevelt as saying, "Franklin finds it hard to relax with people who aren't his social equals." The statement has not been denied at this writing, and even if denial comes, there are facts that affirm it. Of the hundreds of great industrialists and financiers who came to Washington for war work, only those who had *inherited* their wealth were ever honored by the President's friendship. In the landed proprietor's contempt for "people in trade" may also be found the reason for the President's ever evident antagonism to business.

It is safe to say that Franklin Roosevelt owed more to Jim Farley than to any other, yet never once was Jim invited to spend a night in the White House or permitted to share in purely social functions. This was not ingratitude but rather Franklin Roosevelt's inability to forget that both Jim's grandfather and his father had started life as bricklayers. John L. Lewis was another to whom he owed a great deal, and whose friendship might have been retained had the President been able to overlook the fact that Lewis, like all of his forebears, had been a coal miner.

Both the adolescent note and the royalty complex, however, leave Franklin Roosevelt less than understandable until considered in connection with the man's implicit belief in his destiny. Not merely a belief, but an unshakable conviction. Again why not? Here was one struck down in the very prime of life, seemingly doomed to hopeless invalidism, yet who rose from a bed of pain to become Governor of New York and President of the United States. Not merely once but repeatedly. What more natural than for him to think that he had been called? To have implicit faith in his mission, the infallibility of

336

his judgments, and equally full confidence in the justice and wisdom of his actions?

The messianic complex, for it was that, came to dominate him above all else. Not to be re-elected was to thwart divine purpose, and out of the belief came a desertion of standards that would have shocked him in the earlier years when as a young New York legislator he defied the orders of Tammany. Shrewdly, if cynically, he assessed the electorate, and decided that the have-nots outnumbered the haves. This conclusion reached, the class struggle was lifted from its frowsy lower levels and made a determining factor in his bids for continuance in power. According to the specious argument that he developed, if there were have-nots, it was due to no individual fault—no lack of ability, character, and industry—but a status due entirely to the unfairnesses and inequalities flowing from the evil practices of the haves.

As a result, success in business or the professions became suspect. Only on park benches and ancestral estates was true nobility to be found. The possession of competence argued criminality, some trick with loaded dice, and base envies took the place of emulation. Instead of the government owing every man the opportunity to make a living, the living was owed as a right, regardless of individual effort or capacity. Largess, increasingly poured out by boards and commissions without care of the national debt, undermined pride, self-respect, and industry, and added to the tin-cup army that lined up before the federal treasury. The right of every American to climb as high as his abilities would carry him gave way to the amazing theory that the fastest must halt their ascent to keep pace with the slowest. As Donald Richberg phrased it, "superior rights for inferiors."

How else can the labor troubles of today be seen except as the direct result of Franklin Roosevelt's determination to continue in office at whatever cost? Packed boards and biased executive orders made a joke of collective bargaining and destroyed the health of the labor movement by the creation of "political company unions," dependent on White House favor and awarded privileges in return for support. Today, by the gilding process of time, these privileges have taken on the color of inalienable rights.

Only a distinct messianic complex could have constrained the idealist of 1932 to play up the class struggle and enter into shameless deals with the lowest levels of political life. It was not merely that he accepted the support of the notorious city machines and their equally notorious bosses, but he bought it by favors that did not stop short of naming their henchmen to high posts, even the federal bench.

There was also the manner in which he played up to the Negro vote. In the course of one conversation on the subject, I ventured the opinion that the race's main handicap was not social or political discriminations, but the denial of *economic equality*. The American Federation of Labor, I pointed out, was chiefly responsible by reason of its refusal to let the Negro enter skilled trades, and even to allow him full membership in the unions of the unskilled. Why not make that the object of attack rather than screaming about the poll tax, which applied to whites as well as blacks? The President changed the subject without answering.

The messianic complex, while distinctly perceptible in the second term, came into full flowering with the outbreak of the European war. There is no doubt that he meant to take the United States into the war on the side of the Allies, for the Atlantic Charter and Lend-Lease stand as proof. With the staggering victims of German megalomania again holding out imploring hands to America, world leadership would be thrust on him even as it had been forced on Woodrow Wilson, and the God that had spared him in the hour of affliction would enable him to succeed where Wilson had failed.

Only the messianic complex explains the manner in which he viewed the war as *his* war. From the very first he exercised the right of independent action, making decisions without authority of law or without submission to public opinion, and hiding his improvisations under the pretense of military security. Eyes fixed on the new world order that would make him another Prince of Peace, he handed out munitions, planes, ships, and millions with never a thought of exacting promises in return. Had he bargained realistically, demanding agreements with respect to postwar policies, the world might not now be shattered into hate-filled fragments.

Even yet the full story of Teheran and Yalta is not known, but enough has been revealed to prove the abandonment of principles that Franklin Roosevelt himself declared, and for which Americans thought they were contributing their blood and treasure. Pledge after pledge repudiated, that Russia might be persuaded to pay lip service to the United Nations! The Baltic states, which held our promise of undying loyalty, handed over to vassalage; Poland, our devoted ally, mutilated and tortured; a dismembered Germany doomed to spoliation and despair; the body of a betrayed Mihailovich rotting in some ditch; Finland and Czechoslovakia sunk in humiliating sycophancy; Rumania, Bulgaria, Yugoslavia, Albania, and Hungary ruled by Moscow-trained criminals; Manchuria raped, and the United Nations brought to bankruptcy by Russia's veto.

All this while the peoples of the world still thrilled to the sonorous pledges of the Atlantic Charter: "No aggrandizement, territorial or otherwise . . . no territorial changes that do not accord with the freely expressed wishes of the peoples concerned . . . the right of all peoples to choose the form of government under which they will live . . . sovereign rights and self-government restored to those who have been forcefully deprived of them." What stood more plain than that Russia was an absolute distatorship, open in its hate for democracies and frankly dedicated to a philosophy of world conquest? Instead of recognizing this truth, and guarding against it, Americans were asked to believe that Russia was simply "another kind of democracy" and worthy of complete trust without the imposition of terms.

What more obvious, as proved by Hitler, than that a dictator seizes on even a hint of appeasement as a sign of weakness, exploiting it to the utmost? Yet from first to last, fawning approaches surrendered America's dominant position. Five times the President of the United States begged Joseph Stalin for a conference, and the two acceptances were on Moscow's terms.

Winston Churchill had the vision to urge a major offensive against Hitler through the Balkans, seeing it as the one hope of saving eastern Europe and a large part of central Europe from Russian enslavement. Under Stalin's pressure, Franklin Roosevelt turned away from Churchill's proposal and supported the Russian demand for the Normandy invasion.

Granting the necessity of destroying Germany's war potentials, what so evident as that the the recovery of Europe depended on the maintenance of Germany's political and eco-

339

nomic unity? And yet Franklin Roosevelt yielded to Stalin's demand for dismemberment and conceded Russia's right to loot and ravage.

There is this, however, to be said in excuse: Nothing is more exhausting than argument, and the shell of a man that sat in the meetings of the Big Three at Yalta lacked the strength for controversy. All that maintained him was the messianic complex, and under its compulsion he rested content with the smooth, plausible surface of agreements, either shutting his eyes to the substance or else trustful of some miraculous change that would take place before the hour of revelation. His holy mission, for such he felt it to be, *must* have the crown of success, if not in actuality, then in words.

Intimates and even acquaintances have remarked on Franklin Roosevelt's preoccupation with the judgment of history on his record. Those who admired and loved him should be glad that he will not hear it.

CHAPTER 42

Harry Truman's Inheritance

I cannot recall ever meeting Harry Truman during my years as editor of *The Independent*. He took no part in politics as an employee of various firms in Kansas City, and was equally anonymous when he worked the family farm from 1906 to 1917. I knew his father, of course, for he was a rampant Pendergast man, figuring vigorously in every fight between the Goats and the Rabbits.

I also knew Harry Truman's people, for they were scattered all over Jackson County. Solomon Young, his maternal grandfather, wagoned to Independence from Kentucky in 1842, and took up five thousand acres at $1.25 an acre. Another Kentuckian, Captain Jesse Holmes, followed the Youngs in 1844, and bought a large stretch of fertile prairie land. A daughter, Mary Jane Holmes, returning to Kentucky for a visit, married

John Shippe Truman, and persuaded him to make Independence their home. A son of this marriage, John Anderson Truman, married Mary Ellen Young, Solomon's daughter, and these two were the parents of the President.

Nancy Tyler, Harry Truman's great-grandmother, was a member of the party that followed Daniel Boone into the Dark and Bloody Ground, and a tale in common circulation had to do with her heroism. Cut off from the stockade by raiding Shawnees, the girl threw herself flat, feigning death, and did not let out so much as a moan when braves ripped off her scalp. The great Daniel himself praised young Nancy, and the lace cap she wore ever afterward was a badge of honor that all Kentucky gloried in.

With the discovery of gold in California, Solomon Young engaged in the freighting business, plying between Independence and Sacramento, and had wild Jim Bridger as his partner for a time. A shrewd man from all accounts, Solomon bought a Spanish grant in California, selling it later for $75,000, quite a fortune in those days. When he died in 1895 he divided his holdings among his children, and Harry Truman's mother inherited the 600-acre farm near Grandview.

Mrs. Truman's people, the Wallaces, were also a well-known family. One of them, William H. Wallace, enjoyed state-wide fame as a lawyer and orator, his speech in the Frank James trial being generally esteemed as vastly superior to Cicero's best efforts. Old Mr. Gates, Mrs. Truman's grandfather, was equally prominent, for he made Queen of the Pantry flour, its use compulsory in every Southern home.

As the Washington correspondent for *Collier's,* I met Harry Truman fairly often after his election to the Senate, sometimes in connection with articles and at others just for reminiscence. It was at my suggestion that he made his first public argument in support of the merger of the Army and the Navy, and the piece had the strength that came from careful study.

Simple, unassuming, and sincere, in both his looks and his talk, Harry Truman presented the perfect type of sturdy, God-fearing small-town American. The "next-door neighbor" kind, exchanging garden gossip across the back fence. He was humble in his approach to the responsibilities of the senatorial office, and when I saw him in the White House shortly after his elevation to the Presidency there was the same humility and effect of high resolve.

It was in July that I took Henry La Cossitt, the editor of *Collier's*, to call on the President, and for a full hour he talked frankly on both domestic problems and foreign affairs. It was with warmth of feeling that he spoke of Franklin Roosevelt, praising him for his vision and courage, and no doubt was left in our minds that the President meant to adhere to New Deal fundamentals. At the same time, however, he voiced views that plainly indicated independence in thought and action.

People, he said, had developed the "gimme" habit, leaning more and more on government rather than their own effort. Without any lessening of interest in the underprivileged, Uncle Sam must put aside his red robes and white whiskers, and get out of the Santa Claus business. The postwar period held every promise of prosperity, for a banked-up purchasing power would take care of the highest possible level of production. There were also the needs and demands of a world that would have to be rebuilt.

Private enterprise, with the necessary safeguards against monopoly, would be given the green light with every confidence that it would meet the problem of full employment. Public works—worth-while projects and not just improvisations—would be engineered, and then laid on the shelf to be taken down when needed to "fill in any valley of depression."

With respect to the scores of independent agencies, bureaus, and commissions spread around over the landscape, they would either be abolished or else put into some permanent department of government. This done, each department must be headed by a competent man vested with full power and held to full responsibility. If he couldn't handle the job without running to the White House every few minutes, then the thing to do was to replace him. Turning to pressure groups, the President denounced them as a "menace to orderly government."

Our foreign policy would avoid the extremes of appeasement and arrogance. America's interest in every European settlement would be asserted as a right in view of our enormous contributions in men, money, and materials. The stabilization of Europe was a business in which the United States must have a voice

342

and part, for unless settlements were just, the world peace for which America fought could not possibly be assured.

At no point was there unwillingness to concede Russia's right to friendly neighbors. How would we feel, for example, if we had Germany to the north of us instead of Canada? Or to the south of us in place of Mexico? At the same time, a clean-cut distinction should be made between friendly neighbors and puppet states. The Atlantic Charter had given the pledge that territorial grabs would not be permitted, and that the governments of liberated countries must be set up by the peoples themselves, free from outside pressure. Our ace in the hole was the refusal to recognize any government not the result of free and unfettered elections.

What impressed him most as a goal to strive for was a United States of Europe, or at least a federation based on a customs union, a common currency, and the internationalization of waterways. What if the United States were cut up into forty-eight separate units, each with its own military establishment, its own foreign policy, its own currency, and shut off from neighbors by tariffs, passport requirements, and all sorts of export and import regulations? What more certain than trade dislocations, entailing economic disaster, if the wheat and corn belts were denied equitable exchange of their products with industrial areas? If Illinois, wanting to do business with Ohio, would have to send and receive goods by way of Kentucky or Michigan because of restrictions imposed by Indiana? And what if little Delaware lived in sweating fear of absorption by Pennsylvania or New York? The way to a federated Europe was wide-open, for the United Nations specifically approved regional agreements.

When the conversation turned to the national defense, Henry La Cossitt observed that atomic fission had altered, if not entirely scrapped, all of the old concepts. What good were coast fortifications and bases when it would soon be possible for a rocket bearing a warhead of atomic energy to be propelled through space at sixteen thousand miles an hour? The President disagreed, contending that it was only orthodox weapons that would undergo fundamental changes. America would still have need of an army, a navy, and an air force, although operating under unified control. Such unification would be one of his immediate drives, and there were also three other

343

needs that he had in mind: scientific research under centralized direction; industrial preparedness, meaning a plan for the swift mobilization of industry in event of an emergency; and universal training.

The plan, as broadly outlined, was this: Between high school and college, every seventeen- or eighteen-year-old American, without other exemption than some physical or mental impairment, would be called up for a year of training, although the period might be spread out. Emphasis would not be placed solely on military instruction, but rather on the development of sound minds and sound bodies. In plain, a training for citizenship that would at the same time fit every youth for the national defense. A sane preparedness was commanded by every law of self-preservation.

When Henry La Cossitt and I left the White House, it was with the deep conviction that Harry Truman, with his simple, common-sense approach to things, would make a good President, and perhaps even a great one. That was the feeling of the people as a whole, for while Franklin Roosevelt moved in an upper air, the Missouri farmer and county road builder was one of their own kind. A wave of good will swept up from every section.

Interested by the President's mention of a United States of Europe, I went back to him a few months later and asked authorization for an article outlining the plan in detail. He consented, and spoke again with the hardheaded reasoning of a man who wanted to have some idea of where he was going before lifting a foot. Here, for example, are some of the statements that voiced his thought:

With all the good will in the world, how may the United States aid effectively in the rehabilitation and reconstruction of Europe until Europe is in a position to make intelligent use of help from the outside? How may Europe hope for any real recovery when tariffs, trade restrictions and currency confusions prevent the exchange of commodities, and wall off industrial districts from agrarian areas? When factory workers starve while farmers go without clothes and furniture? When the abundance of one area is the famine of another?

Until European countries put by their hates and fears, and recognize themselves as members of a *family*, what more inevitable than armament races? With resources poured into military estab-

344

lishments, where is there any chance of escape from low standards of living, and the mendicancy compelled by mass poverty? Or from the threat of another and more terrible war?

President Truman knows his Caesar, his Charlemagne and his Napoleon, and is equally familiar with the Pan-American movement from its inception. While he would be the last in the world to claim possession of an "international mind," history has always been a passion with him. Essentially a realist, and profoundly convinced that the American form of government is the best in the world, the Pan-American arguments are bound to have an appeal to him.

Count Richard Coudenhove-Kalergi, for years the moving spirit in the drive for European union, rushed at once to London with the article, and on reading it, Winston Churchill regained his former enthusiasm for the project. With the President of the United States demanding federated effort as the price of American aid, the movement could be pushed with every prospect of success. On receipt of a cable from Count Kalergi, I saw the President about a second article, only to find that it was no longer a subject for discussion.

And what of the other declarations of purpose so admirably outlined by the President on his entrance into the White House? The government of Poland, headed by Communists from Russia, many with criminal records, has its ambassador in Washington as the result of a *de jure* recognition. Tito, his hands dripping with the blood of Mihailovich and thousands of other butchered patriots, is also recognized by the United States as the product of "free and unfettered elections."

Chiang Kai-shek, to whom our faith was pledged, still reels under the blow of General Marshall's bland announcement that the difference between the Nationalists and the Communists is that between Tweedledum and Tweedledee. With Russia in possession of Manchuria, industrial Korea, and the ports of Dairen and Port Arthur, Washington refused China the license to purchase for cash some $75,000,000 worth of military supplies.

No word is ever said about Estonia, Latvia, and Lithuania, and while the rape of Hungary brought denunciation from the White House and State Department, the enslavement of Rumania and Bulgaria is accepted as an accomplished fact. The Italian treaty, jammed through the Congress under administration pressure, robbed the wretched country of its ships and put it in pawn indefinitely by admission of Russia's right to reparations.

In 1938 Adolf Hitler forced Austria to pass a law that "all members of the House of Hapsburg-Lorraine shall be, for the sole fact of their belonging to that family, banished forever from Austrian territory, and their property confiscated." In January, 1947, it became known that the votes of the United States and Russia had compelled the re-enactment of this Hitler law as part of the price that Austria would have to pay for peace. Another appeasement by the American representatives at the Moscow conference was agreement to the Russian contention that Austria must admit "war guilt," thereby opening the way for Russia to demand reparations from the impoverished country.

With respect to promised domestic reforms, the President's budget has continued federal expenditures at war levels, and independent bureaus and commissions still litter the landscape, adding to their pay rolls instead of reducing. There has been no break in the alliance between the White House and the CIO, for in his vetoes of the Case Bill and the Taft-Hartley bill, Mr. Truman followed the arguments of the CIO almost verbatim. Nor in either veto was there any intimation as to what he would consider a fair labor bill for the correction of abuses that he himself admitted in general terms. A change indeed from the bold stand against the railroad brotherhoods that won such acclaim from the country as a whole. Nor in his angry, hectoring messages was there any memory of his initial pledge to recognize Congress as a co-ordinate branch of government with which he would endeavor to work in harmony.

Certain changes, of course, were inevitable. Here was a man who had lived drably, a load of debt compelling him to pinch pennies, and after the first days of doubt and humility it was understandable that he would take an almost childish pleasure in the White House, its pool and masseurs, the Presidential yacht and plane, and the expansion of his wardrobe. It was as natural as the joy of a youngster invited to his first big party and shouting, "Oh, goody, goody!" as he peeks through a crack in the door at the cakes and ice cream.

The meagerness of the Truman background also explains the failure to call the best minds of the country to his side. A farmer throughout his formative years, with all of the rustic's

346

distrust of strangers, it was a foregone conclusion that he would surround himself with intimates. It was his misfortune, rather than his fault, that these intimates were to be found only among his wartime buddies, in the Pendergast machine, and on the back benches of the Senate.

Pressure for a continuance of the working agreement between the White House and the CIO is also fairly obvious. Robert Hannegan, chairman of the Democratic National Committee, lacking the ability to build up an organization of his own, made no secret of his dependence on the CIO for money and precinct workers in the 1944 campaign. When Henry Wallace and Harold Ickes both left the reservation and put on war paint, it became more imperative than ever for the party to retain the allegiance of Phil Murray and his aggressive organization in preparation for 1948.

But where the explanation for other and more disturbing changes? The switch from the middle of the road to an extreme left? The revival and even accentuation of the class struggle? His opposition to any tax relief except in the lower brackets? His refusal to proceed against the admitted evil of a colossal and stagnated bureaucracy? The denial of any need for corrective labor legislation? His shocking stand against the investigation of the Kansas City election frauds? The sudden transition to an angry partisanship in his relations with Congress? The abandonment of his sound concept of a United States of Europe, and the continuance of Roosevelt's policy of appeasement until Russia's truculence and insults made the policy untenable?

One day a simple, small-town American, humble before great responsibilities, but highly resolved to discharge them as honestly, fairly, and nobly as his abilities permitted; the next a politician on the ward level, almost servile in his obedience to the party machine. Why?

It was in search of the answer that I went to Kansas City and traced down every fact, friend, and circumstance connected with the life of Harry Truman. Somewhere in that stretch of years, rather than in Washington, lay the explanation. A familiar terrain, for Independence and Kansas City were home towns; and while I had migrated to Colorado in 1909, touch had been retained by frequent visits.

347

CHAPTER 43

How Local Boy Made Good

*W*hen Harry Truman left the Independence high school in 1901, he did not go back to the family farm but sought employment in Kansas City. At various times he worked in the mailing room of the *Star,* clerked in a bank, and served as timekeeper for a construction firm, but in 1905, either discouraged or else answering the call of his mother, he returned to Grandview. There he knew the drudgeries of milking, plowing, planting, and harvesting until 1917. The toilsome life left little time for reading and companionship, and the one excitement seems to have been his membership in a local militia company. On the outbreak of war he managed to have his weak eyes overlooked, and went with his battery to the field-artillery school at Fort Sill, Oklahoma.

The Truman record in France proves both bravery and competence. First as a lieutenant and then as a captain, he took part in the Vosges operations and the Saint-Mihiel and Meuse-Argonne offensives, and was discharged as a major in May, 1919. Nothing is more evident than that the war years were the happiest in his life, for he continued to hold every single member of his battery in close friendship, and both as Senator and President turned to these comrades when there was an office to be filled, regardless of fitness.

Back in Independence and out of uniform, Harry Truman married Bess Wallace, his childhood sweetheart, and faced the problem of earning a livelihood. Without either a trade or a profession, and disliking the treadmill of farm life, he teamed up with a "buddy" and started a haberdashery store. The venture proved a failure, owing to the postwar depression rather than mismanagement, and Harry Truman walked out of the wreck with a debt of $21,000 saddled on his back.

Bankruptcy never entered his thought, for the public opinion

348

of Independence would have frowned on it as dishonest. Only rascals attempted to evade their obligations. Fortunately, young Jim Pendergast, nephew of Kansas City's Democratic boss, had served in Battery D, and went to "Uncle Tom" with a request that something be done for his former captain. As a result, Harry Truman was entered in the race for county judge for the Eastern District.

At this point a flashback becomes necessary. During my days as one of Joe Shannon's Rabbits, Jim Pendergast led the Goats into battle, and lumbering, heavy-jowled Tom, his younger brother, was generally regarded as Jim's heaviest liability. A mistaken judgment, for when Jim died in 1911, Tom showed unsuspected abilities as his successor. Harsh and ham-handed, enforcing orders with his fists, he not only tightened his hold on Kansas City but challenged Shannon's control of the rural districts.

The election of 1922 was a test of strength, and after a rough and tumble fight, with no holds barred, Tom Pendergast elected his entire ticket, and Harry Truman took his seat on the county bench. Notwithstanding the title, the office was not judicial in any sense, being concerned entirely with road construction and public buildings. For a while "Judge" Truman studied law, but quit before completing the course.

In 1924 Shannon led a bolt that turned the county over to the Republicans, but that was his last show of power. Two years later Pendergast won handsomely, establishing his sovereignty beyond dispute, and Harry Truman returned to the county court as presiding judge. Joe Shannon, given a seat in Congress, no longer figured largely in the local picture, and Rabbit subleaders were pacified by an agreement that awarded them a minor share in patronage.

Now Pendergast, as befitted an iron boss, left the slums and bought himself a $150,000 home in the fashionable residential district. With an itch for money that Jim never possessed, he quit the saloon and organized the Ready Mixed Concrete Company and a wholesale liquor firm. These were open activities, but it was no secret that he held a garbage contract and had unpublicized holdings in other concerns that did business with the county and the city.

Upsetting changes, however, soon began to take place in the river wards from which Pendergast derived his whacking majorities in every election. The Italian colony, small in early days, grew steadily, and many of the leaders took up bootlegging after prohibition. By 1928 one John Lazia felt himself strong enough to give battle to Mike Ross, Tom's Irish subboss, and won a smashing victory with the help of blackjacks, knives, and several kidnapings. Pendergast, accepting the situation, acknowledged Lazia as the new leader of the North Side, and the lawless young Italian soon stood out as Number Two in the Goat organization.

Election after election, with Harry Truman running regularly for re-election, consolidated Tom Pendergast's power, but he would have remained a local boss but for the failure of the Missouri Legislature to redistrict the state in 1931. With candidates compelled to run at large, Kansas City's block vote became the deciding factor in the 1932 campaign, and fawning men wore a path to Pendergast's office, knees bent and hats in hand. Picking tried and trusted henchmen for every office from governor down, he put them across by huge majorities, and his Missouri delegation played no small part in the nomination of Franklin Roosevelt. Almost overnight, therefore, the former saloonkeeper sat in the seats of the mighty with Ed Kelly and Frank Hague, and basked in White House favor as a party chieftain.

Meanwhile the Italians had been going places. Bootlegging, with a soft-drink monopoly on the side, had contented Lazia at first, but evidently Al Capone's operations in Chicago gave him ideas. Demanding and getting complete control of the Police Department, he not only kicked off the lid but threw it away, turning Kansas City into a wide-open town in every vicious sense of the term.

No longer relegated to the slums, the red-light district occu-pied a place in the heart of the town, brothels lining Fourteenth Street. Every block had its gaming houses, with poker, black-jack, chuckaluck, faro, and dice games running full tilt. Rat-faced creatures offered marijuana and cocaine as though they had been selling shoelaces, and in restaurants on the main thoroughfares strip teasers entertained tired businessmen, never stopping until they had shucked the last stitch. More than that, Kansas City had become a rendezvous for criminals, operating under the protection of the police and even with their assistance.

350

Pendergast's own home was robbed and the daughter of the city manager kidnapped.

And why did Tom Pendergast, the devout churchman and devoted family man, stand for it? The reason was guessed at the time, but not until his trial did the complete story come out. In his plea for mercy, Pendergast confessed that betting on horse races was a vice that changed to mania, and in one year alone he dropped $600,000. In the beginning of his big play, sufficient funds flowed in from his rake-offs and levies, but as losses mounted, money became a desperate need; and partnership with the criminal scum represented revenue that he had to have.

And why did people not rise en masse against the debauchment of their community? Not only were the conditions there for all to see, but the *Star* ran daily exposures, and every election saw honorable men offer themselves for office. No great amount of research was required to develop the reason. Any citizen who dared to lift his voice had his assessment raised; protesting merchants ran the risk of having their buildings condemned as firetraps; preachers who attacked gang rule were waited upon by wealthy parishioners threatening to refuse further financial support; thugs drove opposition voters away from the polls, and the police stood watch while ballot boxes were being stuffed.

There were some honest men in city and county offices, but these too sat silent. Pendergast ruled, not the people, and all knew that their nominations and elections came through the favor of the Boss. Loss of that favor meant a return to private life, and the dreary business of trying to make a living with Pendergast's hand against them.

What brought the whole rotten business out into the open was the "Union Station massacre" in June, 1933. One Nash, a notorious criminal, chanced to be arrested in Hot Springs, and was being brought through Kansas City. Verne Miller, another equally famous "bad man," was in town at the time, playing golf with detectives between crimes, and decided to arrange a rescue.

Lazia, asked for help, hung back from furnishing plainclothes men, but told Miller that "Pretty Boy" Floyd and Adam Richetti, two well-known killers, were in Kansas City, and gave him the address of their hide-out. These two desperadoes, when interviewed, stated that it would be a pleasure to aid in such a good cause, but wanted to know where the necessary armament could be obtained. Obligingly enough, the police department provided machine guns.

Posted in a car at the station entrance, the rescue squad waited until Nash and his captors came out, and then turned loose a deadly fusilade. An FBI agent, an Oklahoma chief of police, two Kansas City detectives, and Nash himself were shot to pieces, and two other peace officers wounded. As was proved conclusively at a later date, the murderers were hidden by the police for twenty-four hours, and then carefully placed in get-away cars.

As if the massacre had been a signal, the Lazia gang now went "trigger happy." Sheriff Tom Bash, driving home late at night, heard shots and looked around to see Charlie Gargotta, a Lazia lieutenant, standing over a dead body, his gun still smoking. Leaping out of his car, Bash ran up through Gargotta's fire, and in the duel that followed two gangsters were killed. Nevertheless, Pendergast's prosecuting attorney continued the case against Gargotta for five years, and then dismissed it.

In view of Mr. Truman's current insistence that the scandals of the Pendergast regime occurred after his departure for Washington, it is to be noted that in 1933 he was not only presiding judge of the county court, sitting daily in Kansas City, but an increasingly important cog in the Goat machine. This was still his position in June, 1934, when the town shook to the news of Lazia's assassination. Out on bond after conviction for income-tax evasion, the gangster was riddled with bullets as he stepped from his car in the early-morning hours. Whether ambitious members of his own mob shot him down, or whether it was the work of eastern gangsters trying to muscle in, remained a mystery. The papers, it may be added, reverently recorded that Lazia's last words breathed love for Tom Pendergast, his adored chieftain.

That fall the Boss selected Harry Truman as his candidate for the United States Senate. In this connection the favored story is that Pendergast picked him in order to make good on his boast that he could send an errand boy to the Senate. As a matter of fact, Truman was the strongest candidate that could have been named. A Mason, a Baptist, and head of the County Judges Association, he also had a love of junkets that carried him to every corner of the state, rejoicing in fairs and conventions. Above all, he had proved himself fanatically loyal to the Boss, for not once in twelve long years had he faltered in his enthusiastic allegiance.

In many ways the November election was Pendergast's most arrogant show of ruthlessness. The North Side vote mills roared at full blast, and thugs overran the residential districts, beating up judges and clerks, driving citizens away from the polls, and killing four of the opposition by way of a final flourish. All of Pendergast's candidates won by staggering majorities, but Harry Truman polled an almost unanimous vote.

The count in the primary for the Democratic nomination, where Harry Truman was opposed by Congressman John J. Cochran, is particularly illuminating. These were the results in the four wards where Lazia operated under Pendergast's direction: Ward 1—Truman, 17,485, Cochran, 49; Ward 2—Truman, 15,145, Cochran, 24; Ward 3—Truman, 8,182, Cochran, 34; Ward 4—Truman, 9,825, Cochran, 53. A total of 50,637 against 160. The extent of Pendergast's helpfulness may be estimated by mention of the fact that Mr. Truman's margin of victory in the state was exactly 40,745. But for the ballot-box stuffing in the four wards, he would have been a badly beaten man.

Election frauds and gang violences, however, had no power to break or even loosen Tom Pendergast's iron grip on the city. In 1936, by way of proof, the Democratic vote was the highest in history, Pendergast doing even better by President Roosevelt than Hague or Kelly. A dearly bought victory, nevertheless, for it was in this election that the Boss made his first major mistake. Major Lloyd Stark, a famous orchardist and also quite a hero in World War I, had won the Democratic nomination for governor, and throughout the campaign made it clear that he would be his own master if elected. Pendergast ignored these pledges as the usual buncombe, and supported Stark in full confidence that he could control the "apple knocker."

He did not have long to wait for disillusionment. One of the Governor's first acts was to kick out Emmett O'Malley, Superintendent of Insurance and Pendergast's closest friend. Following this, he gave heed to the Kansas City *Star's* charges of ballot-box stuffing, appointing a new election board, and this body soon published some startling figures. With a population of 415,000, Kansas City had 288,000 registered voters, an astonishing percentage of 64.5, and in the First Ward, where men, women, and children numbered only 19,993, there were 21,073 voters. When the board finished its check, 90,000 illegal registrations had been removed from the lists.

A federal grand jury swung into action as a result of the investigation, and Maurice Milligan, United States District Attorney, prosecuted vigorously. In the middle of the trials, however, his term expired, and Senator Truman fought reappointment with tooth and nail. By that time, fortunately, the Kansas City vote frauds were getting national publicity, and President Roosevelt, after some stalling, rejected Truman's demand. Plunging ahead, Milligan gained conviction in 259 cases.

Following up, an honest, courageous circuit judge, Allen Southern, called a grand jury in January, 1939, and ordered an inquiry into the "open and notorious violation" of gambling, vice, and liquor laws. According to his estimates, slot machines netted $75,000 a week, gambling around $20,000,000 a year, and the take from brothels and narcotics was a million a month. When Pendergast's prosecuting attorney attempted to have the grand jury dismissed, Judge Southern asked for his ouster, and Governor Stark forced the Attorney General, a loyal Goat, to take effective action. As in the federal cases, Pendergast furnished bonds and counsel for the indicted men, but 100 out of 166 pleaded guilty. Charlie Gargotta was among those indicted, and Judge Southern handed him a penitentiary sentence for the attempted killing of Sheriff Bash in 1933.

Sensational enough, but the big blow-off was yet to come. A main reason for the discharge of Emmett O'Malley was Governor Stark's suspicions as to the honesty of a certain settlement in 1935. During the progress of a long-standing fire insurance rate case, some $10,000,000 had been impounded, and on the eve of a court decision O'Malley engineered a so-called compromise that gave 80 per cent of the money to the companies and only 20 per cent to policyholders.

Governor Stark, on taking office, began an undercover investigation that soon developed these facts: A "fixer" for the companies had promised Pendergast $750,000 as payment for O'Malley's consent to the settlement, and while the death of the fixer stopped payments short of the full amount, Pendergast received $377,500, of which $62,500 went to O'Malley.

354

This was the information given to the federal authorities, and on April 7, 1939, Tom Pendergast was indicted. As in the case of Al Capone, the charge was income-tax evasion rather than his real crime.

The Boss raised the cry of "political persecution," and taking this as their cue, every loyal Goat protested belief in his innocence. Having put them all out on a limb, Pendergast himself sawed it off, for on coming to trial he made no defense whatsoever, but threw himself on the mercy of the court, pleading age and infirmities. Successfully, too, for the judge imposed a sentence of only fifteen months, although compelling the payment of $372,807 for taxes and penalties.

Now the whole rotten structure fell to pieces with a crash. Particularly was the Pendergast boast of "honest, economical government" shown to be a lie, for investigation developed that Kansas City was almost two million dollars in the red. The "incorruptible" city manager, a man who had sat on the county bench with Harry Truman, was indicted for a city water scandal involving $356,000; the chief of police and the city engineer were also caught in the net, along with other officials; Charles Carolla, Lazia's successor as Pendergast's lieutenant in the river wards, was charged with using the mails in connection with his lotteries, and Jack Pryor, a favored Pendergast contractor, got two years for income-tax evasion.

In 1940, after these events, Senator Truman stood for renomination, and the vote of the four Pendergast wards is worthy of note. With the registration rolls purged, and watchers on hand, just 16,174 ballots were cast as compared to 50,797 in 1934. And Governor Stark, his opponent, received 3,426 as against Cochran's 160.

This was the story that I ran down, checking each detail, during my Jackson County stay. And now for the epilogue. When Tom Pendergast stood exposed as a bribe-taker and profiteer from vice and crime, Senator Truman insisted that the revelation came to him as a terrible shock. Neither in his twelve years on the county bench nor during his annual returns to Kansas City as Senator had he seen anything or heard anything to make him doubt Pendergast's honor and honesty. Nevertheless, despite his shock, he was not one to desert a man who had been his friend when he needed a friend.

This fine loyalty suffered no change even when Pendergast

confessed, and other prosecutions bared the corruption that had flourished under his rule and with his approval. It was as Vice-President that Harry Truman flew to Kansas City to join with other faithful Goats in a last tribute to their beloved leader, and it was as President that he wrote to Jim Pendergast, dead Tom's successor, enclosing membership dues and assuring the organization of his devoted support.

When President Truman came out against the re-election of Roger Slaughter, the Kansas City congressman who had voted against administration measures, it was to Jim Pendergast that he appealed for Slaughter's defeat. The request was granted with the same enthusiasm that had marked the performances of the Goats in other days. The *Star* soon produced evidence of grossest fraud, but the Department of Justice refused to allow any thorough investigation by the FBI on the ground that there was no warrant for federal action. The *Star* reporters, however, continued to dig in the dirt, and produced enough proof of fraud to justify a local grand jury in returning many indictments. That very night a safe in the courthouse was blown open and the impounded ballot boxes removed.

The demand for an investigation of the action of the Department of Justice was defeated in the Judiciary Committee by Democratic votes, the while President Truman maintained a profound silence as to both the frauds and the robbery. Moreover, when a resolution came before the Senate to take the matter away from the Judiciary Committee, the Democrats defeated it by a filibuster.

There is still another illustration of the President's capacity for unwavering and unquestioning loyalty that deserves to be cited.

When the two St. Louis bosses, Bernard Dickman and Bob Hannegan, were deep in a pit of defeat and discredit, he rushed to their defense with the same enthusiasm that had been excited by Tom Pendergast's arrest and imprisonment.

In 1934 the St. Louis machine gave Truman so large a majority that it brought accusations of ballot-box stuffing. In 1936 these suspicions changed to certainty, for the evidence of fraud was so plain that a Democratic governor was compelled to remove the entire election board. In 1940, when Senator Truman ran for renomination, not even his most ardent supporters gave him a chance to win. It happened, however, that both Governor Stark and United States District Attorney Milligan entered the race, and by their split of the antimachine vote, Truman slipped through by a narrow margin. This margin was furnished by St. Louis, but while able to put Senator Truman across, Dickman and Hannegan failed to elect their gubernatorial candidate. What followed tore Missouri wide-open.

Under pressure from the St. Louis machine, the Democratic legislature barred the victorious Republican from taking office, pending an "investigation" by one of its own committees. Governor Stark, held over by this maneuver, denounced the whole business as a "shameless steal," and some weeks later the supreme court of the state, although Democratic, ruled that the Republican was entitled to his seat. When Mayor Dickman ran for re-election he was buried under an avalanche of votes, and Bob Hannegan went with him into the discard.

Again Senator Truman proved that he was not the man to desert a sinking ship. First procuring the job of St. Louis's postmaster for Dickman, he then demanded Hannegan's appointment as collector of internal revenue. Straightway the press of Missouri let loose with everything from brickbats to dead cats, the St. Louis *Post-Dispatch* leading what developed into a holy war. To honor Hannegan with office was to disgrace the state and affront its citizens. The fight raged for months, but Senator Truman stood firm, even going so far as to release this statement: "Hannegan carried St. Louis three times for the President and for me. If he is not nominated, there will be no collector at St. Louis. I think I have enough friends in the Senate to see that no other man gets the job."

Even when Hannegan received the appointment, victory did not check the gush of Senator Truman's loyalty. In 1943 he succeeded in having the St. Louisan elevated to the important post of commissioner of internal revenue, and in 1944 to the chairmanship of the Democratic National Committee. Whatever else may be said about Bob Hannegan, his tireless activities in connection with the nomination of Harry Truman as President Roosevelt's running mate proved conclusively that ingratitude was not one of his sins.

Out of it all, the answer to Harry Truman would seem to stand clear. I do not think there is any question as to his personal honesty, for not once during my investigation was

357

it charged that his hands had been soiled by dirty dollars. His ten years on the county bench, however—the period when corruption was most rampant—and his pleased acceptance of elections carried by force and fraud, plus his antagonism to Maurice Milligan, plus his tears at Pendergast's funeral, plus his Dickman-Hannegan performance, reveal him rather mercilessly as one molded into a fixed pattern of party regularity by years of subservience to a boss. If he will or can break away from the pattern remains to be seen.

CHAPTER 44

The Crash of Standards

From the dawn of time it has been the habit of men to exaggerate the importance of the age in which they lived; nevertheless I have the deep conviction that future historians will write down the first half of the twentieth century as the era that worked more fundamental changes in the life of America than any other. The switch from an agricultural civilization to an industrial order; the sovereignty of the machine, eliminating handicrafts and individual prides; the concentration of population in metropolitan warrens, destroying the neighborhood and its social restraints; the automobile, the linotype, the motion picture; the airplane, the radio, radar, and other advances of science and invention that have made "our distant and detached position" a gibbered reminiscence—all of these changes are within the memory of living men.

But may it not be that these same historians will record that the price paid for these triumphs of materialism was out of all proportion to value? That in the pursuit of physical well-being we jettisoned inherited faiths and abandoned old standards? That in the speed of our forward rush we took no thought as to the soundness and safety of the new footings? That in our intense and excited preoccupation with the *outer* life we lost all sight of the *inner*?

358

Age, of course, grows portentous, looking back with a jaundiced and even censorious eye, and the years have a way of painting the past in imagined colorings; but it seems to me that support for these speculations stands so plain as to make the judgments inevitable. Wherever one looks or listens, there is evidence that in the climb to materialistic heights we have suffered certain coarsenings that add up to a deterioration in character if not an actual disintegration.

Take public opinion as an example. Once the "anger of an aroused people" was more than an editorial phrase, and the betrayals and knaveries of officials were punished by popular judgments that had all the finality of a death sentence. Today even open accusations of corruption, involving millions, furnish no more than a day's sensation and drop into the limbo of forgotten things after twenty-four hours.

I think I may offer myself as a fairly competent witness, for in the course of a long public life I have been accused of almost every offense in the criminal calendar. I am not referring to the whispers that politicians drop into the sewers of gossip— the anonymous indecencies that are part of every campaign— or even to the charges roared from the stump by partisan orators. What I have in mind are open accusations printed on the front pages of newspapers, and equally direct attacks made on the floor of Congress.

My own conscience has never arraigned me, yet not in my most optimistic moments have I ever fooled myself into the belief that my innocence stood clear in the eyes of the people. At no time have I had my day in court or been judged by a jury of my peers, and without these public hearings, vindication travels a hard road. The press has little interest in retractions, not by reason of malice, but because they lack the news value of an accusation. As for members of Congress, not one has ever been known to apologize for a false statement.

It will be asked, of course, why I did not go into the courts. The answer is simple: lack of money. Litigation has become a luxury, for attorneys' fees, court costs, continuances and appeals, reversals and remands, all constitute a gantlet that only the well-to-do may run. When a New York paper carried the charge that I had "extorted" money from a president of Mexico, and another printed the lie that I had tried to "organize a Mexican revolution," I took these falsehoods to various lawyers. The expense was beyond my means, and I was also told that it might be years before the cases could be heard.

As a result, many of the accusations leveled against me gained the look of truth. My Kansas City and Denver years may be passed over, for while I was attacked regularly for everything from malfeasance to high treason, the fights were local. The charges made during and after my chairmanship of the Committee on Public Information, however, received national circulation: faking the story of a submarine attack on our transports; the loot of a federal property worth $600,000; an attempt to steal a $14,000,000 government plant; accepting bribes for the use of my name and prestige, etc.

If the newspapers printed my raging denials it was on the market page, and when I wrote to the attorney general, demanding to know what protection I had against Congressional attacks, he answered: "The privilege which applies to the utterances of senators is absolute, and as far as I am advised, you have no remedy." So then, on the face of things, I stood guilty in the public estimation of crimes that deserved shame and ostracism. Out of my own lifelong attitude to such offenses, I had the conviction that people would spurn me as a leper, and it took all of my courage to leave home and office for the open street.

Looking back, I can say truthfully that neither in my public nor in my private life have I ever been called on to pay the slightest penalty. On the very heels of infamous charges, editors have approached me with requests for signed articles, and no man has ever refused my outstretched hand. Nor is it that I am thick-skinned, for even constant attack failed to give me a protective callus, and every lie saw me die a thousand deaths. Only a fortunate experience, in fact, saved me from hunting out a remote cave in which to spend the rest of my days.

It happened on a morning when every paper in New York front-paged the story about my share in the $14,000,000 plant steal. Sick at heart, I crept out of the house and sneaked into the subway with hat pulled down. In the seat next to me a man was reading the headlines that branded me as a rascal, and I actually cringed while waiting for his outburst of indignation. Instead of that, he turned to a friend after finishing the article and remarked, "This Creel must be quite a guy. He's always making the front page."

Not only is there no such thing as a lash, but the very existence of a forceful, effective public opinion is much to be doubted. We have, to be sure, gusts of anger, spasms of irritation, moments of hysteria, and every now and then the fury of a man hunt, but these excitements do not lend themselves to sustained judgments, and the reactions are usually as sudden and violent as the original emotion.

It might be said with safety that we have even lost the capacity for moral indignation. The employment of WPA money in elections was a scandal that soon blew over without hurt to Franklin Roosevelt's popularity. Even after complete exposure of the criminality of Huey Long's regime, close associates of the Kingfish were sent to the Senate. Henry Wallace, as Secretary of Commerce, issued supposedly authoritative statements that wages could be hiked without increase in prices, and the result was a series of disastrous strikes. At a later date it developed that his figures came from a ouija board or crystal globe, but even the sputter of indignation soon died down.

James Curley was elected mayor of Boston while under indictment for using the mails to defraud, and Attorney General Clark's action in blocking a full-scale FBI investigation of Kansas City's election scandal provided no more than a one-day sensation. No one has ever been punished for the criminal waste of millions in the construction of the Latin-American highway, and equally forgotten is the expenditure of $134,-000,000 on the utterly insane Canol project. Major Theodore Wyman, Jr., Hans Wilhelm Rohl, and the Hawaiian war contracts—a mess largely responsible for Pearl Harbor—are not even memories.

On the international scene, President Roosevelt, Marshal Stalin, and Mr. Churchill gave solemn pledges at Teheran and Yalta that the territorial integrity of Poland and other "liberated" countries would be respected, and that "free and unfettered elections" could be counted on as sacred guarantees. Not in all history were explicit covenants ever more completely dishonored, yet where are the evidences of moral indignation?

Injustice, wherever exposed, once had the power to set America ablaze. I can remember when the whole country shook to the Dreyfus case, a passionate indignation sustained through long years. The murder of Mihailovich, the daily slaughter of hundreds in Russia's puppet states, stirred excitement only during the time that it took to turn a page.

From all of which it might be assumed that we have become a nation of mattoids, but that doesn't happen to be true, at least, not yet. A prime essential to the manufacture of public opinion is full and impartial report on men, measures, and events, and such report is not being furnished. Save for certain notable and splendid exceptions, the press is less concerned with information than with what Woodrow Wilson called "the satisfaction of a vulgar curiosity." Owing to the emphasis on crime, grime, sex, and gossip, information with respect to domestic importances and foreign policies runs a poor second when in competition with the lecheries of Hollywood or some murder case with a rich background of degeneracy.

The charges and countercharges of political parties, played up by partisan papers, also help to create a bedlam in which even orderly, searching minds find it impossible to form accurate estimates. The situation was bad enough when there were only Democratic and Republican "party organs," but it is infinitely worse today when it has become the fashion for slack-jawed heirs to great wealth to pour their money into left-wing sheets.

Automatic support contributes as little to intelligent understanding as automatic attack, and when one side is put forward in flat antagonism to another, the reader is compelled to make a choice between two distorted representations. It is not only that mud screens make for low visibility. Mud itself is distasteful to the normal person, and there is a natural aversion to the wallow. If it is true, as is often complained, that our best men are not in public life, the reason is not hard to find. Why should any citizen take a mud bath publicly when he can go to French Lick and take one privately?

For a while there was the hopeful expectation that the reform of the press might be brought about by the menace of new and powerful competition. The newsreels, however, have failed to take full advantage of their possibilities, and the radio is an even more painful disappointment. With the whole field of public opinion open for conquest, the broadcasting systems have disgusted thinking people with their banalities, loathesome commercials, and their commentators who go beyond the columnists in prejudice and distortion.

362

In common fairness, however, does blame rest entirely on the press? Since no business endures, or can endure, without profitable patronage, may the fault not go back to the reading public? The bigoted "party organ," whether right or left, would not live for a day without bigoted partisans, and there would be no emphasis on gossip, conjecture, and sensationalism unless a goodly number of people *liked* that sort of paper.

This defense of the press, based on the theory that newspapers give readers what they want and demand, is supported by the vast change that has taken place in *manners*. Or, to use the jargon of the sociologists, the change in behavior patterns. Throughout my boyhood, youngsters caught using "bad words" had their mouths washed out with soap, and while profanity was common enough around barbershops and livery stables, even the roughest tongue was guarded in the home.

Not so today. For those sufficiently old-fashioned to retain a liking for good taste and clean speech, ear muffs are now as much a part of wearing apparel as shoes, hats, and shirts. In metropolitan centers, at least, obscenity has become a short cut to smartness and sophistication, and small talk is no longer harmless, but all too often edges over into the malicious and unclean after the first few minutes. Except in homes stigmatized as Victorian or bourgeois, kennel terms are commonplace, and mere dislike expresses itself by denial of a person's legitimacy.

Even degeneracy and perversion have been approved as permissible topics of conversation, and "Lesbian," "fairy," and "homo" are words that even teen-agers prattle glibly. Abnormality is not only mentioned, but charged openly as though it were no more shameful than using the wrong fork, or publicly exploring the nose with a rudely penetrative forefinger. If a demand is made for proof, in nine cases out of ten it develops that the accusation has no better ground than some unfortunate mannerism.

Worse still, periodicals and books have not escaped contagion. The mud at the bottom of human nature, of course, has always been regarded as pay dirt by certain types, but until recently, pornography was a stealthy, undercover business. Today, however, restraints have weakened to a point where the peddlers of vile postal cards and privately printed indecencies are up against the wares of editors and publishers who consider themselves reputable.

Reading some of the "smart" weeklies, for instance, comes close to eavesdropping in a water-front dive. As for novels, many of them drip filth from every page, and that without a single redeeming feature in content. If the authors and publishers arranged a nation-wide hookup and broadcast the confession that they were being dirty for money, the purpose could not stand more plain.

Particularly is this true with respect to "whodunits," once harmless entertainment if not exactly elevating. The "private eye" is now a dissolute, lecherous swine, and brief bursts of lust are the only breaks in his incredible consumption of alcohol in every known form. Sex does not stop at rearing its ugly head, but sprawls sluttishly from cover to cover.

No sane person advocates concealment in connection with the so-called facts of life. I myself have never been able to see any difference between prudery and prurience, or between those who wallow in sex like a cat in catnip and those who ignore sex as though it were unnatural, running around with blankets and blindfolds. Nastiness is revolting, to be sure, but nasty niceness is no more pleasing.

Praise be, we have gone far from those ghastly days when it was assumed that the female form stopped at the chin. True, we have not yet reached the level where the facts of life can be taught in the schools, but the things that *ought* to be talked about *can* be discussed, and *are*. The New Frankness, however, as championed by parlor scatologists, is not interested in developing discussion along helpful lines. Their preoccupation is with the abnormalities of sex that have hitherto been veiled in reticence. This stemmed not out of nasty niceness, but for the reason that their consideration of such vagaries was more suited to the clinic than to the living room.

What adds to anger is the excited cackling over degeneracies as though they were brand-new discoveries. The only thing new about them is their discovery as pay dirt. Pompeii's obscene murals prove that erotomania was old stuff in Christ's day; the Greeks had plenty of words for it; and at the risk of making the Bible sell even better, I might mention that St. Paul, in his Epistle to the Romans, dealt with Lesbianism and homosexuality in unsparing detail.

What blocks reform is the inability to get a clean-cut presentation of the issue, for instead of being a straight-out fight

364

between dirt and decency, all sorts of fake claims muddle and confuse. Ill-smelling books and plays take refuge behind a smoke screen of Art, the authors insisting that they are Bold Souls with the courage to paint Life as It Is. Bosh! Real art does not have to be handled with rubber gloves and treated with chloride of lime. Neither does it proceed on the theory that there are only bedrooms in a home, and that people prefer the sewers to the wholesomeness of the sun.

Dickens and Hugo depicted life from the heights to the depths, crowding their canvases with the vilest as well as the noblest, yet never once do they stoop to the obscenities with which the "realists" cram their tawdry creations. No stream of vileness spews from Bill Sikes and the depraved members of the Patron Minette, yet the reader is never in doubt as to their essential evil. Huish, a character so thoroughly wicked that Stevenson himself shrank from him, stands clear without the aid of revolting dialogue. Passion, and the joy and woe it works among the sons and daughters of men, is the theme of every great classic, but the masters of literature do not confuse it with nymphomania.

Viewed honestly, the claim of realism in connection with pay dirt is the last word in downright balderdash. Lacking all skill in characterization, a hack simply grabs at quick effects by slinging together a lot of pornographic matter. It is essentially latrine literature, and there is as much art about it as if one were to put a dictograph on the seat beside a drunken teamster or place a camera in the parlor of a brothel.

An equal amount of impudence attaches to the claim that rotten plays are written with a High Purpose, and that they have a definite Social Value by teaching Moral Lessons. It is not at all uncommon for the managers of malodorous shows to *invite* prosecution as the most effective form of advertising, and packed houses result in almost every case. Here again an irritating hypocrisy is encountered. By way of justifying attendance, people say, "Of course, the play is unpleasant, but such *perfect acting!* That was what I wanted to see."

The same thing holds true with respect to books, people apologizing for the possession of some piece of filth on the ground that they are reading it for the "style." In the days when Proust's wallows in perversion were the vogue—likewise James Joyce's obscene gibberish—I used to cross-examine these lovers of "style," and rarely was it the case that one of them had ever read the classics. As for the great poets, callow reviewers had taught them that Tennyson, Shelley, Keats, Scott, and Longfellow were demoded.

What are we to do about it? Well, for myself I have never had any faith in the censorship of the press, books, or motion pictures. Every experiment along this line has resulted in failure, creating a tyranny of arbitrary personal opinion. I can remember one state censorship board that actually banned mention of motherhood in movies, forbidding baby clothes, doctors' announcements, and everything else that might let people know that there was a natural process for bringing children into the world.

State statutes and municipal ordinances are of small use. When twelve good men and true, with a few women mixed in, enter the jury box to pass judgment on a dirty book or play, they do not sit in an emotional vacuum, but remain susceptible to outside pressure. From all quarters the "realists" spring to the defense of imperiled art, screaming about blue laws, puritanism, and prudery. As a usual thing, the dirt peddlers go free, for what juror wants to be held up to public scorn as a smut hound?

Another obstacle to effective prosecution is a misconception with respect to free speech and a free press. At no time was it ever meant that a mouth or pen should be above the law. Speech is free only so long as it takes care to avoid libel, slander, treason, and incitation to riot, and the written word is subject to the same restraints and restrictive regulations. No civilized society grants any such thing as an absolute right. I remember hearing a debate on the question some years ago, and an indignant citizen, leaping to his feet, asked if the speaker wanted him to believe that he did not have an absolute right to his clothes and his home.

"Certainly," came the smiling answer. "And here is a quick way to prove it. Just try putting on a red hat ten feet tall or a long coat decorated with pink giraffes. Inside of five minutes you would be arrested for creating a traffic jam, disturbing the peace, and being a public nuisance. As for the home, it is your castle until the city wants to run a street through it, or some inspector condemns it as a firetrap."

By dint of steady pressure on magistrates, juries, and public opinion, however, free speech and free publication have come to be accepted as *absolute rights,* and only in rare cases is the theory disputed.

Where the fight must be waged is not in courts or in board rooms, but in the *home,* and the one way to win is for fathers and mothers to accept the duties imposed on them by the fact of parenthood. A first step in the fight is to get rid of the fustian that children must be permitted to "express" themselves without a hint of parental interference. Some woolly-witted people may take this claptrap seriously, but for the most part it is an excuse for evading responsibility.

Children *have* to be trained, just as gardens have to be weeded. Taste, ethics, and manners are not natural instincts any more than a born knowledge of the multiplication tables. They must be *taught.* Discipline is as essential to the development of character as vitamins for the body, and giving youngsters a free hand, in the name of complete expression, can mean nothing except that the parents themselves want freedom.

Of course there were books that I did not want my young ones to read, plays I did not want them to see, and language I did not want them to use, and their mother and I took care that they did not. We knew, to be sure, that eventually they would read and see what they pleased, but by that time we hoped to have built character strong enough to make them turn away from the mean, the cheap, the vulgar, and the lascivious. And never believe that "riding herd" wasn't hard work.

It does not follow at all that men and women should cease to be human beings when they become fathers and mothers. For parents to surrender their individualities, sinking their lives into those of their children, is as stupid as unnecessary. On the other hand, there *are* high duties incumbent upon parenthood, and it is downright dishonest to escape them or evade them by the plea that proper discipline prevents the child's "expression."

I may be all wrong, and it will not be for the first time, but I hold fast to the belief that those who buy dirty books, attend dirty plays, and help to make yellow journalism profitable stand as the direct result of some gross failure in parental duty. Only when fathers and mothers get back on the job, seeing to it that children express themselves in right ways, will good taste be restored to its appointed place in public life.

And why do I not stress *good morals?* Because they change with all the suddenness of a weather vane. From the dawn of time, every age, race, creed, and even every community has made its own interpretation of morals. What New York accepts without a murmur outrages Boston, and Chicago's conception of the pure and clean excites the pulpits of Keokuk. Hollywood itself gagged at *The Outlaw,* a film built around the mammary appurtenances of the star, but various metropolitan centers hailed it as an epic.

Good taste knows no such whirligig changes. What it was in the beginning it is now and ever will be: to hate coarseness whether in speech or print; to guard the tongue and mind against uncleanness; to feel vulgarity like a wound; to love and cherish the fine; and to prefer the heights to the wallow.

All of this at first glance, may seem sheer irrelevance in a volume so largely concerned with public life and public affairs, but I hold that this chapter follows the others in perfect sequence. The crash of standards, necessarily involving radical changes in people's thought and conduct, is bound to have effect on federal, state, and municipal governments. How else explain the deterioration in the public service, the decline of public opinion as a corrective force, and the loss of capacity for moral indignation? And where else is there explanation for the alarming growth of a movement that derides every ancient faith, and burrows openly for the overthrow of our institutions?

CHAPTER 45

Back to the Heights

At the turn of the century a great progressive movement swept the country from coast to coast, calling to its colors all that was best in America. People looked on injustices and inequities with new eyes, and drove mightily against the greeds and cruelties that had crept into our national life. Along with house cleaning there was also a heart cleaning, men and women dedicating themselves anew to the ideals of democracy.

In the beginning much of it was headlong and fumbling, for our one idea was to kick the "rascals" out of office. All of us were perfectly assured that if we could defeat "bad" men and elect "good" men, we could sit down and wait for the millennial dawn in peace and quiet. And what a kicking there was! Man hunts vied in popularity with baseball, and the muckrake challenged the right of the lawn mower to be regarded as America's favorite implement.

Disillusionment, however, was not long in coming. Looking behind our public servants, we saw the black mass of the party machine, and behind it the shadowy figures of those who had a direct money interest in the making of laws. These men were the real masters, owning both parties through the medium of campaign funds. The boasted sovereignty of the people was nothing more than the privilege of choosing between two sets of candidates selected in backrooms.

As a consequence, the progressive movement turned to fundamentals, and began the drive to restore power to the people. Abandoning the "bad-men" theory, we fought for the initiative, referendum, and recall, the direct primary, the headless ballot, the short ballot, commission government for cities, municipal ownership, and stronger statutes for the control of monopolistic trusts. Out of victory came laws that gave protection to men and women in industry, threw safeguards about children, and took the loaded dice away from big business.

Logically, inevitably, the swift march of the movement split the Republican party, forced the nomination of Woodrow Wilson over the stubborn resistance of the bosses, and put an iron-willed progressive in the White House. Four years of basic reform, then the war that brought the Wilson program to a halt, and after the Armistice the sweep of apathy that welcomed the "normalcy" of Harding, Coolidge, and Hoover.

Not until 1932 was there a recovery of interest in the state of the union—a return to progressivism—and Franklin Roosevelt's election gave rich promise that the Woodrow Wilson program would be taken up where he left off, and carried through to completion. The New Deal, to be sure, often confused action with mere activity, but in the first four years, at least, there was a resurgence of true progressivism.

369

If I have dug far back into the past, it is for the purpose of drawing a comparison between the progressive movement of other years and the so-called "liberal" movement of today. As nothing else, it shows how far we have fallen from the heights. Whatever its faults, the progressivism preached and led by Theodore Roosevelt, La Follette, and Woodrow Wilson was intensely American, its core a love of country and pride in our free institutions.

Present-day "liberalism," as it has the impudence to call itself, is anti-American; for at its back, as cunning as secret, are men and women who give their allegiance to a foreign power. And what of their following? Dancing to the strings pulled by hidden hands is as motley a crew as ever gathered under one banner. Shoulder to shoulder with avowed Communists and subversive aliens stand the weird conglomeration known as "fellow travelers," made up of embittered failures, discredited politicians, crystal-gazers, venal labor leaders, underpaid professors and overpaid actors, feminized preachers eager to gain an effect of virility, perennial sophomores, frustrated incompetents, idle wealth seeking protective coloration, motion-picture stars hopeful of a smoke screen to hide inanity and illiteracy, scatterbrains rejoicing in an emotional experience, and cowardly Esaus willing to trade freedom for a bogus security.

"Liberalism!" Not in all history has a word been so wrenched away from its true meaning and dragged through every gutter of defilement. Where once it stood for the dignity of man—the rescue of the spirit from the debasements of materialism—it now stands for the obliteration of individualism at the hands of a ruthless, all-powerful state, and shames human sympathy as a weakness even as it denies the practicability of ideals.

The progressive movement of other days was self-supporting, its campaigns made possible by the sacrifices of devoted men and women. The new "liberalism" derives its income from forced contributions—many international unions under Communist control going so far as to expel members who refuse to donate—and the largess of rich addlepates who seek to hide their futility behind the pretense of Bold Thinking.

Old-time progressives were instinct with patriotism, and what they fought for was not a change in the democratic ideal, but the remedying of wrongs and perversions that shamed the ideal.

"Liberals" sneer at patriotism as old-fashioned and talk of "revolution" as calmly as though they were ordering a sundae. Albert Einstein, first a German, then a Swiss, and now availing himself of the rights of sanctuary in the United States, has no hesitancy in drawing the issue sharply. In letters begging funds for an organization that urges immediate sharing of atomic-bomb secrets with Russia, he speaks repeatedly of "outmoded concepts of narrow nationalism." Oskar Lange, the Pole who asked for American citizenship and then renounced it to serve as Communist Poland's ambassador to the United States, is another who has contempt for our "narrow nationalism."

It is not as if there were the excuse of ignorance. Henry Wallace and his ilk may prattle that Russia is "just another kind of democracy," but every new day brings evidence that the Soviet system rests on terrorism with its firing squads, slave camps, and ceaseless espionage. Not only individuals are denied freedom, but whole populations, and to cap brazen effrontery, all of the men chosen by Moscow to rule enslaved states have had their pictures in some rogues' gallery at one time or another.

Take the cases of Krasnodebski alias Beirut; Rosenfeld alias Rakosi; and George Dimitrov, the Communists who rule respectively in Poland, Hungary, and Bulgaria. Each of the three fled his native land to escape imprisonment for high crimes, becoming a Soviet citizen and rising to high place in the Communist hierarchy. From 1935 to 1943 Dimitrov was secretary general of the Comintern, and Beirut and Rakosi also held important offices in that controlling body.

Or consider Tsola Dragoicheva, Bulgaria's Tiger Woman, who shares power with George Dimitrov. In 1925 a heavy charge of high explosives was detonated in the great cathedral of Sofia, killing 123 worshipers and injuring 325. Dragoicheva, arrested as a terrorist ringleader, was sentenced to life imprisonment, but managed to escape to Russia in 1932. There she remained until 1944 when she returned to Bulgaria under the protection of a Red army.

It is not as if communism made any attempt to conceal its character or purposes. Lenin and Stalin are frank in their statements that every capitalist country is an enemy to be destroyed, and on every page of their writings they heap scorn on "bourgeois morality," and preach lies, treachery, hate, and ill faith as fundamental tenets of the Communist philosophy. There is

371

also the long record—from 1918 to 1947—that proves the fidelity with which they have put their preachments into practice. Every step of the way is littered with the fragments of broken treaties.

It was in shameless repudiation of a solemn treaty that Red armies invaded Poland in 1939, side by side with Hitler's panzer divisions. It was in violation of a nonaggression pact that Russia declared war on Japan. What greater ill faith than the action of the Russian army in turning away from the gates of Warsaw after having urged the Poles to rise? Or the retention of Manchuria after explicit agreement that the area should be returned to China?

When the United States recognized Russia in 1933, a principal condition was that Moscow should cease its propagandizing in this country. Will even Henry Wallace dare to say that the pledge has been kept? Year in and year out, with never a halt, Russia's agents have infiltrated into every department of government, spying, stealing, and corrupting, and all suggestions that these undercover operators be driven out are met by cries of "Red baiting" and "witch hunting." Others have wormed a way into labor unions, fomenting strikes, and still others are at work among the Negro population, inciting unrest and riot. Through every possible medium—the press, the motion picture, and the radio—they pour a steady stream of poison into the wells of public opinion.

What makes the so-called "liberal" movement even more incredible is the refusal of its leaders to institute a single comparison between the United States and Russia. Other nations have larger populations and richer natural resources, and many were old when this was a wilderness; yet America has outstripped them all. Under our capitalist system, with its "oppressions and exploitations," Henry Wallace's Common Man enjoys the world's highest standard of living, and works and lives under constitutional guarantees that protect his life, his property, his freedom of speech, and his liberty of conscience. It was capitalist America that saved Communist Russia when her millions were driven back close to the Urals, and it is capitalist America today, with only 6 per cent of the world's population, that the other 94 per cent looks to for help. And what more significant than that in the war just ended, when we were in competition with communism, nazism, fascism, and monarchism, America outproduced them all?

Behind the Iron Curtain the Russian citizens, save for privileged party members, live in fear and want, denied every freedom that Americans have come to accept as an inalienable right. Neither life nor property is safe, for the one can be seized by fiat, and the other is taken without process of trial for no greater offense than an indiscreet word. Labor unions are submissive bodies controlled by the state, strikes are punishable by imprisonment or death, and a brutal speed-up system scourges every worker to the limit of human endurance.

Much confusion comes from a distorted definition of capitalism. According to the "liberals," it carries an implication of greed and ruthlessness, and yet the butcher, the baker, the cobbler, the corner grocer, and the army of small shopkeepers are capitalists just as much as the heads of United States Steel or General Motors. Size has nothing to do with it.

It is not only possible but common for the laborer of today to become the capitalist of tomorrow. Only recently I was looking over the lists of the presidents of fifty of America's largest corporations, and every man of them started at the very bottom of the ladder. "Big Bill" Knudsen, for example, who rose to be head of General Motors, came to this country from Denmark without a penny in his pocket, and his first job was that of a roustabout.

It is a list that could be prolonged indefinitely, and few of them would be seen as the result of a flying start or a lucky break. What lifted the majority to the top was industry and ambition, nourished and given courage by the freedom that is in the air that Americans breathe. Freedom to climb from the lowest rung in the ladder to the top; freedom to keep and enjoy what has been earned honestly; freedom to change from job to job; freedom to make the laws under which they live; freedom to voice their views and aspirations; freedom of speech and assembly; and above all, freedom to believe as their faith dictates.

The "liberals" would also have us believe that capital—the money that starts a business and meets the pay roll—is the prime importance. This in spite of the fact that the country is white with the bones of men who made the mistake of thinking that success could be bought. Regardless of the amount of the

373

original investment or the additional sums poured in, every undertaking will end in bankruptcy unless it is backed up by energy, initiative, and industry.

The American Way, to my mind, describes our system far more accurately than capitalism; the way blazed by those men and women who first came to these shores, risking death and incredible hardships that they might found a new order under which every citizen could stand free, and have the right to rise as high and fast as his abilities could carry him.

When they set about the organization of a permanent government, what simpler than to have patterned after some existing system? Instead of that they denied the absolutism of the state and evolved a form that put full emphasis on the dignity of the individual. A revolutionary form, repudiating the Old World dictum that a man must remain in the class and condition to which he was born. A democratic form, declaring the truth that all men are endowed by the Creator with certain indisputable rights.

Above all, a system of government that recognized competition as a law of life, offering prizes for superiorities in industry, ambition, and effort. This profit motive, or incentive note, is a main point of "liberal" attack, and yet, more than any other one thing, it is responsible for our greatness. The social order that does not provide a spur to energize the individual is demonstrably a deadening order, compelling a dull, hopeless lower level. Even the Russians, for all their professed devotion to Marx and Engels, have been forced to admit it, for they themselves now offer the unequal wage, and grant special privileges in the way of food and housing to the superior worker.

We are sneered at, to be sure, as a nation of dollar chasers, but the record proves that Americans have never looked on money as anything more than the symbol of success. Financial genius may be given its day of homage, but no mere money-maker, with nothing to distinguish him beyond his wealth, has ever been honored by election to our highest office, and multi-millionaires, for the most part, do not live in memory beyond the reading of their wills.

Where, in all history, was ever a country more generous with its wealth? It is our profits—the premiums put on achievement by our competitive economy—that have fed the hungry of the world, clothed the naked, healed the sick, housed the homeless, and carried education and sanitation to the far corners of the earth.

Not even the stanchest upholder of the American Way will deny that festering evils still persist, but what simpler than to *fight* them? Where is there excuse for the defeatist whines of of the "liberals"? The ballot is in our hands, and there is not a defect in our system that cannot be cured by intelligent voting. Unlike the Russians and the people of the puppet states, Americans do not march to the polls under armed guards, nor are we bludgeoned, exiled, or murdered for refusing to exercise the franchise in the manner that a dictator commands. Our platforms are free for the discussion of every issue, the press is without a muzzle, and the right of peaceable assembly remains inviolate. Even newspapers and agitators that seek to overthrow our institutions are tolerated out of the sacred guarantees of our constitution.

At twenty, when I enlisted in the progressive movement, I was appalled at the magnitude of the task of reform. Today, at seventy, I am amazed at the swiftness of our approach to equal justice. I can remember when it was a common thing for men to say, "This is *my* business and I'll run it as I please." General acceptance of the truth that all business is vested with a public use now compels industry and finance to operate in a show window.

Today the corporation that treats its employees as mere cogs in a machine cannot hope to meet the competition of a company that admits the partnership relation between workers and management. Our concern for labor, in fact, has carried us dangerously close to a point where special privileges are confused with rights.

No longer do powerful and unscrupulous aggregations of capital, sitting behind the screens, pull strings that make a whole country dance to their fiddling. No longer is competition a dog-eat-dog affair, for the competitive struggle is increasingly governed by rules that command fair play. Income and corporation taxes are fast putting a curb on excessive profits, and heavier inheritance taxes will soon make it impossible for adenoidal heirs to play the fool with money they had no part in earning.

My whole adult life has been devoted to criticism of the barnacled faults of the American system; yet never once have I doubted the wisdom and rightness of the system itself. Self-government is the only form of government that can and will endure. The totalitarian state, whether it proclaims a master race or a master class, does not and cannot possess permanence, for it denies the spirit in man, puts all emphasis on hate, suspicion, and distrust, and upholds a program of gross materialism. Force is its one hope of maintenance, and force inevitably calls for more force to beat down growing revolt. Purge necessarily follows purge, for only death can still the passion for freedom that is humanity's instinctive and ineradicable aspiration.

Today we are spending millions on a Voice of America that, it is fondly hoped, will persuade Russia to "understand" America. Why not a drive to make *Americans* understand America? A crusade that will raise patriotism above "liberalism's" sneers, lifting all eyes to the shining arch of democratic achievement, and away from mean search for flaws at the base? We *are* a great people, and out of the glory of the republic's morning, what may not be expected of the noon? If we are given a recovery of pride, courage, and faith, what height can dismay our climbing feet?

INDEX

377

378

384